Developing Thinking in Algebra

Developing Thinking in Algebra

John Mason, with Alan Graham and Sue Johnston-Wilder

The Open University in association with Paul Chapman Publishing

First published 2005

Apart from any fair dealing for the purposes of research or private
study, or criticism or review, as permitted under the Copyright,
Designs and Patents Act, 1988, this publication may be reproduced,
stored or transmitted in any form, or by any means, only with the
prior permission in writing of the publishers, or in the case of
reprographic reproduction, in accordance with the terms of licences
issued by the Copyright Licensing Agency. Enquiries concerning
reproduction ouside those terms should be sent to the publishers.

Paul Chapman Publishing
A SAGE Publications Company
1 Oliver's Yard
55 City Road
London EC1Y 1SP

SAGE Publications Inc
2455 Teller Road
Thousand Oaks, California 91320

SAGE Publications India Pvt Ltd
B-42, Panchsheel Enclave
Post Box 4109
New Delhi 110 017

Library of Congress Control Number: 2004117187

A catalogue record for this book is available from the British Library

ISBN 1-4129-1170-2
ISBN 1-4129-1171-0 (pbk)

Typeset by Pantek Arts Ltd, Maidstone, Kent
Printed in Great Britain by T.J. International, Padstow. Cornwall

Contents

Authors

John Mason is Professor of Mathematics Education at The Open University, where he was, for some 15 years, Director of the Centre for Mathematics Education. He has had a lifelong interest in thinking mathematically himself, in working with others who want to think mathematically, and in supporting people who want to work with others to think mathematically. He has a particular interest in the central role of algebra as a mode of human thought concerned with detecting, expressing and manipulating generality and has conducted research and workshops over 25 years while developing his ideas.

Alan Graham has written over 20 short plays for BBC Schools Radio under the series title *Calculated Tales*. Over the last 10 years, his work has concentrated on two main areas, Statistics and Graphics calculators. He has published numerous books in these and other areas, including *Teach Yourself Statistics*, *Teach Yourself Basic Maths* and the *Calculator Maths* series. Alan's main goal has been to help make the learning of mathematics both fun and accessible to all, taking in a variety of contexts including music and art.

Sue Johnston-Wilder is a Senior Lecturer at The Open University. She has worked with teachers and student teachers for many years developing materials to promote interest in mathematics teaching and learning. She is particularly interested in teaching and learning mathematics through technology, history of mathematics and applications. She has published several books including most recently *Teaching Secondary Mathematics with ICT* with David Pimm.

Book series

This is one of a series of three books on developing mathematical thinking written by members of the influential Centre for Mathematics Education at The Open University in response to demand. The series is written for primary mathematics specialists, secondary and FE mathematics teachers and their support staff and others interested in their own mathematical learning and that of others.

The three books address algebraic, geometric and statistical thinking. Each book forms the core text to a corresponding 26-week, 30-point Open University course.

The titles (and authors are):

Developing Thinking in Algebra, John Mason with Alan Graham and Sue Johnston-Wilder, 2005

Developing Thinking in Geometry, edited by Sue Johnston-Wilder and John Mason, 2005

Developing Thinking in Statistics, Alan Graham, 2006

These books integrate mathematics and pedagogy. They are practical books to work through, full of tasks and pedagogic ideas, and also books to refer to when looking for something fresh to offer and engage learners. No teacher will want to be without these books, both for their own stimulation and that of their learners.

Anyone who wishes to develop an understanding and enthusiasm for mathematics, based upon firm research and effective practice, will enjoy this series and find it challenging and inspiring, both personally and professionally.

Developing Thinking in Algebra

We can only function because of abstraction. Abstraction makes life easy, makes it possible. Words, language have been created by man… Language is conveniently vague so that the word car, for example, could cover all cars, not just one. So anyone who has learned to speak, demonstrates that he can use classes, concepts. *There are no words without concepts…*

Therefore, how can we deny that children are already the masters of abstraction, as soon as they use language, and that they of course bring this mastery and the algebra of classes with them when they come to school. (Gattegno, 1970, pp. 23–5)

INTRODUCTION

This book is for people with an interest in algebra whether as a learner, or as a teacher, or perhaps as both. It is concerned with the 'big ideas' of algebra and what it is to understand the process of thinking algebraically. By working on and through the content rather than just reading the text, you will be challenged to question your own understanding of algebraic thinking and the processes involved in working on and designing algebraic tasks. If you are a teacher of mathematics, whether a specialist or non-specialist mathematician, you may find that the ways of working used have implications for your own classroom. The book has been structured according to a number of pedagogic principles that are exposed and discussed along the way, principles that teachers have found useful in preparing and conducting lessons.

Throughout the book, tasks are offered for you to think about for yourself, and, possibly after modification, for use with learners. It is vital to work on them yourself so as to have immediate experience of what the text is highlighting. It is assumed and expected that you will adapt and modify both the structure and the presentation of tasks to learners so as to be appropriate to their needs and experience.

It is absolutely vital that you stop and take the time to work on the tasks, even if they seem too simple or too challenging at first. If they seem too simple, you can use strategies suggested in the text for challenging yourself at your own level; if one seems too difficult, you can try some of the strategies suggested for what to do when you get stuck. In either case, these same strategies can be used with and by learners at any age.

Here then is your first task:

Task 0.1 What is Algebra?

What does the word 'algebra' mean to you? Write a sentence or two that captures your present understanding.

Comment

Developing your ideas about what is algebra is part of what this book is about.

There is no 'right' answer to this question at this stage. You may have written something including 'rearranging letters' or 'generalised arithmetic' or if you are an experienced mathematician 'a branch of mathematics concerned with the relations and properties of quantity'. You may have recalled feelings of curiosity, confusion or boredom when you learned algebra at school.

The notion of what algebra is or can be develops through the book. But it is worth stressing at the outset a very definite and clear stand taken by the authors:

> Algebraic thinking (particularly the recognition and articulation of generality) is within reach of all learners, and vital if they are to participate fully in society.

Everyone who gets to school has already displayed the powers needed to think algebraically and to make sense of the world mathematically. They have all generalised and expressed generalities to themselves and others. What they need is encouragement and permission to develop those powers in a supportive setting.

Furthermore, generalisation, being fundamental to mathematics, is a part of every mathematical topic. Put another way:

> A lesson without learners having the opportunity to express a generality is not a mathematics lesson.

STRUCTURE OF THE BOOK

The book consists of fifteen chapters.

The chapters are divided into four blocks, the first three of which have four chapters each, whose contents run roughly parallel, block by block. The first chapter of a block focuses on opportunities to express generalities, and the sections consider different contexts (numbers, diagrams, out of school, and numbers again), with the challenges developing in sophistication and complexity from block to block. The second chapter focuses on two aspects: mathematical themes and natural powers to make sense of the world. The themes chosen pervade mathematics and provide a way of connecting topics that otherwise seem disparate. The particular powers highlighted are possessed and used by everyone, and they need to be activated and developed in order to make sense of mathematics. The third chapter in each block is concerned with the use of symbols in algebra and the fourth makes specific use of tools such as graphics calculators, spreadsheets and graph-plotting software.

In the first three blocks, each chapter has five sections that are each based on a notional two hours of work. The fifth section of each chapter addresses pedagogic issues that have arisen in the chapter.

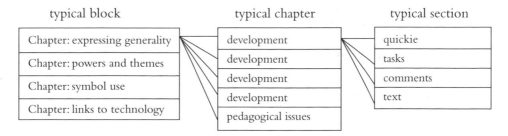

typical block	typical chapter	typical section
Chapter: expressing generality	development	quickie
Chapter: powers and themes	development	tasks
Chapter: symbol use	development	comments
Chapter: links to technology	development	text
	pedagogical issues	

The final block has three chapters that summarise the principles put forward in the book, the powers identified, the mathematical themes illustrated, and the pedagogic issues highlighted along the way.

ACTIVE LEARNING

Rarely is it enough just to read through materials. Learning is a process of maturation, like a fine wine or a good cheese: it takes place over time rather than just at the time of study. Full engagement comes about by actively 'doing' such things as: jotting down ideas; doing tasks and constructing your own examples; trying to make connections; getting involved in detail; standing back to get the 'big picture'; explaining what you are doing, or trying to do, to someone else; being prepared to struggle; acknowledging feelings; and so on. You are strongly recommended to keep a notebook in which you work on the tasks, with a place on the side of the page for making comments and observations. You may find that you also want to develop your own collection of tasks for use with learners, based on suitable modifications of the ones presented, augmented by your observations of what learners respond when you try them out.

Task 0.2 Quickie

Write down a number that uses all of the digits 0 through 9 exactly once.

And another.

And another.

And another which is as big as you can make it.

Comment

What did you do? Did you just provide solutions, or did you become aware of a range of possible choices as you provided yet another example. If you did become so aware, did you note down some thoughts about the effect of being asked for another and another?

When learners are asked to write down an example of something, then after a pause, another, and after another pause, another, many begin to explore beyond the confines of one or two simple examples. They start to become creative and to push themselves, perhaps trying to come up with extreme examples.

Did you think of using exponents (powers)? If not, does that thought change your ideas about the task?

Tasks are designed to generate activity by learners in order to facilitate and stimulate interaction with the teacher. In the case of distance learning materials such as this book, interaction is with comments, with friends and colleagues, and with learners with whom you try tasks out.

Task 0.3 About Tasks

Look at the first two tasks again. What do you notice?

In what way are they similar and in what way different?

Comment

Both tasks asked for some action from you that required you to do some thinking. The first was asking you to think about your understanding – to reflect on where you are; the second to engage in a little mathematics. They were followed by comments that explained something of the purpose behind the task and some suggestions of other things to think about. In neither case was there a model 'solution' – what is important is your response. This is the pattern throughout the book. There is a collection of suggestions on the associated website for when you get stuck on some, but not all of the mathematical tasks.

How you use the 'comments' is up to you but you are advised to 'have a go' before reading them and then maybe amend or augment your reaction to the task. That way you get a chance to engage, and maybe struggle, with the task and then set up an interaction between your thinking and the comments. For some tasks, marked with a ☞ (computer mouse) in the book, you are offered a further stage of interaction, this time with task suggestions that have been provided on the associated website. Each section aims to have a final task that could be used for (self)-assessment purposes. No advice or suggestions are provided for these.

Tasks with 'Quickie' in the title are designed to be just that – a mathematical task that is not too stretching in itself but which provides an opportunity to think about choices and may raise your awareness of underlying concepts. The quickies in a chapter are all related, and are commented upon in the final section of the chapter.

SUMMARY

To use the book effectively you will want to engage with the tasks yourself, and make observations about what you notice both in the activities and in yourself. Getting stuck for a while on a task is excellent, for it provides an opportunity to experience the creative side of mathematical thinking. If a task seems easy, then modify it so as to challenge yourself; if it seems too hard, find some way to simplify it. At the end of each chapter, think about implications for learning to think algebraically in the classroom. You may also want to try out tasks, suitably modified, with learners, and connect their experience with your own on similar but more challenging tasks.

Further task support of Tasks and Quickies marked with
can be found on the website
www.paulchapmanpublishing.co.uk/resource/algebra.pdf

Introduction to Block 1

There are a good many ideas that are introduced in the first block and are developed and extended in subsequent blocks. Chief among these is the notion that algebra provides a symbolic language in which to express conjectured generalities. The power of the symbolic language is that it enables those symbols to be manipulated.

1 First Encounters With Expressing Generality

Chapter 1 introduces one of the central themes of the book:

- Every learner who starts school has already displayed the power to generalise and abstract from particular cases, and this is the root of algebra.

The suggestion made is that expressing generality is entirely natural, pleasurable, and part of human sense-making. Algebra provides a manipulable symbol system and language for expressing and manipulating that generality. The core pedagogic issue is therefore about enabling learners to employ their natural powers in using algebra to make sense both of the world and of other people's use of algebra.

The first three sections of the chapter look at generalities experienced in patterns in numbers, patterns in diagrams, and patterns outside school. Section 1.4 returns to number patterns and suggests things to do when you are stuck on a mathematical problem. Section 1.5 looks at the ideas of the chapter from a pedagogic point of view.

In the quickies in this chapter, you will be asked to write down some numbers. It is important that you do actually write them down, for there is a significant difference between imagining the numbers, and actually writing them down.

1.1 EXPRESSING GENERALITY IN NUMBERS

Quickie 1.1

Write down a number that is 1 more than a multiple of 10. Write down another. Write down another. What are their remainders when you divide them by 10?

Comment

Variations of this task will recur during this chapter. As with all tasks in this book, what matters most is not your specific answer but your response, that is, what you notice about yourself in attempting the task.

What did you notice about how you went about the task? Did you simply write down suitable numbers? Did you find that you were beginning to be more adventurous when you wrote the third number? Were you surprised when you found the remainder?

Were you able to use the experience of the first two to help with the third? Do you have a sense of something that is or might be 'always' true? How confident are you about it?

Almost certainly you found yourself choosing which multiple of ten to add to 1 in order to produce a number, though you may not have thought precisely in those terms. Nevertheless, you have a sense of a generality. Whilst generalising is natural, learners need time to notice that they have a sense of a generality, and time to express generality, to strengthen and to extend their natural powers to generalise.

Number Patterns

One of the most important sources of generalisations is the domain of number, in detecting and expressing number patterns.

Task 1.1.1 Anything plus Anything

A young child observed that 3 + 5 = 5 + 3, that 2 + 4 = 4 + 2, and that 'anything plus anything is anything plus anything'. Express in your own words what you think the child was probably trying to express.

Comment

As it stands, the statement could be interpreted as, for example, taking 'anything' as independent, so that for example 3 + 5 = 17 + 22, yet it seems entirely implausible that the child was thinking this way. The more likely interpretation is that if you select any two numbers, then you get the same answer, no matter in which order you add them.

The child's statement is an expression of generality, transcending the particular instances and dealing with an infinite number of possible cases. The actual expression of generality may, as in this case, need refining to avoid misconstruing it. Often the first attempt to express a generality turns out to be too wide-ranging, which is why any such expression needs to be treated as a conjecture, as something that needs checking in particular instances, and justifying in general, perhaps at some later date. Algebra as language provides ways of being more precise in the expression of generality and, later, for reasoning about properties of numbers.

Task 1.1.2a Mental Multiplication

If you had to multiply 32 by 18, in your head, how might you go about it?

Comment

If you *had* to do it in your head, you might think either of 32 as 30 + 2 and multiply both by 18 before adding, or else think of 18 as 20 − 2, multiplying both by 32, and then subtract appropriately. You might know another way.

It is clear that learners are not expected to memorise all possible calculations with numbers conforming to patterns like $(30 + 2) \times$ *something*. Rather, they are expected to discern a 'general method'. The next task considers possible variations on this theme.

Task 1.1.2b What can be Changed?

What can be changed in the form $(30 + 2) \times$ *something*, and still be of help in doing mental multiplications?

Comment

Perhaps the most salient variation is in the tens: $(30 + 2) \times$ *something* suggests $(40 + 2) \times$ *something*, $(50 + 2) \times$ *something*, and so on. Awareness of the possible change is awareness of a general method, a generality. Furthermore, there is already an implicit generality in changing the other number, the 18, to *something*: it does not matter what the second number is, the multiplication is likely to be easier when split up than when attempted directly. Furthermore, it can be useful if '+ 2' is replaced by '+ 1', or '+ 3', or, depending on mental facility, 4 or even 5. Instead of adding 6, or more, any number could be decomposed as a subtraction of 1, 2, 3 or 4. There are three different features of the original task that can be changed: the tens number, the 'extra bit', and the number to be multiplied by.

Task 1.1.2c What is the Generality?

What implicit generality is being exemplified by the previous methods of doing a multiplication?
Try your articulation out on others to see if they can make sense of it.

Comment

It is quite hard to state a generality succinctly but clearly, even after several attempts. One attempt at a generality might be 'you find a number close to one of the numbers that is easier to multiply by'. Another attempt might be: 'mental multiplication can be done more easily by linking at least one number to a nearby number that is easier to compute with'. Notice that the previous sentence already includes an implicit generality: 'linking at least one number to a nearby number' is not specific, but general. To learn to use this 'mental method' is to come to appreciate and be familiar with a generality.

It is not easy to express the generality, partly because there are several 'things' that could be varied. If care is not taken, you end up like the child in Task 1.1.1, using general labels such as *something* or *anything* to refer to different items.

Not all generalities need to be expressed explicitly, but it is worth noting how often there is an underlying generality that learners are expected to appreciate and to be aware of, even if not explicitly. Learners need plenty of experience of expressing generalities in order to make sure they are appreciating generalities implicit in techniques and concepts, rather than just trying to reproduce those techniques.

The next task demonstrates a general form of task for provoking learners to use their natural powers to generalise.

Task 1.1.3a In Sequence

Fill in the fourth line in this sequence of arithmetic statements:

$(3 + 2) \times (3 - 2) = 3^2 - 4$

$(4 + 2) \times (4 - 2) = 4^2 - 4$

$(5 + 2) \times (5 - 2) = 5^2 - 4$

$(6$

Is it correct? What do you think comes next?
Comment Most people know what is coming next: '+' then a '2' then a bracket, and so on. And the next line and the next line … . Those three dots are called an *ellipsis*, meaning a 'short-form', and were introduced by Isaac Newton to mean 'and so the pattern continues'. But what is that pattern?

When working on tasks such as this, there is often an assumption that the learners 'see what the teacher sees'. Indeed, since many people do not recognise 'seeing' as a description of what they do in their heads, even that assumption needs to be rephrased: 'Learners do not always attend to what the teacher is attending to'.

If some people are 'seeing' or attending to different features than those seen or attended to by the teacher, they may find what the teacher says quite mystifying. It is important for learners to have time to think about, formulate and try to articulate generalities, to themselves and to each other, before expressing to a group or a whole class. At first, it is necessary to call upon them to generalise explicitly in a variety of different contexts. As the practice of becoming aware of generality develops, and as expressing generality becomes a habit, it may not be necessary to call explicitly for generality every time.

Therefore the next task is offered as an introduction to expressing generality.

Task 1.1.3b In Sequence (continued)

Complete the rows in Task 1.1.3 that start (37 … and (987654321 … .

Comment

If you are not sure, write some more rows that follow on from the ones given, not just writing numbers, but paying attention to what you are changing and what you are preserving, that is, to what stays the same. A useful label for this process is *Watch What You Do*. By asking yourself 'what is the same about each row?' and 'what is different and how is it changing?' you can focus attention usefully in order to detect generalities in the form of patterns of relationships.

The brackets are as much a feature of the sequence as are the numbers, and deserve explicit attention. Work with brackets is developed explicitly in sections 3.3 and 7.3.

Rina Zazkis (2001), a researcher in mathematics education, has found that using very large numbers, which are intentionally daunting when it comes to performing arithmetic calculations on them, is a good way to prompt learners to become aware of generality.

Task 1.1.3c In Sequence (again)

Someone far away is thinking of a number, and because you don't know what it is, it is necessary to denote it by something such as a little cloud ☁, to show that someone is thinking of it. Their number is the first number in one of the rows. What does the rest of the row look like? The row starts (☁.

Comment

To display the line with clouds in this text would block you from doing the real work, which is to detect the structure of the rows and expressing it, probably by becoming aware of how you knew what to write down in the previous task. In words, 'cloud plus two' times 'cloud minus two' is cloud squared take away 4.

As you move from row to row, your eye naturally discerns things that are the same every time, and things that change. For example, each line starts with a left bracket. The symbol sequences)×(and)= are common to every line. The symbol also appears to the right of the = sign in each case. By stressing what is changing, and consequently ignoring what stays the same, you invoke your natural power to detect something that is changing and can take different values or qualities, thus experiencing generality.

Indeed, what may be most striking at first is the familiar number sequence 3, 4, 5 … . However, the significant pattern is found, not by following the sequence of counting numbers one by one, but by looking at what is being said on each line: 'The product of "anything" plus 2 and "that same thing" minus 2 is the difference between their square and 4'.

Notice how hard it is to articulate the generality in words, because of the problem of referring to something general more than once. Using clouds makes it clearer, as long as it is agreed that what is in the cloud is fixed (the person does not change the number they are thinking of just yet).

$$(\mathbf{\odot} + 2) \times (\mathbf{\odot} - 2) = \mathbf{\odot}^2 - 4$$

One advantage of the use of clouds with numbers is that it makes the generality much less open to ambiguity. The statement can be 'looked at', but it can also be read: 'two more than the number you are thinking of, times two less than it, is the square of that number minus 4.'

Task 1.1.3d In Sequence (continued further)

What happens if the number another person is thinking of in their thought cloud is 13/3? Does 'it' still work? What is the 'it'?

Comment

What is the range of permissible change for the 'anything', that is, for the entry in the cloud? You may already be convinced that it can be any counting number; introducing a fraction is intended to suggest that it might work for *any* fraction. In which case, why not *any* number? What if you use the square root of 10? One of the purposes and powers of algebra is that it makes it possible to locate and describe succinctly the range of permissible change within which a relationship holds: in this case, two expressions *always* yield the same value.

In every case so far, two expressions such as

$$(3 + 2) \times (3 - 2) \quad \text{and} \quad 3^2 - 4$$

have been equal in value – different ways of expressing the same number. Mathematicians like this sort of regularity, so when they encounter less familiar numbers in the same computation, they look for the pattern to continue. The next task shows how this can lead to some discoveries.

Task 1.1.3e In Sequence (continued backwards)

What happens if you work your way backwards four or more rows?

$(4 + 2) \times (4 - 2) = 4^2 - 4$

$(3 + 2) \times (3 - 2) = 3^2 - 4$

$(2$

$(1$

Comment

The row beginning '(2' is a reminder that multiplying by 0 must give 0. The row beginning '(1' can be interpreted as saying that $3 \times (^-1) = 1^2 - 4 = {}^-3$, which, generalised, leads to 'multiplying a positive by a negative gives a negative'. The row beginning '(0' can be interpreted as saying that $2 \times (^-2) = {}^-4$. The row beginning '(${}^-1$' can be interpreted as saying that $1 \times {}^-3 = (^-1)^2 - 4$, so since by the pattern of the previous rows you would expect $1 \times (^-3)$ to be ${}^-3$, it must be the case that $(^-1)^2 = 1$ in order to preserve the pattern based on the equality of different expressions.

This is the fundamental reason why it is generally accepted that $(^-1) \times (^-1) = 1$: it allows the 'rules of arithmetic' to extend beyond positive whole numbers to negative numbers.

Pause for Reflection

The most important notion in this section is that when a pattern is detected in which some things are changing and others staying the same, there is an opportunity to express a generality, in this case, $(\clubsuit + 2) \times (\clubsuit - 2) = \clubsuit^2 - 4$.

This stated relationship is, for the moment, only a conjecture, because there is only a sense of pattern, an intuition of how numbers work, on which to depend. (How do you know whether it works when, say, $\clubsuit = 987654321$?)

In the next few sections, the notion of expressing generality will be exemplified in contexts other than number patterns.

Task 1.1.R Reflection

What struck you about the work in this first section? Make a note of ideas that you would like to come back to you when preparing for or conducting a lesson.

Comment

Possibilities include:

- pleasure in expressing generality;
- the discovery of properties of numbers such as multiplying negative numbers together arising from expressing generality arising from patterns;
- thinking about what can change whilst some relationship remains invariant.

There are likely to be other things as well.

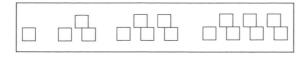

Notice that an alternative perception might be: 'I see two rows, the top row having one brick less than the bottom row. The bottom row has one, two, three, . . . bricks in it, depending on its sequence position'. An alternative is 'the bottom row has as many bricks as the picture number; the top row has one fewer'.

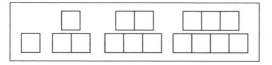

Each way of seeing gives rise to a way of counting, which can be expressed more succinctly (as your confidence grows), until it looks very much like a formula. Thus:

Picture number 37 will have two rows of bricks.
There will be 37 bricks in the bottom row and 36 bricks in the top row.

This can, when appropriate, be shortened to:

Picture 37 needs 37 (bottom row) + 36 (top row) bricks.

Algebraic thinking has already begun. By the time facility has been achieved in being able to find the number of bricks needed in particular cases, sufficient attention is freed to see and express generality.

Task 1.2.2b How Many Bricks? (generalised)

Someone has a picture-number in their head. Tell them how to calculate how many bricks that picture has.

Comment

This is the heart of algebra seen as expressing generality. Where does the generality lie? The point of this task is to lead up to seeing how to count the number of bricks in general, by seeing a structure or pattern in how each and every picture is constructed.

Let the person's picture number be denoted by a cloud. Then there will be ✿ in the bottom row, and (✿ − 1) in the top row, or ✿ + (✿ − 1) altogether. Alternatively, there will be 1 plus a multiple of 2, namely 1 + 2(✿ − 1), or again, 1 less than a multiple of 2, namely 2✿ − 1.

When you express a generality, such as in the last task, it is important to be clear on the status of your expression. Is it a conjecture, or do you have some way to justify it as being always correct? Reference to the structure, such as 'two rows of picture-number bricks then remove one from the top row' constitutes a justification. However, it is always wise to test a conjecture, even an almost certain conjecture, on one or two typical examples, as there can be a slip between 'seeing' or 'having a strong sense of' the structure, and actually expressing that accurately in symbols.

Task 1.1.3e In Sequence (continued backwards)

What happens if you work your way backwards four or more rows?

$(4 + 2) \times (4 - 2) = 4^2 - 4$

$(3 + 2) \times (3 - 2) = 3^2 - 4$

$(2$

$(1$

Comment

The row beginning '(2' is a reminder that multiplying by 0 must give 0. The row beginning '(1' can be interpreted as saying that $3 \times (^-1) = 1^2 - 4 = {}^-3$, which, generalised, leads to 'multiplying a positive by a negative gives a negative'. The row beginning '(0' can be interpreted as saying that $2 \times (^-2) = {}^-4$. The row beginning '($^-1$' can be interpreted as saying that $1 \times {}^-3 = (^-1)^2 - 4$, so since by the pattern of the previous rows you would expect $1 \times (^-3)$ to be $^-3$, it must be the case that $(^-1)^2 = 1$ in order to preserve the pattern based on the equality of different expressions.

This is the fundamental reason why it is generally accepted that $(^-1) \times (^-1) = 1$: it allows the 'rules of arithmetic' to extend beyond positive whole numbers to negative numbers.

Pause for Reflection

The most important notion in this section is that when a pattern is detected in which some things are changing and others staying the same, there is an opportunity to express a generality, in this case, $(\diamondsuit + 2) \times (\diamondsuit - 2) = \diamondsuit^2 - 4$.

This stated relationship is, for the moment, only a conjecture, because there is only a sense of pattern, an intuition of how numbers work, on which to depend. (How do you know whether it works when, say, $\diamondsuit = 987654321$?)

In the next few sections, the notion of expressing generality will be exemplified in contexts other than number patterns.

Task 1.1.R Reflection

What struck you about the work in this first section? Make a note of ideas that you would like to come back to you when preparing for or conducting a lesson.

Comment

Possibilities include:

- pleasure in expressing generality;
- the discovery of properties of numbers such as multiplying negative numbers together arising from expressing generality arising from patterns;
- thinking about what can change whilst some relationship remains invariant.

There are likely to be other things as well.

Comment on tasks

Remember that if you find a task too simple or too familiar, you have an opportunity to devise your own, similar task that stretches and challenges you. One way to do this is to ask what you might change and still have a task that calls upon the same kind of thinking. For example, in Task 1.1.3, some of the invariants in the expressions are the two 2s on the left, and the 4 on the right. Suppose someone suggested changing both 2s to some other number: what then would replace the 4?

1.2 EXPRESSING GENERALITY IN DIAGRAMS AND PICTURES

Quickie 1.2

Write down a number that is 2 more than a multiple of 5. Write down another. Write down another. What are their remainders when you divide them by 5?

Comments

Did your thinking at the start of the last section come back to you?

This section continues the theme of expressing generality, in the context of reading diagrams and pictures. It calls upon your power to imagine change.

Generalising from Diagrams

The following task requires you to imagine a relevant diagram in each case.

Task 1.2.1 What is General About …?

What is general about each of the following statements?

The sum of the angles of any triangle lying in the plane is 180°.

If you know the three lengths of sides of a triangle, you can construct the triangle uniquely.

Comment

In the first statement, the triangle can be *any* triangle whatsoever, however extreme.

In the second statement, the three lengths must belong to a triangle, but otherwise are perfectly general.

Often the generality in a statement is hidden in language such as *a* or *any*. The word *any* can be taken to refer to a specific object, or to an arbitrary choice of object, hence to all such objects.

Opportunities to generalise arise in using simple diagrams. For example, if you have two line-segments or blocks and you put them in line, with the front end of one at the back end of the other, you get a new segment whose length is the sum of the two segments. Furthermore, you can put either of the two segments first, and then the other:

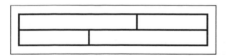

Children learn that the two compound rods will be the same length. Articulating that awareness of the way the world works expresses a generality that is one of the rules of arithmetic: you can add two numbers in either order; the result is always the same.

A similar fact applies to multiplication. To count the number of squares in the following array, you can count how many in each row, and the number of rows, or how many in each column and the number of columns.

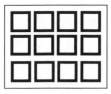

Generalising from Picture Sequences

Opportunities to generalise arise when a sequence of objects is being counted.

Task 1.2.2a Brick Walls

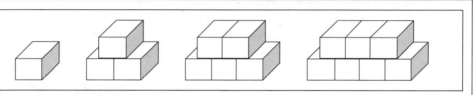

Decide how you are going to continue the picture sequence. The best way to do this is to make or draw some more yourself, first in order to clarify your general rule, and then in order to become aware of *how* you are counting. Once you can say in words how the sequence extends, you have your first expression of generality.

Comment

Once you have specified a way of extending the sequence of pictures indefinitely using a rule, there is a unique answer to counting the number of bricks needed to make any particular wall (such as the thirty-seventh one, which is a typical two-digit number). There are usually many different ways of seeing *how* to do the counting, which therefore provide opportunities for choice and creativity.

The point of counting in individual cases is to become aware of *how* you are counting. Sometimes it is easier to draw a picture to *show how* you are counting, rather than to say it in words. For example, here are two of the many different ways of seeing the brick wall sequence: 'I see one brick, with none, then with one pair, then with two pairs, ... of bricks added on'

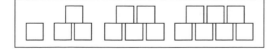

or more deliberately, to emphasise the adding of pairs of blocks, like this:

Notice that an alternative perception might be: 'I see two rows, the top row having one brick less than the bottom row. The bottom row has one, two, three, . . . bricks in it, depending on its sequence position'. An alternative is 'the bottom row has as many bricks as the picture number; the top row has one fewer'.

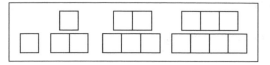

Each way of seeing gives rise to a way of counting, which can be expressed more succinctly (as your confidence grows), until it looks very much like a formula. Thus:

Picture number 37 will have two rows of bricks.
There will be 37 bricks in the bottom row and 36 bricks in the top row.

This can, when appropriate, be shortened to:

Picture 37 needs 37 (bottom row) + 36 (top row) bricks.

Algebraic thinking has already begun. By the time facility has been achieved in being able to find the number of bricks needed in particular cases, sufficient attention is freed to see and express generality.

Task 1.2.2b How Many Bricks? (generalised)

Someone has a picture-number in their head. Tell them how to calculate how many bricks that picture has.

Comment

This is the heart of algebra seen as expressing generality. Where does the generality lie? The point of this task is to lead up to seeing how to count the number of bricks in general, by seeing a structure or pattern in how each and every picture is constructed.

Let the person's picture number be denoted by a cloud. Then there will be ☁ in the bottom row, and (☁ − 1) in the top row, or ☁ + (☁ − 1) altogether. Alternatively, there will be 1 plus a multiple of 2, namely 1 + 2(☁ − 1), or again, 1 less than a multiple of 2, namely 2☁ − 1.

When you express a generality, such as in the last task, it is important to be clear on the status of your expression. Is it a conjecture, or do you have some way to justify it as being always correct? Reference to the structure, such as 'two rows of picture-number bricks then remove one from the top row' constitutes a justification. However, it is always wise to test a conjecture, even an almost certain conjecture, on one or two typical examples, as there can be a slip between 'seeing' or 'having a strong sense of' the structure, and actually expressing that accurately in symbols.

Picture sequences worth counting can come from many sources, such as children's own drawings or traditional designs from different cultures. They can also arise spontaneously at unexpected moments.

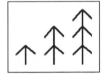

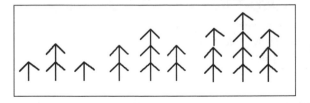

For example, while producing a Christmas picture, children in one class were drawing trees. They soon realised they could make bigger and bigger versions, and that they could count the twigs, or the twig-ends, not just for particular trees, but for any such tree no matter how large. They could even develop forest clumps growing in some regular manner, such as shown here.

Reading Areas

A single diagram can usually be interpreted as illustrating a whole range of possibilities, a generality.

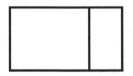

In the diagram, the total area of the large rectangle can also be expressed as the sum of two areas. The sum of the areas of the two small rectangles is the area of the large rectangle. Because no statement has been made about the actual areas, this is a very general statement. An algebraic version of the generality runs along the lines of:

if the height is h and the widths are a and b respectively,
then the total area is both $h(a + b)$ and $ha + hb$.

Although they look different, these two expressions must therefore be equal, at least as long as a and b are possible lengths. No matter how you move the pieces, area is conserved.

This is, of course, the reason why mental multiplication strategies such as those used in Task 1.1.2 always work. The following tasks provide more experience of using multiple expressions.

Task 1.2.3a Finding Areas

Find at least three different ways to decompose this shape into rectangles to find its area.

You have to decide on appropriate lengths for yourself, but the aim is to express a method that works in general, for all 'L-shapes'.

Comment

Did you find yourself wanting to use some specific numbers, or letters, to describe your method or did you use shapes?

For complicated shapes, even in the plane, it is not always easy to discern how to break a shape into rectangles in a maximally efficient manner. Learners often struggle with seeing how to break up a shape into rectangles in order to find its area.

Task 1.2.3b Finding Complicated Areas

Make up a figure from rectangles and draw its perimeter, hiding the component rectangles. Clearly, someone else could partition this shape into rectangles. Now make up a more complex shape that is harder to partition with a minimum number of rectangles.

Comment

The principle behind this task is that in order to gain facility in discerning component rectangles, it is useful to make up your own.

Restricting attention to squares partitioned into squares and rectangles yields useful experience in discerning features, recognising relationships, and expressing generality concerning different ways to calculate total area, as the next task shows.

Task 1.2.4 Reading Areas

Interpret each of the diagrams as general statements about areas in as many different ways as possible.

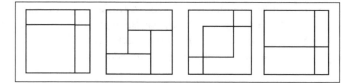

Comment

The first thing you have to do is to 'see' the diagram as made up of components. Selecting different features will lead to different readings.

Paying attention to the range of values that a variable can take is an important part of introducing symbols, because it is easy to forget necessary restrictions. If you add letters, a and b, for the sides of the two inner squares, a and b represent lengths and must therefore be non-negative. The first diagram can be interpreted as $(a + b)^2 = a^2 + 2ab + b^2$. If a denotes the size of the large square and b one of the inner squares (again with a being a non-negative number, and b a number between 0 and a), then $a^2 = (a - b)^2 + b^2 + 2b(a - b)$.

Pause for Reflection

Reading a diagram or picture is actually very similar to reading a symbolic expression:

- you have to discern details that contribute to the overall picture;
- you look for relationships between elements, and sometimes also between diagrams or expressions;
- you express those relationships;

- you ask yourself what can change in this diagram and still the detected relationships hold;
- you identify relationships that can be taken to hold for a whole class of diagrams, expressions, or other objects, and in so doing you construct properties.

Sometimes these happen so quickly that they slip by unnoticed; sometimes learners get stuck because they have not shifted appropriately, or they are stressing different features.

Relationships hold between elements, so it is necessary to stress or foreground those elements, and as a result, to ignore or background other elements or features. Caleb Gattegno (1970), an influential educator and philosopher, suggested that the process of stressing some features and ignoring others is, in itself, the process of generalising.

Task 1.2.R Reflection

What comes to mind as you think back over the work in this second section?

What differences do you find between generalising from a diagram or a sequence of diagrams, and generalising from patterns in numbers? Which do you feel most comfortable with?

1.3 EXPRESSING GENERALITY OUTSIDE SCHOOL

Quickie 1.3

Write down a number that is 3 more than a multiple of 7. Write down another. Write down another. What are their remainders when you divide them by 7?

Write down a 10-digit number that is 3 more than a multiple of 7.

Write down a number that is 3 more than a multiple of 7 and which it is unlikely anyone else reading this book will think of writing down (yes, you *can* do it).

Comments

While carrying out this task, you might have noticed that when asked to construct something, then another, then another in quick succession, you find, that by the time the third one is requested you are starting to be a bit more creative, a bit more extreme (Watson and Mason, 2004).

When, in class, learners hear others describe their third number, they sometimes find themselves thinking 'why didn't I think of that?', or even, 'I would never have thought of that!' But in truth, it takes only a few exposures to these sorts of tasks for most people to begin to relax and explore more extreme cases. For example:

Write down a number with 10 digits that leaves a remainder of 1 on dividing by 10, by 5, by 7.

(Note that 7 might require more thought.)

Write down a number you think no one else in the room will think of writing down.

Write down a number that is very large.

The purpose here is to help learners to become aware that in any situation, when asked for an example, they have a variety to choose from. It is not a matter of selecting the first that comes to mind, but of pausing to consider the entire set from which to make a choice. A choice can be made to be simple, really simple, quite complicated, or really complicated. In making this choice, awareness of the infinite extent, and yet of having a method of constructing any one of them, sets the stage and lays the groundwork for expressing generality.

This section offers a variety of tasks intended to alert you to the pervasive need for expressions of generality in the world outside of school. Customers want to know what something will cost them. Entrepreneurs need to devise pricing policies such as sale discounts and bulk purchase discounts, as well as deciding what mark-up to put on different items. Consequently, entrepreneurs use algebra thinking, even if they do it by using a calculator or a spreadsheet.

Using Symbols

Since using words is both tricky and tedious, especially if you have to keep writing them all down, mathematicians use labels for objects they want to speak about. Most people learn, long before their first lesson in algebra, that 'algebra is about using letters'. Unfortunately, many people never discover what those letters are for, or why they are used. Since it is important for learners to grasp the notion of being able to talk about and manipulate 'whatever number someone else is thinking of, even if it is not yet known', the cloud of section 1.1 provides a useful transitional tool between the informality of words and the formality of letters. After a period of time using clouds, the notion of using a single letter is likely to arise quite spontaneously as a reduction in effort.

Task 1.3.1 From Words to Symbols

For each of the following relationships, express the generality in words and symbols:

The height of a plant at the end of some specified number of days if it grows by 2 cm per day.

The number of days in a specified number of weeks.

The number of minutes in a specified number of hours; specified number of days; specified number of weeks.

The number of fence posts and rails needed to make a 3-rail fence along a stretch of road.

Comment

Make sure that you state clearly that whatever symbol you use, it stands for the number of something or other! How can you check if your conjecture fits the situation? Look out for some similar opportunities when shopping or reading the newspaper.

Whenever a generalisation is first expressed, its status is one of conjecture: it is an attempt to express something. However, it is very likely that there are flaws, either in the expression, or in the insight that is being expressed. Mathematical thinking can only take place within a supportive atmosphere, in which everything said (including everything asserted in this book!) is taken as a conjecture to be tested out in experience.

Task 1.3.2a Value Added Tax (VAT) and Discount

In a discount warehouse, you see an item advertised at 20% off the listed price, but you know that there is a VAT of 17.5% to be added on. Which would you prefer, to have the discount taken off first before the VAT is added on, or to have the VAT added on and then the discount taken off the total? Which do you think the customs and excise would prefer?

> *Comment*
>
> Did you try a particular example, perhaps a simple example such as £1 or £100? You might even decide to make the VAT a more tractable quantity such as 10%, thereby revealing an implicit conjecture that the answer does not depend on the actual discount and tax.
>
> A few calculations will probably produce a conjecture that for the customer, it does not matter: either order gives the same result. But why?
>
> Start with £500. To discount by 20% means to subtract off 20% of the original: (500 − (20% of 500), which is the same as (100% of 500) − (20% of 500), which is the same as 80% of £500. So a discount of 20% applied to 500 is the same as taking 80% of £500, and this generalises by replacing the 500 by any other sum, and the 20% and 80% by any discount and its difference from 100%.

This is an example of implicitly or intuitively 'seeing the general through the particular'. Trying a particular case using objects with which you are familiar and confident is entirely natural. This is what is meant by *specialising*. The purpose of specialising is to move to a simple or simpler particular case in order to 'see what is going on', in order to generalise. Sometimes the simplest possible case can be informative, or perhaps some other extreme and special case, but sometimes you need a less specialised case in order to see what is going on.

An excellent way to investigate the effects of discount and VAT is to use a spreadsheet, on which each step of the calculations can be displayed. A change in one of the values produces an instant change in the answers, enabling learners to experience a number of examples in quick succession, thereby supporting them in expressing generality. This generality remains a conjecture until the equality is proved generally to be true and not just special to a few cases, but the spreadsheet provides an ideal way to do many examples very quickly.

The formulae are displayed here.

	A	B	C	D	E	F
1	VAT	0.175	Price	500	Price	=D1
2	Discount	0.2	Reduction	=D1*B2	VAT	=B1*F1
3			discounted price	=D1-D2	price inc VAT	=F1+F2
4			VAT	=B1*D3	reduction	=F3*B2
5			Actual price	=D4+D3	Actual price	=F3-F4

The process of telling cells what calculation they are to do using the contents of other cells is itself a step towards expressing generality.

Task 1.3.2b VAT and Discount (continued)

Express a generality of which 'so a discount of 20% is the same as taking 80%' is a special case.

What role does the £500 play in the calculations? Express a generality.

Do something similar for 'adding VAT'.

Express a full generality together with an explanation of why the generality is valid.

Comment

Calculating a discount of D% means calculating $(100 - D)$% of the price. Denoting VAT by V, adding in VAT means calculating $(100 + V)$% of the price. So, you are looking for values of D and V for which the following two expressions are the same:

$(100 + V)$% of $(100 - D)$% of the price, and $(100 - D)$% of $(100 + V)$% of £100.

But compounding percentages is multiplication, and it does not matter in what order the multiplication is done. So what the customer actually pays will be the same, whatever the order. This is clearly indicated in the spreadsheet, where no matter what values are inserted for the price, the VAT or the Discount, the Actual price is always the same, no matter in which order it is calculated.

For the customer, the order does not matter. For Customs and Excise, and for the entrepreneur, however, it matters a lot. Customs and Excise get more if the VAT is calculated on the full price rather than on the discount. However, the entrepreneur would lose out. Of course, this is unreasonable, so Customs and Excise declare that VAT is the last thing to be calculated, after all other calculations are done.

Task 1.3.2c VAT and Discount (continued)

The statements about Customs and Excise and the entrepreneur in the previous paragraph are examples of general statements. Do some examples to check these statements. In other words, try some special cases, first to appreciate what the generalities say, then to check that they are correct in particular cases, and then to see why the general statements must always be true.

Suppose a warehouse offers a discount of D% and furthermore, no VAT to be paid by the customer. What is the effective discount being offered?

Comments

Try some examples with a view to generalising!

Other Contexts

Task 1.3.3 Sale!

The following price reductions have been sighted in shops. Put them in order of increasing reduction:

Two for the price of one.

Buy one, get one free.

Buy one and get 25% off the second.

Buy two, get one free.

Buy two and get the cheaper one free.

Buy two and get 50% off the second one.

Three for the price of two.

Make up your own variants and then put them all in order of reduction!

Comment

One approach is to try them all out on an item of say, £100. Another is to work out what fraction of the original price is being charged for each one.

Behind the arithmetic there are generalities lurking: no prices have been mentioned, so these apply to any prices; 'buy one' and 'buy two' suggest 'buy n' where n is some, probably small, positive whole number; 'get one free' and 'get one at reduced price' suggest that you might get two or three at the reduced price (or free), and the reduction could be anything from 100% off (i.e. free) to 0% off (i.e. no reduction).

Task 1.3.4 Customs and Excise

How does a shop work out how much VAT they owe Customs and Excise if all their shop prices are quoted as inclusive of VAT?

Comment

The question is posed in general, so a sensible approach is to try particular cases, and then to look through the particular in order to express the general.

Pause for Reflection

Sorting out discounts and percentage increases requires a cool head, and is informed by checking the calculations on specific numbers. To express the generalities, it helps to use symbols like $D\%$ for discount percentage and $V\%$ for the VAT percentage as an aid to remembering what they represent. Often it is actually clearer to use symbols than to use numbers, because it is then possible to read the expressions. The symbolic expressions are both a statement of what calculation to do, *and* the answer to the calculation!

Pursuing an investigation that requires the learner to process a lot of examples is a far more satisfying way of getting practice than doing a set of exercises.

Task 1.3.R Reflection

What struck you about the work in this section?

Have you begun to notice occurrences of or opportunities for generalising outside of your teaching institution?

1.4 MORE EXPRESSING GENERALITY

Quickie 1.4

Write down an expression for all numbers that leave a remainder of 1 when divided by 10; all those that leave a remainder of 2 when divided by 5; all those that leave a remainder of 3 when divided by 7.

This section considers arithmetic topics that sometimes cause some confusion when treated purely as arithmetic, but which are actually easier to think about when approached algebraically, by generalising.

Remainders

Since remainders cause some confusion, especially when used with negative numbers, this subsection begins by generalising the quickies, and then addresses the question of what it means mathematically to find the remainder on dividing $^-3$ by 5.

Task 1.4.1a Remainders and Multiples

Write down a number that leaves a remainder of r when divided by m. Now write them 'all' down, as a general expression,

Generalise the observation that 2 and 7 have the same remainder when divided by 5.

Comment

Trying particular cases is a good way to get a sense of what is going on and appreciating the structure, leading to an expression of generality. Quickie 1.4 was meant to provide that background. Trying particular cases is also important for testing conjectures, but can never validate a conjecture, unless you try all possible cases. One of the main points of algebra is that you can 'try' an infinite number of cases symbolically.

Task 1.4.1 can be generated by asking yourself what features of the quickie can be varied. The second part is another way of looking at the same situation as part one: two numbers have the same remainder on dividing by m if their difference is a multiple of m.

The point of tasks such as this is to prompt generalisation, so that learners become adept at answering 'questions of this type', that is, that they become familiar with the whole class of questions of which this is a representative.

Task 1.4.1b Remainders and Multiples (continued)

Write down in order, left to right, all the numbers between −13 and 12 that are 2 more than a multiple of 5.

Look for and express to yourself a relationship between successive pairs of your numbers.

Now starting from the right, write down underneath each number its remainder when divided by 5.

What is the same and what is changing? Generalise.

Comment

The positive numbers all leave a remainder of 2 when divided by 5. What does it mean to ask for the remainder when a negative number is divided by 5? The most sensible thing is to expect that it will continue to be the smallest positive number that, when subtracted from the number, makes a multiple of 5. So $^-3$ is 2 more than $^-5$, which is a multiple of 5, so the remainder on dividing $^-3$ by 5 is 2. Remainders always lie between 0 and the divisor.

For numbers of the form $5n + 2$, the remainder on dividing by 5 is always 2. Consequently it makes sense, following this pattern, to define the remainder on dividing n (a positive or negative integer) by a number m to be the number r where $0 \leq r < m$ and $n = qm + r$. The q is called the quotient. In other words, r is the smallest non-negative number you can to add to some multiple of m to get n. The two descriptions, one in terms of adding on and the other in terms of remainders, then describe the same thing.

Task 1.4.1c More Remainders

What is a reasonable meaning to give to the remainder on dividing ⁻3 by ⁻5? What about the remainder on dividing 2 by –5?

Comment

Numbers of the form ⁻5n + 2 will have remainder 2 on dividing by ⁻5, so the remainder on dividing by 5 and by ⁻5 is the same, and more generally, the remainder on dividing by n and by ⁻n is the same.

Fractions

Task 1.4.2a Fractionated

What fraction of the first whole rectangle has been shaded in?

What fraction of the second whole rectangle has been shaded?

What fraction of the third whole rectangle has been shaded (light, dark, both)?

Comment

Many learners struggle with adding fractions. There are many reasons for this, including what fractions mean, why they are needed, cultural antipathy to fractions, and attempts to teach methods without a firm appreciation of images to fall back on.

This task suggests an image that doubles as a method either for adding fractions or for exploring fractions in order to work out a method of adding them. It is important when contemplating using any mediating tool, whether software, diagram or metaphor, to be clear about what learners need to do in order to make effective use of the tool.

Task 1.4.2b Generalising Fractionated

What features of the first rectangle diagram correspond to the fraction shaded as 2/5 (one reading) and as 8/20 (second reading)? In other words, what must someone discern and relate in order to be able to read the diagram as depicting a fraction? What features must all three rectangles share?

How is the third related to the first two?

Comment

It is vital to be explicitly aware of how the fraction is read, in order to be able to decide what rectangle to draw for yourself when given a fraction. Note that reading someone else's diagram and depicting a fraction for yourself are reverse operations. Depicting can be assisted if you are aware of how you go about reading.

Note that great care is needed when using diagrams to represent fractions. The light-shaded rectangles are depicted as a fraction of one rectangle, the dark-shaded are depicted as a fraction of a second, and it is only when they are depicted as fractions of the same whole that you can sensibly add them.

Arithmetic Rules

In Task 1.1.2, it was pointed out that a mental arithmetic strategy for multiplying numbers close to tens is to decompose the number and multiply separately. Another version of this same rule was then illustrated using area diagrams prior to Task 1.2.4. There are several mental strategies that can be hard to verbalise but easy to recognise when the situation arises.

Task 1.4.3 Mental Strategies

The following general statements are taken from Augustus de Morgan writing in 1883. For each statement, construct an example in which it might be useful, then express it in symbols as a generality.

'We do not alter the sum of two numbers by taking away a part of the first, if we annex that part to the second.'

'We do not alter the difference of two numbers by increasing or diminishing one of them, provided we increase or diminish the other as much.'

'If we wish to multiply one number by another, we may break up one of them into parts and multiply each of the parts by the multiplier, and add the results.'

'The same thing may be done with the multiplier instead of the multiplicand (the number being multiplied).'

'If any two or more numbers be multiplied together, it is indifferent what order they are multiplied, the result is the same.'

'In dividing one number by another, we may break up the dividend, and divide each of the parts by the divisor, and then add the results.' ... 'The same thing cannot be done with the divisor' (De Morgan, 1883 pp. 23–4).

Comment

Notice that in the second statement, 'increasing or diminishing' means adding or subtracting, not multiplying or dividing.

Did you construct an example to show that 'the same thing cannot be done with the divisor'? Finding counter-examples to variations is an important component of appreciating what a statement is really saying.

One way to work on these observations with learners is to use diagrams or to use a standard situation that learners can imagine. For example, imagine you have a bag of marbles, but you do not know exactly how many there are. You can remove some marbles with one hand, and some others with the other hand. If you remove one less with the first hand, and one more with the second, you still remove the same number over all.

THOANs

The acronym **THOAN** is a short form for **TH**ink **O**f **A** Number, where numbers are here taken to mean any number with which learners can comfortably do arithmetic, usually whole numbers. A calculator may be useful for trying specific numbers or for extending the range of numbers. In various forms, THOANs have been used since medieval times. Adolescents are often intrigued by a mathematician's ability to predict answers after seemingly complex sequences of calculations. Of course, it is all done with algebra.

Task 1.4.4a THOANs

Think of a number between 1 and 10. Add 1; double the result; add 3; subtract 4; add 5; halve the result; add 6; subtract 7; add 8; subtract 9; subtract the number you first thought of.

Comment

Your answer is 1, no matter what number you started with.

One way to THOAN is to imagine you are moving about on a number-line. Another way is to imagine the numeral in your mind.

Of course, you can vary the ending by asking people for their answer and then telling them their starting number, or subtracting 1 and telling them they now have their starting number.

How can the answer be independent of the starting number? Although each participant starts with a particular number, the leader is ignorant of what they have chosen, and so starts with a symbol that stands for an unknown starting number.

To see why, write down the number you first thought of (a particular number). Now write down each subsequent calculation to form a list, one under the other, as an arithmetic operation but *without* actually doing the arithmetic. (It is important that you actually do this!) Now look through your statements and check for ambiguity. Is it perfectly clear which calculation is to be done first, second, and so on in each line? You will need to use brackets correctly, according to the rules discussed in Tasks 1.1.2 and 1.2.4.

Beside your chosen number in a second column, write a cloud. Now on each subsequent line rewrite the calculation using cloud in place of your chosen number. Be careful not to replace the numbers used in the instructions with clouds. Now do what arithmetic you can with the numbers in your final expression. It will eventually come down to 1, showing that no matter what number you started with, represented by cloud, it all disappears in the end to leave you with 1.

Task 1.4.4b THOAN (generalised)

What aspects of the particular calculation sequence could be varied?

How simple a THOAN could you design?

Comment

After enjoying a sequence of THOANs her brother was playing on a car journey, a 7-year-old girl asked if she could 'do one'. She started in confidently and then realised she did not know what to do! So she decided to make a simple one. After a few 'add three, now subtract three', she alighted on 'Think of a number; that's the number you thought of!' with a variant: 'Think of a number; subtract the number you just thought of; your answer is zero!' She laughed and laughed.

Other THOANs include

THOAN; add 2; multiply by the number you first thought of; add 1; take the square root; subtract the number you first thought of; your answer is again 1.
THOAN; square it; add 4; subtract four times the number you first thought of; take the (positive) square root; add 2; you're left with the number you first thought of.

You can easily make up your own; the more complicated they get, the more dependent you will become on being able to manipulate the expressions in order to simplify them. One of the features of a good THOAN is that it builds up a complicated expression one way, and then undoes the expression in a non-obvious way.

Pause for Reflection

Some important arithmetical ideas have passed by along the way to using the expression of generality in order to make sense of those ideas.

Task 1.4R: Reflection
What aspects of generalising are unclear or problematic for you? Are there any topics you teach that do not involve generalisation in some way?
Comment It is not always easy, or even possible, to articulate what it is that you do not understand. It is easy to say 'I don't understand' in a very general way, but much more useful to try to articulate what it is specifically. If a conjecturing atmosphere has been developed, so that learners are willing to try to express themselves even when they have a tentative suggestion, then it is much easier to be of assistance than if they wait until they are confident before saying something out loud.

Every mathematical topic, by virtue of being mathematical, involves generalisation. For example, a technique is a 'general method' for resolving a class of similar problems; a concept is a generality that has many different exemplars. Thus, every lesson affords opportunities for learners to generalise for themselves.

1.5 PEDAGOGICAL ISSUES

This fifth section highlights some of the observations made in the context of specific tasks offered during the previous four sections. Starting with some thoughts about the quickies, working through issues concerning the nature of algebra, it ends with a reflection on the structure of the tasks used in the chapter.

Quickies

The quickies started out in the form 'one more than a multiple of … ', and moved into the language of remainders. The form of the task one might use with specific learners depends on their competence. For example, with some year 7 pupils at the beginning of the year, Jackie Fairchild[1] formulated the task as in the first part of Task 1.5.1.

Task 1.5.1 Coined Tables

I have a 2p coin, and a large (unlimited?) supply of 5p coins. What values can I make?

How do those values relate to the five times table?

How do they relate to the quickies in this chapter?

Comment

Most year 7 pupils quickly recognise that you can make 2 plus a multiple of 5, and suggest representations such as 2 + [something] × 5. The 'something' could be a box, a cloud (to represent a number that someone is thinking but as-yet-unknown to us), a cloud (to represent anything that someone might choose to think of), a word or short-form (*number* or *numb*) or a letter (such as *n* for number).

One way to familiarise learners with exercising their powers is to use variations on the same task over a period of time.

Powers

You saw in some of the earlier tasks (for example, Task 1.3.2) that specialising means trying out particular cases of some generality, in order to develop a sense of what is going on. Whenever a generality is encountered, it is valuable to try to 'see the particular in the general', that is to seek specific, confidence-inspiring, familiar examples. Specialising is something people do all the time in conversation, especially when they try to offer examples or instances that contradict or support, challenge or extend what is being asserted. Every child who gets to school has already displayed the power to specialise for themselves, spontaneously.

Generalising is the flip side of specialising. It means locating some generality that encompasses a collection of particular cases, which is what the tasks have been about. Whenever a particular object or collection of objects is encountered, it is worthwhile trying to 'see the general through the particular', by asking what can be changed while leaving the idea or technique or problem much the same.

What is Algebra?

This chapter has proposed that algebra is most usefully seen as a language in which to express generalities, usually to do with numbers. Learners will only understand algebra as a language of expression if they perceive and express generalities for themselves. At first this takes time, but in this way learners become effective users of algebra.

Experience with expressing generality in different contexts leads to multiple expressions for the same thing. For example:

- the area diagrams (see Task 1.2.4) are open to several different readings leading to different expressions;
- counting features of picture sequences such as the number of blocks, edges, faces, etc. almost always leads to many different ways of seeing how to count, and each of these yields a different expression of the same generality: the count;
- the sales tax and discount tasks (see Tasks 1.3.3 and 1.3.4) show that there are different ways of calculating tax and price, and care is needed to make sure that the correct calculation is being used.

For each of these examples, the general expression reveals much more than the particular cases.

Pedagogy of the Chapter

The chapter, like most of the book, is structured around mathematical tasks. It is what you notice while doing the tasks that is likely to inform your future use of algebra and your future teaching of it. The sections have been constructed with a number of pedagogical constructs or principles in mind. This provides one important reason that you should actually do the tasks yourself, rather than just thinking about them or imagining yourself doing them – that 'doing' is the only means by which you can experience the pedagogic ideas directly for yourself.

For example, it has been suggested that manipulating familiar objects that inspire confidence is the beginning of getting a sense of structure, and that the structure eventually emerges in the form of a generalisation or expression.

You will learn most from your own first articulations of the emerging generalisation. Remember that all first articulations are likely to be flawed, sometimes seriously. They are best treated as conjectures, for their status is temporary and conjectural. By saying conjectures out loud, and even making a brief note of them, you separate yourself somewhat from them, so you can look at them more dispassionately. By externalising them, using your notebook, they can be pinned down long enough to test them, and perhaps modify or even reject them in favour of a new version.

These ideas are usefully summarised in terms of manipulating–getting-a-sense-of–articulating (MGA) as a cycle or spiral of activity.

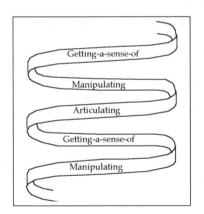

At any time you can specialise to some example that is familiar and confidence-inspiring, manipulating it so as to get-a-sense-of structure leading to re-articulating the general for yourself. Sometimes the first specialising is insufficient, so further specialising is required.

The MGA spiral is thus intimately related to the use of the power to specialise and to generalise that drives mathematics.

You may have noticed yourself, or learners, using 'it' quite often when trying to articulate a generality. For example, 'you take it and you add to it and then you double it'.

In this case, the third 'it' refers to something different from the first two. It is well worth while becoming attuned to learners using 'it' when explaining something, and inviting them to clarify to what the 'it' refers, for often 'it' hides confusion or obscures a switch in what is being attended to.

Task Strategies

Some strategies have been suggested for prompting learners to become aware of possible generalities. These include:

- paying attention to *how* you draw or calculate or count in particular cases (*how* particular cases work) in order to become aware of the *how* as a generality;

- using large unwieldy numbers that no one wants to calculate with in order to direct attention towards structure and away from particular calculations;
- paying attention to and probing the use of indefinite pronouns ('it', 'that', 'this') when learners are explaining what they are doing or thinking (often 'it' and 'this' hide a slide from one object to another, creating confusion);
- explicit use of variation in detail to promote a shift of attention from particulars to what can be varied or changed and still the same idea applies (see for example, Task 1.1.2a);
- ... another and another ... often leads people to expand their horizons and become more creative, even extreme, in the construction of mathematical objects, thus enriching their awareness and their experience;
- encouraging the learner to construct their own extreme or complicated examples to reinforce their creativity, and in becoming aware of a range of possibilities from which to choose, to develop their sense of generality. Being trusted to make choices (and to check conjectures) supports learners in seeing themselves as active, competent doers of mathematics.

Most of the task-types used in this book have been borrowed from the culture of class-rooms and from numerous researchers and teachers, such as Brown and Walter (1983), Prestage and Perks (2001), Watson and Mason (2002; 2004) and Bills *et al.* (2004).

It is vital to challenge learners, but not to over-challenge them with tasks they cannot do, or under-challenge them with tasks that are too easy. The same applies to your work on this book: you should feel able to work on tasks that challenge you, extend those that are easy for you and decide that some tasks are inappropriate for you at this time.

You may feel that the pacing of this chapter has not been quite right for you – perhaps too fast or too slow. Either way, further examples can be found on the associated website (www.paulchapmanpublishing.co.uk/resource/algebra.pdf). The pedagogic significance of the chapter lies in becoming attuned to noticing opportunities, within standard topics, to pause briefly and get learners to express generality.

Final Reflections

Task 1.5.R Reflection

What struck you about the work in this chapter?

What do the following terms mean to you, currently? Try telling someone else, or writing down something about them.

    Specialising

    Generalising

    Expressing generality

    Conjecturing

    Algebra

What aspects of the tasks gave you some pleasure (even just a tiny bit)? Not which tasks, but what happened inside you? How might that happen for your learners?

Note

1   Private communication. This was brought to our attention by Jackie Fairchild.

2 Using Mathematical Powers; Meeting Mathematical Themes

Chapter 2 revisits specialising and generalising, and suggests further powers that all learners display and that play a fundamental role in doing and learning mathematics. The chapter introduces freedom and constraint, reading diagrams and imagining and expressing, while building on the mathematical themes that you met in the previous chapter such as 'seeing the general in the particular' and 'variation'. The chapter ends with a review from a pedagogic viewpoint.

2.1 SPECIALISING AND GENERALISING

Quickie 2.1

2^3 means $2 \times 2 \times 2$; 3^5 means $3 \times 3 \times 3 \times 3 \times 3$. What does 5^3 mean?

What is the same and what is different about $2^5 \times 2^6 = 2^{11}$, $3^5 \times 3^6 = 3^{11}$, and $5^5 \times 5^6 = 5^{11}$? Generalise.

What ought to be the meaning for 2^4, 2^3, 2^2, … ? Generalise.

Comment

What did you attend to in order to work out what the index (the little number above the base) means?

Seeing the General through the Particular

It is important to get a taste of how, from one or two particular instances, it is possible to see through to the general. It is tempting to call the particular cases in Quickie 2.1 *examples*. But of what are they examples? They are only examples *of* something when you have appreciated a generality of which they could be particular instances. For example, $2^5 \times 2^6 = 2^{11}$ is only an example of the laws of indices when it is seen as a particular instance of $x^n \times x^m = x^{n+m}$.

Task 2.1.1 Adding Constraints

Write down a number that, when you subtract 1, the result is divisible by 2. Write down another such number. And another.

Write down a number that, when you subtract 1, the result is divisible by 2 and by 3. Write down another such number. And a harder example.

Write down a number that, when you subtract 1, the result is divisible by 2 and by 3, and by 4. Express all such numbers. Write down another such number. And another.

Keep generating and as you do so, describe what you see.

Comment

Experience with the quickies in Chapter 1 probably helped you to see that in each case the number being sought is 1 more than a multiple of 2, then 1 more than a multiple of both 2 and 3, then 1 more than a multiple of 2, 3 and 4. It is tempting to follow the pattern of multiplying 2 and 3 to get 6, by multiplying the 2, 3 and 4 to get 24. But what is wanted is a number that is a multiple of 2, of 3, and of 4, and 12 meets all of these criteria. Indeed, 12 is not only the smallest positive number with this property, but all other numbers with this property are themselves a multiple of 12.

What is the generality of which this task is an example? First, there is an implicit pattern in the 'divisible by 2, then by 3, then by 4', suggesting carrying on with 5, 6, 7, … . There is no general formula for a number that is a multiple of 2, 3, 4, …, n.

Second, the number subtracted could be altered. If the number subtracted is allowed to change at each stage, then the task becomes much more difficult! The point is that exploring variation in the question can lead to challenging problems.

Seeing the Particular in the General

Hand in hand with detecting and expressing generality is the reverse process of taking a general statement and constructing particular cases. Although it sounds easy, it is not always immediately apparent that something is actually a particular case of something else.

Task 2.1.2a Adding and Multiplying

In general,

$$a + (1 + \tfrac{1}{a-1}) = a \times (1 + \tfrac{1}{a-1}).$$

This looks like a worryingly complex statement to many people.

Try some special cases. For example:

$$3 + (1 + \tfrac{1}{2}) = 3 \times (1 + \tfrac{1}{2}) \quad \text{and} \quad 4 + (1 + \tfrac{1}{3}) = 4 \times (1 + \tfrac{1}{3}).$$

Write down the particular cases when a is 5 and 7. Keep writing down special cases until you get a sense of the generality.

In what sense is the statement $2 + 2 = 2 \times 2$ a particular case of this generality? What happens when $a = 1$, or $a = 0$?

Comment

When *a* is 6, the statement can be written as

$$6 + 1\tfrac{1}{5} = 6 \times 1\tfrac{1}{5}.$$

The point about specialising is to base your confidence in being able to get a sense of what is going on, no matter how off-putting the symbols are at first.

Did you notice any differences between identifying a generality corresponding to a given particularity, in the previous section and specialising a generality for yourself?

When $2 + 2$ is re-written as $2 + 1\tfrac{1}{1}$ it fits the general pattern more clearly.

A good strategy whenever you meet a general mathematical statement, especially one that seems confusing or abstract, is to specialise: to a few simple cases, to an extreme case of some sort, and to a sort of 'middling' case by means of which you can get a sense of what the generalisation is saying. Watching What You Do as you carry out the calculations can assist in detecting the structure and re-expressing that as a generality for yourself.

Task 2.1.2b Seeing the Particular

For each of the calculations in the first two rows, decide whether it is a particular case of one of the generalities in the third row.

$4.1^2 - 3.5^2 = 0.6 \times 7.6$	$3^3 + 2^3 = 5 \times (9 + 6 + 4)$	$4 \times 74 = 280 + 16$
$22 \times 22 = 480 + 4$	$4t^4 - 9t^2 = t^2(4t - 3)(4t + 3)$	$64 - 1 = 7 \times 9$
$a(b + c) = ab + ac$	$a^2 - b^2 = (a - b)(a + b)$	$a^3 + b^3 = (a + b)(a^2 + ab + b^2)$

Comment

What is most useful is to become aware of *how* you went about the task. Were you satisfied with superficial features to distinguish to which generality each particular belonged, or did you check all of the details?

In order to check for a match, you effectively discern details in the particular and locate corresponding elements in the general.

In order to specialise a generality you have to pay attention to each of the elements in the generality which are general, and replace them with particulars. In some algebra texts this is referred to as *substituting* a number for a variable. Instead of constituting a mechanical exercise for learners, however, it can be recast as in Task 2.1.2 as an act of specialising that is useful to perform whenever you are stuck on or confused by a generality.

Task 2.1.3 Odd Sum

Someone announced that the sum of consecutive odd numbers is always the difference of two squares. What do you think?

Comment

A natural thing to do is to try some particular examples (specialise). The examples themselves may be useful if you discover a counter-example (an example that shows the conjecture needs modifying), but examples are most useful when they reveal what is going on. Once you have discerned *that* it seems to work, you can start focusing more specifically on looking for relationships. For example, how are the relevant square numbers related to the sequence of consecutive odd numbers? Then you can try to express that relationship in words, clouds, or symbols according to your preferences and current confidence.

Specialising and Generalising

Specialising and generalising are not just 'things to do' to make tasks interesting. They lie at the heart of mathematical thinking, both when exploring and when trying to make sense of some assertion or conjecture, including assertions coming from authorities such as textbook authors. Whenever you find yourself stalled or stuck when working on a task or when reading a text, get into the habit of asking yourself whether there is a particular case, not too simple, not too complex, that you can use to try to see what is going on. The MGA spiral in Chapter 1 summarises the actions you take, as you *manipulate* a familiar example to try to *get a sense* of what is happening, so as to bring that sense-of to *articulation*, and eventually to express it in some useful mathematical form. That form, that articulation can then become, with experience, a confidence-inspiring familiar object to be used in future specialising.

The famous German mathematician David Hilbert (1862–1943) changed the direction of mathematics research in 1900 by announcing 21 mathematical problems he thought needed to be solved.

> He (Hilbert) was a most concrete, intuitive mathematician who invented, and very consciously used, a principle; namely, if you want to solve a problem first strip the problem of everything that is not essential. Simplify it, specialize it as much as you can without sacrificing its core. Thus it becomes simple, as simple as can be made, without losing any of its punch, and then you solve it. The generalization is a triviality that you don't have to pay much attention to. This principle of Hilbert's proved extremely useful for him and also for others who learned it from him. Unfortunately, it has been forgotten (Courant, 1981, p. 161).

The twentieth century mathematician Paul Halmos said:

> the source of all great mathematics is the special case, the concrete example. It is frequent in mathematics that every instance of a concept of seemingly great generality is in essence the same as a small and concrete special case (Halmos, 1985, p. 324).

> An intrinsic aspect of [teaching] at all levels, elementary or advanced, is to concentrate attention on the definite, the concrete, the specific … We all have an

innate ability to generalize; the teacher's function is to call attention to a concrete special case that hides (and, we hope, ultimately reveals) the germ of conceptual difficulty (Halmos, 1994, p. 272).

Task 2.1.4 One Sum

If two numbers sum to one, then which will be bigger – the square of the larger added to the smaller or the square of the smaller added to the larger?

Comment

A natural response is to try some examples. Choosing special cases makes the arithmetic easy (e.g. 0 and 1, or $\frac{1}{2}$ and $\frac{1}{2}$), but these are not terribly convincing. After all, it might be too extreme. There are so many possibilities. Confidence with fractions might lead to trying examples like $\frac{1}{3}$ and $\frac{2}{3}$; confidence with decimals might lead to 0.3 and 0.7 or 0.2 and 0.8. But what about 1.5 and $^-0.5$?

Having tried a number of examples, it is hard not to be convinced that the two answers will indeed always be the same. But so far, only a few cases have been tried. How is it possible to know for certain that no matter what numbers are chosen (summing to one of course), the two computations will wield the same answer? For the moment there is a conjecture that the answers will always be the same. It is not proved, merely tested in a few cases.

Since there is a lurking generality, the best thing to do is to express that generality. First express the generality in words, then once you are fluent in algebra you can use it as a more economic way of expressing the same ideas. The symbols become entities you can manipulate with confidence as you did numbers.

Let x be any number whatsoever. There is a touch of power in that utterance: 'let x be …'. It is a supremely creative act, and it wields power over all numbers. It also reveals a fact about possible numbers that solve the problem: the second number must be $1 - x$, since they must sum to one.

Then the two expressions to compare are $x^2 + (1 - x)$ and $(1 - x)^2 + x$. Now it is possible to manipulate these expressions in order to see why they always give the same answer, no matter what number is put in place of x. Since $(1 - x)^2$ means $(1 - x) \times (1 - x)$ and since everything in one bracket has to be multiplied with everything in the other, it turns out that $(1 - x)^2 + x = 1 - x - x + x^2 + x = 1 - x + x^2$, which is the same as the other expression. So the two expressions must always give the same values.

The important feature of this task was the natural response of trying some special or particular cases. The purpose of trying them is to get behind the calculations to experience the structure.

Pause for Reflection

Task 2.1.R Reflection

Describe as if to a colleague what it means to 'see the general through the particular'. How does it relate to specialising; particularly where a lot of cases are tried?

Comment

Specialising by trying many cases builds up confidence and experience, which then contribute to a sense of what might be going on. It is not the individual cases themselves that are informative, but how they are interpreted. Taking a single particular case and paying close attention to how it is drawn, calculated, formulated, etc. can reveal what is changing (and how) and what is staying the same, which when expressed, yields a (conjectured) generality. This is 'seeing the general through the particular'.

2.2 FREEDOM AND CONSTRAINT: SEEKING STRUCTURE

Quickie 2.2

If 2^3 means $2 \times 2 \times 2 = 8$, and 2^2 means $2 \times 2 = 4$, and 2^1 means 2, what operation takes you from term to term? What might 2^0 mean?

Comment

Pay attention to what is the same and what is different about each of the instances provided. How are the instances related? Have you noticed the pattern 3, 2, 1, 0 in the indices? Have you noticed a pattern in the value in each case $(8, 4, 2 \dots)$?

This section is concerned with a theme that pervades mathematics: freedom and constraint. Solving equations can be seen as a process of trying to find out whether there is any freedom left in the choices for some variables subject to stated constraints.

Freedom and Constraint

Think of a number, any number. Settle on a specific one. Now think of a number between 23.1 and 23.2. It is highly unlikely that your first number satisfies this new constraint, so you have an experience of how initial freedom can become constrained. Even so, there is considerable freedom despite the new constraint. This section explores this pervasive mathematical theme of adding constraints to initial freedom of choice.

Task 2.2.1 Four Numbers Summing to ...

Find four numbers that sum to 50, and another four numbers. And another. Find four numbers that sum to 37, and another four, and another. Find four numbers that sum to 0.31287. In how many different ways can you find four numbers that sum to a specified number?

Did you allow fractions? Decimals? Negatives?

Comment

At first sight this is an arithmetic task not an algebra task. The algebra arises when you are asked for more examples, and you become aware of a generality as you make your choices.

How did you start? Did you prepare the way by deciding to use two numbers to make 25 and then repeat them, or two numbers to make 20 and two to make 30? Did you take extreme examples such as 1, 1, 1, 47? Or did you set off choosing the first three numbers and only then deciding what the last one had to be? Some people choose four numbers, add them up and then see how close they are to fifty, adjusting one of the numbers appropriately. Others choose three numbers and then work out what the fourth number has to be.

Did the more complicated sums prompt you to change your approach? Were you aware of your approach as a method you could use for any number?

No matter what approach you take, there is an opportunity with a task such as the previous one to experience where there is freedom of choice and, where there are constraints, even to the extent of reducing choice to just one possibility, or even turning out to be impossible to complete. As with most of the tasks in this book, the previous task could be modified to suit learners at different levels: numbers could multiply to make a given total, or their square-roots could add to a given total, or the sines of four angles could add to a given total, and so on. Another way to complexify is to add further constraints.

Task 2.2.2 Constrained Choice

Write down a fraction whose value lies between 3 and 4; whose denominator is a multiple of 5; whose numerator is a multiple of 11, and whose denominator is less than 17. How many can you find? *This may look hard*, so instead, try the following sequence derived from it:

Write down a fraction whose value lies between 3 and 4.

Write down a fraction whose value lies between 3 and 4 and whose denominator is a multiple of 5; find a way to write down all such fractions.

Comment

One way to work on this is to make a list of possible fractions and then look for an expressible pattern in them: $\frac{16}{5}, \frac{17}{5}, \frac{18}{5}, \frac{19}{5}, \frac{31}{10}, \frac{33}{10}, \frac{37}{10}, \ldots$ (repetitions due to simplification have been omitted but might be usefully left in the list). The ones with denominator 5 are of the form $\frac{15+m}{5}$ for $m = 1, 2, 3, 4$; the ones with denominator 10 are of the form $\frac{30+m}{10}$ for $m = 1, \ldots 9$; the ones with denominator 15 are of the form $\frac{45+m}{15}$ for $m = 1, \ldots 14$; and so on. From these local generalisations, a global one can be detected: $\frac{15n+m}{15}$ for n a positive integer and $m = 1, \ldots, 5n - 1$.

By piling on the constraints one at a time, with attention directed to finding not just one example at each stage, but all possible examples, what looks initially as a daunting task becomes manageable. This is a choice that can be made whenever you find yourself stuck on a problem: simplify it in any way that preserves something of the challenge, but makes it easier to think about. Resolve the simplified version, but try to find all possible solutions. Then add back another constraint.

Constraints may be imposed from outside, or they may be imposed by the structure of some phenomenon, such as a multiplication table. But constraints can also be imposed by the learner, sometimes helpfully, and sometimes unexpectedly blocking further progress on the task. Thus there are close links with discerning details, detecting relationships, and making properties.

Seeking Structure

Task 2.2.3a Multiples Tables

Say What You See in the way of patterns and connections in the standard multiplication table.

1	2	3	4	5	6	7	8	9	...
2	4	6	8	10	12	14	16	18	...
3	6	9	12	15	18	21	24	27	...
4	8	12	16	20	24	28	32	36	...
5	10	15	20	25	30	35	40	45	...
6	12	18	24	30	36	42	48	54	...
7	14	21	28	35	42	49	56	63	...
8	16	24	32	40	48	56	64	72	...
9	18	27	36	45	54	63	72	81	...
...	...	...	...	...	...	...	...	...	...

Comments: sample observations–conjectures

In the row starting 2, the units digits repeat 2, 4, 6, 8, 0, ...
In the column starting 5, the units digits alternate 0 and 5.
What will the units digits be in column 3 if it is extended further?
The numbers in the main diagonal top left to bottom right are all square numbers.
What happens along diagonals that move upwards to the right (as in 4, 6, 6, 4)?
In the column headed 2 there are 4 single-digit numbers, then 5 two-digit numbers. What happens subsequently?

Comments: relation to freedom and constraint

The table structure imposes constraints on what numbers can appear in any place. There is a sense of constrained-freedom in the table extending on and on in each direction. Being asked to Say What You See gives learners a wide range of choice as to what to describe and draw attention to. Where learners are given choices, they are more likely to exercise responsibility and to be interested and motivated than when their freedom to choose is severely constrained.

Observations turn into conjectures as soon as someone expects the pattern observed to continue beyond the boundaries of what has been checked. For example, in the row starting 2, 4, 6, 8, you are adding two each time, so after 8 will be 0, then 2, 4, 6, 8 again, over and over. Which entries in that row will end in 2? In 8? Note how this pattern is about stressing the units' digits and ignoring the other digits in the numerals. It is the sense of 'continuing on and on' that gives access to generality.

The invitation to Say What You See can be very useful in generating discussion, drawing attention to different features, and slowing learners down who tend to jump in with the first idea that comes to mind. Inviting people not to use technical terms and not to explain, but just use language to direct everyone's attention to some feature they have noticed exercises the power to express and, at the same time, exercises other people's power to imagine and to follow directions.

Task 2.2.3b Multiples Tables Variant

Say What You See in the way of patterns and connections in the table.

5	10	15	20	25	30	35	40	45	...
10	20	30	40	50	60	70	80	90	...
15	30	45	60	75	90	105	120	135	...
20	40	60	80	100	120	140	160	180	...
25	50	75	100	125	150	175	200	225	...
30	60	90	120	150	180	210	240	270	...
35	70	105	140	175	210	245	280	315	...
40	80	120	160	200	240	280	320	360	...
45	90	135	180	225	270	315	360	405	...
...	...	...	...	...	...	...	...	...	...

Comment

You may wish to connect this to a multiplication table, or to treat it simply as a source of patterns. For example, some learners may concentrate on the fact that some columns alternate the last digit while others are all zeros. The columns with all numbers ending in zeros have 'tables' as the numbers in front of the zero. Others may notice that the second column is double the first, the third treble the first, and so on. What numbers would appear two columns to the left of the first column? What about two rows above the top row?

The software program Monty[1] provides a dynamic presentation of patterns in tables. A spreadsheet can be used effectively to impose windows on tables such as these in order to focus attention on certain patterns.

The next task can be taken as an example of how equation-solving can be seen as starting from great freedom of choice, and then, through imposing constraints, narrowing down the choice. Adding further constraints may limit choices further, or may simply complicate the search for the remaining possibilities.

Task 2.2.4 Doing and Undoing

I am thinking of a number between one and ten; when I add two, I get six. What is my number? How did you find it?

I am thinking of a number between one and ten; when I add two, then divide by three, the answer is two; What is my number? How did you find it?

I am thinking of a number between one and ten; when I add two, then divide by three, then multiply by five, the answer is ten. What is my number? How did you find it?

I am thinking of a number between one and ten; when I add two, then divide by three, then multiply by five, then subtract four, the answer is 6. What is my number? How did you find it?

Comment

'I am thinking of a number' signals a great deal of freedom. Each additional fact is a constraint on the freedom.

The key question is not getting the answers, but 'how did you do it?' Doing and undoing is designed so that, when used repeatedly, learners become familiar with and articulate about how addition and subtraction are related, and also about how multiplication and division are related. There is a natural link with THOANs (Chapter 1) because they involve building up some complexity (doing) and then undoing but not by simply reversing each operation in turn.

Getting learners to complexify something that is initially complicated is one way to prepare them to recognise an appropriate technique when they meet a complicated situation in the future. More generally, given any calculation process that starts from a number and gives a result, it is useful to ask whether it is possible to reverse or undo the calculations sequence so as to be able to answer the question, 'if this was the answer when using that calculation, what was the question?'

Pause for Reflection

Freedom and constraint is a powerful theme because it works on a psychological as well as mathematical level. Mathematics provides a way of expressing freedom of choice (using a letter to denote the choice, or a cloud to denote an as-yet-unknown choice), of imposing constraints, and then for searching to see what of any objects meet all the constraints. Instead of imposing lots of constraints at once, it is often useful to impose them sequentially, both to facilitate working out the consequences of the constraints, and to experience the forced restriction of freedom due to each constraint.

Task 2.2.R Reflection

What examples can you bring to mind of freedom and constraint in everyday life?

2.3 READING DIAGRAMS

Quickie 2.3

What patterns can you see in the table? Extend it downwards and to the right and left.

$2^3 = 2 \times 2 \times 2$	$2^2 = 2 \times 2 \times 2$	$2^1 = 2$	$2^0 = 1$	$2^{-1} = 1/2$	$2^{-2} = 1/(2\times2) = 1/2^2$
$3^3 = 3 \times 3 \times 3$	$3^2 = 3 \times 3 \times 3$	$3^1 = 3$	$3^0 = 1$	$3^{-1} = 1/3$	$3^{-2} = 1/(3\times3) = 1/3^2$
$4^3 = 4 \times 4 \times 4$	$4^2 = 4 \times 4 \times 4$	$4^1 = 4$	$4^0 = 1$	$4^{-1} = 1/4$	$4^{-2} = 1/(4\times4) = 1/4^2$

This section returns to the theme of interpreting diagrams as sources of generalisation and as ways of depicting relationships.

Seeing and Other Senses

It is tempting to use words to do with 'seeing' when inviting people to look at diagrams or to imagine things, but many people prefer either 'hearing' or 'sensing'. Yet the language of 'seeing' is endemic in everyday language. Expressions such as 'I see what you are saying', 'it appears to be the case', and 'Now it is clear', or even 'clearly!' are all predominantly visual at root.

Throughout this book the word *see* is to be taken as broadly as possible, signalling whatever inner experiences are being triggered at the time. Similarly, the word *imagine* is taken to mean whatever inner sense(s) you experience, whether predominantly visual, aural or tactile. Sometimes one may be supplemented by the others; sometimes no one particular sense is dominant yet there is some 'sense of' what is being talked about. The point is that most people have access to all senses, but some people have strongly developed preferences.

Say What You See

A diagram may 'be worth a thousand words', but it is not always easy to work out quite what those thousand words are! When you draw your own diagram, you are expressing something of which you are already aware. The point of drawing a diagram for someone else is so that they experience something, as in 'I see what you're saying'. When you encounter someone else's diagram, you have to make sense of it, just as you do with text. So when using a diagram, either making sense of someone else's, or drawing your own, it is useful to pay careful attention to details and relationships.

The phrase Say What You See is intended to trigger you to pause and to articulate features that you discern in the diagram, and relations between these features, as a strategy to help you make sense of the diagram. It is an example of the MGA spiral at work as you get-a-sense-of and then articulate perceived relationships as conjectures, and express them as generalities.

Task 2.3.1 Say What You See

Say out loud what you see in the picture.

Write out instructions as to how to draw it so that someone else could follow without seeing the picture.

Now try to locate a different way for drawing the picture.

Comment

Did you find yourself giving an overall description (there are five triangles around a pentagon …), or did you start in with some specific details? Did you start in the middle and work out, or start outside and work in? These are all choices to be made when describing to others. Did you try to draw it yourself, without looking at the picture while drawing? There are some implicit relationships that may not be evident until you try to draw for yourself.

If you tried to draw the picture yourself you may have found it helpful to pay attention to how you drew it. And you may easily have made one or more starts that you could not continue because through drawing it you became aware of relationships that you had not spotted just by looking. Saying *just* what you see without trying to label the picture can focus attention on details rather than being absorbed by the overall impression. While the global may be helpful, it can mask details that are essential to appreciating structure, that is, relationships implied or indicated. Attending only to details leaves you caught in particular details. Flexible movement to and fro between details and relationships leads to appreciation of the whole through and with its parts.

The picture is reasonably attractive to many people. But what relationships make it what it is? What about it could be changed, and still it looks much the same? What are the principles that are used to generate it? How might it be extended or varied? These questions are integral to appreciating the picture as a mathematical object.

For example, if you see the picture as generated by a central interior pentagon with its edges extended in a Catherine-wheel manner, each by the same amount, then the outer pentagon is formed by joining up successive ends of the arms. The picture could be extended by doing the same thing to the outer pentagon: extending its edges to make another Catherine wheel. But this raises a question about how far to extend the arms each time. There is no obvious relationship arising from the picture, although one might be tempted to ask whether the opposite edges will always be parallel no matter what extension is used. Aspects of generality creep in at every stage, concerning what choices must be made in order to be faithful to the original diagram, and what choices are arbitrary, or free.

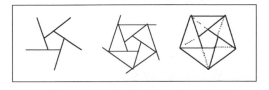

Immediately, more questions arise: if the extensions are scaled down each time by a fixed ratio, will the diagram extend forever or will it be bounded inside some circle. If the latter, what is the smallest radius of a bounding circle compared to the original pentagon?

If you see the picture as an outer pentagon with parts of the chords drawn from each vertex to the next but one in a counter-clockwise direction, then the picture takes on a new appearance, and different extensions and developments are likely. Does the use of the chord construction determine a relationship between the inner and outer pentagon, and, if so, what is that ratio? Most significantly, looking at the picture the first way might not have attracted attention to the chords' property, whereas looking at it this way the chords become more salient.

Notice how having a diagram, especially one that you have drawn for yourself, enables you to 'see through' the diagram to features that could be extended or varied. Diagrams stabilise parts of mental images, enabling you to work *on* the diagram not just gaze at it, to imagine more aspects or elements imposed but not depicted. You get a sense of what is constrained and what is free to change, perhaps within constraints.

The next task involves expressing generality, but it is worth drawing a version for yourself so that you can *watch what you do*, as well as *saying what you see*.

Task 2.3.2 Pattern Wheels

A printer's roller, rather like a wallpaper roller, has some patterns carved on it. It is inked and then run along a strip of paper to reveal:

All you know is that the wheel has gone around *at least* twice. Imagine that it keeps on rolling (the ink stays wet!) and the sequence carries on and on.

Predict the pattern of the twentieth square if the wheel continues to roll; predict the pattern of the hundredth square. Justify your conjectures by reference to the picture and how it is generated.

Note: the statement that it has gone around *at least twice* forces the patterns of each square to be uniquely determined, no matter how far the sequence is extended.

Make up your own pattern sequences and then make predictions. Do enough so that you are confident you can 'do any question of this type'.

How do you direct your attention in order to locate the repeating pattern that appears at least twice in the following?

Comment

Did you notice yourself looking for a consistent way to discern a pattern that repeats from the beginning?

Can you make a similar task in which it is even harder to see what the repeating pattern will be? What makes locating the repeating pattern difficult?

Notice the reoccurrence of *doing and undoing*. Whenever you have a technique or a process that produces a result (a 'doing'), it is fruitful to turn the process around and ask what other starting conditions would produce the same result (undoing). Then you can move on to characterise all possible results from using that process. These are recurrent mathematical themes that will be elaborated as you work through the book.

Pause for Reflection

If you want learners to say 'Oh, I see what you are saying!', or 'Oh, I hear what you are saying!', then it is worthwhile learning to 'say what you see (or hear, or sense)'. In other words, look for opportunities to try to give an account of something you have seen or heard or done, briefly but vividly, so that others can enter into the situation from their own experience. Teachers of mathematics share with teachers of English and history the opportunity to prompt learners to become aware of and to develop their powers to imagine and to express what they imagine to others.

Task 2.3.R Reflection

What for you is the same and what is different about reading text, reading diagrams, and reading symbolic expressions?

2.4 IMAGINING AND EXPRESSING

Quickie 2.4

Following the rules expressed in the quickies so far in this chapter, what ought to be the result of $5^{\frac{1}{2}} \times 5^{\frac{1}{2}}$, and what does that suggest as a meaning for $5^{\frac{1}{2}}$?

You have noticed that $4^0 = 1, 3^0 = 1, 2^0 = 1, 1^0 = 1$

What value does this sequence suggest should be assigned to 0^0?

What does the following sequence suggest is the value of 0^0?

$0^4 = 0 \times 0 \times 0 \times 0 = 0, 0^3 = 0 \times 0 \times 0 = 0, 0^2 = 0 \times 0 = 0, 0^1 = 0, 0^0 = ?$

Comment

Zero is a somewhat anomalous number, because of its multiplicative property, so it is likely to prove awkward when considering powers. The fact that different routes suggest different values of 0^0 leads mathematicians to treat 0^0 as undefined (indefinable, meaningless), because there is no consistent value to be assigned to it.

Imagination is a powerful instrument. It is used to imagine some process continuing; combining together unusual or novel elements in some way; imposing objects mentally on some diagram or scene; imagining some elements changing but preserving some relationships and so on. It is the basis of how people talk to each other (describing what they are aware of), how they predict, and why they are surprised (having not predicted). This section is about some of the ways in which this power can be exploited to pedagogical advantage.

Seeing Beyond the Diagram

Seeing the general through the particular has already been suggested as a useful way of reaching for and articulating a generality: some features are retained as invariant, while others are permitted to be changed or varied. Diagrams, like electronic screens, show particulars, and it is up to the reader to work out what is particular and can be varied, and what is structural and must remain invariant. This section considers the way in which it is useful to look beyond what is actually displayed.

Task 2.4.1a Squared Off

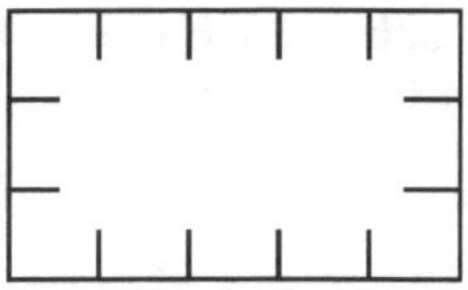

How many of the (implied) small squares are needed to make up the whole rectangle on the left?

Using only your eyes and without touching the figure on the right in any way, how many squares are needed to fill out the whole rectangle?

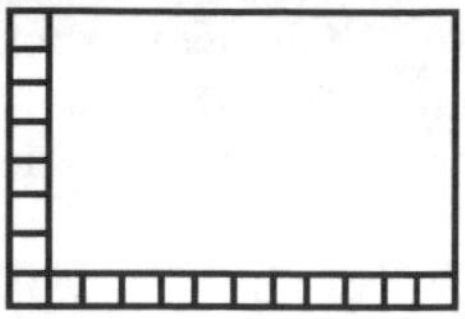

Comment

The issue here is not the actual computations, but seeing what computations are needed. To do this it is necessary to imagine what is not displayed, only suggested. Controlling your eye movements in order to count the squares is also non-trivial for many people. It calls upon directing attention to squares in turn while counting, and retaining one number while doing the count in the other direction. Did you find yourself counting the shorter side first? Might this have been a possibly unconscious strategy to 'do the simpler one first'?

It is not necessary to 'see' the remaining squares outlined, but it is possible to have a sense-of the squares being completed, and to sense that the rectangle is made up of 3 rows of 5 or 5 columns of 3 without actually seeing them completed. Yet researchers (Battista et al,. (1988), cited in Day and Kalman, (2001)) have found that some younger learners do not automatically use their power to imagine. Rather, they focus on what they see directly. They count the spaces around the outside and then add 'a few' for the ones in the centre. This strategy can remain robust even after having filled out the rectangle with tiles and then putting the tiles away.

Three-dimensional objects can cause even more difficulties:

Task 2.4.1b Squared Off Extended

How many unit cubes are needed to make up the following shape (seen from two directions)? Imagine there are no holes.

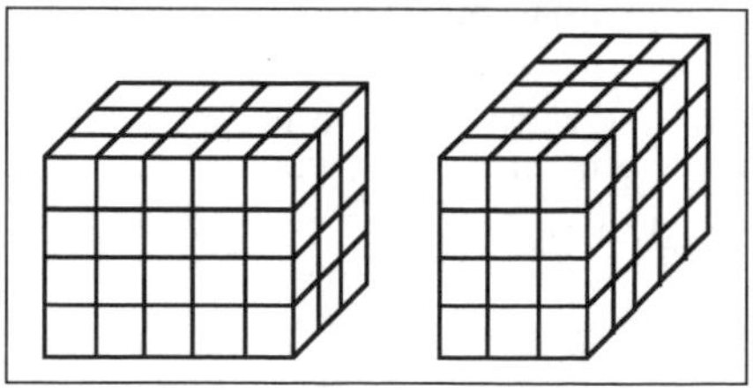

How many unit cubes are needed to make up the following shape (seen from three directions)? Imagine there are no holes.

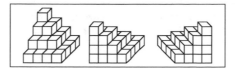

Comment

Why might multiple views be needed? How many views are required to be certain of the number of cubes, assuming no holes?

Many adolescents appear to struggle to 'see' the depiction of a cuboid as a solid and the presumption of the presence of cubes that cannot actually be seen. They seem to be absorbed by what they can actually see. One way to support them in 'filling out' what is depicted is to stimulate them to develop their powers of mental imagery. Indeed, working explicitly with mental imagery can be of help to everyone, and not just in mathematics.

Jerome Bruner (1966) distinguished three forms of representation of abstract concepts and used these to develop a spiral approach to learning. Indeed, it was from his work that the MGA spiral was developed. He suggested that providing learners with concrete physical experiences, in this case perhaps a cuboid made up of unifix cubes, would support them in making initial sense of a concept. However, learners need to internalise their physical 'sense' by forming images (both inner images and outer diagrams and pictures that depict and support those inner images). Bruner called this an *iconic* mode of representation. Thus getting learners to interpret pictures of cuboids as physical cuboids, and drawing pictures to represent a physical cuboid made up of little cubes, while placing the physical versions out of reach, helps wean learners off the need to have the physical model actually present, and encourages and strengthens their mental imagery (in the broadest sense, including visual, visceral, and aural components). Ultimately the images and pictures are replaced by symbols that denote objects.

These three forms of representation − *enactive* (as in 'doing' and 'manipulating'), *iconic* (as in depicting) and *symbolic* (as in denoting but not 'looking like' what is denoted) − not only describe different modes, different ways of thinking, even as different worlds of experience, but also act as a reminder that learners are best served if they are encouraged to overlay the physical with the imagistic, and the imagistic with symbols that can be manipulated.

When something complex or abstract is encountered it is natural to look for some specific example that is familiar and confidence-inspiring. Often this will be in the form of a physical model or representation of the situation, or some pictures or symbols. The important feature is that the example is familiar and confidence-inspiring. Thus symbols and pictures can both serve as manipulable elements, as things to treat enactively. The purpose of manipulating examples is of course to get-a-sense of underlying structure and relationships. This corresponds to Bruner's iconic mode. That growing sense-of is repeatedly articulated in words, diagrams and symbols until it becomes succinct and manageable, and eventually it becomes concrete and confidence-inspiring so as to be used in further manipulation.

Imagining

This subsection features exercises in imagining a number-line and movements both on it and of it. At any time it is possible to stop and make use of a picture, but the longer you persevere without a picture, the stronger your mental imagery will become. Do not forget that the word *imagine* is used here to mean any or all senses you care to employ.

Task 2.4.2a Number-line Movements

Imagine you are standing somewhere on the number-line and facing in the positive or increasing direction. Make a note of where you are. Now imagine going forward 3 steps, then going backward 5 steps, then forward 4 steps, then backward 1 step. How many steps do you need to go (and in which direction) to get back to where you started?

Comment

A variant of this task was exploited by Bob Davis[2] to introduce negative numbers and their arithmetic. He asked learners to imagine a bag containing an unknown number of marbles (or even to have such a bag present). Actions of putting so many marbles in, and taking so many marbles out, were repeated, and then learners were asked to say what action was required to return the bag to the starting number. A bus stopping to pick up and let off passengers is another suitable context.

The focus of discussion is *how* people know how many steps are needed, how many marbles need to be added or taken away, how many people are needed to get on or off the bus to restore its starting number, and that these are independent of what the starting value actually was. It is this invariant that is crucial, permitting a generality to be expressed that it does not matter how many you start with, the sequence of actions will restore that value. The arithmetic is not difficult; what is being offered is a connection between the actions on the number-line and a sense of the movement.

Some contexts permit the use of multiplication as well.

Task 2.4.2b Number-line Movements

Imagine you are standing somewhere on the number-line and facing in the positive or increasing direction. Make a note of where you are. Imagine going forward 3 steps; then backwards by 1; then forwards so as to double your distance from the starting point; then backward 2 steps. How many steps forward or backward do you need to go in order to be back at the starting point?

Comment

Again the actual starting position does not matter: the relative movement required remains the same. The complexity of the movements can be increased substantially, with several actions of 'turning around'. The point, however, is that learners begin spontaneously to generalise concerning the relationships between going forward and backward.

One awareness to be developed through this kind of task is the way that rotation through 180° interchanges the effects of moving forwards and moving backwards. Later this will turn out to mirror the multiplication of positive and negative numbers by negative 1.

Pause for Reflection

> ### Task 2.4.R Reflection
>
> What is the same and what different about imagining points on a number-line and moving up and down it, THOANs, using people getting on and off buses, and using a bag of marbles?
>
> *Comment*
>
> Mathematically they are identical, in that the same operations can be carried out (even on the same numbers) but in different contexts. Offering learners a variety of forms of the same thing (including identical numbers and operations) provides them with an opportunity to notice for themselves that they are all the same. Then they can be challenged to come up with their own contexts for the same operations and numbers, in order to exercise their power to disconnect the numbers and their operations from contexts. If learners become playful, inventing wild and funny contexts, they are exercising choice and creativity, and probably more fully engaged than if they are simply following instructions on pre-assigned tasks.

2.5 PEDAGOGICAL ISSUES

Extending Meaning

The quickies in this chapter have suggested that the index notation for the notion of a positive integral power of a number can usefully be extended to include fractional indices (but only when the base is positive), zero, and negative indices. The 'meaning' adopted is that which allows the rules of manipulation to continue to be valid. This idea of extending meaning has already happened to children in the early years of primary schooling, for counting numbers treated as adjectives (3 pencils, 2 crayons) are turned into objects (2, 3, …) with operations applied to them to create new numbers. Counting numbers are augmented by negative 'numbers'. Then fractions are introduced, and then decimals, extending the initial notion of 'number' from meaning whole number to include decimals. The process of extending meaning continues in higher mathematics. It is important to become attuned to when meaning is being extended, and to become aware of how that meaning is extended.

The Paradox of Examples

If you are confronted with a statement (for example $2 + 2 = 2 \times 2$), it is individual and particular. However, in order to make sense of it, in order merely to interpret it, you have to 'see it' as an example of something with which you are familiar: arithmetic, addition and multiplication, statement about numbers, and so on. The person who writes the statement probably sees it as an example of something, and as a teacher, it is necessary to have some strategies for exposing what it exemplifies so that learners can come to see it also as 'an example'. Three strategies were offered in this chapter:

- stating a generality;
- providing instances in some sort of pattern;
- offering one or more specific instances through which the generality can be seen, by careful choice of the particularities.

For example, in reverse order, the statement

$$3 + 1\tfrac{1}{2} = 3 \times 1\tfrac{1}{2}$$

is rather suggestive of a possible structure, though it becomes even clearer when further examples are given, such as

$$17 + 1\tfrac{1}{16} = 17 \times 1\tfrac{1}{16} \qquad 23 + 1\tfrac{1}{22} = 23 \times 1\tfrac{1}{22} .$$

The interesting pedagogic question is, if you are going to offer various particular cases, which ones might be the most informative.

We could also have presented the generality and invited you to write down some particular cases (to see the particular in the general), in order to gain confidence with familiar examples, get a sense of what is going on, and re-articulate the generality for yourself.

Invariance in the Midst of Change

The human perceptual system is designed to detect change. When you look at a diagram or gaze at a scene, what strikes you is changes, in colour, in texture, in tone, in position (such as through movement). The immediate impulse is to detect change. But change only makes sense where there is something not changing, something which is relatively invariant. Put another way, it takes two to contrast!

Mathematicians make great use of invariance through the way that they state results and analyse situations. For example, in the number-line work in section 2.4, it helps enormously to find out what, if anything, is *not* changing, in order to work out how things are changing (what points are not moved, what points move in the same way). Mathematical diagrams are curious because they are statically presented on the page, but they have to 'come alive' in order to be appreciated. You have to 'see through the particular' by imagining what can change, and how, and what relationships nevertheless must remain the same (invariant). Sometimes an object such as a point or line literally remains fixed; other times it is the position of the point on the line or some other relationship that remains invariant.

Same and Different

Asking learners to step back and consider what is the same and what different about various objects, whether mathematical diagrams, expressions, or even tasks, proves to be a fruitful way to draw learners out of calculations in order to gain further experience of important ideas and concepts. It is another form of the pervasive theme *invariance in the midst of change*. Asking learners to construct their own examples that display similarities with or differences from a given example helps to extend learners' awareness of what is encompassed by specific concepts.

Task Structures

You may have noticed the structure of tasks such as Task 2.1.1 Adding Constraint: each stage adds an additional constraint. If it had started with 'write down a number', then the first stage would have been complete freedom within numbers, then a constraint, then a further constraint, and so on. Any traditional pedagogic task can be seen in a similar light: free choice amongst a class of objects is constrained by various conditions. The task is to construct an object meeting all those constraints (or show that none is possible), and often a useful way to proceed is to think in terms of the constraints being added on one at a time rather than imposed all at once.

Traditional tasks ask learners to find a solution. A valuable shift is to ask learners 'In how many different ways can you find ... ?'. Attention is shifted from merely applying a technique to deciding what constitutes 'different', and to trying to look at problems from different perspectives, tackling them in different ways. One of the principal differences between American and Japanese classrooms is that whereas American teachers tended to ask learners to find answers, Japanese teachers tended to ask learners how many different ways they could use to find answers (Stigler and Hiebert, 1999).

Mathematics as Problem-Solving

School mathematics often reduces to the teaching of techniques that have proved useful in a variety of contexts. But the purpose of those techniques is and always has been to solve problems, whether arising from out-of-school contexts or from within mathematics itself.

> The mathematician's main reason for existence is to solve problems, and … what mathematics *really* consists of is problems and solutions. (Halmos, 1980, p. 519)

> The major part of every meaningful life is the solution of problems … it is the duty of all teachers, and all teachers of mathematics in particular, to expose their students to problems much more than to facts … One of the hardest parts of problem solving is to ask the right question, and the only way to learn to do so is practice. (Halmos, 1980, pp. 523–4)

> A teacher who is not always thinking about solving problems – ones he does not know the answer to – is psychologically simply not prepared to teach problem solving to his students. (Halmos, 1985, p. 322)

You may be able to recall some incidents in your own experience that match Halmos's observations.

As with all the comments in this book, it is vital not to accept what others say at face value. Rather, it is important to look for examples in your own recent or past experience that illuminate or which are illuminated by what you are reading. Then it is important to look for examples that do not seem to fit, in order to appreciate the scope of relevance of what is being offered, for you, at the present time.

Final Reflections

Task 2.5.R   Recalling

Thinking back over your work on this chapter and the previous, can you identify moments that might serve as examples of your use of specialising, generalising, of encounters with invariance in the midst of change, of Say What You See and Watch What You Do?

Were you aware of using or looking for familiar objects to manipulate in order to get a sense of what was going on leading to articulation of that sense?

Notes

1 Monty was originally published by ATM. It is now available on the DfES website www.standards.dfes.gov.uk/numeracy/prof-dev/self-study/UsingICTtosupport mathematics/15343

2 Davis, R., (film), an account of which is given in Mason and Johnston-Wilder (2004a).

3 Using Symbols

Chapter 3 begins by considering the role of symbols in algebra. Section 3.2 provides further experience of detecting and expressing relationships, including properties of numbers. It also considers the issue of what it means for an 'example' to be exemplary, and what this requires of the learner. Section 3.3 highlights the way in which expressing generality often leads to multiple expressions for the same thing, due to different ways of 'seeing' underlying structure. Section 3.4 suggests that algebraic thinking is actually necessary in order to appreciate arithmetic!

3.1 ROLE OF SYMBOLS AND ALGEBRA

Quickie 3.1

Referring to three figures, someone spoke of 'the isosceles triangle' and 'the obtuse angled triangle', while someone else spoke of 'the first triangle' and 'the third triangle'. What is the same and what is different about these two ways of referring? What other ways could you use to refer to those two triangles, say in a telephone conversation with someone looking at the same figure?

Denoting and Labelling

Human beings use symbols in a variety of ways. Here we consider three different uses.

One common use of symbols is as label. In the first diagram, it is quite difficult to talk about the different lines going through the corners of the rectangles, and to direct a listener's attention to the corners of the rectangles that do not yet have a line drawn through them. In the second diagram, the labels on the corners make reference much easier. Attention can be directed precisely (as long as you are clear what each label is referring to).

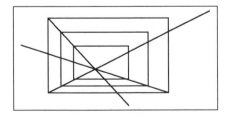 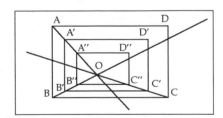

Now observe that the points D, D', and D'' all lie on a straight line.

The fact that A, A' and A" are on a straight line, B, B' and B" are on a straight line, and C, C', and C" are also on a straight line, with the three lines meeting at point O forces the remaining vertices of the rectangles to lie on a straight line, and the rectangles to be in the same proportion (*similar*). The diagram expresses a generality, because the choices of vertices of the rectangles is completely free, subject only to the constraint of the corresponding vertices lying on straight lines meeting in a common point.

Here the labels for points are just that, labels. They are not quantities, and you cannot do calculations with them such as adding or multiplying. They are used to draw attention to features, and then to express relationships such as being on a straight line or forming a rectangle.

By way of contrast, the expression a/b (where a and b are integers and $b \neq 0$) expresses a general fraction. The a and b stand for complete freedom of choice from amongst the integers, subject only to the stated constraint that $b \neq 0$. They act as surrogate general numbers, and are usually referred to as *variables* because the values they represent might vary. Arithmetic computations can be done with these variables because they represent general or free-choice numbers.

In addition to labels and variables, there is a third use of symbol that is the source of much confusion for learners. When stating a measurement, it is necessary to specify the units, as in 3.5 m or 2.1 cm^2 or 0.6 kg. Here the letter is used as an acronym to save print and to reduce clutter.

In summary, symbols can be used as labels to refer to things; as variables standing for quantities (usually numbers) that might possibly vary; and as units of measurement. One of the big confusions in early algebra is between letter as unit of measure, and letter as unspecified or general quantity. Thus 3m for 3 metres is easily confused with $3m$ meaning three times the as-yet-unspecified number m. This is why some learners think $3y$ means three yachts or three yogurts, rather than three times the number represented by y.

Within the class of variables there are special situations in which attention is focused on some quantities varying (so they are referred to as variables) while other quantities are assumed to be fixed during the analysis, but they are expressed generally rather than specifically. The next task gives two examples.

Task 3.1.1 Variables and Parameters

Solve the equation $2x = 5$ for x. Make up a similar question and solve it. And another.

I have a friend who has an equation just like $2x = 5$, but I don't know what numbers she has in place of the 2 and the 5. How can I tell her what the solution will be to her problem; or at least, how to go about solving it?

How many fence posts are needed to make a three-rail fence along a stretch of land if the posts have to be 1.5m apart along the side of a road for a distance of 300m? Generalise.

Comment

For the equation, a suitable generalisation could be: solve the equation $ax = b$ for x (where $a \neq 0$). Here, a and b are generalised constants, called *parameters*. This means that although they can vary (subject to the stated constraints), they are to be treated as constant when solving the equation. Of course at some other time they might become the thing being varied, and so they would become variables in that situation.

Setting up a situation in which someone not present needs to know how to do a calculation can often help learners appreciate the need for a succinct way to express a computation in general. Of course, they are more likely to see what to do if they have experience of expressing generality previously.

In the fence-post situation, the salient feature that varies (suppose you were looking in a catalogue to find the cost of some fencing, or you were a fencing contractor) is the length of the fencing. The distance between posts is constant (more or less: a modelling assumption that there will be slight variations but overall the average will be 1.5m). The number of rails is of course irrelevant. So an expression such as *length*/1.5 + 1 rounded up to next integer, where the length is given in metres, expresses the number of posts needed. But there could be varieties of fencing, with different spacing between the posts. So a further generalisation might be *length*/*spacing* + 1 rounded up to the next integer. Here when the focus is on *length*, the value of *spacing* is deemed to be constant.

Traditionally, school algebra has treated the letters x and y as variables for specifying functions to graph, and various letters to stand for a quantity in a problem whose value is 'as-yet-unknown', a term coined by Mary Boole. She suggested that often in mathematics when faced with a problem, it is useful to 'acknowledge our ignorance' (say of the answer or solution). It can be very helpful to denote what we are ignorant about by a letter ('let x be the number of ... '). This theme is developed through this chapter.

Mathematicians find it useful to develop succinct but informative labels for numbers that are otherwise hard to name except by long-winded phrases. The next task is a reminder about this.

Task 3.1.2a Labelling

What facts do you know about the (positive) square root of 5? What facts do you know about the fifth root of 2?

Comment

The dominant facts are that the square of the 'square root of 5' is 5, and that the fifth power of 'the fifth root of 2' is 2. But it is awkward to have to keep writing long phrases such as 'the square root of 5' when what is wanted is a notation for the number. So mathematicians invent a symbol that signals the operation to be performed. Thus $\sqrt[2]{5}$ is to be read *both* as 'the number that when squared is 5' and as the operation of square-rooting applied to 5.

The next task introduces a function that is not as widely used as the ones mentioned so far, providing you with an opportunity to experience getting to grips with a new function.

Task 3.1.2b Floor & Ceiling

The ceiling function assigns to any real number x the smallest integer greater than or equal to x, and is denoted by $\lceil x \rceil$. Thus $\lceil 2.1 \rceil = 3$ and $\lceil {}^-2.1 \rceil = {}^-2$ (imagine them on a number-line).

The floor function assigns to any real number x the largest integer less than or equal to x, and is denoted by $\lfloor x \rfloor$. Thus $\lfloor 2.1 \rfloor = 2$ and $\lfloor {}^-2.1 \rfloor = {}^-3$ (imagine them on a number-line).

Convince yourself that, for all x, $\lceil x \rceil - 1 \leqslant x \leqslant \lceil x \rceil$.

Under what circumstances is $\lceil x \rceil = \lfloor x \rfloor$, and under what circumstances is $\lceil x \rceil = \lfloor x \rfloor + 1$?

Generalise the observations

$$\left\lfloor \frac{2n+1}{2} \right\rfloor = n, \left\lfloor \frac{3n+1}{3} \right\rfloor = n, \dots \text{ and } \left\lceil \frac{2n+1}{2} \right\rceil = n+1, \left\lceil \frac{3n+1}{3} \right\rceil = n+1, \dots$$

Comment

To internalise new notation requires more than 'seeing it go by'. It is usually necessary to encounter it repeatedly, so that over a period of time you gain experience and become familiar with using it, not just reading it, but using it to express yourself. One way to hasten this is to explore its use: here a few of the many properties have been offered for exploration.

Task 3.1.2c Process and Result

How many other examples can you think of, in which symbols are used to represent both a process or operation, and the result of performing that process or operation?

Comment

Notation for the square-root of five can be generalised to any root of any (positive) number. Similarly, the same process is used for fractions (2/3) and for trigonometric functions, where sin(45°) is both the process of forming the sin (as a measure of 45°) and the answer to that process.

This double use of symbols is no mere convention or awkwardness. It is one of the sources of power for the language of mathematics as both an expressive and a manipulative medium. In algebra, it is vital to be aware of the triple nature of any expression of generality: as an expression of generality, as the process of calculating the result, and the result itself. The next section considers ways in which the triple perception can be developed within arithmetic, before ever mentioning algebra.

As a finale to this section, tackle the next task, paying attention to when you are thinking of a process and when an answer, and to how you are using symbols.

Task 3.1.3 Students and Teachers

At a certain school event there are six times as many students as teachers.

Comment

This problem, and ones like it, have been thoroughly studied (MacGregor and Stacey, 1993). Many people first write down $6s = t$, even when they are told to use s for the number of students, and t for the number of teachers. The sound of the relationship in words is compelling.

Learners who have taken to using their power to specialise to check a generality are likely to discover the error in their first conjecture.

The issue at stake here is that *s* does not stand for *students*, because that would be using it as a short form for a unit of measurement. Thus 6*s* read as six students is using *s* as a measurement unit. It is more useful to use *s* as *the number of students*. Then 6*s* means six times the number of students. When the letter *s* is read as *the number of students*, it is more likely that the expression $s = 6t$ will be produced.

Pause for Reflection

What seems initially like a straightforward enough process of inviting learners to use letters in place of numbers has mystified learners for many generations. Yet the process of denoting and labelling is common and familiar.

Task 3.1.R Reflection

What aspects of symbol use are least clear to you at the moment?

Recall three recent incidents in classrooms that involve labelling or denoting. How did learners respond?

3.2 DETECTING AND EXPRESSING RELATIONSHIPS

Quickie 3.2

Express all the relationships you can detect between the numbers 9, 6 and 3. Do the same for 8, 5 and 3.

This section is about the use of symbols for expressing relationships. In fact this is what you have been doing all along when expressing generality. The first task raises issues about what learners attend to when seeking relationships.

Task 3.2.1 Same and Different

What is the same, and what different about the following six number facts? Express your answer as a general statement.

$3 + 4 + 5 = 3 \times 4$ $\qquad$ $6 + 7 + 8 = 3 \times 7$ $\qquad$ $11 + 12 + 13 = 3 \times 12$

$1 + 2 + 3 + 4 + 5 = 5 \times 3$ $\quad$ $4 + 5 + 6 + 7 + 8 + 9 + 10 = 7 \times 7$ $\quad$ $21 + 22 + 23 + 24 + 25 = 5 \times 23$

Comment

Some people focus on just one instance to try to detect a generality. Often this is possible, but if the example has some misleading coincidences, the expressed generality may need to be modified before it correctly generalises all cases. For example, focusing on the first statement might suggest a generalisation such as $n + (n + 1) + (n + 2) = n(n + 1)$, by identifying the two 3s. Testing it out on other cases reveals that it does not often work.

Notice that there are two forms of testing: testing the algebraic expression by substituting values, to see if it does truly express what happens in particular cases, and testing the expression against other known cases.

Textbooks and teachers put forward mathematical objects as 'examples', but what is involved in appreciating just what is being exemplified? Chapter 2 considered the paradox of example-giving: you cannot see something as 'an example of something' until you know what that 'something' is, but in order to find out what that 'something' is, you need to have some examples. One typical way of breaking into this cycle is to focus on just one of the particulars, with the possibility of detecting relationships which are particular to the one case, but do not hold in other cases. That is why trying several cases or instances, and paying attention to what is invariant and what is changing is helpful in expressing generality. But accumulating lots and lots of examples can turn into busy-work if it is a displacement for seeking invariant structure, for detecting relationships.

Task 3.2.2 What is Exemplary?

What mathematically inappropriate generalisations might $3 + 4 + 5 = 3 \times 4$ suggest to a learner?

What mathematically inappropriate generalisations might $2^2 = 2 \times 2$ suggest to a learner?

What mathematically inappropriate generalisations might $C = 2\pi \times 2$ as the circumference of a circle, suggest to a learner?

What mathematically inappropriate generalisations might the use of £100 as a test case for exploring the effects of discounts (as in Task 1.3.2a.) suggest to a learner?

Make up some more of your own.

Comment

It is amazingly easy to fall into the trap of having the same number playing different roles in examples. To the expert, the difference in the roles may be obvious, but to the learner it could prove distracting, if not mystifying. Young children are constantly making conjectures (for example, in the meaning of words that they hear, or in grammatical constructions) that may not be adjusted for some time.

Expressing Properties

Seeking and expressing relationships is only one phase of mathematical activity, for once a relationship has been detected, the question arises as to what objects or parts of objects have that relationship. In other words, it is possible to start thinking in terms of properties. The next task applies this idea to various types of number.

Task 3.2.3a What Do You Know About ... ?

What do you know about zero? What do you know about one? What is the same and what different about these two numbers?

Comment

At first this question can seem daunting. If this is the case, ask yourself what happens when you calculate with 0 and with 1.

Task 3.2.3b What Do You Know About ... ?

What is the same about the relationships between ⁻1 and 1; between ⁻2 and 2; between ⁻3 and 3. Generalise.

Comment

One thing that is the same is that the sum is zero in each case. Put another way, ⁻n is the number that when added to n, gives zero. There is a subtle but very important shift from being aware of this relationship, to seeing this relationship as what characterises negatives. This property is taken as a definition of negative: the answer to an undoing question associated with $0 + n = n$, namely, what number added to n gives you zero?

This property of the negative of a number is one from which all other properties can be deduced. This subsection concentrates on the shift from relationship to properties; reasoning with properties by making deductions comes later.

Task 3.2.3c What Do You Know About ... ?

What is the same about the relationships between 1/2 and 2; between 1/3 and 3; between 1/4 and 4. Generalise.

Comment

The 'new' number $1/n$ is the number that when multiplied by n gives 1.

Task 3.2.3d What Do You Know About ... ?

What property $\frac{a}{b}$ characterises (where $b \neq 0$)?

Comment

Following the format for reciprocals, a/b is the number that when multiplied by b gives a.

Notice the role of symbols in expressing succinctly the generality that encompasses the many cases such as $\frac{2}{3}$ is the number that when multiplied by 3 gives 2, etc.

Notice that both for negative numbers and for reciprocals, the 'test' for the new number is given in terms of integers, in terms of what is already familiar. The new number has a single property, namely that it 'undoes'. Thus to test for something being a negative, you add the 'thing' and see if you get zero.

You might at this point have some nagging questions. For example:

What is the negative of a negative?
What is the relationship between multiplying a number by ⁻1 and forming the negative of that number?

These questions are typical of those that a mathematician asks themselves. They will be addressed in a later chapter.

Task 3.2.3e What Do You Know About …?

What is the same about the relationships between $\sqrt{2}$ and 2; between $\sqrt{3}$ and 3; between $\sqrt{4}$ and 4. Generalise.

Comment

Did you think to consider the cube root of five, and generally, the nth root of m for positive integral n and m?

The important feature of these tasks is the shift from seeing a relationship between two objects (one undoes some operation on the first) to seeing the relationship as the defining property that characterises an object (negative reciprocal, fraction, root). When you want to check or verify some conjecture, you have to resort to the defining characteristic properties of the objects in question, and to reason with those, rather than bringing in other associations you might have such as approximate values, places where you have seen them used, emotional reactions to them or their use, and so on.

Pause for Reflection

This section has moved a long way, from detecting relationships in particular situations in order to express them generally, through using expressions of fractions to explore an unfamiliar operation, to expressing general properties of numbers.

Task 3.2.R Reflection

What is the most challenging aspect of the section for you?

Comment

These ideas will reappear in Chapter 11. Treating expressions as objects will happen frequently in remaining chapters, so there will be opportunities to become comfortable with ways of interpreting expressions and to develop confidence in treating them as objects.

3.3 MULTIPLE EXPRESSIONS

Quickie 3.3

Write down a typical decimal number. What about it makes it typical? Write down another that is also typical but different in some way. What other possibilities are not represented by your decimals?

Write down a number that uses all of the digits 0 through 9 exactly once. And another. And another. And another that is as small as you can make it.

A principal theme of this section is that multiple expressions for the same thing lead to desire to rearrange and manipulate those expressions in order to reveal and check that they always give the same numerical answer. In previous chapters, there have been many situations in which you are likely to have come up with different expressions for the same generality. One of the delights of tasks that focus on expressing generality is that, in many cases, everyone can find their own expression that at least looks different to others, yet expresses the same thing. This section provides more of such opportunities.

Multiple Names for the Same Thing

There are many situations in mathematics, as well as in life, when there are multiple names for the same thing. Each name signals a different perspective, a different approach or way of thinking.

Task 3.3.1a Multiple Names
In how many different ways can you depict one-half?
Comment
Sticking with the task for even a short while can produce surprise at the vast array of ways of denoting and depicting the number one-half.

The fact that the same person can have several names and nicknames, and that many objects have several labels by which to refer to them, shows that learners have plenty of experience of different names for the same thing and this experience can be drawn upon in learning mathematics.

For example, the number 5 can be written as

$$3 + 2, 3 + 1 + 1, 8 - 3, {}^-2 - ({}^-7), 10/2, {}^-200/{}^-40, 2.5 \times 2, 0.1 \times 200/4, (3^2 + 1)/2 \dots$$

where each particular indicates an infinite class of similar examples. For example,

$$3 + 2 = 4 + 1 = 5 + 0 = 6 + ({}^-1) = \dots, \text{ and } 3 + 1 + 1 = 5 + 0 + 0 = 7 + ({}^-1)$$
$$+ ({}^-1) = \dots.$$

Fractions provide a more complex variation, because different fractions such as $5/2$, $10/4, 15/6, 20/8, \dots$ all have the same value, and so are treated as equivalent.

Traditionally, many learners find expressions such as $3x + 2$ a shock. Being used to arithmetic, where they 'get numbers as answers', they want to achieve a single number and so are tempted to write $5x$, $6x$ and the like, if not 5 or 6, ignoring the x altogether. If learners have had plenty of experience in arithmetic of treating expressions such as $3 + 2$ and $10/2$ as things, as acceptable names for numbers, then they are likely to accept expressions of generality such as $3x + 2$ and $5x + 1 - (2x - 1)$ as things rather than as incomplete operations.

In many situations, different ways of seeing lead to different expressions of generality for the same thing. If different-looking expressions actually express the same thing, then there ought to be a way to see this without having to go back to the original source, just as there are ways to tell whether two fractions are equal without returning to the source that led to them as expressions of a situation.

Task 3.3.1b Multiple Names (continued)

What is the same, and what different about the following three expressions:

$$(x + 1)(x - 3) \qquad (x - 1)^2 - 4 \qquad x^2 - 2x - 3 \qquad x(x - 2) - 3$$

Comment

They are all different expressions for the same quadratic, since they always give the same values no matter what value is used in place of x. The first displays the roots (-1 and 3), the second displays the position of the minimum point as $(1, 4)$ and the third displays the y-intercept (-3); the fourth displays an efficient calculation sequence (subtract 2, multiply by original value, subtract 3).

Often it is possible to detect relationships by simple 'inspection', at least until things get complicated. Then it is worth having a general 'method', as illustrated in the next task.

Task 3.3.2 Identifying Equivalent Fractions

If you start with a fraction, then you can construct equivalent fractions (fractions with the same value) by multiplying top and bottom by the same number. But suppose someone claims to have done this and presents you with two fractions using huge numbers, such as $\frac{3703701}{4938268}$ and $\frac{96496434}{1278661912}$. How could you decide if they did indeed have the same value?

Comment

One method is to perform the divisions and compare the decimal answers. However, there might be long strings of decimals to think about carefully in order to be certain whether the two fractions are identical. Another method, developed by Eudoxus of Cnidus in Greece around 360 BCE, is to perform two multiplications and compare the answers.

Even if you worked with the specific fractions, because of their complexity you were probably thinking of the numbers in the numerators and denominators more as place holders, as slots, rather than as specific numbers. This is what it means to see through a particular case to a generality. It involves thinking about what you 'do in general'. The result is a general method for deciding whether two fractions are the same: multiply the numerator of one by the denominator of the other, and vice versa, and see if the answers are the same. When it comes to expressions of generality, the same thing is needed: a way to tell whether two expressions always give the same value. The techniques for doing this are the rules of algebra, which are themselves the expressions of generality of the rules of arithmetic, as will emerge in section 3.4.

The remaining tasks in this section offer opportunities to work on multiple ways of seeing and hence expressing.

Multiple Routes to the Same End

There are often different ways of getting the same answer. Here is a direct approach!

Task 3.3.3 Key Sequences

Two people were using different formulae on their calculators but getting the same answers every time. One was entering any number, multiplying by 2.7, then adding 3.78. The other was entering the same number, adding a fixed number (the same each time), then multiplying by another fixed number (again the same each time). What fixed numbers was the second person using? Why does it work no matter what starting numbers are used?

Two people were using different formulae on their calculators but getting the same answers every time. One was entering any number, multiplying by some fixed number, then adding a fixed third number. The other was entering the same number, adding a fixed number, then multiplying by a fixed number. What was the relationship between the fixed numbers the two people were using?

Comment

As you probably noticed, the second part is a generalisation of the first part of the task. Notice the effect of using decimals rather than integers: the 'other pair' of fixed numbers being used is not so obvious as it would be in the case of whole numbers. Did you think to try it with whole numbers in place of the decimals? Did you divide 3.78 by 2.7 or did you think to find common factors between 270 and 378? Decimals sometimes obscure or block out strategies that might come to mind with whole numbers.

The two people multiply by the same number, but they add different numbers because one does it before multiplying and the other after.

Could one person add a fixed number before multiplying and the other subtract a fixed number after multiplying?

A further variation for this task would be to allow one person to start with various numbers, and the second to start with one less, or one more, or twice as big, or some other variation, thereby making the arithmetic just a little bit more complicated.

Multiple Expressions of Generality

Task 3.3.4a Multiple Expressions

Take a picture sequence and imagine building each picture from sticks, perhaps like the one shown here (all sticks are assumed to be the same length).

In how many different ways can you work out how many matchsticks will be needed to make the pth picture? How many sticks will be needed to make just the perimeter?

Comment

Did you discern some structure just by looking (Say What You See) in order to form the count? Did you draw one or more examples for yourself and Watch What You Did in order to achieve an expression?

The choice of pictures looking like houses is of course entirely arbitrary. Some learners may like pictures that relate to their experience, while others may prefer more abstract picture sequences. Most learners prefer to make up their own.

Watching What You Do to draw or count a particular case can reveal structure that your body is aware of even if your head is not!

If you happen to 'see' the houses made up as a left end of 4, a right end of 2, and intermediate fillers of 3, as depicted, then your 'seeing' leads to the expression $4 + 3(p - 1) + 2$.

Reversing the process to use an expression in order to 'see' in a way that that expression directly expresses can be quite a challenge, as the next task may demonstrate.

Task 3.3.4b Multiple Expressions

Find ways to see structure in the house-pictures that correspond to the following expressions of generality for the number of matchsticks needed for the pth picture:

$$2 + (p-1) + (1 + 2p + 1); \quad 2 + (3p-1) + 2; \quad 4 + 3(p-1) + 2; \quad 3(p+1)$$

Comment

Trying to see 'through' someone else's expression and looking for different ways to see a general expression are both ways to support flexibility of thinking. Learning to interpret other people's expressions is vital as a teacher when encountering learners' expressions.

The fact that it is more challenging to work from expression to 'seeing' than expressing your own 'seeing' suggests that it is useful to develop flexibility between symbolic and diagrammatic representations. This is taken up in Chapter 8.

Here is a more abstract setting (the pictures do not 'represent' anything), using squares rather than sticks, which may be 'easier' to work with.

Task 3.3.5 Multiple Expressions of Relationships

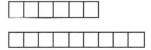

Construct all the statements you can that connect the number of squares in the top row, and the number of squares in the bottom row. For example, 'the bottom row has three more squares than the top row'.

Now interpret the diagram to construct all the arithmetic statements you can about the relation between 9, 6, and 3 that use all three numbers (for example, '9 is 3 more than 6').

Now imagine the diagram to be the fifth in a sequence in which the fourth has 5 on the top row and 8 on the bottom row. Re-express your relationships between 9, 6, and 3 in general, to apply to any member of the sequence.

Comment

Using the language patterns ' … is … less than … ', ' … is … more than … ', ' … is … and …', ' … is … minus …', and ' … and … is … ', ' … minus … is … ' leads to 12 different ways of saying, and hence seeing, the simple arithmetic connection between 9, 6, and 3. How many can you find for the triple 18, 6, and 3?

In order to expose learners to these multiple ways of seeing the same relationship, Nick James invented a game called Trio Tricks.[1] Each person in turn obtains three numbers (the sum of two of them is the third). They score points for each way they can express the relationship, closely checked by the other players.

The purpose of Trio Tricks is to 'keep learners in the situation' long enough that they develop facility and competence, as well as confidence, in locating and expressing relationships. Although pages of exercises have been used by teachers for this purpose for three thousand years, it is much more effective to find tasks that engage learners, such as playing a game like Trio Tricks or using a technique on examples that they construct for themselves. The Trio Tricks task structure can be used in any topic whenever there are different ways of saying the same thing, different ways of using technical terms.

Task 3.3.6 Painted Cube

A cube has been painted on all faces. It is then cut up into 27 cubelets by two plane cuts parallel to each face. How many cubelets are painted on how many faces?[2]

Generalise!

Comment

This has become a traditional course-work task for secondary students in the UK. The common practice is to encourage learners to build up a table for 2 by 2 by 2, 3 by 3 by 3, 4 by 4 by 4 cubes, and so on, and then look for a pattern in the numbers. So-called 'low attainers' are encouraged to make the cubes out of multi-link so they can count all the cubes that have 3, 2, 1, or zero exposed faces.

Dave Hewitt (1992) described the pedestrian 'inchworm' approach of 'making a table and then looking at the table hoping to spot a formula' as *train-spotting* because it is the numbers that are taken as being important, rather than what the numbers signify. By contrast, treating one example carefully (either the 3 by 3 by 3 or the 4 by 4 by 4 cube) and paying attention to the structure, allows the general to be 'seen through the particular' by looking for what is generic in the counting and what is particular to the example.

There are two ways to count all the cubelets: counting them all independently of the how many of their faces are exposed (n^3) and counting them according to how many faces are exposed: the corners (three faces exposed), edges but not corners (two faces exposed), faces but not edges (one face exposed) and interior cubes (no faces exposed), which add to $8 + 12(n-2) + 6(n-2)^2 + (n-2)^3$. So these two expressions must always give the same answer. The rules of algebra ought to enable its users to verify this equality without recourse to the cubelets.

Writing $n = (n-2) + 2$, yields the claim that

$$((n-2) + 2)^3 = (n-2)^3 + 6(n-2)^2 + 12(n-2) + 8$$

More generally

$$(a + b)^3 = a^3 + 3a^2b + 3\,ab^2 + b^3$$

A pattern-spotting interpretative task is to see how the first is a particular case of the second, or looked at another way, how might one account for the coefficients 6, 12, and 8 in the first expression?

Pause for Reflection

The essence of this section is that most situations in which generalities can be expressed can lead to different looking expressions for the same thing. Since they express the same generality, albeit differently, they must always give the same answer. Algebraic manipulation arises spontaneously and, furthermore, the rules for manipulating letters emerge naturally as well. The rules can then be exposed as the expression of generality of the arithmetic of numbers. Historically this led mathematics textbook writers to move directly from arithmetic to algebra as 'arithmetic with letters', missing out the vital experience for learners of expressing generality for themselves.

Task 3.3.R Reflection
Take a topic in mathematics and look for opportunities to get learners to find different expressions for the same generality.
Comment
With sufficient exposure to expressing generality so that they are not only comfortable, but eager to engage, learners will spontaneously invent rules for manipulating expressions.

3.4 ARITHMETIC REQUIRES ALGEBRAIC THINKING

Quickie 3.4
Write down a general decimal that has two digits before the decimal point, and two digits after it.
Write down a general four digit whole number. Now write down the number obtained by reversing the digits. By finding an appropriate way of writing your two numbers, calculate their difference and show that it is always divisible by 9.

Task 3.4.1 In Between?
Write down two different fractions. Now write down the fraction whose numerator is the sum of the numerators, and denominator is the sum of the denominators of your two fractions. Does this new fraction always lie between the two you started with?
What about the fraction whose numerator is twice the numerator of your first fraction plus three times the numerator of your second, and whose denominator is similarly twice the denominator of your first number plus three times the denominator of your second fraction? Express a generalisation.
Comment
If you are struggling with comparing the fractions, you may wish to change the fractions to decimals using a calculator.

Arithmetic is often presented as a process of doing calculations in order to get a single number as an answer. The trouble with this is that it obscures rather than illuminates the method used to work out what calculations to do. It also blocks out the creative potential of arithmetic. This section is about developing the essence of algebraic thinking in and through arithmetic. It builds on the notion expressed by Dave Hewitt and others, that in order to learn arithmetic it is actually necessary to think algebraically. The reason is that arithmetic is not about memorising hundreds of arithmetic facts, but about learning methods of doing arithmetic calculations.

No one teaching arithmetic would expect learners to memorise all possible additions of two two- or three-digit numbers, nor the products of all pairs of two-digit numbers. The whole point of arithmetic is to learn methods, as George Eliot observes in the introduction to an essay about Thomas Carlyle: 'It has been well said that the highest aim in education is analogous to the highest aim in mathematics, namely, not to obtain *results* but *powers*, not particular solutions, but the means by which endless solutions may be wrought' (Eliot, 1855, p. 343). The fact that it is about methods (generalities) signals the presence of algebraic thinking. Unfortunately, mathematics is not always seen or taught in this way: Augustus de Morgan, writing at about the same time, railed against teaching by rote:

> Mathematics is becoming too much of a machinery; and this is more especially the case with reference to the elementary students. They put the data of the problems into a mill and expect the result to come out ready ground at the other end. An operation that bears a close resemblance to that of putting in hemp seed at one end of a machine and taking out ruffled shirts ready for use at the other end. This mode is undoubtedly exceedingly effective in producing results, but it is certainly not soaked in teaching the mind and in exercising thought. (De Morgan, 1865, p. 2)

No one advocates rote learning as a sole approach, but there are many different views about how learning and understanding are entwined! The view taken in this book is that it is through the use by learners of their own natural powers that they both appreciate and are motivated to continue to appreciate mathematics and, in particular, algebraic thinking.

This section looks at the potential to use arithmetic not as a means of getting answers, but of exposing methods, that sets the scene for a transition from implicit to explicit algebraic thinking.

Task 3.4.2 Operation Tracking

Using two columns, with one row for each new operation, record the following operations in the first column, and the answers to the calculations in the second column. 'Start with 4; add 5, multiply by 3, subtract 1, divide by 2.'

In a third column, repeat the operations with 7 as the starting number.

Find a notation that makes it easy to access the operations while at the same time using different starting numbers.

Comment

As an oral starter you can get half the class to write down the operations and *not* do the calculations while the others do the calculations in their heads and write down their intermediate answers: who can remember most easily what the sequence was? How could we record the operation sequence usefully?

Those who do the arithmetic are much less likely to remember the operations than those who record them specifically. Doing the arithmetic buries the operations; a useful notation is one that records the operations but makes it easy to see the steps in the calculation. If the operations really do have to be carried out frequently, then inserting a placeholder for the starting numbers and then doing as many calculations as possible reduces the effort when using other starting numbers.

A spreadsheet is ideal for this sort of situation, because it displays all the intermediate calculations in case they are useful as a check or needed for some related purpose.

A simple record is to make a list of the operations: add 5; times 3; subtract 1; divide by 2. Another approach is to depict each of the operations as a function machine with an input and an output.

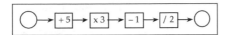

Yet another approach is to simplify the 'machines' to arrows.

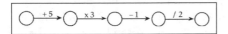

Another is to write down the expressions using brackets.

$$4; (4) + 5; ((4) + 5) \times 3; (((4) + 5) \times 3) - 1; ((((4) + 5) \times 3 - 1)/2$$

Note that each new operation is applied by putting the previous result in a bracket, so that the operation is applied to the full previous answer and not just a part of it.

Focus on answers makes the initial 4 just as important as the sequence of operations; focus on operations makes the initial 4 much less important, since it could change. Recording the operations rather than the intermediate calculations makes sense if there is an expectation that the same operations are going to be used again and again. The notion of repeated use of some calculation sequence is one of the principal forces for movement into algebra.

Once the principle has been established of not doing calculations until a single answer is actually wanted, or, seen slightly differently, not simplifying a calculation until it is needed, practice can be gained by giving responsibility to learners to make up their own sequences. Each person in turn suggests an operation (such as 'times 3'); everyone keeps track of the operations; after a suitable number of operations, the answer is requested, and then the answer is requested for different starting values. Learning to *track* the starting value yet compact the operations makes it easier to work out what happens for different starting values. Once some facility is developed, the starting value can be replaced by some symbol (a cloud, letter or acronym), and algebra has begun!

Task 3.4.3a Number Tracking

If you were asked to apply the same sequence of operations (add 5, multiply by 3, subtract 1, divide by 2) but starting with 6 instead, with the expectation that other starting values would also be used, how might you prepare yourself, and record the process?

Comment

The sensible thing to do is not to do any calculations with the starting value 6, but to track it through the other calculations. This can be done with any of the recording methods: function machine, arrows or brackets.

Input:　　　　6

Add 5:　　　　6 + 5

Times 3:　　　$(6 + 5) \times 3 = 6 \times 3 + 15$ (do other arithmetic but do not touch the 2)

Subtract 1:　　$(6 \times 3 + 15) - 1 = 6 \times 3 + 14$

Divide by 5:　$(6 \times 3 + 14)/2 = 6 \times (3/2) + 7$

Now it is easy to see what would happen if the 6 were changed to a 66 or a 6785. It might not even require an explicit invitation to generalise to have learners suggesting using a cloud:

Inserting a placeholder for the 4, perhaps a cloud, yields

$\cloud$; $\cloud + 5$; $(\cloud + 5) \times 3 = \cloud \times 3 + 15$;

$(\cloud \times 3 + 15) - 1 = \cloud \times 3 + 14$; $(\cloud \times 3 + 14)/2 = \cloud \times 3/2 + 7$

Using an s for *starting number* enables the condensed process to be expressed as $s \times (3/2) + 7$. Of course, operation numbers could be chosen so as to produce a simple formula, as appropriate for particular learners.

Note again that each new operation is applied by putting the previous result in a bracket, so that the operation is applied to the full previous answer and not just a part of it.

Note also that if you track a starting value of 7, you end up with $7 \times (3/2) + 7$. Here the sevens are different! The first one is the tracked starting 7, but the second one is an arithmetic coincidence. If you start with a 3 (or a 5 or a 2), it is important to keep track of which 3 is the starting 3, and which 3 is due to the times operation.

One of the offshoots of such a task, used as a lesson starter for a number of lessons until learners become adept at it, is that it emphasises arithmetic as *operations on numbers* rather than as answer-getting. This is taken up in section 5.

Task 3.4.3b Number Tracking Extended

By altering the numbers but preserving the arithmetic operation sequence ('first an add, then a times, then a subtract, then a divide'), make up some sequences that always give even answers. Then make up some sequences that always give integer answers. What do you notice about the 'divide number' and the others? Try to express a general form for sequences that always yield integer answers. Try changing the order of the four operations.

At any point one of the numbers involved in an operation (say 'add 5') can be changed. Learners will have to start again, but some, anticipating that it might be changed again, can track both the starting value and the 5 when doing the calculations. To get a taste of this, try the next task.

Task 3.4.4 Undoing Operations

Given a sequence of arithmetic operations such as the one used earlier (add 5, multiply by 3, subtract 1, divide by 2) find a starting number that produces 13 as the answer.

More generally, work out a method to find a starting number that will produce a specified result. Characterise the possible integer answers that will arise from an integer starting point.

Comments

This task is an example of the mathematical theme of doing and undoing. The sequence of operations is a 'doing'; instead of always carrying out the sequence, assign the answer and try to undo the sequence to find a suitable starting number. This is the 'undoing'.

As usual, if the task is not quite clear, or how to tackle it is not evident, specialise to a simpler case. For example, simplify the operation sequence to just 'add 3'. How is that operation 'undone'? What about 'times 5', and the others? Now put them altogether, perhaps using function machines of arrows.

What is important is not the 'undoing' of this particular sequence, but the general method of 'undoing' a sequence of operations.

Doing and undoing is a pervasive theme in mathematics, because it is often the case that an 'undoing' problem requires creativity and insight, as well as having multiple solutions, even where the 'doing' is routine and straightforward. Doing and undoing is one way of perceiving the relationship between addition and subtraction, between multiplication and division, between exponentials and logarithms, and between square–roots and squaring.

Pause for Reflection

Task 3.4R Reflection

What opportunities and necessities for algebraic thinking can you detect in the arithmetic that you teach?

What for you are the pros and cons for using large numbers and for tracking numbers through arithmetic computations as roots of algebraic thinking?

How might tracking large numbers be used to highlight the relationship between addition and subtraction, and between multiplication and division?

Comment

Inviting learners to imagine or write down a 'peculiar' number[3] that might be very large, very small, or complicated in some form, and then denote (but not carry out) operations such as adding, subtracting, multiplying, dividing, and where numbers are positive, taking square roots, and then undoing the operations to retrieve the original number again.

3.5 PEDAGOGICAL ISSUES

Quickie 3.5

Write down a general five-digit whole number. Now write down the number obtained by reversing the digits. By finding an appropriate way of writing your two numbers, calculate their difference and show that it is always divisible by 9. What about six-digit numbers?

Comment

The quickies in this chapter have been designed to illustrate how thinking about what is typical about an example expands your awareness of possible variations of the question, in preparation for expressing a general case. Expressing a general form of a number actually deepens appreciation of numbers and of their properties.

Thinking in terms of natural powers is certainly not new: 'The child's own instincts and powers furnish the material and give the starting point for all education' (John Dewey webref, Credo part 1 page 1).

Pedagogic Strategies

Many of the tasks in this chapter have been invitations to detect relationships, to express these using symbols, and to generalise, because ongoing practice in expressing generality is vital if learners are going to develop confidence.

Another and Another

The quickies and some other tasks used a version of 'another and another' because this type of task invites learners to become more adventurous, more creative, and so to explore possible variation of the questions. This in turn makes them more flexible as well as adventurous when working with the same ideas in future.

Same and Different

Asking what is the same and what is different about two or more objects prompts learner to focus attention on details and relationships between details, as a preliminary step towards generalisation and characterising, as in Tasks 3.2.1, 3.2.4 and 3.3.1a among others.

Learner Constructed Examples

Several tasks (3.1.2, 3.2.2, 3.4.1) invited you to construct your own examples, rather than being given them. Constructing your own examples allows you to make choices and so to participate more fully. It is more interesting to work with your own objects than with ones provided by someone else. At the same time, what the learner constructs informs the teacher about possible variations of which the learner is aware and fairly confident. If learners have the opportunity to compare examples with other people's, they may awaken to some possibilities they had not previously considered.

In How Many Ways

Task 3.3.4 used the structure of asking 'in how many ways can you' rather than simply asking for an answer. This can be used to prompt learners to look for efficient methods, or methods that use a particular approach, as well as suggesting to them that sometimes it helps to pause and think about different approaches rather than following the first idea that comes to them.

Pedagogic Constructs

Scaffolding and Fading

Tasks in this chapter used a variety of different prompts to provoke and to promote awareness of generality, and attempts to express that generality. Some (such as 3.1.2) were quite explicit, while others used another and another, or same and different to accomplish the same thing. Correspondingly, in the next block there will not be as explicit and detailed attention drawn to the structure of the various tasks, as you will be expected to consider these for yourself.

Do Talk and Record

All the tasks are intended to get you doing and hence thinking, but experience suggests that thinking can be enhanced if you take opportunities to try to express your thinking to others. In the absence of a willing friend, sometimes a pet, or even a virtual pet can serve. There is something about trying to tell someone else that both clarifies and reveals confusions. Rushing learners to write things down can sometimes block their development, where talking it through first can release thinking. Tasks 3.3.5, 3.3.6 and 3.4.2a implicitly invite talking or some form of expressing before trying to achieve a succinct written record. Writing can also inform and clarify speaking and drawing, as well as informing 'doing', so each mode contributes to the others.

Process into Object

3 + 7 can be thought of as *both* an operation or calculation to be carried out *and* the result of that operation or calculation being performed. Unfortunately it is still the case that emphasis is placed at first on getting or knowing the answer, rather than seeing 10 and 3 + 7 as different names for the same number. One consequence is that 2/3 is then seen predominantly as an uncompleted operation (a division) rather than as *both* an operation (2 divided by 3) *and* the result of that operation. Difficulties are compounded because there are further meanings for the same symbol. The fraction 2/3 can also be seen as an operation *on* other numbers, namely 'calculating two-thirds of'. Indeed, 2/3 only becomes a number when it is interpreted as the *result* of calculating two-thirds of 1, and placed on the number-line accordingly. The fraction 4/6 is quite different in appearance, in meaning as a division operation, even as an answer to that division. The fact that 4/6 of 1 turns out to be the same as 2/3 of 1 is what makes the arithmetic of fractions possible.

An example of the slide from process to object that might have been unfamiliar was in Task 3.4.3 (In Between). Eddie Gray and David Tall (1994) use the term *procept* for any process that is intended to become a concept (and as such, a property of objects). Thus to achieve full understanding, learners have to appreciate both the process and the result of that process, just as an expression such as $2x + 3$ or a calculation like 2/3 or $\sin(x)$ is both a process and the result of that process.

Arithmetic Re-considered

As long as arithmetic is seen to be about getting answers, usually single answers, it provides no access to algebraic thinking. When arithmetic is seen to be about operations performed on numbers, it affords access to, even makes use of, algebraic thinking, because it is supporting awareness of the dual nature of operations as processes carried out on objects (numbers) and as objects themselves. It is making use of learners' powers to see generality through particulars. As these generalities are expressed and articulated, they become objects for further study and use, which is what school algebra is about.

Doing and Undoing

Several of the tasks, such as Task 3.3.3, 3.3.4b, 3.4.3, as well as the characterising of negatives, reciprocals and roots by their properties, are based on the pervasive mathematic theme of doing and undoing. Getting learners to develop the habit of asking their own 'undoing' questions is a good way to promote learner creativity and choice.

Whenever you find yourself doing something and getting an answer, you have choices as to how to put the work into a larger and more comprehensive context. You can look for ways to vary and generalise the question, and you can ask yourself questions such as:

What other starting points will give the same answer?
What sorts of numbers can appear as the answers to these sorts of calculations?

In the case of Task 3.2.3, what starting numbers will produce a specified answer, such as 13, and are there any answers you cannot get if you, say, start with an integer? Often it is the case that there are many different starting values that give the same answer. So finding all of them, and characterising, that is, finding a property that can be used to test numbers without actually doing all the calculations, can turn into opportunities for creativity.

The strategy of reversing a calculation and asking 'if this were the answer, what would the question have had to be?' can lead to creative, and sometimes difficult, mathematics. Indeed many of the really difficult problems in mathematics arise from converting a 'doing' calculation into an 'undoing'.

Pause for Reflection

Task 3.5.R Reflection

Think back to your work on tasks in this and previous chapters, and try to identify movements such as those described by *process into object* and by shifting forms of attention (discerning, relating, property-making).

Notes

1 See for example Block 1 of the course materials *Developing Mathematical Thinking*, Open University, Milton Keynes, which ran from 1984 to 1990. See also Brissenden (1990).
2 Much used currently, this task can be found in *Journey Into Maths* (Bell et al. 1978).
3 The idea of asking learners to construct a particular example, a peculiar example, and a general example was developed by Liz Bills in her thesis (Bills 1996).

4 Depicting Relationships

This is the first of three chapters dealing with alternative ways of representing general relationships (for example, using words, symbols and pictures). Each of these three chapters (Chapters 4, 8 and 12) also looks at how technology can help with teaching and learning algebra; Chapter 8 deals with spreadsheets while Chapter 12 examines the potential of computer graphing packages such as 'Autograph' and 'TI Interactive!'. This chapter focuses on graphics calculators and, in terms of the mathematical content of the chapter, you will be asked to depict linear and quadratic relationships.

The aims are threefold:

- to encourage a fluency in moving between different forms of representation;
- to help you to see how to exploit technology so that attention can be directed towards the meaning of the particular graph under consideration;
- to enable you to reflect more generally on the different formats available for depicting relationships and on exploring some of the strengths and weaknesses of each format.

The intention in the text is to give you an indication of how the technology enhances teaching and learning. The illustrations in this chapter are from a TI–83 graphics calculator. More technical help for specific types of graphics calculator is given on the associated website http://cme.open.ac.uk/algebra.

4.1 STRAIGHT LINE GRAPHS

Quickie 4.1

How many numbers do you need to specify in order to define a straight line by the coordinates of points?

Generalising lies at the heart of algebraic thinking. But there are choices to be made about which representational form might be most helpful to use in depicting a generalised relationship. A relationship may initially be expressed symbolically, such as $y = 3x + 2$ but it can be re-presented in a variety of different forms – for example, in a table, in words or in a picture (as a graph or diagram). Conversely, a relationship that has been displayed in the form of a graph can usually be expressed in symbols, in words or in a table. Consequently, there are many opportunities for working on expressing graphically, expressing symbolically, using words, creating tables and moving between these different forms.

In this section, you are asked to focus on relationships the graphs of which take the form of a straight line. Although straight line graphs occur in their own right, they are also important because if you look closely enough, any smooth curve can be described as almost a straight line under magnification.

Task 4.1.1a Depicting and Symbolising Relationships

Imagine the point (1, 2) plotted on a coordinate grid. Now imagine (2, 4), and (3, 6). Now in your imagination, go to the origin (0, 0) and go a little distance to the right and then twice as far up. Repeat this action of going to the origin then to the right (and to the left) some distance and up (or down) twice as far. Continue doing that until you have a sense of a lot of points.

What is the same about the coordinates of the various points? What is the same about the points as seen lying on the coordinate grid?

Comment

At some point, most people want to use squared paper or graph paper. Resisting for as long as possible may help to strengthen your mental imagery but eventually it is probably necessary to see a graph, which might be produced on a collective graph if you are working with others, or on your own, or by a graphics calculator or computer.

Having joined the points and seen that they lie on a straight line, it is valuable to look at the graph and to imagine *you* are a point travelling along the x-axis. As you slide along, imagine, above you, a point twice as high above the x-axis as you are away from the origin. Now move to the left of the origin and again slide along the x-axis The imaginary point is now below you – its depth below the x-axis is twice your distance from the origin. This sense of a graph as the path traced out by a point moving under a constraint (in this case, y value being twice the x value) is a vital link between the graph as a depiction of the relationship between the first and second coordinates, and the symbolic equation $y = 2x$. In this example, the multiplier was 2. Repeated exposures to this task but with different multipliers (both positive and negative) can enhance an appreciation of the effect of the multiplier on the direction of the graph.

Task 4.1.1b Depicting and Symbolising Relationships (continued)

Repeat the same exercise (Task 4.1.1a) but this time, use a relationship such as 'the y-coordinate is one more than 3 times the x-coordinate'.

Comment

The essential idea is to work on developing a mental image of a point moving along the x-axis, with a corresponding imaginary point above or below it, the coordinates of which satisfy some specified relationship. The underlying equation that defines this relationship normally takes the form $y = $ *some expression*; each point lying on the graph determined by this equation corresponds to a pair of coordinates that particularise the generality.

Plotting sample points in order to 'get-a-sense-of' the graph is only one way of approaching graphing. An alternative is to create a catalogue of standard, known graphs that can then be combined to form a specified graph. For example, the graph of $y = 2x$ takes the form of a straight line passing through the origin. But if the required line is one with the same direction as $y = 2x$ but does not pass through the origin, you need to access the family of graphs of the form $y = 2x + c$ for any chosen value of c.

In contrast to the previous task, straight-line graphs can be drawn on a grid, and learners can be invited to work out a corresponding symbolic equation, which is yet another opportunity to express generality in symbols.

Relationships are often encountered in verbal form. In order to depict a verbal relationship graphically, you need either to build up a table of values showing coordinates of particular points on the graph, or to express the relationship in symbols prior to plotting the graph. But developing versatility between using different representational forms requires practice. The next task should help you move more confidently from words to symbols.

Task 4.1.2 From Words to Symbols

For each of the following relationships, write a symbolic expression and sketch a graph. Also make a note of what problems, if any, you encounter.

The number of people who can fit into a number of buses, where each bus takes 45 people.

The height of a plant at some specified time if it grows by 2 mm per day.

The number of litres, given the number of gallons.

The number of litres per kilometre, given the number of miles per gallon.

The first soccer World Cup took place in 1930. It takes place every four years. Which year and which World Cup will next take place after 2007? Find a general formula. Compare this with a general formula for the (modern) Olympics which also takes place every four years and first took place in 1896.

If each egg box holds six eggs, the number of egg boxes required, given the number of eggs.

The length of time it takes to cook a chicken if it requires 45 minutes per kg plus 20 minutes.

Comment

As you may have discovered when you tried to sketch the graphs of these relationships, some of the contexts (bus passengers and eggs, for example), involve *discrete* data – where you can only have whole numbers (of passengers or eggs) so there is a finite number of possibilities within the range considered. Other contexts (plant height and cooking time, for example) involve *continuous* data – these variables are not restricted and so there is an infinite number of possible heights or temperatures within the range considered.

The nature of this distinction and its implications for graphing these relationships are explored in the next subsection.

Representing Discrete and Continuous Variables

Some variables can take only specific values; say integers (such as 'number of children in the family', or half integers (such as 'shoe size'). These are called discrete variables. Others can take any value on a line segment, and are called continuous variables. This distinction between discrete and continuous data is an example of an idea has already been introduced in Chapter 3 – the notion of the range of possible values of the variable.

Whether or not the variables being depicted are discrete or continuous will affect how their graphs are drawn. For example, it makes no sense for the 'eggs' graph to pass through a point corresponding to, say, 3.5 eggs or the 'number of buses' to pass through a point corresponding to, say, 2.73 buses. So, the discrete examples must be represented graphically by a series of separate (discrete) points, rather than as a continuous line. However, the precise detail of how this is to be achieved will depend on the context of the example. Taking the egg boxes example, suppose you have 17 eggs; how many egg boxes are needed? Clearly, there are two full boxes and five eggs left over. But what do you want to do with the remaining five eggs? If the answer is, 'put them in another box', then you need three boxes. In other words, this context would suggest that, where there are eggs remaining, always round up to the next whole number of boxes. This is often referred to as the 'ceiling function' and this idea was explored in Chapter 3.

The table below (Table 4.1) indicates the match between the number of eggs and the number of egg boxes. These data are then represented as a scatter plot.

TABLE 4.1 Table showing eggs and egg boxes

Eggs	1	2	3	4	5	6	7	8	9	10	11	12	13
Boxes	1	1	1	1	1	1	2	2	2	2	2	2	3

Eggs	14	15	16	17	18	19	20	21	22	23	24	25	26
Boxes	3	3	3	3	3	4	4	4	4	4	4	5	5

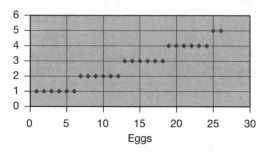

SCATTER PLOT SHOWING EGGS AND EGG BOXES

You have seen how the eggs/egg boxes example can be represented in a table and graphically, but how about algebraically? If E represents the number of eggs and B the number of boxes, an underlying algebraic statement of the relationship between E and B is represented by the following formula:

B	=	E/6
The number of boxes, B ...	... is equal to ...	... the number of eggs, E, divided by 6.

However, as it stands, this formula is wrong five sixths of the time (try it for E = 5, 10, 13, ...). This algebraic formula needs to come with a health warning that, if the value for B is non–integer, it must be rounded up.

Using 'ceiling function' notation, this could be written using special brackets as:

B	=	$\lceil E/6 \rceil$
The number of boxes, B ...	... is equal to ...	... the number of eggs, E, divided by 6, rounded up to the nearest integer.

Contrast this with the graphs representing the continuous data where there is an infinite number of valid points lying between any two points on the graph. For example, the conversion formula connecting the number of litres (L) with the number of gallons (G) is:

$L = 4.55G$

This relationship holds true for all possible values of G, whether integer or non-integer, and so can be represented by a continuous straight line graph.

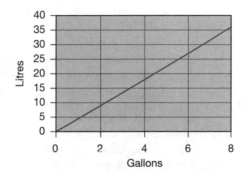

CONVERSION GRAPH FROM GALLONS TO LITRES

The following task brings home the issue of rounding in a surprising way.

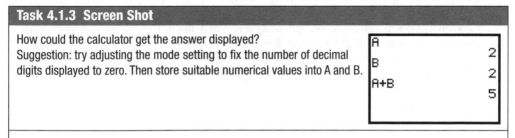

Task 4.1.3 Screen Shot

How could the calculator get the answer displayed?
Suggestion: try adjusting the mode setting to fix the number of decimal digits displayed to zero. Then store suitable numerical values into A and B.

A	2
B	2
A+B	5

Comment

Suitable values for A and B might be 2.4 and 2.4 (remember that the values displayed will always be rounded to the nearest integer). Were you shocked at first? Did that block thinking? Did it engage you?

What is the range of possible values of A and B to give this same output screen?

It is highly likely that someone who is struggling with the use of a calculator might find this daunting enough to block thought. But for someone gaining in confidence, it can act as a spur to activity to try to make sense. Human beings respond to being challenged. A useful teaching strategy is to excite the learner's curiosity by offering them some result or situation that confounds their expectations and that requires some deeper thinking on their part to resolve the conflict. Such a situation is sometimes referred to as one in which the learner experiences *cognitive dissonance* (Festinger 1957). Tasks that trigger cognitive dissonance without overwhelming learners can often trigger mathematical thinking. Indeed, without some sort of dissonance, some need to make sense, learners are unlikely to learn anything. The challenge for the teacher is to walk that fine line between creating a sense of challenge and the learner feeling totally overwhelmed and frustrated.

Linear and Proportional Relationships

This subsection looks at the distinction between two terms that have similar, but not identical, meanings: 'linear' relationships and 'directly proportional' relationships.

Ignoring for the moment the complications raised by discrete data, which were considered in the previous subsection, all of the relationships in Task 4.1.2 were *linear*. In other words, the underlying shape of the graph of the relationship is a straight line.

As you will probably have spotted from your sketches of the graphs, many of these straight-line graphs passed through the origin, but not all. Any linear relationship whose graph passes through the origin with a positive gradient (i.e., sloping from bottom left to top right) is usually referred to as one of *direct proportion*. A relationship of direct proportion can be summarised crudely as: 'If you double this, you double that', 'If you treble this, you treble that', and so on. A simple example of direct proportion is money conversion, say from pounds to pence. There are 100 pence in one pound. If you double the number of pounds you double the number of pence. If you treble the number of pounds you treble the number of pence, and so on.

One of the examples in Task 4.1.2 that was not based on direct proportion was 'length of time it takes to cook a chicken'. There are many ways of cooking a chicken, many of which will be subject to different cooking times. If you consider, say, roasting a chicken at a suitable (fixed temperature), most recipe books will provide a helpful formula linking the weight of the bird to cooking time. This often takes the form of, 'allow 20 minutes plus an additional 20 minutes per kilogram'. So, the connection between time and weight of chicken has both a fixed as well as a variable element. As you should have seen from your graph sketching in Task 4.3, it is this 'fixed' component that ensures that the graph does not pass through the origin. Check your sketch of this example again to convince yourself that this is so.

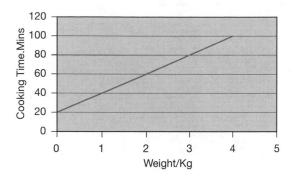

THE GRAPH OF COOKING TIME AGAINST WEIGHT OF CHICKEN

This distinction between proportional and linear relationships is explored further in the Task 4.1.4.

Task 4.1.4 Spot the Difference

Consider the following two relationships and think about what is the same and what is different about them.

The approximate conversion rate between inches and metres is that 1 metre equals 39.37 inches.

To convert temperatures from degrees Celsius to degrees Fahrenheit, multiply by 1.8 and add 32.

Comment

Both these relationships are linear but whereas the first one is based on direct proportion, the second is not. Sketching the graphs will reveal this clearly.

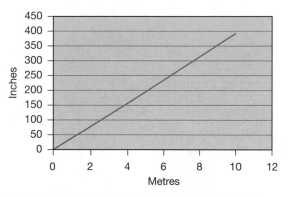

THE 'DISTANCE' CONVERSION GRAPH FROM METRES TO INCHES

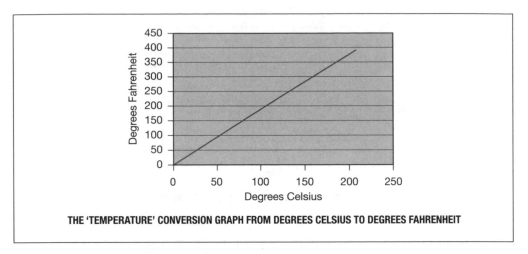

THE 'TEMPERATURE' CONVERSION GRAPH FROM DEGREES CELSIUS TO DEGREES FAHRENHEIT

What these relationships share is linearity. However, while the first relationship is one of proportion, the second is not (it passes through 32 on the vertical axis).

Task 4.1.R Make a Summary

Write, in your own words, what you understand to be the distinction between relationships that are linear and those that are directly proportional. How are these two forms of relationship distinguished graphically?

Comment

All relationships involving direct proportion are represented graphically by straight lines with positive gradients that pass *through the origin*. Such a relationship is a special case of a linear relationship. A linear relationship is represented by a straight-line graph that may or may not pass through the origin. Graphically, the distinction is as follows.

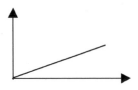

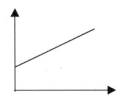

Directly proportional relationships are represented by straight-line graphs with positive gradients passing through the origin.

Linear relationships are represented by straight-line graphs that may or may not pass through the origin (this one does not).

4.2 QUADRATIC RELATIONSHIPS

Quickie 4.2

If you look at a mathematical curve drawn on a set of axes, it could be moved around to occupy different positions relative to the axes. What might be a useful (numerical) measure of the graph's current position?

In this section, you are asked to focus on relationships the graphs of which take the form of a curve known as 'quadratic'. As before, you will be offered tasks that are designed to help you develop your skill and confidence in moving easily between different representational forms.

Task 4.2.1 Depicting and Symbolising Relationships

Imagine the point (1, 1) plotted on a coordinate grid. Now imagine also (2, 4), and (3, 9). Now go to the origin (0, 0) and imagine going a little distance to the right and then go up by a distance that is the square of this distance. Repeat this action of going to the origin then to the right or to the left some distance and then up by the square of this distance. Continue doing that until you have a sense of a lot of points.

What is the same about the coordinates of the various points?

Comment

This task is similar to the one that you carried out in Task 4.1.1 but with a different rule. The key difference is that this time there is no 'constant step size'; rather than the path being a straight line, it curves upwards. As before, it passes through the origin.

The picture that you probably had in mind was:

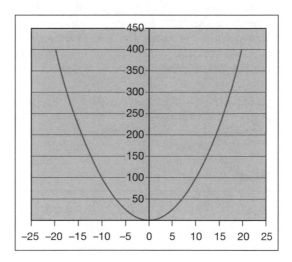

Expressed algebraically, the relationship is written as $y = x^2$ and this equation is the simplest form of the family of equations known as *quadratic*.

Whereas linear relationships are usually associated with straight lines, quadratic relationships are usefully considered in terms of area. Here is a simple example to illustrate this point. If a square has side of length x units, then $y = x^2$ can represent a formula connecting the area, y, and the length of side, x. Lengths are easily compared by eye, but how good are our estimating skills when it comes to comparing areas? The next task will give you the opportunity to find out.

Task 4.2.2 Squares and Circle

Look at the square to the left. Only one of the squares on the right has double the area of the original square. Which one do you think it is?

Look at the circle to the left. Only one of the circles on the right has double the area of the original circle. Which one do you think it is?

Comment

As has been indicated, most people have a good eye when it comes to judging distance: at a glance they can make an accurate estimate of what a doubling would look like in length or height. But when it comes to area, most of us aren't so skilled. In each of the questions in the task, it was the first option that corresponded to double the area of the original shape. In the case of the square, doubling the length and the height of the original square (third option) has the effect of scaling the area by a factor of 4. In fact, in order to scale the area by a factor of 2, you need to scale the dimensions of each side by a factor of $\sqrt{2}$, or approximately 1.41. In other words, a doubling of area is achieved by a 41% increase in both dimensions.

The same is true of the circle example. Doubling the area of a circle involves scaling its radius by a factor of $\sqrt{2}$, which gives a roughly 41% linear increase in each dimension.

Putting the circles together concentrically does not seem to make it any easier, while giving them a common point (the second diagram) at least helps to draw your eye to the ratios of diameters.

Geographers tend to use circles to depict conurbations, with the area proportional to the number of people. Why might these be at best difficult to read, and at worst, misleading?

Just as in section 4.1 you were asked to develop your versatility at moving between various representational formats for linear relationships, the next task asks you to take a *quadratic* relationship and depict it in different ways.

Task 4.2.3 Area of a Semi-circle

Use the following three forms of representation to depict the relationship between the area of a semi-circle and its radius:

(a) an algebraic formula;

(b) a table; and

(c) a graph.

Comment

(a) The formula for the area of a circle is:

$$A = \pi r^2,$$ where A represents the area of the circle and r is the radius.

So, it follows that the area formula for a semi-circle is:

$$S = 0.5\pi r^2, \text{ or } \tfrac{1}{2}\,\pi r^2,$$ where S represents the area of the semi-circle and r is the radius.

(b) Depending on the context, you will need to determine the range of relevant values (for example, is it a tiny semi-circular drawing or large semi-circular playground?).

Here is a table that might be relevant to a playground (the area values have been rounded to the nearest whole number):

Radius (r)/metres	10	15	20	25	30	35
Area (S)/metres^2	157	353	628	982	1414	1924

(c) The graph of $y = 0.5\pi r^2$ is not restricted to a particular range of values and can take both negative and non-integer values. However, since the question deals with the radius of a semi-circle, it makes sense for r to take only non-negative values, as shown here.

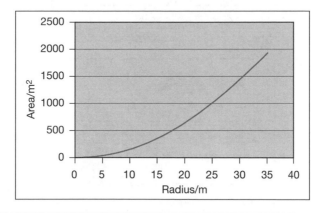

In the next task you are asked to think about some underlying relationships between the speed that a car is travelling and its stopping distance. As with previous tasks of this type, the aim is to explore the variety of different forms of representation that can be used to express the relationship and to reflect on the strengths and weaknesses of each.

Note that the *stopping distance* of a car has two components: the *thinking distance* (how far a car travels before the driver reacts) and *braking distance* (how far the car travels under braking). Overall stopping distance is the sum of thinking distance and braking distance.

Task 4.2.4 A Linear and a Quadratic Relationship

Look at the table of braking data, which was taken from the UK government's Highway Code website.

(a) How does the variable 'thinking distance' relate to a driver's reaction time? If you were trying to explain their connection, might you find it helpful to use a diagram? If so, what diagram might you use?

(b) Make a rough plot of 'Thinking distance' against 'Speed'. How would you describe the relationship between thinking distance and speed? Can you explain why the graph has this shape?

(c) Make a rough plot of 'Braking distance' against 'Speed'. Describe its general shape. From common sense, would you expect the graph to pass through the origin?

(d) Add columns 2 and 3 and put them in column 4. Make a rough plot of 'Stopping distance' against 'Speed'. Describe its general shape. Again, would you expect the graph to pass through the origin?

Speed/mph	Thinking distance/metres	Braking distance/metres	Stopping distance/metres
20	6	6	
30	9	14	
40	12	24	
50	15	38	
60	18	55	
70	21	75	

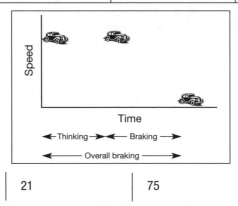

70	21	75	

Typical Stopping Distances, *source*: www.highwaycode.gov.uk, p. 97–101

Comment

(a) The driver's reaction time is the (hopefully small) interval between seeing the hazard and applying the brakes. Typically, this is roughly 2/3 of a second for the average driver.

The driver's thinking distance is how far the car travels during this interval. The whole notion of 'thinking distance' can be a tricky concept to grasp, mostly because not everyone is aware that there really is a measurable gap between thought and action.

Here is a diagram drawn by one teacher when explaining these ideas to Key Stage 3 pupil.

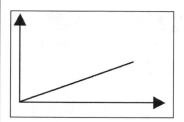

During the 'Thinking' phase (i.e. between pictures 1 and 2), the car continues at a steady speed. Only during the 'Braking' phase does it slow down. The final picture in the diagram is when the car is at rest.

(b) The 'Thinking' distance sketch should look roughly as follows – a straight line passing through the origin, where the vertical axis is 'distance travelled during thinking time' and the horizontal axis is ' car speed'.

This can be explained as follows. A driver's reaction time will be more or less fixed, regardless of the speed that the car is travelling. This means that a car travelling at, say, 40 mph during the 'thinking' phase will travel twice as far as a car travelling at 20 mph. In other words, there is a directly proportional relationship between thinking distance and speed.

(c) With 'Braking' distance, as speed increases in fixed steps, the distance increases in everincreasing steps. The graph will still pass through the origin but would then curve upwards, like this. *Note*: the vertical axis is 'distance travelled during braking time' and the horizontal axis is 'initial car speed'.

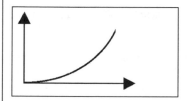

Braking distance is non-linear because doubling the speed does not double the braking distance. Although it could be a quadratic relationship, there are other families of curve that might fit these points. This point is taken up again in section 4.4 of this chapter. It makes sense that the curve should pass through the origin since a car travelling at zero mph should have a zero braking distance!

(d) Stopping distance is also non–linear and again a quadratic curve should fit these points. As with braking distance, it makes sense that the curve should pass through the origin (a car travelling at zero mph should have a zero stopping distance).

You will return to this example in section 4.4 where the graphics calculator will be used to uncover the underlying equations representing braking distance against speed and stopping distance against speed using the calculator's quadratic curve-fitting facility (known as quadratic *regression*).

Graphs, formulae and tables all have their uses. Learning to move between them is valuable for three main reasons:

- This experience makes you more versatile in your ability to choose suitable representations for a particular situation.
- Different learners have different preferences in terms of how they can best make sense of relationships (using words, pictures tables or symbols) and as a teacher you need to be aware of these choices and have some facility with all of them.

- It helps you gain insight about the *general* properties of these various representational forms and their respective strengths and weaknesses.

But most significantly, graphs offer opportunities for expressing and appreciating generality. Indeed, you do not appreciate a graph unless you recognise the generality that it is depicting.

Task 4.2.R: Make a Summary

Write, in your own words, what you understand to be the distinctive features of relationships that are quadratic.

Comment

All quadratic relationships are represented graphically by a symmetrical U-shaped graph which may or may not pass through the origin, and which may or may not cut the *x*-axis. What other features have you observed?

4.3 LINEAR RELATIONSHIPS AND THE GRAPHICS CALCULATOR

Quickie 4.3

How few numbers to you need to specify a straight line?

How does your answer relate to the equation $y = mx + c$?

Can you think of another way of specifying a straight line with only two numbers other than using $y = mx + c$?

There is, and almost certainly will be in the future, a growing range of electronic devices that can be used to support and promote mathematical thinking. The following two sections illustrate just a few of the many possibilities, based on a graphics calculator.

The examples used in this and the following sections can be applied to most makes of graphics calculator. However, the screen shots used are based on a particular make of calculator – the Texas Instruments TI-83/TI-84 family – so if you are using another model, be aware that some of the screens may look slightly different. Please do not just read this section passively! You will gain far more if you can get your hands on a graphics calculator and try to create these screens for yourself.

Term-to-Term Sequences

One common way of generating a number sequence is to set up a starting number and then apply some rule to take you to the next term. This rule is then applied to each term, thereby generating the sequence. For obvious reasons, this approach is often referred to as the 'term-to-term' method. An alternative approach is to define a rule for calculating the value of any given term, based on its position in the sequence. This way of generating number sequences is the position-to-term method. Both these approaches are explored below.

Task 4.3.1 Number Sequences

The recent memory of a graphics calculator can be used to generate sequences. The calculator stores the latest answer in a store called ANS.

(a) On a graphics calculator, enter the number 0 and press <ENTER>.

Then press + 3 <ENTER>.

Finally, keep pressing <ENTER> to see the 3-times table on the screen.

(b) Now clear the screen and try to display the 7-times table.

 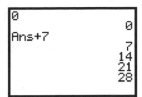

(c) Try the three below and then generate some times tables of your own.

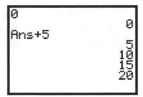  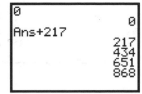

(d) So far, all the number sequences began with zero. They can, of course, begin with any starting number. Try these and others like them.

 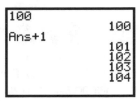 

(e) Spend a few minutes thinking about which numbers will, and will not, be represented in these last three sequences (in part (d)). For example, will the number 63 be included if you extend the first sequence? How about 72? How might someone express a rule for predicting which numbers will be included and which will not?

Comment

Notice that all of these sequences are essentially 'linear' in nature – that is, the number added each time is the same, so they increase in fixed steps. But how many of these sequences are based on direct proportion? Put another way, if you were to travel backwards along the sequence, would you pass through zero? (As has been remarked several times in this chapter, it is this 'passing through zero' that is characteristic of directly proportional relationships.)

There are two main ways in which a linear sequence can be generated on a calculator. The first you have just seen – you enter a starting number (say, 3) and then keep adding the same fixed number (say, 6) term to term. The essential characteristic of this approach is that each number in the sequence is created from the number that precedes it. The next subsection describes a second approach for generating linear sequences on a calculator that is referred to as 'position-to-term' sequences.

Position-to-Term Sequences

Another method for generating sequences is to use a sequence formula. Here, each number in the sequence is calculated by a formula that is based on the number's *position* in the sequence. For example, consider the formula $3n + 1$. The first number in this sequence is the value of $3n + 1$ when $n = 1$. This gives the value $3 \times 1 + 1 = 4$. The second number in the sequence is the value of $3n + 1$ when $n = 2$. This gives the value $3 \times 2 + 1 = 7$. Continuing in this way gives the number sequence 4, 7, 10, 13, 16, … . Each term value is 1 more than a multiple of 3.

A calculator command such as **seq** on the TI-83 will generate number sequences by this method.

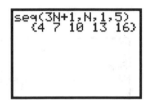

The four items contained in the brackets following the **seq** command, separated by commas, are known as the *arguments* of the command. The **seq** command may seem rather complicated at first, but learners quickly adapt to it. Its syntax can be explained as follows:

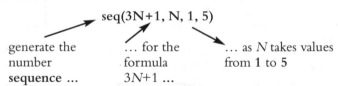

seq(3N+1, N, 1, 5)

generate the number sequence …

… for the formula $3N+1$ …

… as *N* takes values from 1 to 5

Task 4.3.2 Number Sequences Using the Seq Command

Explore the **seq** command to create some sequences of your own. For example, start by altering only the first argument to create the sequence: 9, 15, 21, 27, 33. Then try varying some of the other arguments to see the effect. Create sequences that get smaller as well as larger.

Comment

Note that the letter used on a graphics calculator to generate a sequence is quite arbitrary. However, the letter used as the second argument in the **seq** command must match the one chosen to set up the sequence formula in the first argument. For example, the first **seq** command below is valid but the second is not.

seq(2B–3,B,1,10)   A valid command because the same letter, B, is used throughout the command.

seq(2B–3,C,1,10)   An invalid command because two different letters, B and C, have been used.

Sequences in Graphs and Tables

A feature of the sequences just discussed is that they are discrete – i.e. they are based on using only integer values of N. You saw in Section 4.1 that with discrete data like these, it makes no sense to talk about the value of the 'two and a half'th term or the value of term value 71.3. Thus, when representing such a sequence graphically, it should appear as discrete points (called a *scatter plot*) and not as a continuous graph. In Task 4.3.3, you will be guided through plotting the term values of the formula $3N + 2$ against their term positions. The position numbers (1, 2, 3, ...) and the term values (5, 8, 11, ...) for the first ten terms must first be stored into separate lists and then these two lists will be displayed as a scatterplot.

Task 4.3.3 Depicting the Formula 3N+2 as a Scatter Plot

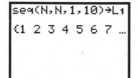

Step 1: Generate the 'position' numbers 1 to 10 and store them in list L1.

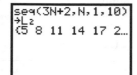

Step 2: Generate the first ten 'term' values in the sequence and store them in list L2.

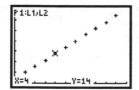

Step 3: Set up statistics plot facility to display the values in L1 and L2 as a scatter plot, choose a suitable graphing window from the Window menu and display the graph on the graphing screen. It should look something like this.

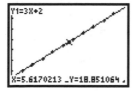

On the Y= screen, enter the equation Y1 = 3X + 2, as shown. Then return to the graphing screen to see the continuous graph passing through the points of the scatter plot. How is scrolling along this line different from scrolling along the scatter plot?

Comment

The numbers displayed at the bottom of the graphing screen correspond to the X and Y coordinates of the current cursor position. Note that when the scatterplot is selected, these are integer values (reflecting the discrete nature of a number sequence) but they take non-integer values when the continuous function $Y = 3X + 2$ is being traced.

Task 4.3.R How was the Calculator for You?

Look back through this section and make a note of the main areas where the calculator may have been able to support your thinking about any of the following:

> term-to-term sequences;

> position-to-term sequences;

> discrete and continuous relationships.

Comment

If you are a calculator novice, you may have felt that the calculator failed to support your thinking as too much of your attention was directed at understanding the various commands and trying to locate them on the appropriate screen menu. However, with a little experience of using these commands, your confidence will grow and you will start to notice a shift of attention away from 'How do I do … on the calculator?' to 'What if I were to … ?' and ' I wonder why it displays this … ?

One potentially valuable feature of the calculator is the way in which its commands and menus are organised and presented – their very structure encapsulates the essence of the mathematical ideas they represent. An awareness of this on the part of the student can provide a most fruitful 'way in' to what the underlying mathematics is about. For example, the four arguments of the command **seq** represent the four key things that you need to be aware of when considering a number sequence based on a 'position-to-term' formula, namely: the underlying formula, the variable or letter on which the formula is defined, the term number to start the sequence and the term number to end the sequence.

4.4 QUADRATIC RELATIONSHIPS ON A GRAPHICS CALCULATOR

Quickie 4.4

How many points are needed to determine a quadratic curve passing through them?

How many numbers do you need to state in order to specify a curve by the coordinates of points?

As you saw in sections 4.1 and 4.3, a key characteristic of linear relationships is that, for a given step size, the values increase (or decrease) by a fixed amount. In fact, only linear relationships have this property. In this section, you will use the calculator to explore one of the many families of relationship that are non-linear – the quadratic relationship.

Stopping Distance

In Section 4.2, you were asked to sketch the graphs of thinking distance, braking distance and overall stopping distance against speed. In this section, you will be guided through a similar exercise using the graphics calculator. However, supported by the calculator technology, you will have the opportunity to explore these relationships in greater depth than would be possible from a sketch alone.

Task 4.4.1 Graphing the Braking Data on a Graphics Calculator

Enter the data for speed, thinking distance and braking distance given in Task 4.2.4 into lists L1, L2 and L3, respectively.

Using a suitable window, set the STATPLOT menu to plot L3 against L1 using a scatter plot. It should look something like this.

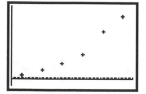  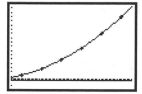

You can now use the calculator to fit a quadratic model to these points by using the quadratic regression facility; the quadratic equation is stored on the Y= screen and its graph is displayed on the graphing screen as shown here.

Comment

You can now use the calculator to generate the overall stopping distance data by adding the data in L2 and L3, storing the result in list L4.

Task 4.4.2 Stopping Distance

From the home screen, enter L2 + L3 -> L4 and plot the data in L4 against L1 as a scatter plot. Then, use the calculator's quadratic regression facility to fit a quadratic model to these points. The quadratic equation is stored on the Y= screen and its graph is displayed on the graphing screen as shown here.

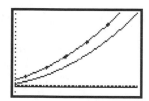

(a) Try to explain what is displayed on the graphing screen.

(b) Does the overall stopping distance curve pass through the origin?

(c) Do the braking distance curve and the overall stopping distance curve have the same shape?

Comments

(a) The screen shows two graphs. The lower one represents braking distance plotted against speed, while the upper curve represents overall stopping distance plotted against speed. The smooth curves are the calculator's best guess, based on using quadratic regression, of the two relationships. Not surprisingly, for any given speed, overall stopping distance exceeds braking distance. The widening gap between the two reflects thinking distance that increases as speed increases.

(b) Note that this time the curve does not appear to pass through the origin. However this may be an illusion because **Xmin** is currently set to some number other than zero (the calculator may have chosen something like 15 or 20 for **Xmin**. Adjust the Window settings so that the true origin is displayed (i.e. set **Xmin** to zero) and see what happens to the display when speed = 0 mph.

Clearly it is consistent with common sense that when travelling at 0 mph the stopping distance should be 0 metres.

Task 4.4.R Quadratics on a Calculator

Look back through this section and section 4.2 and make a note of the main areas where the calculator may have been able to support your thinking about any of the following:

- the general shape of a quadratic;
- what happens to the graph when you change the constant.

Comment

The graphic calculator gives learners access to a greater number of cases of quadratic graphs than would normally be the case when using pencil and paper.

4.5 PEDAGOGIC ISSUES

Quickie 4.5

How few numbers can you use to specify a quadratic graph?

What about higher-order functions such as a cubic, a quartic, ... ?

Comment

Three numbers are needed to specify a quadratic curve; usually these are taken to be the values of a, b and c in the standard form of the quadratic equation: $y = ax^2 + bx + c$. By extension, four numbers are needed to specify a cubic curve, five to specify a quartic, and so on.

The slope of a straight line is really a ratio of two numbers (vertical rise and horizontal run), but the value of that ratio can be specified as a single number. Taking slope as specified by a single number, then two numbers are sufficient to pin down a particular straight-line graph. The usual format is to use the so-called 'standard form' of a linear equation, $y = mx + c$, where m represents the slope and c the y-intercept (i.e. where the line cuts the y-axis). Alternatives to this approach could be to specify the *angle*, rather than the slope of the line or to provide two points through which the line must pass. (In order to satisfy the 'two numbers only' criterion, you might use the points where the line intersects the y and x axes, assuming it does not pass through the origin. If it does pass through the origin an indication of the slope is needed.)

What Makes Graphing Difficult?

The fact of a straight line is not hard to grasp. What makes it difficult is the variety of ways in which a straight line and its corresponding graph can be understood and interpreted. For example, a straight-line graph can be seen both as a collection of points and as an object in its own right.

Graphs depict relationships between two quantities (usually denoted by x and y). To read a relationship from a graph it is useful to think of it as a set of all points satisfying a constraint (namely that the y value and the x value are related). As your eye moves along the x-axis, it is free at any time to move up (parallel to the y-axis) to the curve, leading to a point on the curve that satisfies the relationship being depicted. This relationship may also be recorded symbolically using an equation. It may not be obvious to many students that the height of the curve at that point is actually the particular value of y in the corresponding equation.

The graph can also be seen as an object and as such it has a shape – for example, linear (straight line), quadratic, parabolic, and so on. The graph has, or corresponds to, an equation, which can be thought of as a constraint on the freedom of the points that make up the shape.

Straight-line graphs have the property that they can be expressed symbolically using a linear equation, and determined by two distinct points on the line or by a point and the slope. Indeed, a straight line is determined by the choice of *any* two distinct points on that line – as a property abstracted from a relationship, this is something that takes time to appreciate.

The Graphics Calculator as a Tool for Teaching And Learning

In looking at a calculator screenshot, you first have to discern and recognise elements such as axes or commands to work out what the screenshot is showing. Then you have to discern relevant components and relate these to the text. (How was the screen produced? What are the various parameters? What is being depicted in a graph?) The instructions to use specific calculator commands are not particular to the specific sequences, graphs and tables of course, but apply more generally. Did you notice yourself generalising, or at least recognising that 'this is what this instruction does', or were you caught up in following the text to the extent that you did not always notice 'what the command did and how it was used' in a form that would enable you to use it yourself another time?

Distinguishing between Discrete and Continuous

Earlier in this chapter, the distinction was drawn between discrete and continuous data. This is a distinction that even young children can engage with. There are practical situations where it crops up naturally (differentiating between foot size and shoe size, for example) but it will also crop up when they are drawing graphs.

It is very tempting to 'join up' points that represent discrete situations in order to display some trend or pattern. But 'joined up graphs' imply that every point on the curve is a possible data point of the depicted relationship. So displaying discrete data as if they were continuous can be misleading. (Watch out for it in newspapers and in school reports to governors!) 'Continuous' can also be mistaken for 'discrete': as Task

4.5.1 demonstrates, it is possible to be misled by a calculator into thinking that out-puts are discrete when what is happening is that rounding, perhaps even severe rounding is taking place.

Mathematics as Making Sense of Phenomena

In Chapters 1 and 3 you explored a range of contexts in which expressing generality was not only possible, but captured the phenomenon. In this chapter you saw how an electronic screen such as a graphics calculator can be used to present a phenomenon (depict a relationship), that then needs to be interpreted. It was also demonstrated how a phenomenon in the material world can be modelled by detecting and express-ing relationships either as symbolic expressions (equations, perhaps) or as graphical relationships. The screen shot in Task 4.5.1 was intended to be a surprise, but it is hoped that there have been other surprises along the way, because it is only when there is a surprise, a discrepancy between expectation and perceived, that sense-making is activated and people are moved (motivated) to 'sort things out'. The term *cognitive dissonance* was used to refer to a surprise; a mismatch between expectation and perception. Nitas Moshovits-Hadar (1988) suggests that every mathematical 'fact' or 'result', every technical term, signals a surprise that was experienced by someone, which led to its development and use, and that it is possible to re-enter and re-create that surprise for learners. This is an example of what John Dewey (1902) referred to as the principal role of the teacher; to *psychologise the subject matter*; that is, to present phenomena that bring the subject matter to the attention of learners in such a way as to make it possible for them to recognise the phenomenon as something that needs explaining, and which affords access to making sense using the powers and experi-ence they have available.

Reflections

If you are not very familiar with a graphics calculator, it might be worth going back and reviewing the keystrokes you made and what they did. The shift from 'what they did' to 'what they do' is the shift from being aware of relationship in a specific instance to 'recognising something as a property'. If you experienced any uncertainty about keystrokes and their use, then you have a taste of why it is that learners don't always seem to learn from being given instructions.

Using a graphics calculator enables learners to achieve quickly results that might take rather longer if laboriously worked out by hand, especially when it comes to plotting. The tool is designed to mediate between the learner and the task, but as with any tool, it is easy to become caught up in the details of using the tool and miss the reason for using it, namely to understand or appreciate some mathematical idea, or to model some situation in order to resolve certain questions. Consequently it is vital, after using a tool, to pause and reflect by considering what it is that the results tell you, and at the same time, to check against your intuition that the results seem to be reasonable and roughly what you expect, since there may have been some mistakes in the keystrokes!

Manipulate–Get-a-Sense-of–Articulate (MGA) and See–Experience–Master (SEM)

Pausing and reflecting is a contribution to two versions of a learning spiral: manipu-late; get-a-sense-of; articulate (MGA) and see–experience–master (SEM). In the

MGA spiral, learning is seen to be enhanced by manipulating familiar objects (in the case of this chapter, an example might be simple number sequences of the form 'something more than a multiple of') in order to get a sense of what might be going on (with the calculator). Having seen the calculator used for simple sequences, further experience was available when encountering less familiar sequences such as those based on the quadratic relationship. Here the calculator was becoming more familiar, enabling you to use it to get a sense of what quadratic sequences are about. Now you are being urged to think back over what you have done and to try to bring to articulation both what distinguishes direct and indirect proportion as linear relationships, and how these differ from quadratic relationships.

Notice also that it is useful to think in terms of learners meeting ideas and gaining experience with those ideas over a period of time before being expected to display mastery. This is usefully summarised by the three-term framework of *See–Experience–Master*. When you first see or meet an idea, it is like a lump, undifferentiated, or like an express train going through a station, all speed and power but no detail. With continued exposure to the same idea it begins to become familiar, and eventually to be incorporated into your thinking. A related way of describing this uses the MGA framework. With experience, through manipulating familiar, confidence-inspiring objects, you begin to get a sense of what some notion entails, what some technique involves. For example, you become more familiar with a graph as an object but also as a set of points. As your familiarity grows, you become more articulate, more able to make use of the terms and the constructs in order to express your thinking.

Multiple Representations

Some learners have strong preferences for visual information and others for symbolic. All learners benefit from information being given in parallel forms that are seen to be equivalent.

Drawing on examples from previous chapters, the sequence in Task 1.2.2 can be represented in four different ways as follows:

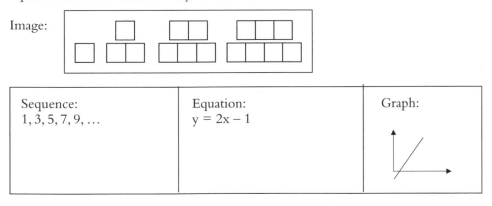

| Sequence:
1, 3, 5, 7, 9, … | Equation:
$y = 2x - 1$ | Graph: |

Similarly the sequence from Quickie 1.3, can be represented in four different ways:
Description: Numbers that are 3 more than a multiple of 7.

Sequence: 10, 17, 24, 31, …	Equation: $y = 7x + 3$	Graph:

Technology gives an advantage in that parallel representations are quickly generated, and the effects of making changes can be compared in each representation.

Introduction to Block 2

The next four chapters revisit similar ideas to those in the four chapters of Block 1, but with added sophistication. Since expressing your own generalities is considered to be an essential foundation for all of algebraic thinking, since it is something that improves with practice and experience, and since it underlies the learning of all other mathematical topics, it continues to be stressed and developed in this block, especially in Chapter 5.

Chapter 5 continues the theme of Chapter 1 by providing further exposure to contexts in which generalising (and specialising) can be encouraged.

Chapter 6 continues the theme of Chapter 2 by focusing on the natural power to organise and characterise things by their properties.

Chapter 7 continues the theme of Chapter 3 by developing the notions of multiple expressions for the same generality, and expressions of constraints on a generality, as routes to and motivation for the rules for manipulating algebraic symbols, and the roles that symbols play in mathematics.

Chapter 8 continues the e-tool theme of Chapter 4 by developing the use of spreadsheets as a tool for providing background experience for variables and for exploring different representations of relationships.

5

More Experience of Expressing Generality

Chapter 5 exemplifies the See–Experience–Master framework introduced in Block 1, by revisiting the act of expressing generality in situations somewhat more varied than previous examples. The contexts are drawn from numbers, geometrical relationships, and outside school. The tasks invite you to notice how what you attend to changes as you work.

5.1 EXPRESSING GENERALITY (NUMBERS)

Quickie 5.1

Write down an expression for the angle between the hour hand and the minute hand when the hands indicate that the time is an exact hour.

Comment

Did you think to try some particular cases either to check your expression or to provide insight into what it should be? By paying attention to *how* you work it out in one or two cases, you can move to expressing that method in general.

This section considers the shift from using a letter to denote a general number, to using it to express an as-yet-unknown number.

Percentages

The most general case can be seen as the least constrained: objects being considered, such as numbers, can be any number whatsoever. Interesting things start to happen when some constraints or limitations are placed on the numbers, such as that they must be an integer, being between five and seven, being odd, or meeting some other condition. Here there is opportunity to experience and express the effects of constraints.

The next three tasks revisit 'doing and undoing' in the context of expressing generality.

Task 5.1.1a Discount

Choose a number; add 10%. What must you multiply your starting number by in order to achieve the same result? Try several examples. What about subtracting 10%?

Comment

Most people would manipulate calculations on one or more specific prices (such as £100) in order to get a sense of what might be going on, before articulating a generalisation.

The essential awareness associated with % is that adding $i\%$ to a number is the same as multiplying by $1 + i/100$. Subtracting $d\%$ of a number is the same as multiplying by $1 - d/100$. For example, subtracting 10% of a number is the same as multiplying by 0.9. Pause and make sure that this example does specialise the general case, and that the generality describes your findings!

Task 5.1.1b Compounded Percentages

Suppose that you add 10% of something and then add 10% of that. What is the overall percentage increase? What happens if you add 5% and then 10%. Generalise.

If there is a tax of 10% but a discount of 10%, what is the overall effect as a % of the starting price? Generalise.

Comment

Were you able to go straight to symbols this time? The point of manipulating numbers is to gain confidence; once you become confident to use symbols, they form 'confidently manipulable objects' in the same way that numbers do!

It is tempting to conjecture that the compound percentages will be the sum of the percentages (after all, you are calculating 10% and then adding it on). But the second calculation is 10% of the new number and so the result is slightly larger, by 10% of the previous increase.

Task 5.1.1c Undoing

When you add a particular percentage, what must you subtract to get back to the original number? Try some cases. Generalise.

Comment

Did you think to make sure your generalisation also works when you first subtract a percentage, and then find what percentage of the result to add back on to achieve the starting value?

Being asked to 'undo' or 'reverse' a task is an invitation to express a relationship: what percentage reduction will 'undo' a percentage increase and what percentage increase will undo a percentage reduction? In effect it is asking what an inverse or reverse % key would have to do.

Notice how the three Tasks 5.1.1a to c were structured so as to prepare you for the 'undoing' question. With exposure to such structured tasks, you would expect to develop the confidence to engage in undoing for yourself in other situations.

The relationship between tax and discount to return the original price is an example of a constraint: knowing one value (percentage increase) constrains, indeed determines the other (percentage decrease). The essence of the relationship is that if the reduction is to undo the increase (or vice versa), then

$(1 - d/100)(1 + i/100) = 1$ (applying the decrease to the increase makes no change to the starting number).

This relationship between two otherwise freely chosen numbers constitutes a constraint. If either is specified, the other is determined.

As you may have found in Task 1.1.1 in Chapter 1, the fact that addition and multiplication are commutative (you can multiply numbers in either order) means that it does not matter in what order you perform the calculations of percentages.

Dimensions of Possible Variation

Every task can be augmented by asking learners to look for and express underlying implicit possibilities for variation. A single, simple idea, suitable initially for young learners developing their arithmetic skills, suddenly explodes into a rich collection of tasks that learners can invent and explore for themselves using the notion of dimensions of possible variation: in any question, what aspects could be changed?

Take an idea for a single task, and see for yourself how it might be developed using the notion of dimensions of possible variation.

Task 5.1.2a Different Routes

Write down any number. To the right of it and above, multiply by 3 and then add 5. To the right and below, add 5 and then multiply by 3. Your two answers will differ by 10. Why?

Comment

Note that the difference of 10 is independent of the starting number, so that 10 is invariant while the starting number changes. Looked at one way, this task invites two expressions of generality and a relation between them; looked at another way, it invites a single expression of generality that relates the results from different routes.

This and many similar tasks can be turned into magic with an audience. The audience secretly specifies the input, and openly chooses the two operation numbers and one of the output numbers. You then predict the other output number.

Task 5.1.2b Different Routes Developed

What dimensions of possible variation could be exploited to generate a whole domain of tasks similar to this one with the same aim, namely to alert learners to the fact that operations performed in different orders give different answers, but that there may be a relation between those answers?

Comment

At a surface level, it is vital for learners to appreciate and to come to think of spontaneously for themselves what dimensions of possible variation and associated range of permissible change are available in any task. Here, possible dimensions of possible variation include the 3 and the 5, and the operations of multiplication and addition could all be changed, and more operations could be compounded. Thus this task could be transformed from a very simple, straightforward exploration inviting an expression of generality, into a challenge to construct two compound operations that always differ by a constant. The core of all such tasks is to go beyond expressing generality (generalising a single calculation) to locating and expressing relationships between expressions, for example, $(x + 5) \times 3 - (3x + 5) = 10$, which can also be seen as a single expression of generality.

Notice that the tax and discount tasks could be seen as examples of this more general structure.

Note that the task *Different Routes* does not require learners to be able to manipulate symbols, but exposure to various versions of this task over time is likely to provoke the conjecture that it should be possible to see why the difference is always 10.

Making Sense of Arithmetic

Expressing generality is central to all of mathematics, including arithmetic. The calculations in the next task suggest ways of carrying out mental calculations that people have suggested at various times.

Task 5.1.3 Specialising and Generalising	
Match the particular calculations in the left with the correct corresponding general statements on the right (*not the one aligned with it!*). Then show that the implied generalities *always* work. There is an additional opportunity to generalise to three digits in as many ways as you can.	
$83 \times 87 = 7221$	The product of two two-digit numbers for which the product of the tens digits and the product of the units digits is the same, is the same as the product of the numbers with their digits reversed.
$26 \times 31 = 62 \times 13$	To multiply two numbers together, subtract the square of their difference from the square of their sum and divide by four.
$36 \times 76 = 2736$	To multiply two two-digit numbers with the same tens digit and with their units digits summing to ten, multiply the tens digit by one more than itself and append the product of the units digits.
$57 \times 23 = \dfrac{(57 + 23)^2 - (57 - 23)^2}{4}$	To multiply two two-digit numbers with the same units digits and with their tens digits summing to ten, multiply the two tens digits and add the units digit, then append the square of the units digit.
What is the same, and what different, about the calculations in the left column?	

Comments

To show that a 'method' *always* works requires writing down a general expression for the two numbers, including any constraints, and then using algebraic manipulation to justify the 'always'.

Note that the last calculation on the left shows how with only a table of squares of numbers, you could perform multiplications by simply squaring, subtracting, and dividing by 4.

Getting learners to pick an item from a collection and to say what distinguishes it from the others is useful for learning about what learners are attending to, and what is likely to help them refine and become aware of their power to discern. Here, the verbal expressions suggest general properties of numbers and their multiplication.

In addition to providing opportunities to express generality, the tasks in this section have also been suggesting that mastering arithmetic actually involves algebraic thinking: every 'method' is in fact a generalisation.

Pause for Reflection

Task 5.1.R Reflection
It is a reasonable conjecture that one of the features that makes certain tasks more attractive than others is the extent to which the learner is able to make choices, including taking opportunities to specialise and to generalise, to explore dimensions of possible variation and their associated ranges of

permissible change. Other conjectures claim that it is being clear what the tasks is asking you to do, or not being too challenging, that makes tasks attractive. How do these fit with your experience so far?

Is there any aspect of arithmetic that you can think of that does not, implicitly, involve learners in appreciating generality?

Comment

If 'expressing generality' is overused, then it may lose some of its initial attractiveness for learners. However, it is reasonable to expect that the greater the sense of generality, the more attractive generalising will be, since people get pleasure from encompassing a wide range of possibilities under one idea or method.

5.2 EXPRESSING GENERALITY (DIAGRAMS)

Quickie 5.2

Write down an expression for the angle made between the 12 o'clock position and the minute hand of a clock when the time is *m* minutes past an hour. Does it matter which hour?

Comment

Did you think to try some particular cases either to check your expression or to provide insight into what it should be? By paying attention to *how* you work it out in one or two cases you can move to expressing that method in general.

Arithmetic lends itself naturally to expressing generality. But generality pervades all of mathematics, not just arithmetic. This section demonstrates that geometrical diagrams and graphs, as well as picture sequences, are natural contexts for generality.

Diagrams and Graphs

Euclid, who lived in modern day Alexandria from around 325 to 265 BCE, collected and edited the geometrical knowledge of his predecessors. The next task invites you to depict what is being described verbally.

Diagrammatic sources for expressing generality go beyond the purely geometrical;

Task 5.2.1 Interpreting Euclid

In Book II, Euclid enunciates the theorem that:

If a straight line is bisected, and a straight line is added to it in a straight line, then the square on the whole with the added straight line and the square on the added straight line both together are double the sum of the square on the half and the square described on the straight line made up of the half and the added straight line as on one straight line.

Note your first reactions to reading the theorem.

Break the statement of the theorem down into small parts and build up a geometrical diagram to illustrate it. You may easily find that, once you see what is going on, you will wish to start the diagram again.

Express the theorem in symbols and then relate the result to one part of Task 5.1.4 (Specialising and Generalising).

Comment

Articulating geometrical relationships without using a diagram (as we think Euclid did) is very difficult, not only for the author, but also for the reader. Making sense of someone else's articulation involves discerning small steps and implementing them on your own diagram. Where there appears to be ambiguity, you have to be prepared to try several versions.

---

they include both picture sequences in which the number of components of different kinds needed for the *n*th picture can be counted, and tabular arrangements of numbers. The next subsection includes an example of picture sequences, and the one following considers arrays of numbers.

Task 5.2.2a Imagining

Imagine a straight line lying on a plane that has a pair of coordinate axes painted in it. Imagine a copy of the line resting on top of the original, perhaps as if it were on an overlay or acetate sheet.

Now slide the copy parallel to the *x*-axis. What happens to its equation as it slides? (You might want to choose another original line with an easier equation, at least to start!)

Start again and this time, slide the line parallel to the *y*-axis. What happens to its equation?

Start again and this time, slide the line parallel to the line $y = x$. What happens to its equation?

Comment

Of course it seems challenging and abstract at first, but you have the opportunity to choose what particular cases to consider, and how far to generalise for yourself!

What is the same about all the lines, geometrically, and what is the same about their equations?

Task 5.2.2b Imagining More

Imagine a straight line lying on a plane that has a pair of coordinate axes painted in it. Make sure your line crosses both the *x*- and the *y*-axes. Imagine a copy of the line resting on top of the original, perhaps as if it were on an overlay or acetate sheet.

Now rotate the copy about the point where the original crosses the *y*-axis. What effect does this have on the equation?

Start again, and rotate the copy about the point where the original crosses the *x*-axis. What effect does this have on the equation?

Comment

This time the constants stay the same but the coefficient of *x* (the slope) can change, whereas before it was the slope that was staying the same and the constants that were changing.

Remember to 'Say What You See' in your imagination.

Counting in Picture Sequences

In section 1.2 there were examples of picture sequences in which the number of components were to be counted. Because it is a fruitful domain of exploration for learners who can construct their own picture sequences using their own chosen elements, here are some more examples of the sorts of things one might count.

Task 5.2.3a Picture Sequence

The pictures displayed are the first and the third in a sequence, and are made up of segments and squares.

By saying to yourself what you see, give a verbal description of how to draw any picture in the sequence that is consistent with these being the first and the third.

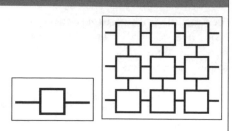

How many segments and how many squares are required for the nth picture in your sequence? How many T-junctions will there be (the first has 2: ⊢ and ⊣ but there are also ⊥ and ⊤)?

In how many different ways can you express the numbers, as a result of stressing different aspects of the pictures?

Comment

One way to count is to associate the number of squares with the square of the picture number, and the number of segments as n rows of $n + 1$ segments and n columns of $n - 1$ segments. This does actually work for the two given cases.

It is vital to decide on a rule that generates all the pictures in a sequence, because often there is no unique rule determined by a few examples. In the case of the picture square in task 5.2.3a, one rule is that there is a square array of squares, and adjacent squares are joined by segments, and there are leading and trailing segments on the left and right ends of the diagram.

Another rule is that for odd-numbered pictures the rule is as just stated, but for even-numbered pictures the rule is to have the same number of squares as in the previous picture, but with segments sticking out of the top and bottom squares as well. An even more extreme rule would allow any pictures at all in the even places, making it very difficult to predict the number of components required!

Sometimes differently expressed rules will yield the same pictures, and hence the same counts; at other times there will be different pictures and so different counts. What matters is agreeing what the rule is so that different expressions of the count are known to be expressing the same thing!

Task 5.2.3b Perforations

Perforated sheets of stamps make it easy to separate them. Suppose a block of stamps has 4 perforations along the top and bottom of each stamp and 3 down each side, as well as one at each corner. In how many different ways can you count the number of holes in a block of stamps?

Comment

Trying special cases is helpful, but even more helpful is Watching What You Do when you count the special cases, because you are looking for a general method of counting no matter what the block size!

Each way of organising the counting involves stressing certain aspects (and consequently ignoring others), leading to different expressions. Looking for different ways to count reinforces the experience that there are usually many different ways of 'seeing' how to count something, leading to different looking expressions of the general. Thus Say What You See, and Watch What You Do are versions of paying attention to what is changing (details) and what is staying the same (structure), experienced through specialising (doing particular cases carefully) in order to generalise.

Multiplication Displayed on a Grid

Diagrams have been used in this section for different kinds of mathematical phenomena: geometrical relationships, things to count arising from picture sequences, and now, layouts for arithmetical calculations.

In Chapter 2, reference was made to using mental methods for multiplying. For example 32×58 can be seen as $(30 + 2) \times (60 - 2)$. It is also popular to display multiplications in a grid format, as one step between mental methods and long multiplication.

Task 5.2.4a Same and Different Multiplications

What is the same, and what different about the two multiplications displayed?

×	70	5	
100	7000	500	7500
20	1400	100	1500
3	210	15	225
	8610	615	9225

×	$7x$	5	
x^2	$7x^3$	$5x^2$	$7x^3 + 5x^2$
$2x$	$14x^2$	$10x$	$14x^2 + 10x$
3	$21x$	15	$21x + 15$
	$7x^3 + 14x^2 + 21x$	$5x^2 + 10x + 15$	$7x^3 + 19x^2 + 31x + 15$

Comment

Did you remember to *Say What You See* carefully, before jumping to conclusions?

Did you do your own similar example, and did you 'Watch What You Did' in order to detect or check structure?

What general principles are being exemplified?

Notice that the bottom right cell acts as a check on arithmetic because it can be calculated by two different routes.

Replacing x by 10 in the right-hand table yields the left-hand table.

One general principle is that for any given array the column sums and row sums all add to the same overall total. Another general principal is that arranging calculations in a table can make it easier to keep track of what has to be done, but it is useful to have a 'story' to tell so that when you encounter the table again, you are familiar with reading what it says.

This tabular extension of the mental methods in Chapter 1 forms an intermediate step between mental method and a long multiplication layout but it retains the powers of ten in the cells. Many learners will have been introduced to the Gelosian tabular form of multiplication, which omits the powers of ten, and is exemplified in the next task.

Task 5.2.4b More Same and Different Multiplications

The multiplication method shown here for multiplying 75 by 123 is sometimes known as Lattice or Gelosian multiplication.

What is the same and what different about this method and the method of Task 5.2.4a.

Why does this method always work?

		7	5	×
		7	5	1
	07	14	10	2
9	19	21	15	3
2	31	15		
2	5			

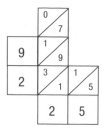

So $75 \times 123 = 9\ 225$, and $(7x + 5)(x^2 + 2x + 3) = 7x^3 + 19x^2 + 31x + 15$

Comment

The multiplier, 123, has been moved to the right-hand side in order to leave room for the answer, because Gelosian multiplication, on which this is based, traditionally moves from top right to bottom left.

The double digit numbers 07, 19, 31 and 15 are diagonal sums from the interior cells of the thick square (the working section). The 'single digits' are obtained by diagonal addition, that is by adding the digits in diagonals as shown in the table to the right. This further diagonal addition only makes sense when the base used for numbers (base ten) is the base used for the cells. Therefore moving to the algebra, the last 'diagonal' stage does not apply. But the rest works well. As long as the cell entries are treated as coefficients of powers of x, the table records all the products as coefficients for powers of x.

Notice the difference between making sense of someone else's layout, and creating your own!

Pause for Reflection

Task 5.2R Reflection

What similarities and what differences did you notice between interpreting a geometric diagram as a generality, reading a picture sequence with a view to counting components, and reading a tabular array of calculations? Were you aware of dimensions of possible variation (DofPV) in the same way or to the same degree while engaging in the three types of task? Were you aware of slipping between discerning, relating and property-making while engaged in the tasks?

Comment

It seems that some learners perceive geometric diagrams as particular rather than general, perhaps because they are not familiar with the notion of changing positions of points and lines while retaining relationships. By contrast, numbers, whether in a tabular array, or arising from counting, are more familiarly associated with generalisation.

Awareness of dimensions of possible variation, of the possibility that some feature could be different without changing the approach or method, can lie below the surface of explicit consciousness, or can lie above it. Different degrees of confidence with different representations certainly play a part, for when attention is fully occupied by details there is less room for being aware of DofPV and generalisation. One of the important things that a teacher can do for learners to is to remind them that the particular is interesting only to the extent that it illustrates or 'speaks' the general. Every act of generalisation, every awareness of a DofPV involves discerning features, both those that could change and those that are to remain invariant, and detecting relationships amongst these.

5.3 EXPRESSING GENERALITY (OUTSIDE SCHOOL)

Quickie 5.3

Write down a time when the angle between the hour and the minute hands of a clock is zero.

Write down another such time.

And another such time.

Comment

Finding one time for a zero angle can be achieved by thinking about clock faces. Others are more difficult to find. A general method will be developed in section 5.5.

This section returns to sources for expressing generality coming from situations and phenomena outside school. It suggests, with a few examples, places where algebraic thinking plays a role in life outside the classroom.

Particulars and Generals

As suggested in Section 1.3, whereas customers want to know particularities, entrepreneurs need to have formulae for calculating prices. Not paying attention to these formulae can result in losing money, as the first task shows.

Task 5.3.1a Reduced for Quick Sale

A supermarket advertised packets of mince tarts at 80p per packet with a second packet half-price. As the sell-by date approached, a further reduction was made to 50p per packet while retaining the 'second packet for half-price' sign. What then do you expect to pay for two packets? Express a general formula for your calculation of the cost of an even number *p* packets of tarts.

In fact, the supermarket charges you 60p for two packets. What is going on?

Comment

The supermarket checkout is programmed to compute the price for two.

It does this by subtracting half of the difference between the cost for two and the reduced price for two (20p) from each item once there are two or more items. The checkout uses the same method even when the further reduction is made, so the new price is 30p (50 − 20) each for two or more.

Here is an account of an interaction arising in a similar situation.

Task 5.3.1b Reduced for Quick Sale

Another supermarket had Sharon fruit on sale at 85 pence each, or two for £1. As the sell-by date approached, they were reduced in order to clear. Alan Parr[1] reported purchasing two of these fruit, expecting to pay the reduced price for each. On inspecting the bill he discovered that he was supposed to receive 40p back, but the checkout person ignored the negative sign and asked him for 40p (despite the posted price). Eventually he added two packs of gum at 25p each, and since the bill now came to 10p he happily paid and left. The supermarket had actually refunded him for 'buying' the fruit!

What was the clearance price?

Comment

Again the supermarket formula is to subtract a certain amount from each item once there are more than two. When the further reduction was made, the formula was not adjusted. So, denoting the reduced price by r, the adjusted price for two became $2(r - (2 \times 85 - 1)/2)$, which turned out to be -40p. So the reduced price r must have been 15p. It became not only cheaper but profitable to buy two and throw one away rather than to buy just one!

What are the relevant DofPV in these situations? They include: original price, second item at specified reduction, reduced price near sell-by date.

You might expect that containers with twice the quantity would be cheaper than two half-sized containers, but that is not always the case. Shopping affords plenty of opportunity for algebraic thinking as well as for arithmetic, simply by generalising the relationships that are displayed.

There are of course many other situations involving formulae.

Task 5.3.2 Formulae for Situations

Each of the following provides an opportunity to express a formula that the entrepreneur can use to work out what the customer is to be charged (ignoring extras such as sales tax, etc.). Work on some of these to get a sense of the range of opportunities for learners to express generalities relevant to the world in which they live.

Plumber charges in terms of fee for turning out, fee per hour, cost of parts.

Emergency response in terms of time to make call, time to alert agency, time to prepare vehicles, time to reach site (average speed of travel specified).

Hiring tools in terms of fixed charge and cost per day.

Car hire charges at so much per kilometre and so much per day.

Cost of salad in terms of tare weight (weight of container), total weight, cost per gram.

The length of time it takes to cook a chicken if it requires 45 minutes per kg plus 20 minutes.

The first International Conference on Mathematics Education (ICME) took place in 1969. The next was in 1972 and thereafter has been every four years. Find a general formula for the year of the nth conference (n is ≥ 2).

The brakes of a railway train are put on when it is going at 45 mls/hr (miles per hour) and its speed now diminishes at the rate of 10 mls/hr. every minute until it stops.

    (i) Write a formula for the speed of the train after a given time expressed in minutes (V, t).

    (ii) Write this rule so that it will apply to any original speed and rate of decrease (V, V_0, r, t).

    (iii) Write a formula for the speed of the train if, after its speed has been decreased at a certain rate for a given time, the brakes are taken off and the speed increases at a given rate for a given number of minutes (V, V_0, r_1, t_1, r_2, t_2). (Nunn, 1919, p. 13).

Comment

Did you notice how the chicken cooking situation was the same as in Task 4.1.2 in Chapter 4?

    The strategy of 'do as many as you feel you need to in order to be able to generalise, to do another task of this type' is a powerful way to hand control and choice to learners while at the same time getting them to practise.

Task 5.3.3 Situations Graphed

Interpret the first of the following graphs as depicting a physical situation in which distance from a point is graphed against time (*x*-axis is time, *y*-axis is distance).

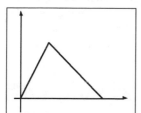 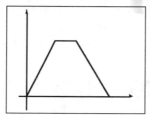 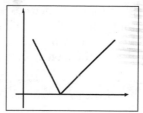

Now do the same but this time interpret the graph as speed against time (*x*-axis is time, *y*-axis is speed).

Now do the same but this time interpret the graph as speed against distance from a point (*x*-axis is distance, *y*-axis is speed).

Repeat for the other graphs, including one of your own.

Comment

Did you find your choice of context changing, or was it always the same? How adventurous, how extreme could your situations be?

    Did you find yourself following a point moving along the graph and saying to yourself, for example, 'here the distance is increasing … here it is decreasing'?

    The point is to gain confidence in reading graphs, by imagining a point moving along the *x*-axis and then tracking what the corresponding *y*-value is, and therefore what it means.

    It is very tempting to associate features of a situation that are *not* what is being graphed, and then to interpret the up and down of the graph in those terms. For example, in reading a graph of speed against time, it is tempting to some learners to follow their first reactions by assuming that the trip involves going up hill and then down hill.

Motivation: Reality and Context

Although mathematical techniques arise as the result of someone finding a method to solve a class of problems arising in some context, ever since printing was developed, most mathematics textbooks have isolated or abstracted problems from their contexts, and at best only introduced the contexts as applications once the techniques are mastered. Some people like to use real or realistic contexts as an introduction, from which mathematical problems are extracted and methods for resolving them are devised or presented. Some people want mathematics to arise only from real situations in which learners can alter (hopefully improving) their environment or their life, thus experiencing the power of mathematics in their lives. Some people see this as desirable when possible, but are content to make use of manufactured contexts when no others are available. Some people make use of both of these sometimes, but see number and geometry, and especially generality as intrinsically pleasurable and motivating, when learners' own powers are being called upon and extended.

It is sometimes difficult to distinguish between authentic adult activity which makes use of mathematics appropriate to school, real problems which learners themselves face, and phenomena to which learners can be expected to, or helped to, relate. For example, although most children have not been on a canal barge, it is not difficult to get them to imagine being on a barge sufficiently vividly to enable a question to be posed, as in the next task.

Task 5.3.4 Barging

Imagine you are on a canal barge that is moving along at a steady pace. You jump off the bow onto the footpath while the barge is moving, and walk in the same direction as the barge is moving until the stern comes opposite you, when you jump back on. How far have you walked compared to the length of the barge? You may find you have to introduce some general or unknown numbers for various explicit and implicit measurements in the problem.

What might make this task more authentic, more real, more realistic, more vivid as a phenomenon, in the senses above?

Comment

Being shown an animation (perhaps even a video!) might make it more of a phenomenon to help learners make it real for themselves and hence to engage with the task. Getting learners to raise their own questions about the situation might be expected to be even more motivating. Posing a different question more connected with working on a canal barge might move the problem towards the more authentic. Finding some comparable situation in learners' own lives would move the task towards real problem solving.

Although this section appears short, it is intended to act as stimulus to collecting situations in which generality is implicit but usefully expressed.

Pause for Reflection

Task 5.3.R Reflection

Have you begun noticing opportunities for, or at least surmised the existence of, formulae in places you had not previously been aware of them? What other situations can your learners come up with?

5.4 EXPRESSING GENERALITY (NUMBERS AGAIN)

Quickie 5.4

Write down an expression for the angle made between the hour hand and the 12 o'clock position when the time is m minutes past the hour of h o'clock (h is a positive integer constrained by $0 < h \leq 12$).

Comment

Did you take into account that as the minute hand moves, so too does the hour hand? Did you either check your expression on some particular cases or use particular cases to gain insight?

Here is another situation in which the task is presented in terms of particular cases, and the task is to locate, experience and express a generality.

Task 5.4.1a Going With and Across the Grain

Extend the table entries both downwards and leftwards, then extend your leftward extensions downwards and check them against leftward extensions of your downwards extensions.

								4	8	12	16	20	24	28	32	36
								3	6	9	12	15	18	21	24	27
								2	4	6	8	10	12	14	16	18
								1	2	3	4	5	6	7	8	9
								0	0	0	0	0	0	0	0	0

Comment

Here, going with the grain means either following patterns up or down columns, or across rows; going across the grain means recognising that going up or down a column and then across a row gives the same result as going across a row and then up or down a column. The fact that these always agree indicates why it is that the rules for multiplying negative numbers are the way they are.

Mathematicians need the rules of arithmetic for positive whole numbers to extend to negatives, fractions and decimals, in order that arithmetic remains consistent (and useful). Since for positive numbers proceeding along a row and then up or down a column gives the same result as proceeding up or down and then across the row, the same property is demanded when the table is extended. This is an example of the way in which mathematicians extend the meaning of a term such as *number* beyond its initial connotation.

Task 5.4.1b Going With the Grain: Extending Tables

Extend the table upwards and downwards by several rows, by retaining what is the same and varying what is changing systematically (going with the grain). What does each row tell you?

$7 \times 3 = 21$	$3 \times 7 = 21$	$21/7 = 3$	$21/3 = 7$
$7 \times 4 = 28$	$4 \times 7 = 28$	$28/7 = 4$	$28/4 = 7$
$7 \times 5 = 35$	$5 \times 7 = 35$	$35/7 = 5$	$35/5 = 7$

Comment

Did you fill in columns or rows? Most people find columns easier and faster, perhaps because there are some features that are invariant and hence can be filled in without thinking. In this case, filling in columns is 'going with the grain', following an evident pattern of numbers in sequence.

The value of the activity of filling in the table comes when attention is directed 'across the grain', which in this case means to the relationships between entries in each row, which illustrate the commutativity of multiplication and the relationship between division and multiplication as inverse operations.

The characteristic of going with the grain is being caught up in an almost mechanical activity of repeating invariant items and following an evident pattern such as the counting numbers. The characteristic of going across the grain is interpreting relationships and seeing through each particular to a generality.

Task 5.4.1c Going With the Grain: More Extending Tables

Extend the table upwards, downwards and to both sides (going with the grain). Predict the entry, say, 35 cells to the left and 6 cells up from the marked cell. Write in both the calculation and the answer.

		$3 - 0 = 3$	$3 - 1 = 2$	$3 - 2 = 1$		
			$2 - 1 = 1$			
			$1 - 1 = 0$			

Comment

Did you find yourself almost automatically alighting on the sequences 3, 2, 1 and 2, 1, 0 in the central column, and find yourself extending them downwards? A little less obvious is the pattern of subtractions of 0, 1, 2 in the row. Once noticed, they invite continuation: subtracting 3, 4, 5, ... to the right, and −1, −2, ... to the left.

Where a pattern does not immediately jump out, it is useful to ask yourself what is changing and what is staying the same?

Task 5.4.1d Going Across the Grain

If the table extended in all directions, where would you expect to find 5 − 4? 4 − 5? 37 − 36? Select two of your own and work out where they would be found. Write down a rule for locating any given subtraction. What does the table tell you about subtracting?

Comment

'Going across the grain' here means looking at the table as a whole for meaning in relationships between entries that link entries together in some way other than the filling out of a sequential pattern. In this case, it means getting a sense of where any particular entry might be, and also discovering how adding and subtracting negative numbers has to work in order to preserve the pattern going with the grain.

There is a significant difference between a 'table' collection of subtraction or other drill arithmetic questions, and developing a table with patterns such as in these tasks. Here there is underlying structure to be discerned and appreciated. The tasks are of little value unless learners spend time going across the grain seeing generalities through the particulars.

Spreadsheets are under-used technological tools for developing algebraic thinking. A spreadsheet is particularly helpful for exploring tables such as those encountered in the previous three tasks.

Spreadsheet Sequences

Spreadsheets are very useful when the same operation is to be carried out repeatedly on successive values. It is also a model or method for laying out calculations, because it is possible to display all intermediate calculations, and to see these change as input values are changed, without the tedium of doing the calculations yourself.

The tasks in this subsection show how a spreadsheet can be used to good effect to produce sophisticated number sequences. Using a spreadsheet does more than produce sequences, however. By setting up their own sequences, learners are introduced to what amounts to expressions of generality, because the spreadsheet layout forces you to think in terms of operations on as-yet-unassigned values that will be in particular cells.

Suppose you were to enter numbers and formulae into a spreadsheet as follows:

	B	C	D	E	F	G	H	I
1	starter							
2		1	1	1	1	1	1	1
3	3	=C2+B3	=D2+C3	=E2+D3	=F2+E3	=G2+F3	=H2+G3	=I2+H3
4	5	=C2+B4	=D2+C4	=E2+D4	=F2+E4	=G2+F4	=H2+G4	=I2+H4
5	–7	=C2+B5	=D2+C5	=E2+D5	=F2+E5	=G2+F5	=H2+G5	=I2+H5

Here is the spreadsheet that would result:

	B	C	D	E	F	G	H	I
1	starter							
2		1	1	1	1	1	1	1
3	3	4	5	6	7	8	9	10
4	5	6	7	8	9	10	11	12
5	–7	–6	–5	–4	–3	–2	–1	0

Task 5.4.2 Spreadsheet Sequences

Say What You See happening in each row. Connect this with the way the cell formulae were set up.

Express to yourself in words what the spreadsheet has done. Express in symbols the entry that would be in the hundredth cell along, and the nth cell along. Predict the entries in the nth cell in a row whose starter was s.

Comment

Notice how the symbols used to refer to cell entries are treated as labels (cell D4 refers to or labels the value that is in that cell). This is slightly different to thinking of a symbol like x as 'having a value'. Researchers have studied the use of spreadsheets as an introduction to expressing generality, and have found that learners respond very quickly and competently to the use of cell reference labels to refer to their contents. After that, letters such as x or n could be treated as the names of cells that have an as-yet-unknown value stored in them.

One benefit of the spreadsheet is that changing a single cell can change all the values instantly, producing a phenomenon to make sense of and then to predict what will happen when a different value is inserted in that cell. For example, try predicting the effect of changing the entry in cell B3 to something else.

Table Patterns

Structured tables are a popular source of contexts for expressing generality while developing familiarity with the table structure. For example, the hundred square, or a calendar, especially when extended, provide opportunities for looking for relationships between entries.

	A	B	C	D	E	F	G	H	I
1									
2		3	4	5	6	7	8	9	10
3		10	11	12	13	14	15	16	17
4		17	18	19	20	21	22	23	24
5		24	25	26	27	28	29	30	31
6		31	32	33	34	35	36	37	38
7		38	39	40	41	42	43	44	45
8		45	46	47	48	49	50	51	52
9		52	53	54	55	56	57	58	59
10		59	60	61	62	63	64	65	66

Task 5.4.3a Table Patterns

Examine the table to see how columns and rows are related. You may recognise it as similar to a calendar except that there is an extra column to the right that repeats the first column on the left. Imagine that the table is extended further both to right and to left, and both up and down.

Select any four cells in the arrangement shown at the right. The cell shown shaded is meant to be obscured so that only the contents of the other four cells are visible.

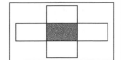

Calculate the sum of the upper and lower, and the sum of the left and the right. What do you notice? Why must this always happen?

Calculate the product of the left and the right, and subtract the product of the top and the bottom. What do you notice? Must this always happen?

Comment

The best way to justify an 'always' is usually to express what is happening as a generality. In this case, denote the contents of the top cell by t, express the entries in the other three cells, and then perform the calculations. The conjecture that two expressions must always be equal, or that the difference between two expressions must always be constant leads to a desire to be able to manipulate expressions in order to justify such conjectures. Manipulation and rearrangement is taken up in Chapter 7.

What is the range of permissable change encompassed by the 'this always' in the addition relation? Does it apply equally to the multiplicative relation.

This example is based on the numbers going up in steps of 1, and an addition of 7 going down the columns. These are examples of things that can be varied.

There is another dimension of possible variation, namely the 'cross' arrangement of cells selected. Almost any arrangement of four cells will produce an additive relationship that is invariant for any table, the invariant itself depending only on the three values that determine the table, and many will produce a multiplicative invariant as well.

Task 5.4.3b Your Own Table Patterns

Experiment with arrangements of four cells to find additive invariants. Express the invariant in terms of the numbers that generate the table. Try using six or more (even numbers of) cells.

Experiment with arrangements of cells to find multiplicative invariants. For example, take any cell, the cell two to the right, the cell three down, and the cell two to the right and three down, forming a rectangle. Multiply the diagonally opposite cell entries and compare. Express the invariant in terms of the numbers that generate the table.

Pause for Reflection

The power of a spreadsheet to generate complicated sequences is immense! A spreadsheet is excellent as a vehicle for presenting sequences as phenomena with parameters that can be easily changed, and so inviting generalisation. It also provides a stepping stone in the use of labels to refer to values that are as-yet-unknown, since they are whatever happens to be in the cell at the time of evaluation of the sheet.

Task 5.4.R Reflection

What aspects of expressing generality were highlighted for you in working with a spreadsheet?

What differences do you see between using cell references and using letters to express generalities?

5.5 PEDAGOGIC ISSUES

Quickie 5.5

Using your experience of the previous quickies in this chapter, write down an expression for the angle between the minute hand and the hour hand of an analogue clock in terms of the time the two hands 'show'.

Not so quick: how many times in a twelve-hour period is the angle between the hands 0°? 90°?

Comment

Did you take into account that angles are a measure of rotation in a given direction (usually counter-clockwise in mathematics), but that nothing was said about which side of the hour hand the minute hand was located at any given time?

The quickies in this chapter concerning clock hands illustrate a subtle difference between expressing generality, and expressing relationships amongst 'as-yet-unknowns'.

Pedagogic Strategies

This section looks further at a subtle shift in the use of symbols from expressing a generality to representing as-yet-unknown values; at some potentially confusing aspects of the language used when generalising; and at the role of context in assisting and blocking generalisation.

Doing and Undoing

Turning a 'doing' into an 'undoing' is a strategy for extending or creating an exploration that challenges thinking while at the same time promoting understanding of the technique or concepts involved. It was used in Task 5.1.2a particularly.

Same and Different

Whenever there are two or more objects present, it can be helpful to consider what is the same and what is different, or, put another way, what is changing, and what is staying invariant. To do this requires you to stress some features and consequently to ignore others, which is the basis for generalisation. Tasks 5.1.5a, 5.1.7 and 5.2.5a made particular use of this.

Say What You See; Watch What You Do

Whenever you want to detect some underlying structure or to generalise some process or pattern, it can help to 'say what you see', that is, to be explicit about what features you can discern, as a step to finding relationships between those features. It is often useful as a strategy to pull yourself out of the details of doing calculations, manipulating objects, in order to focus on getting a sense of structure, of what might be going on. Tasks 5.2.4a, 5.2.4b, 5.4.2, 5.4.3 and 5.5 used this particularly.

Dimensions of Possible Variation

Asking yourself 'what is the same and what is different?' about two or more objects or situations is a useful way of focusing your attention in order to subsume a multiplicity of 'things' into a general class, what is often called a *concept*. By stressing what is changing while other features stay more or less the same, you become aware of what is called a *dimension of possible variation*.[2] This means, a feature that is allowed to change, and still the objects concerned fit the concept under consideration. Thus meeting a number of things of different colour leads to the notion of colour. The extent or range of change permitted in that feature is referred to as the *range of permissible change*. It is important to note that different people, and especially, different learners, may be aware of different *dimensions of possible variation* and within any one dimension, may be aware of different ranges-of-permissible-change. Thus one person on hearing the word number may think 'counting number' while another thinks 'integer', or 'real number'.

Mathematical tasks are never finished, just put to one side for a time! In other words, you can almost always fruitfully consider what features could be changed or varied (DofPV) and in what ways (RofPCh). Tasks 5.1.5a and 5.3.2 used this strategy explicitly. In Task 5.3.2 the notion of context as a DofPV was explicitly varied.

Learner Constructed Objects

Constructing your own objects is much more interesting that dealing with someone else's, particularly in a textbook. Tasks 5.3.3 and 5.4.3b explicitly invited you to construct your own examples, but this invitation is implicit whenever you specialise in order to get a sense of what is going on in order to re-generalise for yourself.

In How Many Ways?

This strategy was used explicitly in Tasks 5.2.4a, 5.2.4b, 5.2.4c, because it draws attention to multiple approaches and reminds learners that it is often worthwhile considering several approaches and explicitly choosing one of them, rather than diving into calculations immediately.

MGA and DTR

The whole point of becoming explicitly aware of the interplay between specialising and generalising is so that the learner can take initiative whenever they get stuck, to specialise (to construct their own particular cases or examples) to confidence-inspiring familiar objects. Manipulating these, whether they be physical, diagrammatic or symbolic, is not an end in itself, but a step on the way to 'getting a sense of' underlying structure and hence to becoming aware of, and then articulating, a generality. MGA is not a sequence of steps but rather acts as a reminder about the interplay between all three aspects of coming to understand. The attempt to articulate informs the manipulating and clarifies the sense being made. When planning lessons or parts of lessons for a classroom, Do–Talk–Record (DTR) acts as a reminder that expecting written records too quickly can be daunting for many learners, and that talking about what they are thinking, trying to articulate more and more succinctly and clearly their growing 'sense of' supports and is supported by the development of written records.

SEM

Chapter 5 exemplifies the See–Experience–Master framework introduced in Section 4.5, by revisiting the act of expressing generality in situations somewhat more complex than previously. The contexts are patterns in numbers, geometrical relationships, and outside school. The tasks invite you to notice how what you attend to changes as you work.

Language of Generalisation

Algebra provides a language in which to express generalities precisely and concisely, to the extent that they can be manipulated in order to facilitate reasoning.

English is rather peculiar when it comes to expressing generality, for the words used are often quite ambiguous. Consider, for example, the assertions 'the angles of a planar[3] triangle add up to 180°' and 'the product of two odd numbers is always odd'.

Does the first speaker mean a specific planar triangle she has in mind, or does she refer to all possible planar triangles? The little word '*a*' can be used both ways. The second speaker can also be misinterpreted, by taking him to mean that there are two odd numbers, and every time you multiply them, their product is odd.[4] Other words that are used in mathematics for generality include *any*, *all*, and *whenever*.

Consider the assertions

'there is a number that is smaller than any positive integer';
'any positive integer is bigger than some number'.

The second could mean that for any positive integer, there is some number smaller than it, or it could mean the same as the first statement, that there is a number that is smaller than any, and all positive integers. Mathematicians find it convenient, in order to guard against ambiguity, to put all the generalities and claims for existence at the front, rather than tacking them on the back, or worse, having some at the front and some at the back. Thus the first statement would be rendered carefully as: 'There exists a number n such that for any positive integer p, $n < p$.' The second would either be the same, or would be rendered carefully as: 'For any positive integer p there exists a number n such that $p > n$.'

In the heat of the moment when, for example, speaking and writing at a board, it is all too easy to remember the 'alls' and 'anys' only after the main idea has been stated, and so to confuse learners who are either struggling to make sense of what is said, or are blissfully unaware of the ambiguity or even of the generalities being expressed. When you catch yourself uttering a potentially ambiguous statement you can choose to pause and check what sense learners have made of it, and perhaps get them to participate in rephrasing it with symbols, in a more formal form. Formality of expression is not part of a plot to make ideas obscure, but rather part of an attempt to reduce potential ambiguity.

Pause for Reflection

Task 5.5.R Reflection

Reflect back on the examples you have seen so far of dimensions of possible variation.

Work on some of your own.

In what ways, if any, has the notion of expressing generality developed or changed as a result of working on this chapter?

Rehearse in your own words the similarities and differences between 'using a letter to express a generality' and 'using a letter as an as-yet-unknown'.

Notes

1   Email communication
2   See for example Watson and Mason (2004).
3   *Planar* means 'lying in a plane'. The angle sum for triangles on a sphere or other curved surface is not invariant!
4   This is similar to the classic question: 'What do you get when you multiply 7 by itself 7 times?'; answer: '49 every time'.

6 More on Powers, More on Themes

Chapter 6 returns to the subject of mathematical powers and themes initiated particularly in Chapter 2, but now providing more explicit experience of their use and their role in learning and doing mathematics. Section 6.1 focuses on characterising things, which requires placing attention on properties. (The properties of a square are what makes it a square rather than something else.) Section 6.2 introduces 'figurate' numbers, numbers that arise from counting objects in drawings; square and triangular numbers are familiar examples. Section 6.3 demonstrates the use of powers and themes in some standard curriculum topics. Section 6.4 indicates a connection between summing sequences and finding areas.

6.1 CHARACTERISING

Quickie 6.1

The sum of three consecutive numbers is always divisible by 3. Is any number that is divisible by 3 also the sum of three consecutive numbers?

One of the many powers that all children display is the power to organise, classify and characterise things. This power is vital for dealing with what happens moment by moment, for recognising something as having been seen or heard before, and for using language. This section draws attention to tasks that make use of this power.

Characterising Possible Answers

Almost any task or problem that produces a numerical answer can be used to generate a new task, by characterising the numbers that are allowed as answers to that problem.

Task 6.1.1 Repetitions

Consider an operation such as 'double and add one'. Repeatedly apply it to the current answer, doing this a specified number of times. Can any pre-assigned whole number be reached by applying this operation to some whole (starting) number? By applying it twice? Thrice? ... ? If so, how do you choose the starting number; if not, which ones can be reached?

Comment

Did you then try the operation on lots of starting numbers or did you look at the structure of the process? How could you get a pre-assigned even number? How could you get a pre-assigned odd number?

Task 6.1.1 started as a calculation and generalisation task, but then turned the question around to ask what properties characterise the numbers that can be reached by using the calculation. Put succinctly, the 'doing' of calculations is converted into an 'undoing': what starting values will reach a pre-assigned ending number. The next task uses a similar move to produce characterisation questions that can be approached through generalising patterns or through reasoning with the general.

Task 6.1.2a Number Forms

What numbers arise by multiplying two numbers that differ by 2 then adding 1?

What numbers arise by multiplying two numbers that differ by 4 and adding 4?

What numbers arise by multiplying two numbers that differ by 6 and adding 9?

Generalise.

Comment

The aim is not to find a list of numbers, but to recognise a type of numbers, and to express the generality for each of the questions, leading to a generality that subsumes all of them at once.

One approach is to try many particular cases and then look for some property shared by all the answers; another is to work with the general, to express the generality and then rearrange the expression so as to reveal some underlying structure. For example, n and $n + 2$ represent any two numbers differing by 2. Multiplying and adding 1 yields $n^2 + 2n + 1$, which is the same as $(n + 1)^2$, so all such numbers are perfect squares, and furthermore, all perfect squares can be thought of as 1 more than the product of two numbers differing by 2.

The next task is a more challenging version of the previous one.

Task 6.1.2b More Number Forms

What numbers arise by multiplying four consecutive numbers, then adding 1?

Comment

Although the calculations are more demanding, experience on the previous task might alert you to possible patterns. Justifying your conjecture requires more extensive symbol manipulation than in tasks so far.

The principal point of these tasks is that with every 'doing', that is, with every technique that solves a particular problem, there are opportunities to try to classify or characterise the numbers that can arise from the use of that technique. This is a strategy that can be used with learners who frequently complete exercises more quickly than others, to keep them engaged and developing their mathematical thinking. Characterising also promotes using algebra to reason about infinite classes of numbers rather than just doing arithmetic with particular numbers, as in the next task.

Task 6.1.3 Characterising

What positive whole numbers have an odd number of factors?

What straight-line graphs have their slope equal to their y-intercept? Half their y-intercept? More generally, t times their y-intercept?

What pairs of straight lines through the origin have their slopes the reciprocal of each other?

Comment

Did you try some particular examples, perhaps systematically?

With the first part, you might have started working systematically through the numbers 1, 2, 3, … , or you might have worked on numbers with one prime factor, two prime factors, and so on.

Again, for the second part, trying a few cases (decide on the slope, then work out the equation using the constraint, then perhaps plotting), it soon becomes clear that all lines through the point $(^-1, 0)$ have their slope equal to their y-intercept and vice versa, so these properties characterise each other. Generalising to other multiples simply changes the fixed point on the x-axis: what straight-line graphs have their y-intercept a constant more than a constant multiple of their slope? However, using DofPV to generalise and vary the task suddenly produces a much harder question: changing y-intercept to x-intercept changes the family of straight lines from all those through one point, to all the tangents to a cubic polynomial, an exploration well beyond the scope of this book.

For the third part, a pair of lines through the origin with reciprocal slopes are reflections of each other in the line $y = x$, because reflection in that line interchanges x and y coordinates, and so interchanges the numerator and denominator of the slope calculation. Being reflected-pairs characterises those pairs with reciprocal slopes.

The essence of those tasks is to take a property and try to find some other way to describe the objects (numbers, lines). For example,

characterise numbers with exactly three factors;
characterise fractions whose decimal representation cannot terminate in zeros;
characterise numbers that are two more than a multiple of three, in terms of remainders. (Remember Chapter 1?)

Calculating the number of factors of a number can be thought of as an operation or a function applied to numbers. Calculating the decimal representation of a fraction can be thought of as an operation or a function applied to fractions. Calculating three times a number and adding two can be thought of as an operation, or a function applied to numbers. In each case, you are characterising the objects that can arise as a result of applying the function.

6.2 FIGURATE NUMBERS

Quickie 6.2

The sum of five consecutive numbers is always divisible by 5. Is any number divisible by 5 always the sum of five consecutive numbers?

Nichomachus of Gerasa (now northern Jordan), who lived around 100 AD (also known as 100 CE, which denotes 'Common Era' to non-Christians), coined the term *figurate numbers* for numbers arising from counting objects displayed in regular, usually equally spaced geometric patterns[1]. Apparently Nichomachus used the symbol α (alpha, the first letter of the Greek alphabet) as the object to make up his patterns, so that the task was to predict the number of alphas needed to make the *n*th picture.

$$\alpha$$
$$\alpha \quad \alpha$$
$$\alpha \quad \alpha \quad \alpha$$
$$\alpha \quad \alpha \quad \alpha \quad \alpha$$

The ancient Greeks used alpha for the number one as well as for the first letter, and it was the first letter of the Greek word for number, *arithmos*, so there were lots of reasons for using alphas. Below, in the modern style, circles and squares are used instead.

Gnomons

A *gnomon* is the angled object used at the centre of a sundial. In this subsection, gnomon shapes are constructed from different objects (circles, squares). The gnomon number for a particular shape refers to the number of objects it contains.

Task 6.2.1 Gnomon Numbers

For each of the picture sequences, decide on a rule that generates these and subsequent pictures in the sequence. How many objects (circles, squares) are needed to make the *n*th picture?

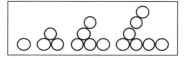 

Comment

The best way to count is first to draw a more complicated one and to Watch What You Do as your body takes over the repetitive task of drawing. The way in which you draw the object can often suggest an underlying structure that is useful for expressing a generality.

If your rule is, start with one, and add on two new ones for each succeeding picture, then your expression of generality for the number needed for the *n*th picture will be $1 + 2(n - 1)$ (if you see two arms and a single core circle or square) or $2n - 1$ (if you see two arms overlapping in a single object) or something equivalent. The specific expression you use will reflect your choice of how to see each picture being constructed.

Notice how you need the third or fourth pictures at least in order to detect that the sequence is intended to be gnomons (as distinct from other shapes) and thus determine a general rule.

The reason for asking for a general rule in words for how to draw the pictures is that any finite sequence of numbers can be extended in infinitely many different ways. A rule might be 'the next number is whatever I feel like saying', which, although extreme, illustrates the point. The point about using picture sequences for counting objects is that there is a background structure, coming from the pictures, which is what the formula is expressing. But there has to be explicit agreement as to what the rule is for drawing the pictures before it makes sense to try to count or express a generality. If you were given only the first two pictures, there are numerous ways you could imagine extending the sequence.

An advantage of pictures is that it is usually pretty hard to see ways of describing more than one rule that accounts for three or four pictures in the sequence. Although it is common to be given the first few terms of a sequence, it is often more interesting to be given a few sporadic examples, such as the third and the fifth, or the third, fifth and sixth terms of a sequence. The task then is to try to see what is the same about the terms, and what is 3-ish, 5-ish, or 6-ish as appropriate, about the examples given.

The gnomon numbers are of course just the odd numbers. But the gnomon shape is useful for decomposing other shapes. For example, the following shapes are particular instances of ways of combining gnomons.

Task 6.2.1a Using Gnomons

In Task 2.1.2 (Adding and Multiplying) the sum of consecutive odd numbers was connected with the difference of two squares.

Draw a picture of consecutive odd numbers as consecutive gnomons and then interpret your diagram as indicating the difference of two squares.

Comment

Starting with the largest of the consecutive odd numbers as a gnomon, the others tuck neatly in the corner. To count the number of squares making up the sum, you can imagine filling out the gnomon stack to a square and then removing the ones you don't want: the difference of two squares!

Task 6.2.1b Using Gnomons

The three pictures are each the fifth of a sequence, obtained by sticking gnomons together. Decide a rule for drawing the pictures in each sequence, and express the count in terms of gnomon numbers.

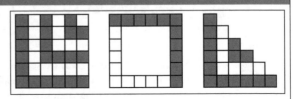

Comment

The square with alternate gnomons shaded displays a square of size 6 as the sum of the gnomon numbers (counting from the top right-hand side of the square) $1, 3, 5, 7, 9, 11$; that is, the sum of the first six odd numbers. It suggests more generally that the sum of the first n odd numbers is n^2.

The second picture suggests that two consecutive gnomons can be put together to form a frame, so the sum of two consecutive odd numbers is divisible by four (here the fifth and the sixth gnomon are the same as four times five).

The third picture suggests that the sum of every other gnomon makes a triangular shape.

Triangular Numbers

Numbers that arise from counting objects in triangular arrays such as in the previous task or like the following are called triangular, for obvious reasons. They turn out to be the building blocks for other counting problems, as well as forming a particular but generic example of arithmetic progressions (discussed in Chapter 11). Here the first five triangular numbers are depicted in terms of the number of objects (circles, squares) in the picture.

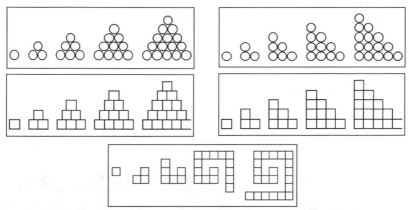

One of the features of picture-counting is that pictures that look different can end up with the same count.

Task 6.2.2a Triangular Numbers

Describe in words the formation of triangular number pictures in each version. Describe in words what is common to all of the sequences depicted above.

Comment

Triangular numbers arise from adding on one more object than was added on at the previous step, or at step *n*, adding *n* new objects. In other words, the *n*th triangular number is the sum of the first *n* consecutive numbers. In Task 6.2.1a, they are displayed as the sum of alternating or odd gnomon numbers.

Did you notice one or more false starts in seeing the spiral as triangular numbers? Many people find that describing in words precisely how to draw the spiral is not quite as easy as it seems at first. It may help to shade in the 'even numbers' in each case.

Task 6.2.2b Expressing Triangular Numbers

Each of the following diagrams suggests a way to express the fifth triangular number, and hence the general triangular number (the sum of the first *n* natural or counting numbers) in terms of *n*. Interpret each diagram in general, perhaps by drawing a different version (that is, a version corresponding to a different *n*) and Watch What You Do when drawing, in order to contact the underlying structure.

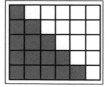 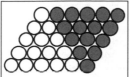 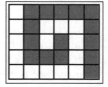

Comment

Two copies of the fifth triangular number form a rectangle or parallelogram that is 5 rows of 6. More generally, two copies of the *n*th triangular number form a rectangle or parallelogram that is *n* by *n*+1. Thus the *n*th triangular number must be $n(n+1)/2$. The curious, and at first unexpected, feature of this formula is the presence of the 2 in the denominator. Triangular numbers must be whole numbers, so how can this formula work?

The explanation of course is that either *n* or *n* + 1 must be even no matter what value *n* takes, so the answer is indeed always an integer. The reason that triangular numbers are so useful as building blocks is that any quadratic formula that always gives integer values for all values of *n*, can be written in terms of sums of triangular numbers.

The next two tasks show how triangular numbers can be used to decompose other figurate numbers arising from different polygons.

Task 6.2.3a Polygonal Numbers

Say What You See in the table below, and extend the table both down and to the right, at least in terms of verbal descriptions of what picture should appear in each cell. Do not forget to work 'across the grain' as well as 'with the grain' (following a row or a column is going with the grain; going across the grain means relating each individual to the row and the column in which it appears).

What might *digonal* numbers be, if they label the row above the triangular numbers? What about *monogonal* numbers in the row above that?

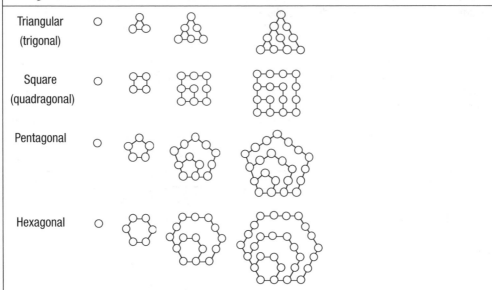

Triangular (trigonal)				
Square (quadragonal)				
Pentagonal				
Hexagonal				

Comment

Digonal numbers would be the counting numbers, adding one new circle for each new column, and *monogonal* numbers would be the constant sequence 1. Looking at the other sequences in this way, to form the *n*th number from the *n* − 1th number, you add 1 for digonals; *n* for triangular (they might usefully be called trigonal); $2n - 1$ for the square (quadragonal?); $3n - 2$ for the pentagonal; $4n - 3$ for the hexagonal; and more generally, $pn - (p - 1)$ for the pth polygonal number sequence.

Looked at another way, in the first column the nth row is arrived at from the $(n - 1)$th row by adding 0 in column one, 1 in column two, n in column three, and the nth triangular number in column four.

A *generic* example is a single instance or particular through which a generality can be perceived and expressed. In the next task, a single instance of a picture from a picture sequence is all the evidence for generalities to be expressed concerning the shading of the particular.

Task 6.2.3b Nichomachus' Figurate Numbers

Using the following pictures as generic examples, express a method of decomposing polygonal numbers of any size as sums of trigonal (triangular) numbers.

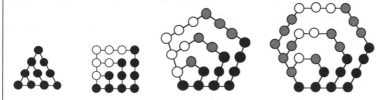

Use your observations to justify the use of the labels in the following chart, which is the way Nichomachus presented his version of figurate numbers.

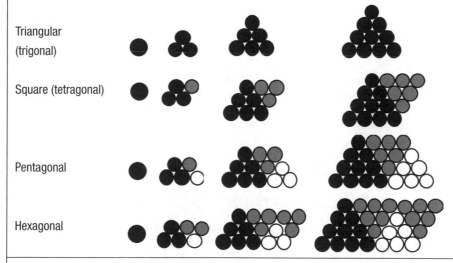

Triangular (trigonal)

Square (tetragonal)

Pentagonal

Hexagonal

Comment

It may take a moment or two to see what is going on, and how the chart fits with the polygonal versions in the previous task. Again it is clear that the first few terms are highly uninformative. It is only when you get to an example that distinguishes itself from other possible versions that you get a sense of underlying structure. In the fourth row and first two entries it is quite difficult to see how the grey circles fit in, until you look at bigger examples, or look at the pattern by going with the grain in the columns.

The figurate numbers offer much more than opportunities to express generalities while counting. In each case, the underlying idea has been to characterise the numbers that arise from the corresponding picture pattern.

There are many more kinds of figurate numbers. You can for example, move into three or more dimensions. You can also consider numbers arising from objects lying in ever more rings around a central object. Apart from the pleasure of finding a systematic and structural way of counting in order to express a generality, you can characterise the number sequences in various ways as above.

It is sometimes unexpectedly easy to ask very difficult mathematical questions. For example, what numbers are both square and triangular? To answer this requires some heavy mental machinery inappropriate for most learners at school, although pupils who are interested will be able to explore these ideas on a spreadsheet.

Pause for Reflection

Task 6.2.R Reflection

Why is it important to have explicit agreement on how a sequence of numbers or diagrams continues before trying to express a generality about the sequence members?

Comment

Often a generality can be located by 'seeing through the particular', perhaps even a single, *generic* example. The problem when teaching is that what seems generic to one person may be overlooked by others, so it may be necessary to impose or indicate structure, such as was done with the shading of the polygonal number diagrams.

Triangular numbers are particularly stressed in many national curricula. The reason is that they form basic building blocks for more complicated objects. The way Nichomachus dissected polygonal numbers into triangular numbers is just one illustration of this.

An important strategy in mathematics is to ask 'undoing' questions, and to try to characterise the answers that can arise to the corresponding 'doing'. This applies not just to figurate number sequences, but to any situation in which there is a technique for getting answers.

6.3 USING POWERS IN CURRICULUM TOPICS

Quickie 6.3

The sum of seven consecutive numbers is always divisible by 7. Is any number divisible by 7 always the sum of seven consecutive numbers?

This section turns attention to the curriculum topic of area and perimeter, with the aim of demonstrating that every mathematics lesson contains one or more opportunities for learners to experience, if not express, a generality. The notions of area and perimeter are chosen because they are related to the use of diagrams for 'reading algebra', and because some learners have difficulty in distinguishing between them and in remembering how to calculate them.

Using Learners' Powers

In selecting or modifying tasks that will present the subject matter in a form in which learners will be able to move from initial exposure to repeated experience and eventually to mastery, it can help to think in terms of learners' powers:

What tasks would get learners specialising and generalising for themselves, in this topic?

What tasks would get learners imagining and anticipating some mathematical relationship, and then expressing that in words, pictures, and eventually, symbols?

What tasks would get learners ordering, organising or characterising mathematical objects according to concepts that are used in the topic?

What tasks would get learners conjecturing and convincing, first themselves, and then others?

Structuring tasks so that learners are making choices and constructing objects for themselves engages their creative potential, and so harnesses their emotional energy. Specialising in order to appreciate a generality, and seeking counter-examples to other people's conjectures offers opportunities for learners to experience the freedom that comes from making choices and learning to make sensible and useful choices.

Area and Perimeter Related

Although area is usually used for measuring land, there is at least one culture in which it is conventional to compare the amount of land used for a vegetable garden by the perimeter (Bishop, 1998)[2]. Tasks that involve assembling shapes from squares while seeking the largest or smallest perimeter are designed to develop learner awareness that area is preserved under cutting up a shape and re-assembling it, whereas perimeter is not, as well as to practise calculating areas. The tangram puzzle is intended to develop a sense of the invariance of area under moving pieces around. But it can also be used to prompt learners to work on discerning and relating, by seeing a complex shape as made up of component pieces. This is done by displaying an outline and asking learners to make it up with tangram pieces.

Task 6.3.1 Grid Lock

On a piece of square grid paper, draw a 6 by 1 rectangle. Now find all shapes you can with the same area and the same perimeter as this piece, under the constraint that the boundary of the shape lies on the grid lines, and does not intersect itself (the shape does not fall into two pieces). Can you find a shape with the same area but smaller perimeter? Try the same task on triangular paper.

Comment

There are several shapes with area 6 and minimum perimeter.

You may have noticed that shapes with minimum perimeter and fixed area have no internal grid points. All grid points are on the boundary or outside the shape.

Once learners are aware that area does not change when pieces are moved about, they are ready to develop formulae for areas of shapes, because the formulae are all based on the area of a rectangle, and the formulae all involve generality, which is not always fully appreciated by learners.

Task 6.3.2 Jigsaw Areas

Use the diagrams to interpret formulae for the area of a parallelogram, triangle, and trapezium, using the area of a rectangle as the product of the two edge lengths.

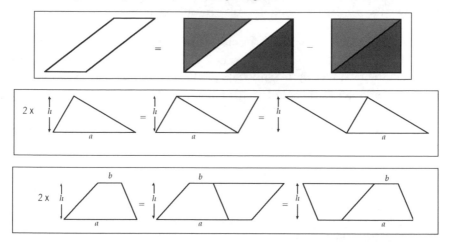

These diagrams have power as justification for area formulae only when their full implicit generality is appreciated.

In each case, express verbally what can change while keeping the calculations identical.

What is the same about the diagrams for the area of a triangle and for a trapezium?

Comment

In the first 'diagram equation', the area of the parallelogram is displayed as the difference between the areas of two rectangles. Denoting the base and height of the parallelogram by a and h respectively, and the 'overhang' by b, the area of the parallelogram can be read as $(a + b)h - bh = ah$, which is independent of the amount of overhang. It is important that learners appreciate the scope of this generality: the overhang can be gigantic, the parallelogram very thin, but the formula for the area still applies.

In each case, the top of the figure (a side in the case of the parallelogram, a vertex for the triangle, and a pair of vertices for the trapezium) can slide along the top side, without changing the area calculation. Imagine the most extreme version you can, with the top vertex of the triangle, for example, a long way from the base. Still the area is the same. There is a small but significant emotional buzz available from appreciating the generality and from the ability to find areas of very extreme looking triangles!

The triangle diagram is a special case of the trapezium diagram in which a is zero. So it makes sense to think of a triangle as a special kind of trapezium just as a square is a special kind of rectangle. Both the area and the perimeter formulae reduce to those of the triangle when a is zero.

It is more useful to be able to reconstruct a diagram when you need it than to memorise either the diagram or the formula. Both will come with the familiarity gained by learners who have worked at making sense of the diagrams and the implicit generality for themselves.

Area and perimeter together provide opportunities for exploring dimensions of possible variation.

Task 6.3.3   Area and Perimeter

Which of the following statements about a rectangle are always true or only sometimes true:

You can make a rectangle with the same perimeter but larger area.

You can make a rectangle with the same perimeter but smaller area.

You can make a rectangle with the same area but larger perimeter.

You can make a rectangle with the same area but smaller perimeter.

If a statement is only sometimes true, construct an example to show this, and try to describe the range within which it is true, and within which it is false. If it is always true, show how this assertion can be justified, perhaps by showing how to make the object specified.

Seeing a shape as made up of familiar parts, such as rectangles is just as important as knowing formulae for areas. The next task illustrates a task structure in which the learner is asked to make up a mathematical object with a specified number of components.

Task 6.3.4a   Areas of Rectilinear Regions

What is the minimum number of measurements needed in order to find the perimeter of the following figures? What is the minimum number of measurements needed in order to find their areas?

Design a figure that requires 15 measurements in order to work out its area. Work out a method for drawing a figure that requires precisely n pieces of information (what values can n take?). In how many different ways can the area be calculated given those measurements? What different sets of 'minimal measurements' will still enable the area to be calculated. Try to express a general principle.

Construct a shape that requires the use of at least 7 sub-rectangles in order to calculate its area from measurements that you give.

Comment

One person conjectured that if you count the number of corners on a staircase and subtract 2 you get the minimum number of measurements needed to find the area. What do you think?

The aim of the task is to stimulate learners to 'see' figures decomposed into rectangles, and to see that there are several ways of doing it. Asking learners to create the most complicated object they can within certain constraints not only invites creativity, but allows them to challenge themselves at their own level, and to extend their sense of the Range of Permissible Change.

A similar task can be constructed for focusing attention on perimeter:

Task 6.3.4b   Perimeters of Rectilinear Shapes

The perimeter of the shape shown is $4a + 2b$. Why? What is it about this shape that makes it have that property? How complicated an example can you draw with this same property? Bring to articulation what it is that makes the perimeter depend only on the two outside measurements.

Comment

You could even try to characterise shapes that fit inside a rectangle that is a by b and have a perimeter equal to, say $2a + 3b$ by trying to describe how to draw them.

Notice the movement from seeking relationships between sides of the particular figure and discovering that the perimeter depends only on the outside measurement, to seeing 'having perimeter depend only on outside measurement' as a property that many different figures can have. It requires a small but subtle shift in thinking.

Pause for Reflection

This section has focused on area and perimeter, showing how tasks that are designed to highlight or illuminate important aspects of the topic can be constructed to call upon learners' powers and in particular to release or afford opportunity for expressing generality by learners.

Task 6.3.R Reflection

Try to capture in a few words the effect on you of encountering opportunities for expressing generality within the topic of area and perimeter. What did you notice about shifts from discerning components that make up a shape, to seeking relationships amongst components, to promoting certain features as properties that other shapes could have?

Comment

Perhaps some of the underlying generalities were obvious to you. The issue is whether they are as obvious to all learners!

Switching from seeing area (or perimeter, or both) as a feature of a shape, to thinking about shapes with a given area (perimeter, or both) is typical of the shift in what is attended to, and how, that is essential in order to think mathematically. It involves a shift from recognising relationships to promoting properties. Mathematical reasoning begins when properties are taken as 'what is known' and used to make deductions about the whole class of objects that have the given property or properties.

6.4 AREAS AND SEQUENCE SUMMING

Quickie 6.4

The sum of four consecutive numbers is always divisible by 2, but not always divisible by 4. Is any number divisible by 2 the sum of four consecutive numbers? Is any number divisible by 4 the sum of four consecutive numbers?

This section connects figurate numbers to area calculations, and along the way suggests that it can be informative to interpret algebraic formulae in diagram form as well as to interpret diagrams as algebraic formulae.

Arithmetic Progressions

An *arithmetic progression* (AP for short) is a sequence of numbers with a constant difference between consecutive terms. In other words, the next term is obtained by adding a specified constant to the previous term. For example, the sequences

1, 2, 3, 4, … in which the constant difference between consecutive terms is 1;
5, 2, ⁻1, ⁻4, ⁻7, … in which the constant difference is ⁻3;

are examples of *arithmetic progressions*.

Task 6.4.1 General Term of an AP

The rows of the figure represent successive terms in an AP. You can take the top row as the first term, so the successive differences are positive, or you can take the bottom row as the first term, so successive differences are negative.

What is the first term, the constant difference, and how many objects are in the rth row, from each perspective?

Comment

Some people report 'seeing' the columns first, rather than the rows. One way to overcome this is to reveal the rows one by one, either top down, or bottom up!

This should rings bells with the work done in Chapter 1 and subsequently concerning numbers that are of the form something more than a multiple of something (here, three more than a multiple of two).

Textbook authors have found a variety of ways of posing questions about APs designed to get learners to use the formula for the nth term given the first term and the constant difference. The next task invites you to explore the DofPV that might be available.

Task 6.4.2 Deducing an AP and Specifying APs

How much information do you need in order to specify an AP precisely? For example, if you are told the third and the seventh terms, is that enough? Could any two numbers be the third and seventh terms, and still belong to an AP? Generalise by considering 3 and 7 as DofPV.

One person said they had an AP in which two of the terms, in order, were 9 and 3 and there were two terms in between. Is this enough to pin down their AP exactly?

Specify an AP for yourself, work out some obscure pieces of information about it, then make sure that that information uniquely specifies your AP.

Comment

Being told two of the terms, and which terms they are puts two constraints on the first term and the constant difference, and so determines the AP completely. However, being told two terms and the fact that they are, say, two apart in the sequence, is not enough to determine the AP exactly.

Summing an AP

Arithmetic progressions occur quite often, for example as formulae for the cost of a telephone line in terms of the initial cost and the cost per month. It often happens that it is useful to be able to add up the terms of an AP without actually doing the adding. An example of this occurred in section 6.2, where the triangular numbers were introduced as the sum of the whole numbers from 1 up to some n. In this section that summing process is generalised.

There is an often told story that Carl Friederich Gauss, who became one of the most productive and influential mathematicians of all time, was as a young boy given the task of adding the numbers from 1 to 100 so as to keep him occupied while other learners got on with their work. According to the story, the teacher was astonished when Gauss claimed to have the answer almost immediately. The story suggests that he thought of using the doubled trapezium idea of Task 6.3.2, but with numbers.

Task 6.4.3 Gauss' Method

Write out the terms to be summed from an AP. Then write them down again in reverse order. Now add the pairs, which in the case shown is 14 each time. Notice that twice the sum is 5×14, so the sum is 35.

3	5	7	9	11
11	9	7	5	3

Comment

Notice how you are given a single example and invited to see through the particular, treating it as generic, to a generality.

It is vital, having encountered an idea once, to have multiple exposures, before expecting to gain mastery. But being set a collection of routine exercises does not always achieve useful multiple exposures, because learners quickly follow a template without actually thinking about what they are doing. It is usually more effective to ask learners to find different ways of approaching the same task, and to ask them to construct their own examples, or even better, to invite them to explore a situation in which they naturally construct and 'do' examples for themselves in order to find out what is going on. These task-structures are illustrated in the following task.

Task 6.4.4 Integrating APs and Diagrams

Find at least two different ways to work out the sum of the first 100 even numbers, including one by factoring and then using a known fact about the sum of the natural numbers, and one by using Gauss's method directly.

Construct some APs for yourself, and find their sum. How 'complicated' can you make your examples?

Find two different methods for summing the numbers that are a more than a multiple of m, starting with a and ending with $a + tm$.

Comment

Taking out a common factor of 2 leaves the first 100 natural numbers whose sum is 5050 so the required sum is 10100.

Notice that the invitation to make a 'really complicated' example leads learners to challenge themselves, to make choices, and to exercise creativity, while at the same time revealing the DofPV and corresponding RofPCh, which they think they can handle. An ideal result is for learners to realise that there are no particularly 'complicated' examples, just complicated arithmetic.

Using Algebra to Suggest Diagrams

The previous work used diagrams to work out how to sum an AP. Now we use the sum of an AP in different forms to suggest corresponding diagrams.

The trapezium method of summing diagrammatically looks as follows:

which in its full generality could be expressed as $\frac{n(a+b)}{2}$. Notice that the diagram suggests the multiplication of n by $(a + b)$ before dividing by 2. But this formula can be rearranged, leading to other diagrams as in the next task.

Task 6.4.5 Areas and Sequences

Find a way to depict the sum of an AP that leads directly to $\frac{n}{2}(a + b)$ as an expression of the sum (the first and last terms are summed, and half the number of terms is a multiplier).

Do the same for $n\left(\frac{a+b}{2}\right)$.

Comment

It is not as difficult as it might seem at first. Take one of the rearrangements and arrange for the diagram to perform the halving on the appropriate bit.

Pause for Reflection

This relatively short section offered at least two insights: that diagrams can be useful for achieving formulae, and that formulae can be rearranged to suggest diagrams. Calculating areas and summing APs are very closely related.

Task 6.4.R Reflection

What surprised you most in this section?

How might you arrange for learners to experience similar surprise and pleasure?

Comment

Being excited yourself is certainly valuable for motivating learners, as long as your excitement is neither overwhelming nor cloying. Learners are often very fragile about their self esteem and self image. Someone whom they respect and trust may inspire them, but over enthusiasm may put learners into a state of feeling they are not up to the challenge.

6.5 PEDAGOGIC ISSUES

Quickie 6.5

The product of two numbers differing by two is always one less than a perfect square. Express the statement in symbols and decide whether it is sometimes, always or never true.

Comment

Did expressing the statement in symbols help with thinking about the validity? Did you try some examples? Did you try any extreme examples?

Quickies Reviewed

The quickies in the previous sections of this chapter are closely related. Here they are, assembled in one place:

> The sum of three consecutive numbers is always divisible by 3. Is any number divisible by 3 the sum of three consecutive numbers?
>
> The sum of five consecutive numbers is always divisible by 5. Is any number divisible by 5 always the sum of five consecutive numbers?
>
> The sum of seven consecutive numbers is always divisible by 7. Is any number divisible by 7 always the sum of seven consecutive numbers?
>
> The sum of four consecutive numbers is always divisible by 2, but not always divisible by 4. Is any number divisible by 2 the sum of four consecutive numbers? Is any number divisible by 4 the sum of four consecutive numbers?

Note the use of '*is any*' here in its mathematical sense meaning *every*, not meaning 'are there any at all?'.

Task 6.5.1 Quickies Reviewed

Look back over the quickies for this chapter and express a generality that deals with the odd cases, and one that deals with the even cases.

Comment

It is to be hoped that you had already anticipated this task at least as a conjecture, if not actually attempting to validate it. If you can get your learners to the point where they anticipate generalities as conjectures, then you really have established algebraic thinking. The rest is extending experience, developing techniques and facility with those techniques, and encountering useful relationships, such as that indicated in the quickie for this section.

One of the features of these statements is that they offer a characterisation of numbers divisible by *n*, namely that these are precisely (in the odd case), and some of, (in the even case) the numbers that are the sum of *n* consecutive numbers.

Pedagogic Constructs

Self-esteem and Self-image

Many learners, especially those who end up in bottom sets, cover over their weak self-image with bravado behaviour. In summarising her lifetime's research into self-esteem of adolescents, Carol Dweck (1999) suggested that some learners seem to have a view of intelligence and of themselves, which is self-limiting. They see intelligence as a fixed quantity (of which they have only a limited supply). Consequently, when something goes wrong they immediately assume that they are near their personal threshold, so they shut down. They adopt an 'I can't' attitude, and then produce defensive behaviour, which is usually offensive to the teacher and to other learners.

By contrast other learners see intelligence as something that develops in response to challenge. They do not even think in terms of 'failure', merely in terms of opportunity to learn and develop. What Dweck and her many colleagues demonstrated in their research is that learners can be persuaded over time to adjust their way of describing themselves, and hence their way of seeing themselves, from 'I can't so I won't' into 'I can if I try hard enough'. Replacing the language of 'can't' and of 'failure' by one of 'challenge' and 'opportunity' can have a significant impact on the self-esteem and self-image of learners.

Didactic Transposition

The desire to try to convey personal enthusiasm for, and pleasure in, some mathematical topic or technique or insight is one of the things that gets people into mathematics teaching, and it is one of the pleasures of teaching to see learners maturing and beginning to get pleasure from thinking mathematically. However, there are also some traps. Your desire for learners to learn can block you from supporting those learners effectively.[3] One of the ways that things go wrong was identified by Yves Chevllard (1985),[4] though he was not the first to write about it. He coined the expression *didactic transposition* to refer to the transformation that takes place when an expert's pleasure and insight is turned into teaching materials.

What usually happens is that the expert's awareness is transposed into instruction in behaviour: the teacher tells learners to do a series of tasks that are meant to reproduce the experience of the expert. However, the expert made choices, followed leads that went nowhere, and was driven by a desire to find out something. The tasks set to learners, and this includes all the tasks in this book, are things for learners to do, one after another. After all, learners tend to take the view that their job is to do what they are asked to do, in the belief that this will produce the learning required. In other words, there is an implicit contract between teachers and learners, a contract that is not always as helpful as it might be. Sometimes teachers have to work hard at altering the contract, seeking ways to intrigue, seduce, provoke, and cajole learners into taking initiative.

How do these ideas apply to this book so far? The tasks in this book are designed to promote the reader into taking initiative by not always giving full or even any answers, by suggesting the reader construct mathematical objects for themselves, and by promoting the exploration of Dimensions of Possible Variation at every turn. There are none of the traditional pages of exercises, nor short explanation, and then several or many similar tasks. There is no 'copy and complete'. Rather, the reader is constantly being challenged to simplify and complexify, to specialise and generalise.

Pause for Reflection

Task 6.5.R   Reflection
In what ways does the notion of *self-esteem* fit with your experience of working on this book?   Of working in classrooms?   What for you are the salient ideas from this chapter?

NOTES

1 See for example http://mathworld.wolfram.com/FigurateNumber.html.
2 Papua New Guinea studies by Alan Bishop.
3 See for example Mason and Johnston-Wilder (2004a).
4 See also Brousseau (1997).

7

Symbol Manipulation

Chapter 7 develops further the strategies suggested in Chapter 3 for the need to manipulate algebraic expressions to arise naturally, leading to investment and involvement in clarifying the 'rules of algebra'. Section 7.1 considers different types of expressions, or different roles that expressions can play. Section 7.2 displays the rules of algebra as the generalisations of the rules for arithmetic. Section 7.3 focuses directly on manipulation by offering opportunities to explore symbol manipulation, including experience of using different expressions to perceive the source context differently (as experienced in Chapter 5, section 5.2). Section 7.4 considers some of the manipulation errors that learners classically make when they have not participated in the expression of the rules of arithmetic as generalisations.

7.1 TYPES OF EXPRESSIONS

Quickie 7.1

In how many ways can you rewrite $2x + 3$ as the sum of two quantities using only the symbol x, positive whole numbers and addition signs?

Comment

Did you consider different order as being sufficiently different to be worth counting? The decision is yours.

This section considers different types of expressions, or, looked at differently, different roles that expressions can play.

Expressing Generality in Order to Count

Most counting tasks admit several ways of counting, and hence reaching expressions of generality. The following task is particularly rich in affording opportunities for multiple ways of seeing.[1]

Task 7.1.1a Hexagons

Assume this is the fifth picture in a sequence. How many different ways can you count the number of circles needed in order to make the nth picture in the sequence? Make sure you decide first what the rule is for describing how the sequence is formed; then pay attention to *how* you 'see' this picture with an eye to the generality.

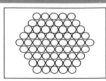

Comment

Did you think of using triangular numbers to help you? What (if any) is the relationship with hexagonal numbers (in Chapter 6)?

It is vital to make sure that each 'way of seeing' does actually generalise, since sometimes what looks general is not (as will be revealed in the next task). Trying your method of seeing on another case (say $n = 4$ or 6) may increase confidence, but is no guarantee. In order to be certain, you have either to show that your way of seeing is structural and not particular, or show that the expression can be manipulated to produce another expression that is known to be correct.

Being so rich, the *Hexagons* task is an ideal setting for interpreting other people's ways of seeing.

Task 7.1.1b Hexagons Again

Translate the following shadings of the fifth hexagon in a sequence of larger and larger hexagons into a way of expressing the number of circles needed to make the nth hexagon. Check that they do actually work on another case, and also on the special case $n = 1$.

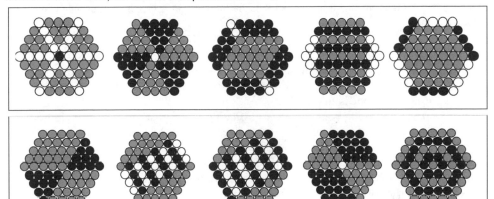

Shade in the blank hexagons so as to display the count expressed by the following expressions:
$1 + 3n(n - 1)$; $3n^2 - 3n + 1$; $3(n - 1)^2 + 3(n - 1) + 1$

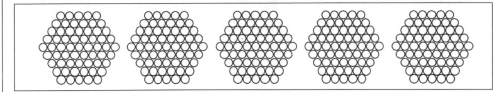

Comment

The first shading suggests an expression of 1 (for the centre) plus $6(n - 1)$ (for the unshaded spokes) plus 6 times the $(n - 2)$nd triangular number, or $1 + 6(n - 1) + 6(n - 2)(n - 1)/2$.

Great care is needed to make sure that what looks general is actually general and not highly particular. One test for this is when the expression achieved is clearly different to expressions obtained by detecting different underlying structure. For example, shading 3 might suggest an expression such as $n^2 + 4(n - 1) \times 2 + 4$, or even $n^2 + 4(n - 1)(n - 2) + 2(n - 2)$, which are both wrong because the shading just does not generalise to other sizes of hexagon.

Once learners have articulated a desire to be able to manipulate expressions, they can be asked to work out the rules from some examples for themselves. The next sub-section considers expressions as objects in order to show different roles they can play.

Expressions as Objects

It is vital that learners develop the flexibility to see expressions in three different ways: as expressions of generality, as 'answers' to a general calculation, and as descriptions of calculations to be done to get specific answers to specific questions. The next task offers some experience of this.

Task 7.1.2a Ordering Expressions

Write the following expressions on cards, one on each. Then place them in some order, for example, as

$2x + 3 \quad 3x - 2 \quad 19$

Now find for values of x for which the expressions are shown in their correct order (smaller to larger).

What are the boundary values at which the expressions stop being in order and two of them become equal?

Make up three expressions that are always in the same order no matter what values of x you substitute.

Make up two expressions and a number so that the three are in a specified order only when x lies between 1 and 2.

Comment

Testing specific values of x to see if they 'work' is a form of specialising. The purpose of the specialising is to reveal something more general: the entire set of numbers for which the three expressions are indeed in order.

Notice that by focusing your attention on finding values that meet some condition, you found yourself repeatedly making choices of values to try, and substituting them in for x. So you gained worthwhile practice in substitution while at the same time extending your sense of what you can do with expressions. Making up expressions of your own involves you in making further choices, and then doing more substituting

Notice that the role of the x here is predominantly as a variable rather than an as-yet-unknown, yet when testing for equality, you are finding specific values for the variable.

Task 7.1.2b Ordering Expressions

Imagine a number-line with just 0 and 1 marked on it. Now add a point somewhere called x. Imagine that the point x moves uniformly back and forth along the number-line.

Now add a second point, which is at $2x$. As your point x moves, imagine the movement of the point $2x$. Now add a third point $1 - x$. Is it to the left or to the right of $2x$ (which depends of course on where x is). Now imagine x moving. Try to get a sense of where the other two points coincide and then change position. Which is to the left of which?

Comment

Imagining the relative movement as x moves is probably a bit of a challenge. Getting a sense of how the two other points move as x moves is useful of itself.

'Number-line movements' is an ideal phenomenon for presenting as an interactive animation[2]. Then you can try to work out, from the movements, what the expressions are likely to be, as well as thinking about which values of x put them in a given order. Learners can be shown just one of the dependent points moving in response to the movement of x, and invited to 'say what they see' before conjecturing which point it is, with justifications, or learners can be shown several labelled points and asked to 'say what they see' and then justify the labels.

The ordering tasks are useful if learners gain experience in thinking of x (and other labels) as denoting values that vary as x varies, rather than being fixed.

Learners are prone to making slips in details when doing calculations, often because their attention is on the process not the details. Sometimes 'slips' are actually deeper misconceptions of 'the rules' of manipulation. Where learners have participated in the unfolding and articulation of those rules, they are less likely to form misconceptions, but they can still make slips. It can be useful to exploit rather than try to avoid classic errors, as the next task illustrates.

Task 7.1.3 Exploiting Errors

Someone claims that $2(x + 1) = 2x + 1$. Someone else claims that $2(x + 1) = 2x + 2$.

What is the range of permissible change for x in each case, so that the equality is valid?

Comment

The first one is *never* valid, that is, there are no values of x for which it is a true statement. The second one is always valid, no matter what number you substitute for x.

Learners who are treated to instruction in techniques without appreciating the source and purpose of those techniques are very likely to develop a *laissez-faire* attitude to mathematics, disowning responsibility for or care about whether things make sense, or whether answers are consistent. Algebra offers a focus for adolescents who both want to be safe within rule structures, and want to challenge those rules, because it offers opportunities to be creative, opportunities to construct rules that will make 'everything turn out consistently', and opportunities to test things out for themselves rather than depending on the authority of the teacher. Here, in a class accustomed to specialising as a way of checking things, it will be evident that there is something wrong, and by being empowered to check things for themselves, they can avoid mistakes in the future. In Chapter 7, the focus is on ways in which learners might come to decide on the rules for manipulating symbols.

An *equation* specifies that two expressions are to be equal, and implies that there are only a few restricted values of the variables that make the equality true. An *identity* states that two expressions are *always* equal; that is, that they always give the same values.

Task 7.1.4 For What Values?

What is the range of permissible change for the values of the letters that preserve the following equalities?

$2x = x + x$ $x^2 - y^2 = (x - y)(x + y)$ $z - 1 = (z^2 - 1)/(z + 1)$ $3w = 2w + p$

Comment

The first three equalities are preserved for all values of the letters. Only the last one is prob-lematic, because p might, but might not, have the same value as w. One of the things that causes confusion when algebra is introduced simply as 'arithmetic with letters' is that w and p both represent unrestricted choices of number. They might actually in some instances have the same value, but they might not. Just because two letters are different, it does not mean that their values *must* be different; by contrast, the same letter *always* means the same current value.

As with each task, there are opportunities to make up your own examples that are as simple as possible yet illustrate the point, or as complicated as possible trying to obscure the point. Both are valuable in order to appreciate the scope and range of permissible change involved in different DofPVs.

Task 7.1.5 Recognising Types of Relationships between Expressions

Identify each of the following as an identity, equation, expression, or inequality.

$3x + 4$; $3x + 4 = 7$; $3x + 4 = (2x + 1) + (x + 3)$; $3x + 4 \leq 7$; $3x + 4 \geq 5x - 2$

For each category (identity, equation, expression, or inequality), make up two examples: one that is in some sense typical, and that helps distinguish that category from the others, and the other that is as complicated as you can make it.

Comment

Probably the hardest to distinguish are the identity and the equation, since they depend on finding the set of values that satisfy the statement. The purpose of constructing your own examples is to reveal to yourself the dimensions of possible variation of which you are intu-itively aware; the complicated example contrasts with the simple, typical one, but serves to reveal what it is about the typical one that is seen as typical.

Pause for Reflection

On encountering an expression, it is necessary to discern the components that make it up, as part of seeing it as a calculation procedure. It is also important to see it as the answer or result of a calculation. On encountering equations and inequalities it is first necessary to discern the expressions being related, and then to see them as being related by equality or inequality. If the component expressions are seen as a jumble of symbols and not as a single object (the result of a calculation) then the notion of equality or inequality specifying a constraint on the expressions, and consequently on the variables involved, is likely to be missed entirely.

Task 7.1.R Reflection

Which do you find easier, finding several different ways of seeing that give rise to different (but equivalent) expressions, or trying to see in a way that is expressed by someone else's expression?

Comment

Situations rich in multiple expressions offer an opportunity for learners to construct their own expression and then to challenge others to 'see the generality that way'.

As a teacher it is vital to be able to put aside your own way of seeing in order to try to enter a learner's perspective. Developing flexibility is also useful for learners, so that diagrams can be used to think about expressions just as expressions can be used to interpret diagrams.

7.2 GENERALISED ARITHMETIC

Quickie 7.2

The expression $30x^3$ can be written as $(6x)(5x^2)$. In how many different ways can you rewrite $30x^3$ as the product of two quantities using only multiplication, positive whole numbers, and x raised to positive integer powers?

What exactly are numbers? How would you set about recognising a number? This section addresses these questions by prompting reflection on what you can do with numbers. There is a long history of philosophical enquiry into what constitutes a number, or indeed any other abstract idea (health, hope, charity). The Greek teacher Socrates, who flourished in Athens around 420 BCE, was ultimately put to death for being too radical in the way that he promoted questioning of fundamental beliefs. Some of his encounters with students were recorded by Plato in the famous dialogues (see, for example, Grube 2002). One of the abiding themes of those dialogues is that asking for definitions of abstract ideas is rarely fruitful; more fruitful is asking what you can do with these things, or how you would recognise them. Socrates urged his students to apply this to abstractions such as truth, beauty, justice, etc. In this section, it is applied to numbers.

Properties of Numbers

In Task 1.4.3 (Mental Strategies) there was a flavour of an approach based on quotes from Augustus de Morgan identifying some of the strategies that can be used to enable arithmetic to be done mentally.

Task 7.2.1 What Is A Number?

To address the question 'what is a number?', it may be more helpful to consider what you can do with numbers in the way of arithmetic. Start by confining yourself to whole numbers, then consider other numbers. For example, you can add whole numbers.

Comment

If you confine yourself to whole numbers then you can certainly add one to any number, to get the 'next number'. Curiously, it turns out that essentially everything else about the counting numbers follows from this one idea, that every number has a 'next'.

Once you go beyond 'adding one' you can of course add and multiply, and sometimes you can subtract and sometimes you can divide numbers. You can also use them as labels (as in clock times or house numbers), as approximations to measurements (as in 3*m* or 4*gm*), but these are not arithmetic uses. You can also exponentiate (raise one whole number to a whole number power).

Having identified operations on numbers, there arises the question of what sorts of numbers are being considered. Is it whole numbers (counting numbers), or integers (positive and negative and zero), or fractions (positive, or positive and negative and zero) or decimals, or perhaps even some other objects?

The whole numbers provide a sensible starting point, before seeing what extensions have to be made to include negatives, fractions, and decimals.

The important thing to notice in arithmetic is that whereas you can always add any two whole numbers and get another whole number, you cannot always subtract any whole number from a specified whole number and still always get a whole number (positive) answer. When the operation can always be performed and the answer is of the same kind as the objects you operated on, the property is known as *closure* (as in the case of adding); when the answer is sometimes not of the same kind, the property is known as *lack of closure* (as in the case of subtraction).

Task 7.2.2a Closure

Compare and contrast the following pairs with respect to being closed under the specified operations:

positive whole numbers under multiplication, and positive whole numbers under division;

integers (positive, negative and zero) under subtraction, and whole numbers under subtraction;

fractions (positive, negative and zero) under addition and subtraction, and positive fractions under addition and subtraction;

positive fractions under multiplication and division, and whole numbers under multiplication and division;

decimals under addition, subtraction, multiplication, and division (other than by zero), and decimals with only two decimal places, under addition, subtraction, multiplication and division (other than by zero).

Comment

In each case the first of the pair is closed under the operations specified, whereas the second is not. The sense implied by the pairs presented in the task is that negatives are introduced in order to permit subtraction to be closed; fractions are introduced to permit division to be closed (other than by zero). One of the 'nice' things that happens is that having introduced negatives to permit subtraction, subtracting negatives does not require further extensions: the integers turn out to be closed under subtraction; having introduced fractions to permit division, dividing fractions (other than by zero) does not need further extension: fractions are already closed under division (except by zero).

Task 7.2.2b Closure Extended

None of the following collections of objects is closed under the indicated operations. What larger classes of objects would you need to use in order to achieve closure under the specified operation?

Squares being cut in half (according to area) by a single straight line parallel to one side.

Triangles being cut into two pieces with equal perimeter by a single straight line parallel to one side.

Circles being cut into two pieces by a single straight line through the centre.

Comment

This task was intended to produce a little bit of surprise: algebraic ideas apply to objects other than numbers, even though this section is particularly focused on numbers. An inner aspect of the task (see section 7.5) is encounters with extending a collection of objects so as to be closed under a specified object. For example, cutting a square in half by area using lines parallel to the edges of the square produces rectangles, and cutting these similarly in half produces more and more rectangles. But can any rectangle be produced in this way, starting from a square? Suddenly the task becomes quite challenging. Partly this is due to the implicit task to try to construct a rectangle that could not arise from repeatedly cutting the rectangles arising from starting with a square.

  Cutting a triangle into two pieces with equal perimeters yields a triangle and a trapezium, so the operation is not closed.

  Cutting a circle through its centre yields two semi-circles; cutting these through the centre of their arcs (the centre of the old circle) yields sectors of the circle; cutting a sector of a circle through the centre of the arc yields more sectors of the same circle, so although circles are not closed under this operation, sectors of a circle, or even of circles in general, are closed under the operation.

A possible DofPV is to permit the cutting line to be any line, not necessarily parallel to an edge of the figure (whether squares and rectangles, or triangles). Instead of an operation of cutting a shape you can start with a square of a specified size and then adjoin copies edge to edge, to produce the shapes known as polyominoes like 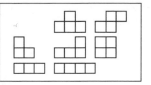 the ones illustrated, which have resisted counting, and which produce difficult jigsaw and other combinatorial problems.

  Having agreed that whole numbers are closed under addition, integers are closed under addition and subtraction, fractions are closed under addition, subtraction, multiplication and division (other than by zero), there are relationships to be observed between the these operations.

Task 7.2.3 What Properties Do Numbers Have?

Express in symbols the following arithmetic facts about numbers:

  If you add two numbers in either order you get the same result (*commutativity of addition*)

  If you multiply two numbers in either order you get the same result (*commutativity of multiplication*)

  If you add two numbers and then add a third, or if you add the first to the sum of the second and third you get the same result (*associativity of addition*).

  If you multiply two numbers and then multiply by a third, or if you multiply the first by the product of the second and third, you get the same result (*associativity of multiplication*).

  If you multiply a number by the sum of two numbers or if you add the products of the first number with each of the second and third, you get the same result (*distributivity of multiplication over addition*).

Comment

The facts given are relationships that hold for all pairs of numbers and the specified opera-tions, so they are properties of numbers. Notice the subtle shift from detecting a relationship that holds, to seeing that relationship as a property of all objects. Indeed, those properties will, shortly, be taken as characterising number-ness: any collection of objects that satisfy those properties when expressed in symbolic terms so as to remove the need to be what you might recognise as numbers, is considered to be a collection of number-like objects, or numbers, for short!

Probably the most important aspect of expressing these generalities in symbols is stressing the *for any*:

For any two numbers a and b, $a + b = b + a$ and $a \times b = b \times a$.

For any three numbers a, b and c, $(a + b) + c = a + (b + c)$ and $a \times (b \times c) = (a \times b) \times c$.

For any three numbers a, b and c, $a \times (b + c) = a \times b + a \times c$

Finally, as explored in the next task, there are two special numbers whose proper-ties are worth noting.

Task 7.2.4 Special Numbers

What properties do zero and one have with respect to all other numbers?

Comment

Zero is important with respect to addition because of what it does (or perhaps does not do) when added to other numbers. One is important with respect to multiplication for the same reason. Furthermore, with every number N there are two associated numbers: one that when added to N gives zero, and one that when multiplied by N gives 1 (for $N \neq 0$). These are called the *additive* and *multiplicative inverses* of N respectively. Zero is the *additive identity* and one is the *multiplicative identity*. The significant feature about numbers is that they all have an additive inverse, and all but zero have a multiplicative inverse. There are examples of collections of objects that satisfy these properties but which are not as familiar as ordinary numbers.

What is the multiplicative inverse of 2/3? Of what is 3/4 the multiplicative inverse? In both cases, the search is for something that, when multiplied by the given number, results in 1 – the multiplicative identity. This is why to divide by a fraction, you 'turn it upside down and multiply'! What you are really doing is forming its multiplicative inverse, which con-verts the division into a multiplication.

The real significance of the special numbers zero and one emerges when the oper-ations of subtraction and division are linked to their counterparts, addition and multiplication, via these special numbers.

Task 7.2.5 Inverse Operations

Construct particular examples of the following statements in order to make sense of them for yourself, then express them generally using symbols.

Subtracting a number is the same as adding its additive inverse.

Dividing by a number (other than zero) is the same as multiplying by its multiplicative inverse.

The multiplicative inverse of the additive inverse of a number (other than zero) is the same as the additive inverse of the multiplicative inverse of the number.

The next task may provide an opportunity to experience what it is like for learners to encounter a collection of symbols: the statements and ideas can be sorted out as long as you take your time and use your own powers, specialising and generalising, conjecturing and convincing, imagining and expressing what you imagine.

As a further example of inverse operations, consider exponentiation (the subject of the Quickies in Chapter 2). The *logarithm of a number n base b* (written $\log_b(n)$ where the b is assumed to be positive, and is usually omitted if it is clear from context) is defined to be the 'power to which the base b must be raised in order to give the number n'.

At first encounter this is a real mouthful. You may need to check out some special cases, say when b is 10. Thus $\log_{10}(100) = 2$ because $10^2 = 100$.

Task 7.2.6 Logarithms

Using the definition, interpret the following statements in terms of logarithms:

$3^2 = 9$; $2^3 = 8$; $10^3 = 1000$;

What base is implied by the statement $10^{\log(100)} = 100$?

Make up your own examples, both simple and complicated.

Decide whether the following expressions are always, sometimes or never true.

$\log_b(b) = 1$ $\log_b(b^n) = n$.

In what sense are powers of b and logarithms to base b inverse operations?

Decide whether the following expressions are always, sometimes or never true.

$\log_b(a^n) = n\log_b(a)$ $\log_b(n \times m) = \log_b(n) + \log_b(m)$ $\log_b(n) = \log_a(n)/\log_a(b)$

Comment

The purpose of this task is to provide some opportunities to struggle with a concept defined in terms of its inverse, in order to appreciate the struggle that some learners have over subtraction and division. Thinking in terms of inverse operations is usually more fruitful than resorting to other ways of thinking about operations.

Powers of b and logarithms to base b are inverse in the sense that either operation applied to the number n, then followed by the other operation, results in n again. The identity involved is the identity function, which sends each number to itself.

Whenever you encounter a complicated or abstract idea (here the definition of logarithm to base b), you have the option of doing the following: try it out on some familiar special cases to try to see what is going on in order to reconstruct and re-generalise for yourself, and rehearse the language pattern until it comes naturally and fluently. As learners develop the habit of taking this initiative themselves, their learning will become much more efficient.

This subsection has invoked a shift from relationships between numbers to properties of numbers. The aim was to become aware both of properties that hold for all numbers, not just for particular ones, and properties that hold for particularly special numbers (zero and one). Properties of zero and one characterise them, and in the next sub-section, the properties of numbers in general will serve to characterise what is meant by 'number'.

From Properties to Axioms: Arithmetic and Algebra

In order to capture the full arithmetic on numbers (which means extending numbers at least to include fractions if not decimals) it is usual to resort to a different collection of axioms, based on abstracting the properties of both addition and multiplication and their inverses, that is, of what you can 'do' with numbers.

A collection of objects satisfies the axioms of algebra if:

there are two operations (which here will be called addition and multiplication) for which:

addition and multiplication are closed, commutative, and associative, and multiplication distributes over addition;

there are two numbers (which here will be called zero and one) such that

zero is the additive identity and one is the multiplicative identity;

to each number there is an additive inverse, and to each number other than zero there is a multiplicative inverse.

Strictly speaking the axioms given here specify what is called a *field*. There are other systems of axioms that mirror just the integers. An additional axiom is required if you want to characterise the real (decimal) numbers[3].

The move from properties to axioms can be experienced in the move from being aware of the relationship between, say, $\sqrt{3}$ and 3, to seeing the positive root of three, $\sqrt{3}$, as having the property that its square is 3, to taking as the only thing you know about $\sqrt{3}$ is that its square is 3, from which you then make deductions. For example $\sqrt{13 + 4\sqrt{3}} = 1 + 2\sqrt{3}$, can be checked by squaring the number on the right. All you need to use is the fact that $\sqrt{3}^2 = 3$.

Task 7.2.7 Symbolising
Express the axioms for algebra in symbols for yourself.
Comment You should end up with the same statements that arose from Task 7.2.3 (What Properties). These are the axioms of algebra, the rules for manipulating symbols.

Pause for Reflection

This section could be seen as abstract and technical, but its main message is that by looking at relationships between numbers involved in operations it is possible to discern some relationships that are always true (possibly with the exception of zero), and these relationships can be turned into properties that all number have. The deft and powerful move made by mathematicians is to isolate these properties and to declare interest in any collection of objects that satisfies those properties. The properties listed are then called *axioms*. *Algebra* at tertiary level, as *abstract algebra*, is the study of properties of collections of objects that satisfy these axioms and other axioms similar to them, using symbols to reason about those properties.

Task 7.2.R Reflection

Articulate in your own words any differences you noticed between thinking about particular numbers, thinking about numbers in general, writing down relationships between operations and numbers (such as that adding can be done in either order), thinking of these as properties of numbers, and treating these properties as axioms.

Explain in your own words, as if to a colleague or friend, what axioms are, and how they differ from properties and relationships.

A relationship is a statement about how two or more objects are connected or related (for example one number is twice another number); a property is a relationship that can hold for one or more collections of objects (the property of being twice another number); an axiom is a property assumed to hold for all objects (for every number there is another number that is twice the first).

7.3 MORE MANIPULATING AND REARRANGING

Quickie 7.3

The expression $x^2 y^3$ can be written as $(xy)(xy^2)$. In how many different ways can you rewrite it as a product of two quantities using only multiplication, and positive whole numbers for the powers?

Having felt the need to be able to manipulate symbolic expressions, the issue now is how to gain fluency. 'Doing' lots of exercises, which means, literally, exercising 'mental muscles', may contribute to fluency if it is done reflectively, or against a clock to try to develop speed. But expertise in manipulation is most likely to arise through continued use to demonstrate that different expressions of generality really do give the same result. In Chapter 12 the case will be made that explorations that call upon the learner to construct their own examples on which to use a technique, in pursuit of some greater exploration, are more likely to result in the development of competent fluency than possibly mindless 'doing' of large numbers of similar exercises. Since the main stumbling block in algebraic fluency is the use of brackets, attention here will focus on tasks designed to highlight the need for and use of brackets.

Using Brackets

Task 7.3.1 Four Fours

How many different numbers starting 1, 2, 3, … can you make using just four fours, and the operations of +, −, x, and ÷? Using a calculator will emphasise the importance of using brackets, as will checking someone else's calculations, because of the need to state unambiguously what the calculation is.

Comment

This is not really an algebra task at all! It may however be useful for learning to use brackets to good effect.

Task 7.3.2 Bracketing and Convention

Without a convention as to the order in which to apply the operations, the expression $4 - 3 + 2 - 1$ is highly ambiguous. In fact, there are five different ways of inserting brackets so that each operation is unambiguously performed on just two quantities at a time. For example, $(4 - 3) + (2 - 1)$. Try reading the numbers and operations out loud using only pauses to indicate how the terms are to be bracketed.

How many different values can be made by bracketing differently? Do the same with the following sequences

$$4 - 3 + 2 - 1 \quad 4 + 3 - 2 + 1 \quad 4 \times 3 + 2 \times 1 \quad 4 - 3 \div 2 - 1$$

Make up sequences like these (alternating + and −; alternating + and ÷; alternating x and ÷; alternating − and ÷). In the case of alternating − and +, what relationships have to hold so that all the answers are positive? In the case of alternating − and ÷, what relationships must hold so that all the answers are integers?

What is the maximum number of distinct answers you can get when alternating − and +; when alternating + and −?

Why do you get more different answers when alternating − and ÷ than when alternating + and x?

Comment

Reading with pauses is fine for the reader but very hard for the listener, which is why brackets are used. The purpose of these tasks is to stimulate learners to explore, making necessary use of bracketing along the way, so that they become familiar with the effects of bracketing and with inserting and removing brackets correctly according to the rules of algebra.

The notion of going with and across the grain can be used to get learners to practise a technique by varying the numbers for themselves, and trying to spot patterns. In the case of bracketing for example, learners can generate entries in a table such as the following. The value is in the spotting, conjecturing and validating patterns (going across the grain) not in clerically filling out the table (going with the grain).

Task 7.3.3 Multiplying Brackets With and Across the Grain

What is the same and what different about the entries in the table?

	$(2a + 8)(5a + 3)$ $= 10a^2 + (6 + 40)a + 24$		
$(2a + 7)(5a + 2)$ $= 10a^2 + (4 + 35)a + 14$	$(2a + 7)(5a + 3)$ $= 10a^2 + (6 + 35)a + 21$	$(2a + 7)(5a + 4)$ $= 10a^2 + (8 + 35)a + 28$	
	$(2a + 6)(5a + 3)$ $= 10a^2 + (6 + 30)a + 18$		

Extend the rows to left and right, and the columns up and down, making sure that the extensions are all consistent when they intersect!

Now, thinking across the grain, what do the cell entries suggest?

Make up your own array, varying a different pair of numbers in place of the two chosen here.

Comment

Initially the table looks very complicated. By discerning what is the same about nearby cells, and what is different, a sense of pattern and structure begins to emerge. As relationships between adjacent cells, and between cells in the same row or same column come to attention, structure is revealed. Extending rows and columns can be done by attending locally to what is changing and what staying the same; by going across the grain through making sense overall, and by linking the expressions on either side of the equal signs. Valuable experience can be gained concerning how bracketed terms are multiplied together.

Expressing Equality and Inequality

Saying that two things are equal arises very commonly in mathematics, as does comparing two quantities.

Task 7.3.4a Equalities

In how many ways can you express in symbols the fact that two quantities, say a and b, are equal?

Comment

Surprisingly there are three distinct ways, with variants of each! You can write $a = b$, or $b = a$, which expresses the equality directly. Secondly, you can write $a - b = 0$ or $b - a = 0$ according to your preference, for if two things are equal then their difference must be zero. You can also write $a/b = 1$ or $b/a = 1$ (assuming neither a nor b can be zero), for if two things are equal, then their ratio must be one.

Instead of immediately writing down the $a = b$ form, it is often useful to write down the $a - b$ form. This is especially true when setting up an equation from a problem. If all the terms are on one side of the equality, the manipulation is usually much easier.

Some people go to great lengths to elaborate the balance metaphor for equations, in which an equality sign is seen as a fulcrum, and the terms on either side have to remain balanced. However, it is not always clear to some learners why the balance metaphor is invoked. The idea is that the equation expression can be adjusted as long as the balance is maintained, so adding the same to both sides, or multiplying by the same on both sides preserves the balance and are acceptable operations to perform. By using the form $a - b$ the need for a balance is obviated. The manipulations must be rearrangements of the expression through expanding or factoring, collecting or distributing.

Task 7.3.4b Inequalities

In how many ways can you express the fact that of two quantities, say a and b, a is always greater than b, or that a is always greater than or equal to b, or that a is never less than b?

Comment

The previous task on equality suggests a direct expression, a difference expression, and a ratio expression. When might a ratio version be useful, either for equality or inequality?

Pause for Reflection

Gaining facility and competence in manipulating symbols is not a simple issue. It is not something that can be done and finished in a short space of time; rather, it is something that is acquired, developed and maintained through use.

Task 7.3.R Reflection

What more do you feel you need to do in order to be confident and fluent with the use of brackets?

What kind of task would be most effective to support learners? Construct one for yourself, and then see if it is effective.

The framework See–Experience–Master is intended to act as a reminder that learners do not often master something on second or third exposure, much less first encounter. Consequently, when planning lessons it is wiser to look for maturation over the longer term than short-term success. Maturation is achieved by engaging learners in tasks that call upon them to construct specific instances in which the techniques to be mastered are required. Sets of exercises are only useful when learners are encouraged to go across the grain, that is, to make overall sense, to articulate what is the same and what different, and to express various dimensions of possible variation of which they are aware.

7.4 IDENTIFYING ERRORS

Quickie 7.4

The expression $(3x + 4y)$ can be written as the sum of three terms, none of them zero, using only positive whole numbers, for example as $(x + y) + (2x + 2y) + (y)$. The expression x^3y^4 can be written as the product of three terms, none of them one, using only positive whole powers, for example as (xy) $(x^2y^2)(y)$. What is the same and what different about the various ways of writing the two expressions in these forms?

Make up an expression consisting of the sum of two terms that can be written both as the sum of two terms and as the product of two terms, in at least two different ways each (not including changing the order).

Classroom Atmosphere

Making slips is perfectly natural, especially when you are in a hurry and your mind is on other things (such as the main task not the subtask). Other errors start off as unthinking slips but turn into practices and habits. In order to support learners in becoming independent learners rather than dependent on a teacher being present, it is useful to establish a way of working in the classroom, what has come to be called, a 'community of practice', which is a classroom ethos that supports learners taking initiative, as well as cooperating and collaborating, all structured so as to promote mathematical thinking.

Central to productive mathematical work is a *conjecturing atmosphere*. This means a working environment in which everything said, whether by a learner, teacher, or in a text, is taken as a conjecture, as something to considered, tested, and justified. In a conjecturing atmosphere, people are happy to have an opportunity to speak when they are unsure, because they know that others will suggest modifications: in a conjecturing atmosphere suggestions are not wrong, but rather conjectures that may need modifying. If someone says something you do not agree with you first test it out on some examples, and if you find a counter-example you suggest it to the originator and ask for comments. In a conjecturing atmosphere, if you are sure of yourself, you take opportunities to listen to others and to suggest modifications or counter-examples.

Another aspect of a conjecturing atmosphere is that people naturally try particular and special cases to test out conjectures, including their own conjectures. This means wanting to check their work for themselves, not waiting to have it checked by the teacher. Research in Australia by Kaye Stacey and Mollie McGregor (2000) revealed that learners who lack confidence and who expect not to get things right are much less willing to check their own work than those who expect to get much or most of it correct. The reason is, of course, that if you find you have a lot wrong, you have to do something about it, which means more work. It is much easier to hand over responsibility to the teacher, thereby becoming more detached, less involved, and more dependent.

Tasks that enable learners to be creative and to make choices are more likely to stimulate learners than tasks that are repetitive and routine. Tasks that involve expressing and testing generalities, and that involve making sense, not simply repeating actions over and over, are much more likely to attract learners to be active participants. Tasks that call upon users to use those powers not only afford the possibility of pleasure stemming from the use of those powers, but strengthen and develop those powers so that they become even more effective.

Working On and With Errors

The thesis of this book is that learners who are regularly called upon to experience, express and test generalities are much less likely to make the kinds of errors that appear so often on tests and exams. Instead of waiting for learners to make a few mistakes, it is also possible to 'take the bull by the horns' by working on errors proactively.

Task 7.4.1 Exposing Errors

A learner announced that she thought that adding one number to another always made the answer bigger than the first number. Her teacher disagreed. Find some examples in which adding does not make bigger. Try to express a generality about when adding does not 'make bigger'.

A learner announced that whenever you multiply two numbers, the answer is bigger than either of them. The teacher disagreed. Find some examples in which multiplying does not make bigger.

A learner repeated something a teacher said to him: 'You can't take a large number away from a small number.' When can you and when can't you?

Someone's father said 'A fraction has to be smaller than a whole, because it means "part of".' Find some examples in which a fraction can actually be larger than 1.

Comment

By proactively confronting possible errors and misconceptions within a conjecturing atmosphere, learners not only learn to check and test conjectures and to check their own work, but to develop strategies for pausing and checking when, in the midst of some calculation, they run up against an uncertainty. Rather than writing down the first thing that comes to mind, they can develop the habit of pausing and checking against a special or particular case.

The strategy offered here is to collect 'howlers' that learners make, and then to fashion them into the format of 'someone once said that … '. Furthermore, it is possible to turn some errors into an opportunity for exploration.

Task 7.4.2a Exploiting Errors

$\frac{16}{16} = \frac{1\cancel{6}}{\cancel{6}4} = \frac{1}{4}$ Something is wrong with the crossing out, even though the answers are correct. What is being done incorrectly?

Find other instances like this one where incorrectly cancelling digits gives the correct answer.

Comment

Did you think to express a generality and then try to solve for one of the variables? Did you think to try three digit numbers?

Task 7.4.2b Exploiting Errors

Check the 'calculations' and construct some more examples of when this incorrect method gives the correct answer (Elgin 2004).

$$\frac{5}{4} - \frac{9}{12} = \frac{5-9}{4-12} = \frac{^-4}{^-8} = \frac{1}{2} = \frac{15-9}{12}! \qquad \frac{3}{6} - \frac{4}{12} = \frac{3-4}{6-12} = \frac{^-1}{^-6} = \frac{1}{6} = \frac{6-4}{12}!$$

Comment

Did you try simplifying 9/12 and then doing the same incorrect calculation? It does not work, so whatever is going on depends on the particular form of the fraction, not on the value of the fraction. Multiplying top and bottom of either fraction by the same amount preserves the correct calculation of the difference, but changes the incorrect calculation. However, multiplying both numerators or both denominators by the same amount preserves both the correct and the incorrect calculation. So one approach is to use a 1 in the denominator of the first fraction.

Looking for sameness and difference, for what relationships might be hiding, one possibility is that the second denominator is a multiple of the first denominator; furthermore, the second numerator is (divisible by) the square of that multiple, and the first numerator is (divisible by) one less than twice that multiple. All this can be uncovered by starting with general fractions, imposing the condition that the second denominator is a multiple of the first, which is taken to be 1, doing the correct and the incorrect calculations, and imposing the constraint that the answers must be the same. This reveals a relationship between the numerators, and the observation that $\frac{2x-1}{1} - \frac{x^2}{x} = x - 1$ whether you use the correct or the incorrect calculation.

Very often taking an error that someone makes and asking for a classification of when (if ever) that wrong calculation could give the correct answer serves three useful purposes: it provides you with an opportunity to explore for yourself, it alerts you to making sure that the tasks you set learners do not fall into the category of it being possible to get the right answer by the wrong method, and it can be used with learners to reinforce their awareness that it is a wrong calculation as they try to find instances where it gives the correct answer, since to do this they have to contrast the correct and the incorrect methods.

Classic Errors

Researchers have collected the wide range of errors and slips made by learners over the years. Some of them have persisted for hundreds of years.[4]

$1/a + 1/b$ is added to get $1/(a + b)$ or $2/(a + b)$. This was commented on in the nineteenth century (Hart 1981) as an example of something learners do even though they would not do the same thing with numerical fractions.

$(a + b)^2$ is expanded as $a^2 + b^2$; $(a + b)^3$ as $a^3 + b^3$; etc.

$3x + 4$ is contracted or compacted to 7 or $7x$, ignoring the letter completely; $2a + 3b$ becomes $5ab$ or $6ab$.

$2a + 3b$ is treated as 2 apples + 3 bananas making perhaps, 5 fruit. Known as fruit salad algebra, the 2 in $2a$ is strictly speaking a verb (double) or at best a noun, multiplied by a, where as in 2 apples, 2 is an adjective. This error shows up when single letters are treated as short forms for objects starting with that letter, so in $3y$ the y is seen as standing for yachts, yams, or yogurts but not for a number.

Confusing $2cm$ or $2m$ and $2 \times m$ where m is a number.

Treating a as 1, b as 2, and so on, rather than as standing for *any* number whatsoever.

Treating letters as always having a single value rather than as standing for any or all numbers.

Thinking that x and y, being different letters, must stand for different numbers.

Thinking that two occurrences of the same letter can stand for different numbers, such as, 'let $2n$ be any even number; then $2n + 2n$ represents the sum of any two even numbers'.

Thinking letters stand only for whole numbers, and not for fractions or decimals.

Thinking algebra is only to do with arithmetic.

Confusion between $a \times b$ and $a + b$ written as ab; not seeing 2 3/4 as 2 + 3/4 but confusing it with juxtaposition in algebra as $2 \times 3/4$. Using ab to represent a two digit number, instead of $10a + b$.

When x is 3, interpreting $4x$ as 43.

Applying operations in order from left to right (so $2 + 3 \times 4$ is 20) rather than using the convention that multiplication and division bind more strongly than addition and subtraction. Calculators and computer software are contexts in which these errors crop up particularly.

Using idiosyncratic notation such as $x + 2 \times 3$ to mean the area of a rectangle with edges $x + 2$ by 3, instead of using brackets. Not even realising that $1 + (2 \times 3)$ and $(1 + 2) \times 3$ give different values, especially when larger numbers are involved.

Confusing $12 \div 4$ and $4 \div 12$ (reading one as 4 guzinto 12 and the other as 12 divided by 4).

Not accepting or recognising $l \times b$ as an answer to the area of a rectangle, which is l by b, because they expect a single symbol or even a number as an answer.

Task 7.4.2c Exploiting More Errors

From the errors listed above, choose one that you recognise from your own learners, and one that you think most of them will not make. Construct tasks that test for those errors. Try to have some tasks be more subtle and others more direct. Then slip them into a test as appropriate, and see what learners do. It would be excellent to write down your predictions before handing out the test.

Many of these errors can be accounted for by learners being desperate to finish quickly and so writing down whatever first comes to mind; by learners unconvinced that mathematics has any meaning or any importance; by learners convinced that their job is to finish tasks as quickly as possible without actually thinking about them.

Pause for Reflection

Task 7.4.R Reflection

What errors have you made recently, or seen recently? How would you account for those errors? Try to characterise some possible situations in which the error does actually give the correct answer.

7.5 PEDAGOGIC ISSUES

Quickie 7.5

What is the same and what is different about the Quickies in this chapter?

Pedagogic Constructs

Inner and Outer Aspects of Tasks

Dick Tahta (1981) distinguishes between the *outer task* (what learners are overtly invited to do) and *inner aspects* of the task (what learners are likely to encounter). In this case, one inner aspect is the fact that different expressions can express the same thing. If inner aspects are made explicit before the task is tackled, then the learner knows what to look for and so is unlikely to experience it fully as an insight. Rather, their work becomes oriented to 'doing what is expected' and they are reinforced in 'seeking what the teacher/author' intends. Guy Brousseau (1997) has developed a comprehensive approach to developing classroom materials and to analysing teaching and learning, which has at its core the *contract didactique*: if the learners do what the teacher tells them to do, then learning will take place. Of course this contract has hidden clauses, because it is necessary for the learners to be active, and to be trying to make sense not just of the tasks but of what they are doing as a result of the task, what they encounter while doing the task. The didactic contract leads to a *didactic tension*:

> The more clearly the teacher specifies what learners are to do, the easier it is for learners to display that behaviour without generating it for themselves.

In other words, if learners are told clearly what they are to do, they will find ways of doing it that avoid internalising, appreciating, or realising (in the sense of 'making real to and for themselves') what the task was intended to do. As you saw earlier, Brousseau builds on an insight of Yves Chevellard (1985) called the *transposition didactique*, which suggests that when a relative expert such as an author or teacher has an insight, develops an awareness, and then constructs materials for teaching, there is an inevitable transformation or transposition of the expert's awareness into instruction in behaviour (telling learners what to do). The result is that learners, in their urge to complete tasks (high achievers want to complete them quickly and get them out of the way, low achievers proceed slowly so as not to incur extra work), circumvent inner aspects of the tasks and merely contact the outer aspects.

Inner aspects include mathematical themes encountered and used, powers for making mathematical sense of situations, and personal propensities (such as diving in without thinking; thinking about it without actually getting down to do things; rushing to finish so as to get on to something else).

For access to original sources of affordances, inner and outer aspects, and the *situation didactique*, see Mason and Johnston–Wilder (2004a).

Pedagogic Strategies

Seeking Opportunities for Multiple Expressions

The need to manipulate expressions arises when learners recognise that different looking expressions can express the same thing, and so must always give the same values. Consequently it is useful to collect examples of situations that enable everyone in the class to have a different expression and yet for all of those expressions to be correct. Hexagons (Task 7.1.1) was a particular example of this richness, but they arise in most mathematical topics.

Treating Expressions as Objects

Because expressions of generality have three different aspects or roles (generality, calculation instructions and 'the answer') it is vital that learners become familiar with all three aspects. Treating them as objects, as 'the answer' helps learners to see expressions as objects in their own right and not just as processes of calculation. Consequently, the strategy of placing several expressions in order and then working out what this constraint implies about the range of permissible change of the variable(s) serves several purposes: it exercises the process of substitution, it treats expressions as objects, and it provides exposure to the theme of freedom and constraint.

Exploring in Order to Exercise

In section 7.3, tasks were proposed that involve the learner in using brackets while exploring some different but related goal. Tasks that involve the learner in constructing examples on which to use a technique is much more effective in exercising that technique than is doing a set of exercises that are directly and specifically focused on that technique. The whole point of gaining facility is to be able to perform the technique or to carry out the method without giving it much thought. Exploration that involves creation of many special cases enables the learner to focus on the greater goal while at the same time wanting to get the answers to the particular cases, whereas learners have no particular interest in the answers to routine sets of exercises.

Exploiting Learners' Errors

One way to exploit errors, and to draw learners' attention to them without being critical, is to invite them to find instances in which the correct and the incorrect calculations do give the same answer. You might be fearful that rehearsing the incorrect calculation might make it even more robust, or that if it often gives a correct answer learners will adopt it. However, by contrasting correct and incorrect answers, the learners are also exercising the correct method; they are also using their natural powers and exercising their creativity in trying to construct other examples, which is much more pleasurable than simply rehearsing the correct calculation on a collection of examples assigned by the teacher.

Notes

1 Wendy Hoskin drew our attention to its particular richness. See Mason (1988) for this and many more situations for expressing generality.

2 See CME website: cme.open.ac.uk It was programmed by Roger Duke, based on ideas of Al Cuoco and Ken Ruthven.

3 Based on Leslie Booth in *Routes to Roots of Algebra* (J. Mason, A. Graham, D. Pimm and N. Gowar 1985) pp. 66–8, itself based on research at Chelsea College (CSMS and SESM) led by Kath Hart (Hart, K. (ed.) (1981) *Children's Understanding of Mathematics*).

8 Changing Representations

In the final chapter of Block 1, Chapter 4, you were presented with a range of forms of representation for depicting relationships. These were:

- words;
- symbols;
- tables;
- pictures (graphs and diagrams).

As Chapter 8 is the final chapter in Block 2, you are invited to return to these themes but with a slightly different emphasis: here the focus is on representations.

The sections are structured around moving *to* a particular representation, with opportunities to notice peculiarities that characterise each mode – symbols, graphs, tables and diagrams – words are the focus of Chapter 10. These themes and their interconnections are illustrated here by a regular tetrahedron, showing the representations as vertices.

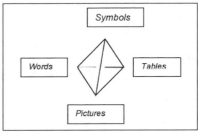

Simply by studying this diagram and relating it to the text above, you have already engaged with the key theme of the chapter of 'changing representations'. In this case, the particular interconnection is represented by the front left edge linking 'Words' with 'Pictures'.

Two other important themes of this chapter are the role of spreadsheets in depicting relationships and certain issues that affect students when moving from one format to another, an issue that is taken up in section 8.5.

8.1 TO SYMBOLS

Quickie 8.1

Spend a few minutes deciding what you think these signs refer to. Then check your answers with the list below.

(i)   (ii)   (iii)   (iv)

Quickie 8.1 (continued)

(v)   (vi)   (vii)   (viii)

(ix)

(i)   Yin and yang – a Chinese philosophy in which the universe is believed to be run by a single principle, the Tao, or Great Ultimate, which is a balance of two opposing forces.

(ii)   Male and female symbols.

(iii)   A road sign indicating a roundabout ahead.

(iv)   The 'cosmic egg' contains all of the numerals and alphabetical letters. It symbolises that all that can be numbered or named is contained in one form from the beginning and contains all human wisdom.

(v)   Wheelchair access.

(vi)   British kitemark indicating a certain standard of quality.

(vii)   Recycling symbol.

(viii)   Solar symbol (found on a Chinese drum, first century AD).

(ix)   The musical notation extract represents the opening notes of the French national anthem, *La Marseillaise*.

Choose two of the nine representations above and think about their design features; how do they represent the underlying idea? What has been stressed and what has been ignored?

Comment

Signs that are familiar, are 'obvious'; those that are unfamiliar can be very opaque indeed. Sometimes it is useful to distinguish between an *icon* and a *symbol*. An *icon* depicts what it represents in a manner that fits with the culture in which it is used: the roundabout sign is an example, because in cultures familiar with roundabouts the picture speaks what it refers to, whereas in cultures unfamiliar with roundabouts it is likely to be mysterious. In order to understand an icon, you need only be a member of the appropriate culture. To understand a *symbol*, you need to be told what it means, or otherwise inducted into its use.

This section focuses on the strengths and weaknesses of the symbolic mode of representation. You will look at a variety of shorthand notations, both mathematical and non-mathematical.

Jerome Bruner distinguished three different modes of representation, namely *enactive*, *iconic*, and *symbolic*, which can be thought of as three different 'worlds' in which people operate. *Enactive* refers to physically doing things, to overt behaviour, though it can be usefully extended to include symbol manipulation. *Iconic* refers to diagrams and pictures, which depict and which can easily be read without much if any instruction; symbolic, as the name suggests, refers to the use of abstract symbols. A picture of a cloud for a number that someone else is thinking of but which is not otherwise known is an *iconic* representation of an as-yet-unknown, whereas using a letter for the same purpose is *symbolic*. Bruner used his three modes of representation to suggest progression for learners, moving from manipulating objects (counters, rods, sticks, folding paper) to imagining moving the objects about, to denoting the movement of the objects by symbols.

A common complaint about algebra is that it is abstract. For those who become familiar with it, it is abstract in the way that 2 is an abstract representation of two apples. The point of algebra, or indeed of any shorthand notation, is to remove context, and deliberately so. This is the strength of any specialised notation: by abstracting an idea from its source and expressing its essence concisely, it becomes both rich and manipulable. That is not to argue that the context and the human dimension of situations are unimportant, but there are circumstances when it is valuable to *ignore* these aspects in order to *stress* underlying structure.

There are many shorthands beyond the world of algebra where richness and manipulability are evident, such as those in the next task.

Task 8.1.1 Everyday Shorthands

Try to identify the source of these shorthands and what they mean:

(a) PAS, MOT, fsh, £4500 ono.

(b) K1, P1, M2, C4F.

(c) det hse, lge gdns, gd decs, fsbo.

(d) WLTM tall N/S m, 40s, GSOH.

Comments

(a) Second-hand car sale: power-assisted steering, Ministry Of Transport Test, full service history, £4500 or near offer.

(b) Knitting pattern: Knit 1 (stitch), Purl 1, Make 2, Cable 4 forward

(c) Selling a house: detached house, large gardens, good decorations, for sale by owner

(d) Dating: would like to meet a tall non-smoking male, in his 40s with a good sense of humour.

How easy did you find this exercise? Clearly your ability to work out the code will be largely determined by how familiar you are with the context (second-hand car sales, knitting, and so on).

It would probably have been an easier exercise if you had been told the four contexts from the outset. The reason is that you would then have a narrower range of words to choose from when trying to match the initials. Without knowing the context, it may appear to be just a sea of letters with no underlying point or purpose – a common view of algebra held by many pupils and adults alike, who have not experienced expressing generality with symbols.

Task 8.1.2 Mathematical Shorthands

Below are three relationships, all expressed in different formats: words, table and a graph. Think about the underlying relationship being expressed in each case and re-present it using algebraic symbols.

(a) To work out a suitable dosage of certain medicines for a child, the rule is: divide the child's age by '12 more than her age'; then multiply the result by the full adult dosage. For example, an adult dose of a particular cough linctus is 15 mg. The dose for an eight year old child would be calculated as follows:

$(8/(8+12) \times 15 = 6$ mg.

(b) The following handy table will calculate prices inclusive of value added tax (VAT):

Price without VAT	£1.00	£2.00	£3.00	£4.00	£5.00
Price including VAT	£1.18	£2.35	£3.53	£4.70	£5.88
Price without VAT	£6.00	£7.00	£8.00	£9.00	£10.00
Price including VAT	£7.05	£8.23	£9.40	£10.58	£11.75

(c) The monthly charge for a telephone land-line, including the rental and the cost of making (national) calls, is summarised in the graph in Figure 8.1.

Comments

(a) $C = F \times A/(A+12)$ where child's dosage$= C$, the full adult dosage $= F$ and the age of the child $= A$.

(b) $V = 1.175N$ where the price including VAT $= V$ and the net price excluding VAT $= N$. The rate of VAT is taken to be 17.5%.

(c) The underlying relationship here is that there is a fixed monthly rental of roughly £17 and national calls are charged at 2.17 pence per minute (i.e. £1.30 per hour). This can be expressed as the following formula:

$C = 17 + 1.3H$ where C is the monthly charge (£) and H is the number of hours.

Recall from Chapter 3 that algebraic symbols are shorthand labels for quantities, not the symbol for the actual objects. For example, when using an algebraic shorthand for 'eight apples', the letter a stands for the number of apples (8) and not the 'measurement unit' (apples). This is a source of some confusion in many students' understanding of algebra that is sometimes referred to as 'fruit salad algebra' and was discussed in more detail.

For the remainder of this section you are asked to look at some particular standard types of representation and how they are expressed in symbols.

Direct and Inverse Proportion

In Chapter 4 you met examples of linear relationships of the form $y = ax + b$. A particular subset of this family of relationships contained those straight lines *that pass through the origin*; these were referred to as proportional relationships.

Where such lines have a positive gradient (i.e. their direction is from bottom left to top right) they are referred to as *directly proportional* relationships.

Remember that two quantities, x and y, are in direct proportion if multiplying x by a certain factor changes y by the same factor (for example, doubling x doubles y and vice versa).

Algebraically, a directly proportional relationship takes the form: $y = ax$, or sometimes $y = kx$ (where the values a, or k, are referred to as the 'constant of proportionality').

A feature of a directly proportional relationship is that it can be roughly explained in terms of the phrase, 'the more of x, the more of y'. However, this is potentially misleading; the two relationships $y = 3x$ and $y = 3x + 2$ can both be roughly explained as 'the more of x, the more of y', but only the relationship $y = 3x$ is one of direct proportion.

Inversely proportional relationships are those in which doubling x divides y by two, and more generally, multiplying x by a factor divides the corresponding y by the same factor. In other words, the product of the two quantities is constant. So direct proportion says that the ratio of the two quantities is constant (invariant), and indirect proportion says that the product of the two quantities is constant (invariant). Medieval university mathematics curricula consisted largely of learning rules for solving problems involving several quantities, some varying directly, and some inversely.

Sometimes people try to explain inverse proportion by the rough-and-ready slogan 'the more of x, the less of y'. However, this statement is too imprecise; it could be applied to a variety of different relationships and not all of them are inversely proportional. For example, consider the following statement: 'I start with a certain amount of spending money and the more I spend, the less I have left.' This is a relationship of the 'the more of x, the less of y' quality but it is not a relationship of inverse proportion. To aid precision, an algebraic formulation is often helpful and this is true in this case. Algebraically, an inversely proportional relationship takes the form: $xy = k$ (or it is sometimes rewritten as $y = k/x$) where k is constant.

Here are two examples:

The more quickly I run, the more distance I travel (directly proportional).
The more quickly I run, the less time it takes (inversely proportional).

Task 8.1.3 Direct and Inverse Proportion

Write the following relationships in the form of: 'the more … the more' or 'the more … the less'.

(i) The length of a hammer handle and the effort needed to pull out a nail.

(ii) The weight of flour and the number of loaves of bread it will make.

(iii) Converting temperature from degrees F to degrees C.

(iv) The number of (cooperating) workers and the time needed to finish a task.

(v) The number of postage stamps you buy and the amount you pay.

(vi) A rock band charged a fixed fee of £300 plus £100 per hour. The relationship between total fee and the number of hours they play.

(vii) The relationship between the average travelling speed and the journey time.

(viii) For a fixed journey time, the relationship between the journey-distance and average speed of travel.

(ix) For a fixed mass of material, the relationship between the density of the material, and the volume it occupies.

(x) When weighing samples of a certain material, the relationship between the size of sample and its weight.

Sort the ten examples into the headings 'direct proportion', 'inverse proportion' and 'non-proportional'.

Comment

(i) The longer the hammer handle the less effort needed to pull out a nail.

(ii) The heavier the flour the more loaves of bread it will make.

(iii) The more the temperature in degrees F, the more in degrees C.

(iv) The more workers the less time needed to finish a task.

(v) The more postage stamps you buy the more you pay.

Task 8.1.3 Direct and Inverse Proportion (continued)

(vi) The more hours the band plays, the more the fee.

(vii) The more the average travelling speed the less the journey time.

(viii) The more the journey-distance the more the average speed of travel. (Note that the question specifies 'for a *fixed* journey time'.)

(ix) The more the density of the material, the less volume it occupies.

(x)   The greater the size of sample the greater its weight.

The relationships can be classified as follows:

Directly proportional   (ii), (v), (viii), (x)

Inversely proportional   (i), (iv), (vii), (ix)

Non-proportional   (iii), (vi)

Some people prefer to use symbols to express relationships; others prefer words and others prefer pictorial representations, which are the subject of the next section.

Task 8.1.R Reflection

Think about your own use of symbols. What role do the symbols play in these cases?

Comment

The symbols that you use may take the role of shorthand, manipulable generalities or you may have thought of other roles.

8.2 TO GRAPHS

Quickie 8.2

Which of the following characteristics do you particularly associate with graphs as ways of depicting relationships:

(i)   enabling exact answers;

(ii) providing an overview;

(iii) exploiting symbols;

(iv) exploiting position and shape.

Comment

The two key features normally associated with graphical forms of representation are options (ii) and (iv) above. However, this depends on the reader discerning the appropriate elements and seeing the graph as representing these. A graph is not traditionally used as a precision tool for finding exact answers though experience of technology and the ability to 'zoom in' allows more accuracy (option (i)). Graphs are not predominately a symbolic medium of communication (option (iii)). Indeed, you may find learners who struggle with graphs are confident with symbols, and vice versa.

Unit Pricing

The term 'economies of scale' refers to the fact that it is often possible to get a reduction in unit price when buying in larger quantities. Taking the example in Figure 8.2, the unit price for buying one pint of prawns is £1.50, whereas the unit price drops to £1.25 (per pint) when two pints are bought. This phenomenon of offering a 'reduction for bulk purchase' is very common, whether you are buying the family-sized toothpaste tube, a tin of beans or a cereal package.

However, this sort of bulk discount does not always apply, even where you might expect it to, as emerged in section 5.3.

Some key features of pricing, and unit pricing in particular, can be helpfully represented graphically.

Taking the prawns data as an example, it is first set out as a table.

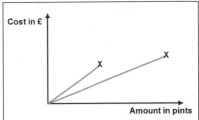

Amount in pints	Cost in £	Unit price per £
1	£1.50	£1.50
2	£2.50	£1.25

Now, the data in columns 1 and 2 of this table can be plotted as a graph – a rough sketch of this graph is shown in Figure 8.3.

Task 8.2.1 Prawns

Look at the points on the sketch graph in Figure 8.3.

(a) Which point corresponds to which price?

(b) What feature of each point indicates its unit price?

(c) What might you expect to pay for half a pint of prawns?

(d) Alternatively, the price can be thought of as paying 50 pence towards the cost of a container and £1.00 per pint of prawns. Sketch the graph that represents this relationship.

Comment

(a) The short line corresponds to the price of 1 pint and the longer (lower) line to the price of 2 pints.

(b) The key to a graphical understanding of unit price is that the *slope* of the line indicates the unit price – the steeper the line the greater the unit price.

(c) Intermediate points within the lines don't have much practical meaning. For example, a point lying halfway along the shorter line would correspond to half a pint of prawns and a price of £0.75. These prawns are not available in half pint sizes and even if they were, there is no certainty that they would be sold at 75 pence.

(d) The graph should start at 50 pence on the vertical axis.

Task 8.2.2 Petrol and Cereals

The two sketches in Figure 8.4 represent the cost graphs for three sizes of cereal packet (small, medium and large) and three petrol purchases representing different quantities of petrol. One is appropriate and the other is not.

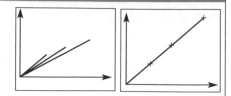

(a) Decide which sketch corresponds to which situation and give a reason for your choice.

(b) What practical meaning can be attached to other intermediate points lying on these two lines?

(c) Redraw the sketch for which the intermediate points have no meaning

Comment

(a) The first sketch corresponds to the packets of cereal and the second sketch to the petrol purchases. Note that the unit price of the petrol is fixed, regardless of the amount bought, and so the slopes of the three lines are the same. With cereal packages, on the other hand there are economies of scale to be made.

(b) Intermediate points are meaningless for the cereal example as they suggest amounts and prices that are not available. However, there are many other valid intermediate points in the petrol example. Note: these comments suggest that, for the cereal example, the use of line graphs is not appropriate since they imply a continuity that is not present here. An alternative would be to express each price/amount combination as a separate point that is not joined to the origin. This would help to emphasise the discrete nature of these data.

Absolute Value

In this subsection, you are asked to explore the 'absolute value function'. It is included here to illustrate a particular piece of algebraic shorthand, albeit one that is normally associated with more advanced work in mathematics.

The absolute value (or modulus) function is a mathematician's way of capturing the *size* of a number while disregarding its *sign* (i.e. whether it is positive or negative). It is simply 'the positive value of'. For example, the absolute value of 3 is 3, but the absolute value of $^-7$ is 7. The absolute value of x (sometimes referred to as the 'modulus of x' or simply 'mod x') is written as x contained inside two vertical lines, thus: $|x|$.

The modulus can also be considered as the distance of the value from zero on the number-line. If you consider the equation $|x - 1| = 2$, this can be interpreted as defining a point, x, on the number-line that is distance 2 from 1. There are actually two such points, $x = 3$ and $x = ^-1$ and this illustrates the fact that equations involving a modulus will usually have several solutions.

Task 8.2.3 Plotting the Absolute Value

Sketch the graph of $y = |x|$. What is the same and what different about that and the line $y = x$?

Now imagine the graph of $y = |x - 2|$ before sketching it.

Comment

If you find it difficult to get started on this task, you might like to switch to another format; for example, a table of values. Some suggestions for sketching these graphs are given here.

It may not be immediately obvious why this zig-zag pattern has resulted from this function. In order to grasp what is going on, try to build up to the function gradually by picturing in your mind the following graphs in turn:

$y = x$; $y = |x|$; $y = |x| - 2$; $y = ||x| - 2|$.

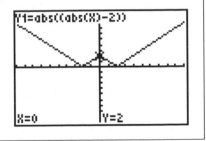

With sufficient experience of using graphic representation, the learner begins to discern and interpret essential elements such as slope and points of intersection with less reliance on the tabular representation.

Pause for Reflection

Task 8.2.R Reflection

The mathematics of the modulus function is more advanced than much of the mathematics in the rest of this chapter. How did you feel about being asked to tackle this mathematical ideal? Were there learning issues for you that could inform your teaching in the future?

Comment

Research has shown that teachers who continue to engage in learning and doing mathematics themselves make better teachers of mathematics (Ahmed 1987).

8.3 TO TABLES

Quickie 8.3

Write down one strength and one weakness of laying out information in the form of a *table*.

Comment

Whereas graphs and formulae are powerful general forms of representation that are good at drawing attention to the overall pattern of the relationship, the main feature of a table is that it lets you quickly find information about a *particular* value. So, the strength in using a table is to find a particular piece of information, while its weakness (in comparison to a graph or formula) is that it is a poor way of considering the overall underlying relationship.

This section looks at some of the strengths and weaknesses of a table for conveying information about relationships. Because spreadsheets are a very efficient way of organising information into tabular form, much of the content of this section will relate to spreadsheet use.

Task 8.3.1 From Formula to Table

In Task 8.1.2 you saw the following formula used for calculating a child's drug dose, based on the age of the child and the amount of the adult dose: $C = F \times A/(A+12)$ where C is the child's dose, F is the full adult dose and A is the child's age.

Create a spreadsheet table suitable for calculating the dose of a particular cough linctus for children aged 1 to 10 (using intervals of 1 year), assuming that a full adult dose is 10 mg. Round the answers to the nearest mg.

Adapt the spreadsheet so that the full adult dose is entered into a separate cell and this cell reference is then used in the calculation for the child dose.

Comment

Your solution might look something like this.

	A	B	C
1	Age/years	Child's dose	Full Adult Dose
2	1	1	10
3	2	1	
4	3	2	
5	4	3	
6	5	3	
7	6	3	
8	7	4	
9	8	4	
10	9	4	
11	10	5	
12			

	A	B	C
1	Age/years	Child's dose	Full Adult Dose
2	1	=$C$2*(A2/(A2+12))	10
3	2	=$C$2*(A3/(A3+12))	
4	3	=$C$2*(A4/(A4+12))	
5	4	=$C$2*(A5/(A5+12))	
6	5	=$C$2*(A6/(A6+12))	
7	6	=$C$2*(A7/(A7+12))	
8	7	=$C$2*(A8/(A8+12))	
9	8	=$C$2*(A9/(A9+12))	
10	9	=$C$2*(A10/(A10+12))	
11	10	=$C$2*(A11/(A11+12))	
12			
13			

Spreadsheet screens showing child dosages based on a full adult dose of 10 mg

The advantage of setting the full adult dose in a separate cell is that you need only adjust the value in this cell to create a new table based on any dose you choose, as you will see in the next task.

Task 8.3.2 Adjusting the Full Adult Dose

Adapt the spreadsheet to create child dose tables corresponding to full adult doses of 15 mg and 20 mg.

Comment

It is a moment's work to adjust the value in cell C2 to 15 and 20, respectively, giving the spreadsheet tables shown opposite. This example indicates something of the power of a spreadsheet once it has been set up properly. By storing the full adult dose value *in a separate cell* (in this case, cell C2) the problem can easily be adapted to fit different data. There are strong parallels here with the shift from arithmetic to algebra. A one-off calculation involving arithmetic is merely that – a one-off, capable of solving only the problem in hand. However, generalise the problem by representing the key variables using letters rather than numbers and you create a formula that can be applied across a wide variety of situations. It is this urge to look for general solutions that seems to be the chief characteristic of mathematical thinking.

◇	A	B	C
1	Age/years	Child's dose	Full Adult Dose
2	1	1	15
3	2	2	
4	3	3	
5	4	4	
6	5	4	
7	6	5	
8	7	6	
9	8	6	
10	9	6	
11	10	7	

◇	A	B	C
1	Age/years	Child's dose	Full Adult Dose
2	1	2	20
3	2	3	
4	3	4	
5	4	5	
6	5	6	
7	6	7	
8	7	7	
9	8	8	
10	9	9	
11	10	9	

Simulating dice scores

This subsection looks at another powerful spreadsheet command that has wide applications in mathematics. This is the command that rounds a (decimal) number *down* to the nearest integer. On a spreadsheet it is called int (i.e. the integer part of). As you will see later in this subsection, it is also known as the 'floor' function.

A spreadsheet context in which one might wish use the int command is any investigation involving the generation or simulation of dice scores.

Task 8.3.3 Dice Rolling

Imagine rolling a die twelve times.

(a)   Write down a typical string of outcomes that you might get.

(b)   Now write down the constraints that effect these outcomes.

Comment

(a)   A typical string of outcomes might look like the following: 3, 2, 1, 3, 6, 5, 6, 2, 4, 1, 1, 2.

(b)   There are at least three important constraints: the outcomes are integers; the outcomes lie in the range 1 to 6 inclusive; the outcomes are all equally likely (although it is unlikely in a short sequence of rolls that each outcome will occur exactly twice). One constraint that does *not* apply to this situation is that an outcome is affected by the outcomes that occurred earlier in the sequence. On the contrary, each outcome is *independent* of all the other outcomes – an important characteristic of any *random number generator* (such as dice, coins, spinners, etc.).

Task 8.3.4 Simulating Dice Scores on a Spreadsheet

You are now asked to simulate dice scores on a spreadsheet. To do this you will start with the random command =**rand()** and then make a series of adjustments to it. As you work through the steps below, try to keep in mind that you want to end up with a command that works in the same way as a die, namely that it generates the integers 1 to 6 so that each outcome is equally likely.

(a)   Open a new spreadsheet screen (Figure 8.20) and enter into cell A1 the command =**rand()**. Now select cell A1 and fill down as far as cell A12. As you might have already guessed, the random command =**rand()** generates a random decimal number between 0 and 1.

(b)   In order to increase the range of values to 0–6, try multiplying the command by 6. Enter into cell B1 the command =**6*rand()**. As before, select this cell again and fill down as far as cell B12. Look at the outputs and consider how closely these match dice scores.

◇	A	B
1	0.30569203	0.05318038
2	0.41276885	1.55250396
3	0.01416711	2.4093565
4	0.34656254	5.55813776
5	0.80206927	5.73887772
6	0.33362259	4.78604118
7	0.71877674	0.9784136
8	0.3176692	4.26796404
9	0.04055743	0.94281444
10	0.52582184	2.64854797
11	0.30765618	2.65755867
12	0.70264242	1.15167154

Task 8.3.4 Simulating Dice Scores on a Spreadsheet (continued)

(c) In order to restrict the output to integer values, try taking the integer part, using the command =**int**. Enter into cell C1 the command =**int(6*RAND())**. As before, select this cell again and fill down as far as cell C12. Consider how closely the numbers in column C match dice scores.

(d) The fatal flaw with the numbers in column C is that they are integers in the range 0–5, rather than 1–6. A simple solution is to add 1 to the command in part (c). Enter into column D 12 simulated dice scores. These are shown alongside a spreadsheet screen showing the formulae required to complete the spreadsheet.

◇	A	B	C	D
1	0.59279103	4.23847357	5	6
2	0.01203784	5.3168778	1	1
3	0.4349889	0.32485329	0	5
4	0.23732741	5.65210797	4	6
5	0.00382146	4.62037687	0	1
6	0.74187478	5.98915482	1	5
7	0.16354061	2.75744855	5	2
8	0.34369809	4.17020093	2	6
9	0.67025715	0.81126803	0	4
10	0.80679289	0.73123883	4	6

◇	A	B	C	D
1	=RAND()	=RAND()*6	=INT(RAND()*6)	=INT(RAND()*6)+1
2	=RAND()	=RAND()*6	=INT(RAND()*6)	=INT(RAND()*6)+1
3	=RAND()	=RAND()*6	=INT(RAND()*6)	=INT(RAND()*6)+1
4	=RAND()	=RAND()*6	=INT(RAND()*6)	=INT(RAND()*6)+1
5	=RAND()	=RAND()*6	=INT(RAND()*6)	=INT(RAND()*6)+1
6	=RAND()	=RAND()*6	=INT(RAND()*6)	=INT(RAND()*6)+1
7	=RAND()	=RAND()*6	=INT(RAND()*6)	=INT(RAND()*6)+1
8	=RAND()	=RAND()*6	=INT(RAND()*6)	=INT(RAND()*6)+1
9	=RAND()	=RAND()*6	=INT(RAND()*6)	=INT(RAND()*6)+1
10	=RAND()	=RAND()*6	=INT(RAND()*6)	=INT(RAND()*6)+1

SIMULATED DICE SCORES IN COLUMN D

This dice score simulation raises questions about some of the other possible functions that can be applied to any decimal number to output a corresponding integer value. There are three useful functions that might be used:

The *floor function*, also called the greatest integer function, gives the largest integer less than or equal to x (see task 2.1.2b). It is often denoted as $\lfloor x \rfloor$. For example, applying the floor function to the number 7.31 gives the result 7. This is written as follows: $\lfloor 7.31 \rfloor = 7$

In many computer languages, the floor function is called the *integer part* function. On a spreadsheet it is denoted by the =**int()** and the =**rounddown()** commands, but these two commands work in slightly different ways; the **int** command will round to an integer value whereas the **rounddown** command allows the user to set the number of decimal places to which the rounding should occur. Note that another term for rounding down is *truncating*.

The *ceiling function* gives the smallest integer greater than or equal to x. It is often denoted as $\lceil x \rceil$. For example, applying the floor function to the number 7.31 gives the result 8. This is written as follows: $\lceil 7.31 \rceil = 8$ (see task 2.1.2b).

On a spreadsheet this function is denoted by the =**roundup()** command. Like the **rounddown** command, it allows the user to set the number of decimal places to which the rounding should occur.

The *nearest integer function* of x is the integer closest to x. Since this definition is ambiguous for half-integers (4.5, 6.5, etc.), there needs to be a convention. The most common method is to round up. There is an alternative convention, used in statistics, that half-integers are always rounded to even numbers in order to avoid statistical bias. On a spreadsheet, this function is denoted by the =**round()** command. For example, the command =**round(4.26,1)** will round 4.26 to one decimal place, giving the number 4.3.

Task 8.3.5 From Floor to Ceiling

The symbol $\lceil x \rceil$ denotes the smallest integer greater than or equal to x. The symbol $\lfloor x \rfloor$ denotes the largest integer less than or equal to x.

(a) Sketch the graphs of $\lceil x \rceil$ and $\lfloor x \rfloor$ on the same sketch. Then check your sketches using a spreadsheet.

(b) Did anything surprise you? If so, what was it and why were you surprised?

Comments

To get you started on the first of these graphs ($y = \lceil x \rceil$), try the following steps:

- Enter ⁻3 in cell A1 and ⁻2.9 in cell A2.
- Select cells A1:A2 and fill down as far as cell A61.
- In cell B1, enter the command **=roundup(A1,0)**. Notice that there are two 'arguments' contained inside the brackets. The first, A1, is the number to be rounded and the second (in this case, 0) is the number of decimal places to which the rounding is to take place. So, this command rounds the value in A2 up to the nearest integer, i.e. to 0 decimal places.
- Select cell B1 and fill down to cell B61. You now have, in columns A and B, the data needed to plot the graph $y = \lceil x \rceil$.

Pause for Reflection

Task 8.3.R Reflection

What have you learned about moving to and from tables as a form of representation?

What special properties are there of information stored in a spreadsheet that distinguish it from data stored in a table on paper?

8.4 TO AND BETWEEN DIAGRAMS

Quickie 8.4

By now you have seen that the first two blocks of the book have been organised into parallel chapters around four themes: expressing generality, mathematical powers, symbols and forms of representation.

Create a diagrammatic representation of the first 12 chapters to emphasise this pattern.

What mathematical properties have you exploited to emphasise this pattern?

Comments

A possible diagrammatic representation might look something like this:

1	5	9
2	6	10
3	7	11
4	8	12

The following mathematical properties underpin this diagram:

- Repeating patterns (it repeats every fourth chapter).
- Use of a diagram in which the repeating pattern is depicted by the position of the numbers.

This section looks at some of the strengths and weaknesses of a diagram for conveying information about relationships.

Task 8.4.1 Older Than

Five people are standing in a row. The first (left-most) is three years older than the second who is two years younger than the third who is five years younger than the fourth who is one year older than the fifth.

Without writing or drawing, can you get an idea of who is older, the first or the fifth person? What is your reasoning? Can you put them in increasing order of age?

Think back to the three forms of representation used by Jerome Bruner – enactive, iconic and symbolic. Find a way of representing this information in each of these ways. What possibilities are afforded by the different representations?

Comment

It is difficult to keep all of this information in your head in order to process it as a whole and some form of representation would be useful to get a handle on it.

Representing the Information Enactively

A suitable enactive representation might be to use rods, with each new rod length defined in terms of the previous rod. In order to compare the five rods at the end, it is necessary to mark off the units. Notice that the actual lengths of the rods are irrelevant (it is only their relative lengths that matters) so the left-hand portions of the rods have been deliberately not marked off in units.

DIAGRAMMATIC REPRESENTATION OF THE FIVE AGES

Representing the Information Iconically

Here you are looking for some sort of diagram or picture. One possible approach would be to use the number-line as shown (A is the first person and E is the fifth).

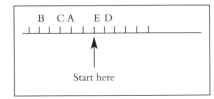

Representing the Information Symbolically

A symbolic representation might involve letting the first person be x years old. The age of each person can then be worked out as follows.

First person	x
Second person	$x - 3$
Third person	$x - 3 + 2 = x - 1$
Fourth person	$x - 1 + 5 = x + 4$
Fifth person	$x + 4 - 1 = x + 3$

From the algebraic symbols, it is easy to see that the fifth person is (three years) older than the first person and the order of their ages, from youngest to oldest is: second, third, first, fifth and fourth. Notice that these results hold true regardless of the value of x. This point is mirrored in the other two solutions where the starting point of the comparisons is arbitrary.

Transitivity and Transitive Ordering

Some ideas are difficult to explain in words but a helpful diagram can make the idea more accessible.

In this section you are asked to consider the concepts *transitivity* and *intransitivity* through the medium of two simple games and then to explore how a diagrammatic representation of the games can help reveal their mathematical structure.

Transitivity in mathematics is a property of relationships in which objects of a similar nature may connect to each other according to the relationship in question. A particular relationship is transitive if, whenever object A is related to B and object B is related to C, then object A is also related to C. For example, the relationship 'is older than' is necessarily transitive since, if A is older than B and B is older than C, then A is also older than C. The relationship 'is the parent of' is not transitive – check it out for yourself!

Most measurement is transitive (length, weight, time, temperature, and so on) but occasionally one's expectation of transitivity is confounded. For example, in soccer, Bolton Wanderers might have beaten Chelsea and Chelsea might have beaten Manchester United, but do not bet against Manchester United when they take the field to play Bolton Wanderers!

A classic two-player *intransitive* game that is played all over the world is 'Rock, Paper, Scissors'.

Contrary to the photograph:

Rock beats (blunts) scissors;

Scissors beat (cut) paper;

Paper beats (covers) stone.

Expressed mathematically:

R > S and S > P but R < P.

SCISSORS SPEARS ROCK!

The two players face each other and at the same instant choose to display one of the three objects, forming their hand into an appropriate shape, as shown in the photographs overleaf.

PAPER

ROCK

SCISSORS

PAPER COVERS ROCK

ROCK BLUNTS SCISSORS

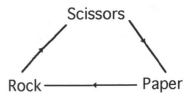

SCISSORS CUT PAPER

The pictures are taken from two people playing 'Rock, Paper, Scissors'.

Task 8.4.2 Diagrams for Transitivity and Intransitivity

Use arrow diagrams to indicate the transitivity or intransitivity inherent in the following two games:

(a) Two people roll a die and the higher score wins.

(b) Two people play 'Rock, Paper, Scissors'.

Comment

Here are two possible diagrams. In each case, the arrow indicates 'is greater than'. For example, A —>—B means 'A is greater than B'.

6 —>—5 —>—4 —>—3 —>—2 —>—1

Scissors

Rock ————←———— Paper

Rolling a die: a transitive game   'Rock, Paper, Scissors': an intransitive game
Notice that the diagram is *linear*.   Notice that the diagram is *cyclic*.

In this task, the form of representations used (in this case, linear and cyclic) helped you to see at a glance the nature of the underlying relationship (respectively, transitive and intransitive).

Pause for Reflection

Task 8.4.R Reflection

Recall an example from your personal life where a diagram proved to be helpful to you. What in particular did the diagram provide that words or symbols could not?

Comment

The guides that accompany self-assembly furniture may not always be very clearly worded but the drawings and diagrams are usually very helpful. In particular, these diagrams mark out the stages of assembly by showing visually what you need to achieve step by step. These diagrams also provide useful information that cannot easily be explained in words, such as the correct orientation of various components and the match between holes and their appropriate screws.

8.5 PEDAGOGICAL ISSUES

Quickie 8.5

Can you think of a practical everyday example (outside the world of education) where *you* created a picture, a graph and an algebraic formula as aids to your thinking. If you can think of some examples, make a note of them for future use in your teaching. If you are unable to think of any worthwhile examples, consider the implications of this in terms of how mathematical skills are 'sold' to students as useful life skills.

This chapter has been mostly about the range of different formats available for depicting a relationship – words, pictures (including graphs and diagrams), tables and symbols. Each form of representation has its particular strengths and weaknesses, depending on the context and the purpose for which the information is to be communicated.

What then are the implications of these representations for teaching and learning? Specifically, what is it about the notion of depiction that you feel your pupils really need to know? Here are two possible answers to this question, which form the basis of this final section: stressing and ignoring, and awareness of modes of representation.

Stressing and Ignoring

Quickie 8.1 illustrates forcefully the way in which people's attention changes when trying to make sense of something. There is an immediate sense of a whole. Certain details also stand out, almost instantly. It sometimes requires an effort of will to attend to other details that do not immediately strike attention. In this way the brain automatically and naturally stresses some features and ignores others. The ones stressed tend to be those features that resonate most strongly with past experience.

The same thing happens when looking at a picture, a poster, a text, a screen or a collection of mathematical symbols. Some features are stressed, while others are effectively ignored. This can be tested by asking learners to Say What You See when looking at a picture, animation, or even a collection of exercises or a mathematical expression. How often have you read a page of text containing a table of data and found your eyes 'jumping' over the table almost as if it were invisible. Sometimes it even emerges when learners are asked to read out some text containing mathematical symbols with which they are not perfectly familiar. In each case, some things will get mentioned, while others seem to be ignored.

Caleb Gattegno suggested that stressing and ignoring is the basis for generalisation and abstraction. For example, in the sequence

$$2 \times 3 + 1, 2 \times 4 + 1, 2 \times 5 + 1$$

it is entirely natural to become aware of some features changing and others staying the same. By stressing what is invariant in the midst of change, attention is drawn to structure, here expressed in general as $2 \times n + 1$.

Task 8.5.1 Stressing or Ignoring Drugs

In Task 8.1.2, you looked at the following formula for calculating a child's dosage, C, based on the full adult dose, F, and the child's age, A:

$C = F \times (A/(A + 12))$

When a relationship is represented algebraically like this, what is being stressed and what is ignored?

Comment

An algebraic formula stresses the nature of the interrelationships between the variables under consideration. For example, the full adult dose, F is multiplied by a factor $A/(A+12)$. For all children's ages that you might consider, this factor will always be a number less than one, so the Child's dose is inevitably less than the adult dose. Furthermore, the fraction $A/(A+12)$ will be smallest for small values of A and largest for large values of A. (If you are not immediately convinced by this, try substituting some values for A into the fraction.) So, a simple analysis of the structure of this formula confirms what commonsense would dictate – it ensures that the child's dose is always smaller than the adult dose and also that the younger the child, the smaller the dose. This may seem like a fairly obvious example, but there are many other situations such as government funding formulae for school, where insight into the nature and weightings of the variables may provide educators with very striking insights into what is really valued by government.

Note that it is uniquely the symbolic form of representation that provides this sort of information – other forms of depiction such as a table or graph could never provide such insights.

What is ignored by an algebraic formula is the context from which the letters have been taken. The point has already been made in this chapter that the whole point of algebra is to use symbols to deal with the relationship in the abstract so that underlying structures can be analysed without the 'noise' created by its context.

Awareness of Modes of Representation

Clearly, in the area of mathematical representations, pupils need to master a number of practical or technical skills. But it is not enough merely to be able to manipulate a formula, draw a graph, handle data in a table and so on. When they have acquired a degree of mastery of their various forms of representation, pupils must develop skills in knowing which type of depiction to choose. This means that they need to be aware of the range of possible formats available and to know something about their strengths and weaknesses, and learn to use one to inform the other. It also requires some flexibility of thinking so that they can move between formats as required.

It may come as something of a surprise to some learners to discover that for many problems there is not always a single best method of solution. Here is an example taken from the Open University residential course MEXR624, Developing Mathematical Thinking at Key Stage 3, Module 2: Targeting thinking.

Task 8.5.2a Farmyard

A farmyard contains both chicken and sheep. The farmer knows there are 26 heads and 74 legs. How many chickens and how many sheep are in the yard?

Students were invited to tackle this question collectively, using as many different forms of solution as they could think of. They tried a wide range of approaches, including using logic, acting, drawing a picture, and guessing and checking. Here are some of their solutions.

Equation 1: If c is number of chickens then

$26 - c$ is number of sheep.

$2c + 4(26 - c) = 74$ (number of legs).

Solve for c, and find $26 - c$.

Equation 2: Let c = number of chickens, and s = number of sheep.

Then, $c + s = 26, 2c + 4s = 74$.

Solve for c and s, algebraically or graphically.

Logic: Each of the 26 heads has at least 2 legs. That uses 52 legs, which means that $74 - 52 = 22$ are left over. So, 11 have 4 legs; i.e. there are 11 sheep. The remaining 15 $(26 - 11)$ are therefore chickens.

Acting: 26 people stand up on 2 feet, that uses 52 legs; these legs currently represent 26 chickens. Now one at a time as I count in twos, one person is to move to the sheep 'pen' and raise their arms. $54, 56, 58, \ldots, 74$. Stop! Now count the sheep and the chickens.

Now add 2 legs to each, then add more in twos, counting as you go from 52 until you reach 74.

Guess and improve: half each, 13 chickens (26 legs) and 13 sheep (52 legs). Total legs = 78, too many, try one less sheep and one more chicken, 14 chicken, 12 sheep, (2 x 14 + 4 x 12)=76 legs, still too many, try 15 chicken, 11 sheep, …

These students were quite amazed at the many interesting solutions they came up with; of course no single one of them was 'the correct' method of solution.

Task 8.5.2b Ease of Generalisation

Returning to the farmyard question, follow each approach in turn but in the general case where there are *H* heads and *F* feet. Which approaches lend themselves most easily to generalisation? What is a learner learning if they use a method for which generalisation is difficult?

Three Modes

Whereas previous chapters have drawn attention to symbols, images (drawing, pictures, diagrams, graphs, tables) and physical objects as ways of expressing mathematical structures (relationships), this chapter has drawn attention to transitions between these different forms of representation. In particular, you have worked with Jerome Bruner's three modes of representation, *enactive, iconic* and *symbolic*. In this section you are asked to consider the relevance of Bruner's ideas to your own teaching.

The enactive mode means that learners physically manipulate objects that have become familiar to them. This includes such physical activity as moving coloured rods around, using an abacus, pouring water between containers, handling objects such as polygons and polyhedra, and so on. But it also includes manipulating 'things' that have become objects through familiarity. Thus, numerals such as 7, 77 and 700000007 are abstractly symbolic when first encountered in primary school but, as the learner gains in confidence and experience, these numerals become familiar and object-like as numbers, so that they can be manipulated mentally, almost as if they were physical objects.

The iconic mode refers to images that 'look like what they represent', although they may need to be placed within a familiar cultural context to be so readily interpreted. A picture of a bundle of ten sticks can easily stand for or represent an actual bundle of ten sticks; a drawing of some rods, even a graph of a relationship, can, for those familiar with what is being represented, have the quality of 'speaking without effort to interpret' what they represent.

The symbolic mode refers to labels and signs that by convention are used to represent something else. Thus letters represent sounds and strings of letters represent words that you have to have learned to interpret, because the choice of sign or symbol is entirely arbitrary and conventional.

These three modes are conveniently labelled as EIS, which is a (symbolic) shorthand for Enactive–Iconic–Symbolic. The elaboration above suggests that these modes are not fixed, but rather change with the experience of the learner: what is symbolic at one time can become enactive through familiarity.

The empty number-line is an example of the use of something physical that moves through iconic to symbolic form: young children moving themselves along a number-line, then moving their finger, then imagining moving their finger, then moving a mental point. At first the number-line has numbers on it, but over time learners develop familiarity so as to be able to impose numbers as required on the blank sheet.

Connections with Specialising and Generalising

Notice links between EIS and specialising and generalising. The purpose of specialising is to manipulate familiar objects in order to get a sense of what is going on more generally. In other words, people quite naturally look for something familiar to manipulate (move into an enactive mode) during which time certain features are stressed and consequently others are ignored. Articulating what is being stressed is expressing generality, and when denoted succinctly, uses symbolic mode of representation. Along the way various iconic substitutes may be employed.

Connections with MGA

As long ago as Plato (500 BCE), people extolled the use of enactive representations when teaching arithmetic (using physical objects to count, manipulate, etc.). Bruner described teaching as a movement between modes. Learners are given familiar objects to manipulate (are shown or encounter some phenomenon, perhaps a moving image on a screen or something happening physically). Ways of recording the phenomenon are developed, usually through some sort of more or less iconic representation (perhaps a picture). For example, using a cloud to represent a number that someone is thinking of, but which is not actually known, is using a cultural icon of a speech or thought bubble. Bruner referred to using objects physically, then having them just out of reach so as to support mental images of using them, and drawings of their use, until the recording in pictures becomes tedious and learners move naturally to succinct symbolic labels.

Task 8.5.2 Enacting Algebra

By its nature, algebraic notation is a symbolic form. Using Bruner's EIS model, can you think of situations where algebra might be seen as being used 'enactively' or 'iconically' by a learner?

Comment

The use of small boxes, each containing a particular but unknown number of matches can be made the basis of tackling early algebraic equations *enactively*. For example, the photographs in Figure 8.30 shows how a student, Lucy, set up the equation $3x + 4 = 13$ and went on to solve this equation by removing matches and boxes from both sides of the equal sign while always maintaining the equality of the equation (she did not, of course, open the boxes during the solution phase!). Once Lucy had mastered the principle of enacting equation-solving in this way, she began to draw the boxes and matches on paper and solve the equations iconically. Eventually she made the switch from pictures to symbolic notation. For this particular student these enactive and iconic experiences were an essential foundation on which she was able to build her symbolic skills. Note that the teacher provided her with several boxes, each containing the same number of matches, but this number was unknown to Lucy in advance.

The set-up: the equation $3x + 4 = 13$ is modelled using boxes and matches.

… suggesting that there are 3 matches in each box.

The first simplification – removing 4 matches from each side.

Finally, one of the boxes is opened to reveal that Lucy had indeed solved the equation correctly.

Sharing out the 9 matches among the three boxes …

Task 8.5.3 Bringing it All Together

An important awareness for students to achieve is the equivalence of different forms (verbal, symbolic and graphical) in the representation of a given relationship. Can you devise a card game that might help students to develop these multiple perspectives?

Comment

One solution might be to prepare a set of cards that contained depictions of, say, ten different relationships in word, graphs and symbols (making 30 cards in all). The cards could be used in a game format (maybe 'Happy Families' or 'Pelmanism'). Examples of such cards are given in the appendix to this chapter.

Pause for Reflection

Task 8.5.R Reflection

In what ways have your views about algebra remained the same, and in what ways have they changed, as a result of your reading and work so far?

What contributions are made to your learning by reading the text, reading tasks, doing tasks, reading comments, discussing and trying out with others?

How might your observations inform how you work with other learners?

APPENDIX

Take a number, double it and add 3.	Take a number and subtract 4.
$y = 2x + 3$	$y = x - 4$

Notes

1 Private communication. This was brought to our attention by Jackie Fairchild.

Introduction to Block 3

The four chapters in Block 3 revisit the ideas from previous blocks, but with further sophistication.

Chapter 9 continues the themes of Chapters 1 and 5 by providing further exposure to contexts in which generalising (and specialising) can be encouraged. Chapter 10 continues the themes of Chapters 2 and 6 by focusing on the natural power to organise and characterise things by their properties.

Chapter 11 continues the themes of Chapters 3 and 7 by developing the notions of multiple expressions for the same generality, and expressions of constraints on a generality, as routes to and motivation for the rules for manipulating algebraic symbols, and the roles that symbols play in mathematics. Chapter 11 also addresses the teaching of reasoning.

Chapter 12 continues the e-tool theme of Chapters 4 and 8 by developing the use of graph plotters as a tool for exploring different representations of relationships.

9 Yet More Expressing Generality

Chapter 9 provides a visit to expressing generality from new areas. Every mathematician can benefit from regular practice in 'seeing through the particular to the general' and expressing those generalities in several different forms. It is also useful to take an expression arising from a context, and to try to 'see' the situation through the structure of the expression. Section 9.1 studies the greatest common divisor and the least common multiples of two numbers. Section 9.2 is based in triangles. Section 9.3 is based in school subjects other than mathematics. Section 9.4 considers tables of data and considers when there is sufficient, or insufficient, information to reconstruct a table when some values are obliterated. Section 9.5 is about the opportunities afforded, by every teaching page of every mathematics textbook, to generalise in order to appreciate what the page is about.

9.1 MULTIPLES AND FACTORS

Quickie 9.1

Show that $2^{\left(2^2\right)} = (2^2)^2$ but that $3^{\left(3^3\right)} \neq (3^3)^3$

In this chapter, the arithmetic operations *greatest common divisor* (GCD) and *least common multiple* (LCM) are introduced as contexts in which to work on expressing generality. They also illustrate two ways of thinking about numbers: in base-ten notation and as products of primes.

LCM and GCD/HCF

For any two whole numbers, there is a smallest number they both divide into without remainder (*lowest common multiple* or LCM), and a largest that divides into both (*greatest common divisor* or GCD, also known as the *highest common factor* or HCF). There are also two different ways of presenting numbers: in base-ten notation (e.g. 8568) and as a product of factors (e.g. $2^3 \times 3^2 \times 7 \times 17$). It seems that many learners do not 'see' $2^3 \times 3^2 \times 7 \times 17$ as 'a number', just as a calculation to find a number. When presented as a product of factors, finding the LCM and the GCD/HCF is relatively straightforward:

Task 9.1.1 Prime Factored

Find the LCM and the GCD/HCF of $2 \times 3^2 \times 5$ and $2^2 \times 3 \times 5^2$.

State in words a procedure for finding the LCM and GCD (or HCF) of two numbers presented in factored form as a product of powers of primes.

Comment

If learners do not think of $2 \times 3^2 \times 5$ as a number, they are likely to multiply out before looking for factors, overlooking the fact that they are given all the prime factors and their multiplicities already. Trying to say in words how you work your way through the primes finding the highest power of each is not easy to make precise. It can take time for learners to bring to articulation the sense that they are getting as they manipulate particular examples. Trying to say it to someone else can be helpful before trying to record it in words and or symbols.

To exercise thinking in terms of products of factors, the next task involves pattern spotting using this form. If learners have not worked with numbers in factored form, they are unlikely to think to use factored form when tackling a question in which factoring makes spotting connections and relations a lot easier.

Task 9.1.2 Seeking Structure

Given that there is a pattern in the following sequences, find a rule that will generate the sequence, and that will continue indefinitely. Specify a direct way to calculate the nth term:[1]

$2, 2^2 \times 3, 2^3 \times 3^2 \times 5, 2^4 \times 3^3 \times 5^2 \times 7, \ldots$
$2, 2 \times 3, 2^2 \times 3, 2^2 \times 3^2, 2^3 \times 3^2, 2^3 \times 3^3, \ldots$
$2, 2^2, 5, 2^3, 2 \times 5, 2^4, 2^2 \times 5. 5^2, 2^3 \times 5, 2^5, \ldots$
$1, 4, 27, 256, \ldots$

Make up your own sequence using powers.

Comment

If you are not used to thinking of numbers as products of powers of primes, then it may take a while to get used to looking at the structure and letting go of thinking about the sizes of the numbers. For the first sequence, the power of each prime increases by one each term, and the next prime has a power of 1. For the second sequence, the next term is the previous term multiplied either by 2 or by 3, alternately. So the $2n^{\text{th}}$ term will be $2^n \times 3^n$, and the $(2n - 1)$th term will be $2^n \times 3^{n-1}$.

For the third sequence, think 2s and 5s and size of numbers.

For the fourth, think factors!

Sometimes it is useful to see numbers in the order and sequence of counting; sometimes in terms of products of factors, or even of products of powers of primes.

Both LCM and GCD/HCF involve thinking multiplicatively about numbers, so perhaps they are related in some way?

Task 9.1.3 LCM and GCD

What relationships can you find between the GCD (or HCF) and the LCM of two numbers?
What about the GCD (or HCF) and LCM of three numbers?

Comment

Did you try some particular pairs of numbers or did you think more generally? Did you think in terms of the sizes of the numbers?

Finding LCMs and GCD/HCFs by factoring works well for smallish numbers, but can be very demanding for large numbers, especially if the factors are unfamiliar. Since computers need to be programmed to simplify fractions with large numbers in the numerator and denominator, and since GCDs often shows up unexpectedly, it would be really useful to have a mechanism for finding GCDs starting from numbers presented in base-ten notation. That is the subject of the next subsection, because it turns out to have surprising links to other mathematical topics.

Task 9.1.4 Diagonal

A diagonal is to be drawn between the opposite corners of a rectangle on a square grid. In the diagrams shown, the 3 by 4 diagonal crosses through 6 grid squares, and the 4 by 6 diagonal crosses through 8 grid squares. How many grid squares will the diagonal cross through in general?

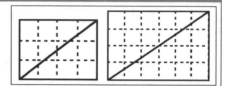

Comment

It may not come as any surprise, given the preceding comments, that the GCD is involved. Note the use of two examples to indicate the meaning of 'the diagonal crosses through' suggests that you try as many particular cases as you need to so that, perhaps by Watching What You Do, you see a way to count the number of relevant grid squares. Some people find that it is possible to work with 'the general case' without actually doing any particular cases.

It is fruitful to look at the sequences of number of grid squares crossed on each row; this is probably how the Athenian astronomer Meton (fifth century BCE) worked out the number of years between the moon appearing at the same time and the same place in the sky (19 solar years is 235 lunar months, which is correct to within two hours). This cycle can be found represented in medieval Books of Hours, and links the Julian calendar with lunar calendars.

Euclid's Algorithm

Euclid describes a process for finding the GCD, which has become known as *Euclid's algorithm*. The following tasks are intended to provide you with sufficient experience that you can formulate Euclid's algorithm for yourself.

Task 9.1.4a Square Removal

Given a rectangle, you can remove the largest square possible, and then repeat with the resulting rectangle. Keeping track of the number of squares of each size leads to the *square removal sequence* associated with that rectangle (for example, 10 squared, 10 squared, 7 squared, etc). At one end of the rectangle, draw the largest square possible and shade it in. What remains apart from the square is a new rectangle. Continue 'removing' the largest square possible until you finally remove a square. Make a note of the square removal sequence.

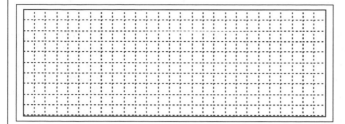 On squared paper, draw some rectangles of your own and become familiar with the process of producing 'square removal sequences'. Under what conditions do you get the same square removal sequence?

Comment

Either by deliberately trying similar rectangles (sides in the same ratio), or by thinking about what is happening, you may see that the square removal sequence depends only on the ratio of *a* to *b*.

Much of mathematics is about making sense of phenomena, including characterising the objects that arise as the result of using a technique. In this case, a natural mathematical question is 'what sequences of numbers can be the 'square removal sequence' for some pair of numbers?', and more generally, what links there might be between the 'square removal sequence' and the original pair of numbers?

Task 9.1.4b Number Removals

Start with a pair of numbers, such as 51 and 30. Remove the smaller from the larger, and repeat removing the smaller from the result as many times as possible without going negative, and make a note of the number of times you removed it (so 51 − 30 = 21: record [1]). Repeat with the new number and the number previously 'taken away' (so 30 − 21 = 9 record [1, 1]). Keep going until you reach 0 (so 21 − 2 × 9 = 3, record [1, 1, 2]; 9 − 3 × 3 = 0 record [1, 1, 2, 3]). Notice that the last number recorded divides both the starting numbers.

Repeat with other number pairs until you are familiar with the process.

Comment

The number that results is the GCD. Did you find the result surprising?

Task 9.1.4c Euclid's Algorithm

Formulate for yourself a technique for finding the GCD of any two numbers. Try to link the diagram and the number manipulations. Try to express your thinking to someone else.

Comments

Would you have preferred just to have been told how to do Euclid's algorithm and given some examples to try? If so, you would have been assiduous in 'doing enough so as to become familiar'?

The word *algorithm* comes from the sound of the name of the author of the most famous Arabic textbook on what is now called algebra, Abu Ja'far Mohammed ibn-Musa al-Khwarizmi (c. 790–c. 850). The word *algebra* is derived from a word in the title of his book, al-jebr, meaning 'the operation of adding the same thing to both sides'.

The remaining question is what square removal has to do with the ratio of the sides of the rectangle, and with the GCD of pairs of numbers.

Book X of Euclid is thought to be by Eudoxus (400–347 BC), who explored the ideas presented here, though without, as far as is known, using 'square removal' diagrams. He used it to explore square roots of numbers, which turn out to have repeating 'continued fractions' that can be used to find solutions to equations such as $x^2 - 2y^2 = 1$, as Pell (1611–85) and others were later to discover. The problem of finding numbers that are both square and triangular can be reduced to this form.

Pause for Reflection

Task 9.1.R Reflection

What did you find out about yourself as a result of this section?

Would you have preferred to be told Euclid's algorithm, or did the 'square removal' help to give it meaning and to support it diagrammatically?

What might this suggest about the tasks you set learners?

Comment

Is it satisfying to be told some 'facts', whose status is currently conjectural for you, and to leave it at that? It is useful to locate what, if anything, blocks you from pursuing an exploration of Euclid's algorithm. Similar factors may be blocking your learners.

9.2 TRIANGLES

Quickie 9.2

Decide which of the following bracketings give the same values for all $a > 0$, and which do not.

$$a^{\left(a^{\left(a^a\right)}\right)}, \quad a^{\left(\left(a^a\right)^a\right)}, \quad \left(a^a\right)^{\left(a^a\right)}, \quad \left(\left(a^a\right)^a\right)^a, \quad \left(a^{\left(a^a\right)}\right)^a.$$

Comments

Trying particular values of a could be fruitful, especially if you are using a calculator or software.

Trigonometry lies at the intersection of geometry and algebra. In this section, some examples are used to show how trigonometry calls upon algebraic thinking.

Diagrammatic Arithmetic of Segments

Early Greek mathematicians saw number both geometrically in terms of lengths, areas and volumes, and arithmetically as the manipulation of quantities to do with trade. Part of the famous books of Euclid can be seen as the manifestation of arithmetic within geometry, possibly because the Greek mathematicians had discovered that the ratio of the diagonal of a square to its edge is not the ratio of two integers. If there were more numbers than could be achieved by fractions, then geometry was a more suitable context to investigate pure arithmetic. Beginning with line segments as denoting numbers, arithmetic was conducted geometrically.

Addition and subtraction of line segments is not so difficult, since you can abut one segment onto another, in two ways, one to make a longer segment, the other to track backwards. Multiplication and division require some geometrical knowledge, provided by the core theorem of Thales (pronounced 'talees'), which provides the basis for trigonometry as well as for multiplication and division of segments.

Task 9.2.1a Thales

An angle is cut off by a pair of parallel lines, as shown.

Then the two triangles are similar (in proportion) and so

$$\frac{x}{x+y} = \frac{a}{a+b} \text{ and } \frac{y}{x+y} = \frac{b}{a+b}, \text{ hence } \frac{x}{y} = \frac{a}{b}$$

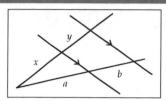

The converse is also true: if $\frac{x}{y} = \frac{a}{b}$ then the lines must be parallel, assuming of course that none of the denominators is zero.

Verify for yourself (algebraically) the truth of these statements.

Comment

The fact that the vertex angle stays the same as the parallel lines move about forces a scaling relationship between the two triangles, so $x + y$ is the same multiple of x as $a + b$ is of a, from which the rest follows. It is also possible to work entirely algebraically. For example, if $x/a = y/b$ then

$$\frac{x}{x+y} = \frac{x}{x + \frac{bx}{a}} = \frac{ax}{x(a+b)} = \frac{a}{a+b} \text{ as long as } x \neq 0 \text{ and } a \neq 0.$$

To use Thales' theorem to do segment arithmetic, for example, in a dynamic geometry package, write $y = \frac{bx}{a}$. By making a the unit length, and using an arbitrary non-zero angle, a segment of length bx can be constructed by drawing a line parallel to a given line through a given point. Similarly, by taking b to be of unit length, the quotient x/a can be formed. So segments can be constructed with lengths equal to the product and quotient of any two non-zero lengths.

Another vital use of Thales' theorem is in showing how trigonometry works: the fact that ratios depend only on the angle at the vertex and not on the particular choices of parallel lines means that ratios of sides can be used as a measure of angle. Since sines, cosines, tangents etc. are ratios of sides of triangles, those ratios are independent of the particular scale, and so depend only on the size of the angle.

Diagrammatic Arithmetic of Areas

Ancient Greek mathematicians were very interested in areas. In order to be able to do arithmetic with them, you need to be able to add areas. But areas come in all sorts of shapes. The Euclidean programme can be seen as the following:

Show how to decompose any polygon into triangles, so that the area of the polygon is the sum of the areas of the triangles.

Show how to convert any triangle into a rectangle of the same area and back again.

Show how to convert any rectangle into a square of the same area and back again.

Show how to add two squares to make a third square (Pythagoras' theorem).

Once this is achieved, any two polygonal regions can be converted (laboriously, but in principle) into squares of equal area, the squares added, and then if need be, the result converted back into a triangle of specified shape.

Breaking a polygon into triangles is not too difficult, namely by cutting off a triangle and so reducing the number of edges of the polygon. The difficulty lies in trying to specify a general rule for cutting off a triangle when the polygon might not be convex.

Converting a triangle into a rectangle is not too difficult, as depicted here:

Task 9.2.1b From Triangle to Rectangle

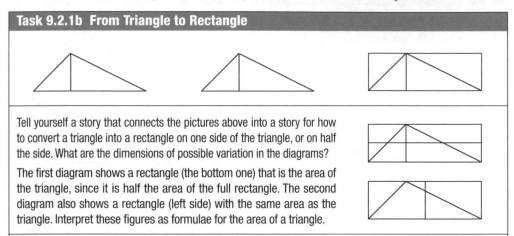

Tell yourself a story that connects the pictures above into a story for how to convert a triangle into a rectangle on one side of the triangle, or on half the side. What are the dimensions of possible variation in the diagrams?

The first diagram shows a rectangle (the bottom one) that is the area of the triangle, since it is half the area of the full rectangle. The second diagram also shows a rectangle (left side) with the same area as the triangle. Interpret these figures as formulae for the area of a triangle.

Comment

Denoting the base by b and the altitude by h, the sequence of three figures above the task can be interpreted as saying that the area of the triangle is $(bh)/2$. The first figure in the task suggests a reading of $(b/2)\,h$ for the area of the triangle, while the third suggests $b(h/2)$. The differences are irrelevant algebraically, but illustrate how rearranging an expression can lead to other ways of seeing.

The Euclidean programme now requires the conversion of a rectangle into a square of the same area, which is most easily seen using Pythagoras' theorem:

Task 9.2.1c From Rectangle to Square

Tell yourself a story that connects the pictures below into a story for how to convert a rectangle into a square of equal area.

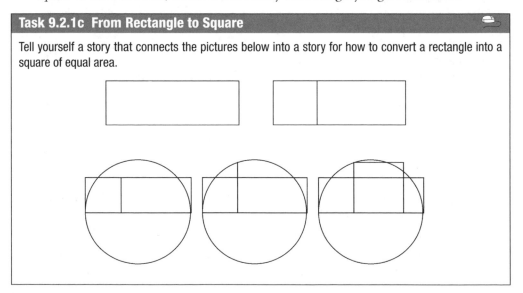

You will probably need to use Pythagoras' theorem on three different triangles that you will need to create for yourself by inserting some line segments!

Work out how to convert a square into a rectangle on a given base (all you can do is draw circles and find the midpoint of a line segment). Write down the instructions.

Comment

At first converting back seems easy, but it can take time to find just the right way of starting from what you know (a square, and an edge for the rectangle) and finding the appropriate circle to draw.

   You might find the geometrical reasoning needs to be supplemented by algebraic (symbols). Historians suspect that for Euclid and colleagues, the experience would be quite different, since right into medieval times and beyond, up until the time of Isaac Newton (1643–1727), mathematicians were more convinced by geometrical than symbolic reasoning.

   Note that the generalities being discussed concern *any* rectangle not just a specific one.

Pythagoras' theorem shows how to construct a square whose area is the sum of the areas of two given squares.

Task 9.2.1d From Two To One

Given two triangles, outline a sequence of constructions for constructing a third triangle on a given base with area the sum of the areas of the two triangles.

Comment

Notice how the task sequence 9.2.1 amounted to an exposition of a technique, but you are expected to go back and bring that sense to full articulation.

Pythagorean Spirals

One of the many important consequences of the Pythagorean theorem is that it gives an elegant construction of square roots. This can be done using the area manipulations in the earlier subsection, but Pythagoras does it with lengths. Combining Pythagoras with the arithmetic of segments means that you can construct any number made from adding, subtracting, multiplying, dividing, and from taking square roots, starting from a unit length. In other words, you can construct lengths corresponding not only to, say 15/13 but also $\sqrt{1+\sqrt{2+\sqrt{3+\sqrt{4}}}}$ and any variations.

   Construction of square roots using right-angled triangles makes spirals with mathematical content, as the next task shows.

Task 9.2.2 Pythagorean Spirals

Starting from an isosceles right angled triangle, erect a new right-angled triangle with the hypotenuse as one side and a unit length as the other, with the one vertex always in common, as shown.

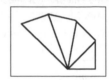

Work out the lengths of all the hypotenuses. Will the spiral ever complete a full revolution? If so, estimate the number of triangles required; if not, what is the limit?

Alternatively, construct an isosceles right-angled triangle each time, as shown are on the left, or more generally, make a scaled copy of the same triangle each time.

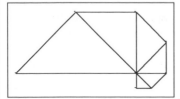
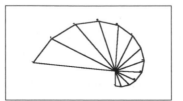

Draw diagrams that display segments with the following lengths: $\sqrt{2}, \sqrt{1+\sqrt{2}}, \sqrt{1+\sqrt{1+\sqrt{2}}}, \ldots$

Use a calculator to see what happens to the lengths as the sequence continues.

Comment

These constructions work very well using a dynamic geometry package.

Pythagorean Triples

The study of properties of numbers has at its core the triples of whole numbers that satisfy Pythagoras' relation. For example, there is an ancient Babylonian tablet (Plimpton 322 in the University of Columbia Museum in New York) that appears to list, in order of increasing angle, the triples of whole numbers making right angled triangles.

Source: http://aleph0.clarku.edu/%7Edjoyce/mathhist/image/plimpton322.jpeg.

The purpose of the next task is to work at following algebraic reasoning deriving a formula for generating these triples. Pay attention to what you need to do in order to follow and appreciate the reasoning. If you get stuck, try specialising using the triple 5, 12, 13, or the triple 8, 15, 17 to see what is being said.

Task 9.2.3 Pythagorean Triples

The aim is to find all triples of whole numbers that have no common factors and that satisfy the Pythagorean relationship: $a^2 + b^2 = c^2$.

If both a and b were even, then c would also be even so there would be a common factor. Assume therefore that b is odd. Write $a^2 = c^2 - b^2 = (c - b)(c + b)$.

Suppose $(c - b)$ and $(c + b)$ share a common factor $p \neq 2$. Then p would also be a common factor for both b and c (add and subtract the two expressions), which would mean it was also a factor of a, that was ruled out at the start.

Suppose c and b are both odd, in which case $(c - b)$ and $(c + b)$ share a common factor of 2. Otherwise, c is even and $(c - b)$ and $(c + b)$ share no common factors other than 1.

It follows then that either $(c - b)$ and $(c + b)$ must both be 2 times perfect squares, since they cannot share any factors other than 2 and their product is a perfect square, or else $(c - b)$ and $(c + b)$ must themselves be perfect squares because they share no factors and their product is a perfect square.

Consequently

> either $c - b = 2m^2$ and $c + b = 2n^2$ for some whole numbers n and m,
> or $c - b = m^2$ and $c + b = n^2$ for some whole numbers n and m (both odd).

From this (by adding and subtracting), $c = m^2 + n^2$ and $b = m^2 - n^2$, which makes $a = 2mn$, or else, $c = (m^2 + n^2)/2$ and $b = (m^2 - n^2)/2$ making $a = mn$. But in the latter case, b turns out to be even, since the difference of the squares of two odd numbers is always divisible by 4. So the second case is ruled out because b was assumed to be odd.

Finally therefore, any triple of whole numbers that satisfy the Pythagorean relationship can be generated by giving values to m, n and p in the triple $[2pmn, p(m^2 - n^2), p(m^2 + n^2)]$.

Check algebraically that these triples do satisfy the Pythagorean relationship. Use the formula to find some Pythagorean triples that you did not already know about.

What did you notice about following the argument?

What is the role of the p suddenly introduced at the end?

Comments

The p stands for any common factor shared by all members of the triple.

Did you find yourself checking each step, but not knowing where it was leading? Were there any specific steps that caused an obstacle? Were you able at the end to think back and reconstruct the steps for yourself? Did it help to carry a particular example with you while reading, or to construct some triples from the formulae?

The whole reasoning turns on the relationship $(x + y)^2 = (x - y)^2 + 4x$, which also figured in the diagrams in Chapter 6. Here, by making xy a square, the sum of two squares is also a square, and furthermore, the reasoning shows that this is the *only* way that the sum of two squares can be a square.

Learners need to reconstruct lines of reasoning for themselves, to be active learners of mathematics. One role for school algebra is to enable general arguments such as this one to be worked through, appreciated and understood. The process is by now a familiar one: working with the general as far as possible, then making use of one or more particular cases to try to get a sense of what is going on, articulating that sense, and trying to use it to re-generalise for yourself.

Pause for Reflection

This section has provided several opportunities to follow reasoning about general numbers without being given particular cases as illustrations. Experience with expressing generality makes it easier to let go of particular numbers and to reason in general than if algebra is presented simply as arithmetic with letters for solving problems.

Task 9.2R Reflection

What differences did you find between the expository nature of the tasks in this section with the exploratory tasks in section 9.1? How might this inform your choice, design, and use of tasks with learners?

9.3 GENERALITY IN OTHER SUBJECTS, AND IN LIFE

Quickie 9.3

Recalling that in index notation, $\sqrt{3} = 3^{\left(\frac{1}{2}\right)}$, show that $(\sqrt{3})^{3\sqrt{3}} = (3\sqrt{3})^{\sqrt{3}}$.

Comment

Take a breath and think your way through. The trouble with using a calculator is that you cannot be sure that the numbers will be the same in all decimal places, beyond those which the calculator can display. This is an opportunity to think multiplicatively, to 'specialise' not by inserting more familiar numbers as such, but by converting the root notation to something a bit more familiar.

As suggested in earlier chapters, algebra is needed by people formulating policies and procedures, and by anyone when repeating the same sort of problem over and over. That is why there is a *formula* for solving quadratics: people recognised that such equations arise again and again so it is handy to have a formula rather than having to go through the detail each time. This section illustrates this theme with examples drawn from various school subjects and from ordinary life.

Formulae from Life

Task 9.3.1 Temperature

In a holiday brochure, it stated that at a particular resort the temperature could change by 10°C (50°F) in a single day. Does this seem correct?

    Note: the temperature in Fahrenheit being F, the temperature in centigrade is $C = 5(F - 32)/9$. What is F in terms of C?

Comment

Rearranging formulae is a favourite pastime of algebra text authors. But it only makes sense when you are familiar with expressions of generality and when you have sufficient confidence to treat the letters as objects involved in arithmetic computations. By seeing the formula as a sequence of operations performed on the as-yet-unknown value F, those operations can be undone in reverse order while at the same time applied to C, resulting in a formula for F in terms of C: $F = 9C/5 + 32$.

To find the temperature change you do *not* simply find out what $10°\,C$ is in Fahrenheit! Rather, you form two values C_1 and C_2 and impose the condition that their difference $C_1 - C_2 = 10$. Then the corresponding difference in Fahrenheit temperatures is found to be

$$(9C_1/5 + 32) - (9C_2/5 + 32) = 9(C_1 - C_2)/5 = 18°\text{ Fahrenheit.}$$

The reason is that the two scales are in the ratio of 9 to 5, but one is translated from the other. 0°C is 32°F.

Task 9.3.2 Bundling Up

If a string around a bundle of uniform sized sticks measures s cm, not including any knots etc., how many more sticks will there be when the string is twice as long?

If a spaghetti measurer for a single portion involves a hole with a diameter of 2.5 cm, what diameter hole will measure twice as much spaghetti?

If asparagus sells at 80p a bunch, what should be charged for a bunch twice the diameter?[2]

Comment

These are examples for which it is important to remember that when the perimeter or diameter are doubled, the area goes up by the square of two.

Task 9.3.3 Snooker

Snooker commentators and expert players can look at a table and say immediately the maximum number of points available. Work out a formula for doing this when there are r red balls left on the table, given the following information.

There are 15 red balls, each worth 1 point and six 'colours' with the following values: black 7, pink 6, blue 5, brown 4, green 3 and yellow 2. Balls are potted alternately red, colour, red, colour, ... When potted, the red balls are not returned to the table but the colours are. When all the reds have been potted, the colours are potted in ascending order of value but now they are not returned to the table once potted.

Comment

Note: snooker players do not use a formula; they become intensely familiar with the numbers. Can you from your formula suggest a rule for minimising what needs to be remembered and still easily work out how many points remain on the table when there are r red balls left?

Task 9.3.4 Exclusion

It was reported that during 1992 in a certain county, although black students were only 10% of the school population, 40% of school exclusions were black. This means, it said in the report, that black students are 6 times as likely to be excluded as white. Justify, comment and construct a general method for making similar calculations from other similar data.

Comment

The first problem is to work out what is going on. A diagram may help, as may careful articulation of what is being compared.

There are many opportunities to explore the general form or method of specific calculations used to make assertions in the media. Formulae also play a significant role in other school subjects.

Task 9.3.5 Pizza

A pizza company offers three sizes: small (9.5 inches, 6 slices), medium (11.5 inches, 8 slices) and large (13.5 inches, 10 slices). The prices advertised are given in the table for four different sets of toppings. Which looks like the best buy for say, three people, four people? What appears to be the pricing policy?

	Small	Medium	Large
Simple	7.49	9.99	12.49
Traditional	8.25	11.49	13.49
Mixed toppings	8.99	11.99	13.75
Full house	9.25	12.49	13.99

Comment

While the customer is concerned about specifics, the entrepreneur is concerned about policy, and the consequences of that policy. Algebra is useful for framing policy, and is very useful for exploring consequences.

Formulae in Other Subjects

Many different subjects in the curriculum benefit from, and even depend upon, use and appreciation of formulae.

Task 9.3.6a Heart Beat

A typical heart beat rate for adults is 84 beats per minute for females, and 78 for males. It can rise to 200 beats per minute with exercise. The heart beats around 170 cm^3 of blood per beat at rest, and up to 300 cm^3 per beat with exercise.

If the left and right ventricles differed in the amount of blood by .01% per beat, then after 15 minutes how much more blood would be in one side of the heart than the other if the body did not take corrective action?

Comment

This is typical of a context in which excess information is given (amounts of blood in a beat, with and without exercise, and so on). The learner has to sort out the wheat from the chaff. But there is also an opportunity to generalise: to develop a formula for the amounts of blood pumped under different conditions by men and by women.

Task 9.3.6b Making Sense of Formulae

In each case, for each variable, rearrange the formula so as to have a formula for that variable expressed in terms of the others.

Population densities of people, animals, insects, plants etc.: density (d), mass (m), Volume (V): $d=m/V$.

Distance (D), velocity (V) and Time (T): $D = VT$.

Electrical Potential (E), Current (I), Power (P) and Resistance (R): $E = IR$, $P = ER = I^2R$.

At constant volume, pressure of gas divided by absolute temperature is invariant; at constant pressure, volume divided by absolute temperature is invariant. $PV = kT$.

Force (F), Mass (m), Acceleration (a): F = ma.

Gravitational force of attraction (F), gravitational constant (g), Masses of two bodies (M), distance between the bodies (d): $F = gM_1M_2/d^2$.

The velocity ratio of a pulley system is the number of strands not counting the free end; the velocity ratio of an inclined plane is the distance travelled/vertical distance achieved; the velocity ratio of a lever is the effort in/load (compare crowbar, wheelbarrow and elbow); the efficiency is the useful energy output/total energy input = mechanical advantage/velocity ratio = (load/least effort to move load)/(distance moved by effort/height moved by load).

Transpiration rate (a twig soaking up water): rate = mass loss/time.

Capillary tube: the thinner the tube, the higher the water rises.

Heating a substance changes that substance: mass before/mass after is invariant for the same substance in different quantities.

Energy needed to heat a mass of water through a specified number of degrees is proportional to the mass and to the temperature change (as long as there is no change of state involved).

Comment

Learners are often offered a triangular mnemonic to help them remember which way round a formula like D = VT goes. An alternative is to be deeply aware of the meaning of each term (V is metres per second, for example) in order to recall one basic relationship (V = D/T), and to develop confidence in rearranging formulae. By using formulae from other subjects within mathematics, learners can be helped to make connections between different subjects, and to appreciate the power they are developing in their algebraic thinking because of its use in other areas.

One of the important features of formulae such as these is the fact that they state invariants. For example, the fact that density is mass divided by volume means that if you take different sized samples of the same 'stuff', then the ratio of mass to volume remains invariant, although the sample size may vary. This is not at all obvious at first, but it lies behind most scientific formulae. Indeed, much elementary science is about seeking invariants. To appreciate invariants, learners have to be aware of what *can* change and still preserve the invariance. In the case of motion, at uniform speed, the distance may vary, and hence the time, but the ratio of distance to time will remain constant.

Pause for Reflection

Teachers of subjects that use mathematics have always complained that learners do not seem to recognise mathematical formulae or methods for rearranging them when they arise outside of mathematics. There may be several factors at play:

Learners have a vested interest in denying knowledge of something so that the teacher will go through it yet again.

Knowledge gained in one context is strongly situated, to the extent that it does not come to mind unless the situation is very similar to that in which it was learned.

Learners do not appreciate the significance of the formulae in the subject, what is invariant and what permitted to change.

Task 9.3.R Reflection

What could be done in your lessons to help learners treat formulae as statements of invariance in the midst of change?

Comment

In secondary school, it might be possible to engage teachers of other subjects in discussion about how they focus learners' attention on what is invariant in the midst of change. In primary school, it would be useful to be on the lookout for invariants in different topics, as this is usually where mathematics makes a contribution to other topics. It might be possible to construct some experiments in mathematics lessons that involve changing some features and discovering an invariant.

The notion of density can be found in most subjects, from population densities of people, animals, plants, microbes, and chemicals, to average word, sentence and paragraph length, average number of adjectives or adverbs per sentence, and so on.

9.4 SUFFICENT AND INSUFFICIENT INFORMATION

Quickie 9.4

Recalling that $\sqrt[3]{4} = 4^{\left(\frac{1}{3}\right)}$, show that $\left(\sqrt[3]{4}\right)^{4^{\sqrt[3]{4}}} = \left(4^{\sqrt[3]{4}}\right)^{\sqrt[3]{4}}$.

In this section, there is a fresh slant on the theme of freedom and constraint while making use of doing and undoing. This produces a task structure that encourages learners to explore the 'undoing' of arithmetic operations as a route into solving equations and also into exploring arithmetical structure of operations.

Two Operations

In this subsection, the generic class of tasks can be formulated at any level of difficulty.[3] Two arithmetical operations are selected; for the purpose of illustration, addition and subtraction are used in the first instance.

Whenever two numbers appear in the middle row of the diagram, the sum is entered into the top box and the difference (left subtract right) goes in the bottom box.

Task 9.4.1a Reconstructing

Suppose that two of the entries in the diagram above have been erased. Is it possible to reconstruct the other entries?

Comment

If the top and bottom boxes are erased, the other entries can be reconstructed. What other choices are there? Work out a general rule for reconstructing the entries in two boxes given the entries in the other two boxes, for different choices of boxes.

Did you find yourself doing particular cases? Did you stick at trying erasing different pairs, and perhaps find yourself starting to reason in general rather than using particulars?

Did you go straight to erasing the middle numbers and trying to reconstruct them from the top and bottom numbers, or did you erase one of the middle numbers and one of the top or bottom first. To work up to the hardest version by first keeping one of the middle numbers makes it easier.

Working with letters rather than numbers demonstrates the power of algebraic symbols as a language in which to express general methods. Without algebra you are confined to illustrating methods by using particular numbers, which can sometimes be misinterpreted.

A further feature of using letters in place of numbers is that you move from detecting and expressing relationships between the entries in the boxes, to treating those relationships as properties. Notice that it is sufficient information to know any two of the values in order to be able to reconstruct the others. Is that true for other operations?

Task 9.4.1b Dimensions of Possible Variation

What other pairs of operations could be used in place of sum and difference?

What other dimensions of possible variation might be available?

Comment

Using multiplication and division is very similar to using adding and subtracting; using addition with multiplication leads to quadratic equations when the middle numbers are erased, but erasing just one of them leads to rearranging useful interim rearrangements from which learners can work out for themselves rules for manipulating equations in order to isolate particular variables.

More middle numbers could be introduced, making the relationships a little more complicated. More layers could then also be added.

Task 9.4.1c Reconstructing Challenge

The operations this time are LCM (above) and GCD/HCF (below). Can you reconstruct the middle numbers given the top and bottom numbers? Are there any constraints on the pairs of numbers that can be used for the top and the bottom in order to be able to reconstruct the middle pair?

Comment

Since the GCD/HCF divides both the middle numbers, it must also divide the LCM.

Exploiting Tables

Various tasks in previous sections have made use of sequences to be generalised, and some were extended to tables giving interlinked sequences running up–down and left–right. Here tables are used to introduce the solving of simultaneous equations and to work on factoring.

One of the important ideas to emerge is whether there is sufficient or insufficient data to 'solve' the equations uniquely. This idea is applied to tables in a slightly different way in the last task of the section.

Task 9.4.2a Tabled Equations

In the table, predict the entries in all the visible cells, and in the cell that is 12 to the right and 7 up from the outlined central cell.

$= -12$					$2x + 3y =$		
			$0x + 2y = -4$				
		$-1x + 1y =$	$0x + 1y = -2$			$3x + 1y = 7$	
			$0x + 0y = 0$	$1x + 0y = 3$	$2x + 0y = 6$		
	$-2x - 1y =$						
							$4x - 2y =$

What makes it possible, and easy, to work out the values of expressions in different cells?

Comment

The fact that you are told the value of x and the value of y makes the other cells easy to evaluate, once you know what the expressions should be.

The question facing mathematicians from Diophantos in about 500 CE to François Viète in the fourteenth century, was how to cope with situations where the information given is not so easy to work with.

Task 9.4.2b More Tabled Equations

Suppose now that you are given the same underlying table, so the expressions are the same, but the values might be different:

					$2x + 3y = 1$		
		$-1x + 2y = 10$					
		$-1x + 1y =$	$0x + 1y =$				
			$0x + 0y = 0$	$1x + 0y =$	$2x + 0y =$		
	$-2x - 1y =$						
							$4x - 2y =$

What other cells can you fill in?

Comment

Did you think to try a simpler case first? What entries would make it easy, but not quite as easy as in the first case? What about being told the value for $3x + 3y$ and for say $4x - 4y$?

Did you try adding the two expressions and their values, and then entering the results in the appropriate cell? What other operations could you perform on the expressions and on their values?

The aim is to empower the learner to simplify for themselves in order to re-complexify, to re-generalise, and so to enable them to reconstruct techniques for solving equations for themselves when they need them, rather than relying on imperfect rote memory.

Notice a connection with Euclid's algorithm for GCDs: by taking suitable multiples of two equations and then subtracting or adding, the coefficient of either x or y can be eliminated, making it possible to solve for the other variable.

There are many ways of presenting this task structure. The expressions could be presented first, inviting expressions of generality of what expression appears in any specified cell, including the cell a to the right and b above the marked cell, even when a and b are negative.

The cells in the same row as the marked cell could be worked on first, to establish the pattern of x, $2x$, $3x$, and so on; the same could be done with the column containing the marked cell, for the ys.

The aim when getting started is to use learners' propensity to 'go with the grain', and detect what the expressions should be, and from the information about the values, work out what the values of the expressions should be as well.

Task 9.4.2c Tabled Equations Developed

If all the values are erased except for two of them, is it always possible to reconstruct all the other values in the table?

Comment

Trying out some simple cases reveals that if the two values are in the same row or column as the marked (zero) cell, then it is not possible to reconstruct all the values. In fact, it soon transpires that if the two given values lie on a straight line through the zero cell, then it is not possible to reconstruct any cells other than those on the straight line.

A thorough exploration of the possibilities involves learners in discovering how to solve equations for themselves. A similar table layout can be used to discover how factoring quadratic expressions works.

Finally, here is a task that exploits the notion of sufficient and insufficient information. It is a worthwhile challenge, because there is more structure to discover than first appears.

Task 9.4.3 Tabled

135	267	402
157	−198	−41
292	69	361

Here is a 2 by 2 table with row and column sums. What is the maximum number of entries that could be rubbed out and still the full table could be reconstructed? Find a way to describe all the sets of cells whose contents could be erased, and still the table reconstructed.

Generalise to r rows and c columns plus the row and column of sums.

Comment

Did you think to try simpler numbers first, or to use letters instead of numbers?

Did you start by rubbing out all the sums? Clearly you cannot then erase any others. Did you think then of exchanging one sum for one entry, and seeing how to reconstruct the table, in order to build up to erasing as many as possible from the core 2 by 2?

Were you able to think generally about a table with r rows and c columns plus the row and column of sums?

Comment

If you erase the entries in a two by two subgrid, then you introduce ambiguity or freedom. There is not sufficient constraint to determine all the entries uniquely. That idea extends however.

Pause for Reflection

This section may have seemed relatively straightforward, but it contains the seeds of tasks that engage learners in discovering techniques for themselves as a result of 'going with the grain' and then making sense and reflecting on the implications of what they have discovered. At every stage there are opportunities for learners to express generalities, which they have reached through the use of their powers to specialise and to generalise, to imagine and express and so on.

Task 9.4.R Reflection

What other mathematical objects in the curriculum could be presented in a tablular form with opportunities for learners to express generalities and to discover techniques for themselves?

Comment

Whenever there are two distinctions to be made, there is an opportunity for a table: for example, the number of people of each sex and above or below a given height, or making some choice.

9.5 PEDAGOGICAL ISSUES

Quickie 9.5

What is the same and what is different about the quickies in previous sections?

$2^4 = 4^2, (\sqrt{3})^{3\sqrt{3}} = (3\sqrt{3})^{\sqrt{3}}, (\sqrt[3]{4})^{4\sqrt[3]{4}} = (4\sqrt[3]{4})^{\sqrt[3]{4}}, (\sqrt[4]{5})^{5\sqrt[4]{5}} = (5\sqrt[4]{4})^{\sqrt[4]{5}}, \ldots$

Extend the sequence and generalise. Verify that your generalisation is correct by using the laws of indices.

Comment

It may help to replace the 4s in the first expression by 2^2. The aim of the quickies in this chapter was to promote multiplicative thinking, and experience with the use of the laws of indices. They provided an opportunity to go beyond 'being scared' by the notation, to trying to work out what they mean, and so to use number symbols in an unfamiliar context as symbols rather than as familiar numbers. The notation for roots effectively specifies the only properties you know about the number. Thus $\sqrt[3]{4}$ has the single property that its cube is 4.

Using Powers: The Role of Pattern-seeking in Mathematics Lessons

One conjecture being offered in this book is that everyone gets more pleasure from the use and development of their own powers than they do from carrying out routine tasks that offer no opportunity for personal choice or initiative. Pattern–spotting is part of the human inheritance, part of what makes humans the social and cultural animals that they are. Detecting patterns and relationships is natural and pleasurable.

It is important that teachers have a strong idea of what possibilities are afforded by a task or a lesson, and that they reflect afterwards on the extent and degree to which those possibilities emerged. The language of mathematical themes and powers is intended, and has been found useful, for augmenting and enriching the topic and concept-specific language associated with a task.

Inner and Outer Tasks

In order to talk sensibly about the issue of explicit and implicit objectives, it can be helpful to think about *inner* and *outer* aspects of tasks. The *outer* aspects are overt and explicit: what you are asked to do. The *inner* aspects are what you might encounter: mathematical concepts you might need to call upon or meet for the first time, mathematical themes which might arise, mathematical powers which might be called upon and mathematical techniques which might prove useful. It also includes the possibility of becoming aware of your own personal propensities such as 'diving in without thinking', 'hesitating before engaging in anything' and so on.

Task 9.5.R Inner Aspects

What personal propensities came to the fore in your response to the tasks in this section? In this chapter? Are there any responses that you would like to alter or gain more flexible control over?

Mathematical Themes

Invariance in the midst of change is closely allied to dimensions of possible variation: each can act as a trigger to the other. In this chapter, as in the next, there are tasks which invite you to stay with the general rather than going immediately to the particular. The quickies offered an opportunity to use specialising in a metaphoric way, by asking yourself 'what does this notation mean?' and to convert the notation into something a bit more familiar (using fractional indices) so that you can use your expertise with fractions to make sense of the assertions.

Task Structures

Some of the tasks in this chapter have been relatively expository; the task has been to make sense of what is presented and to use that in some way. The important aspect of any task is not usually in the doing of the task, but in making sense of it. There is an analogy with the notion of 'with and across the grain': doing a task is going with the grain, following instructions, carrying through techniques. But if a learner is to feel confident that they could do a similar task again in the future, they need to become aware of what 'similar' might mean and how it might be identified, and to be able to reconstruct the reasoning if not the technique, in case the details do not come readily to mind. Consequently it is valuable to 'go across the grain' by considering what it is about a task, about a use of a technique, which is general.

NOTES

1 Idea due to Rina Zazkis
   Brown (2002), 'Patterns of Thought and Prime Factorisation', in Campbell, S. & Zazkis, R. (Eds) *Learning and Teaching Number Theory: research in cognition and instruction*, Journal of Mathematical Behaviour Monograph, Ablex, Westport, pp.131, 137. See also their book.
2 This version is due to Henry Dudeney, a famous Victorian puzzle constructor.
3 Idea due to Nick Andrew.

10 Solving Problems

This chapter develops the theme of use of mathematical powers in the context of solving problems posed in story format, using algebraic thinking.

The first section considers the transition from arithmetic thinking to algebraic thinking. The second section develops the theme of using letters to stand for the as-yet-unknown in problems, and its relations to expressing generality. The third section considers story problems whilst section 10.4 suggests ways of exploiting such problems. Section 10.5 raises pedagogic issues connected with the teaching of problem–solving.

The key issue as far as learners is concerned, is what story problems are for. The case made in this chapter is that they provide an excellent opportunity for expressing generality as well as being intriguing as intellectual puzzles.

History of and Attitudes towards Story Problems

Story problems have a very long history: the oldest of Egyptian papyri, Babylonian tablets, and copies of Chinese and Indian manuscripts all feature them (see Karpinski, 1965; Sanford, 1975). For example, from a Babylonian tablet dated about 1700 BCE:

> I found a stone, but did not weigh it; after I subtracted one-seventh, added one-eleventh, and subtracted one thirteenth, I weighed it: 1 *ma-na*. What was the original weight of the stone? (Tablet R.YBC 4652, in Nemet-Nejat, 1993. p.100)

Surely this is a mathematician showing off ability to add and subtract fractions, not a practical problem. Story problems have been confused with puzzles ever since, some people seeing them as mathematics used to model situations, and others as intellectual challenges.

Diophantus in about 250 CE is the first person on record as collecting problems systematically and posing them with some degree of generality using only numbers as the context.

The mathematician and philosopher Alfred Whitehead (1948, p. 134) had a suggestion that has been echoed by many since: 'By examples I mean important examples. What we want is one hour of the Caliph Omar, to burn up and utterly destroy all the silly mathematical problems which cumber our text-books. I protest against the presentation of mathematics as a silly subject with silly applications.'

Story problems have been used in a variety of ways:

to show off the arithmetic skills of the problem poser (for example, in some Babylonian tablets and Egyptian manuscripts, demonstrating skills in dividing by 7, 13, 17, and 19; see Robson 2000);

to show how a technique is used to solve a class of problems, as when the solution is followed by 'Do it like this' in 4000-year-old problems found on Egyptian papyri (Gillings, 1972, pp. 232–3) or by offering several related worked problems (Gillings, 1972, p. 154), or as Girolomo Cardano (1501–76) put it in his highly influential book *Artis Magne*[1] 'We have used this variety of examples so that you may understand that the same can be done in other cases' (Witmer, 1968, p. 37);

to demonstrate the range of applicability of specific techniques;

to provide a context so that the solver can more readily locate the required calculations (but this leads to students using inappropriate information derived from their knowledge of the context; see Cooper and Dunne, 2000);

to provide cultural information about what authors have assumed is familiar, interesting, or relevant to their students (see, for example, Butler 1838, written for the use of young ladies);

to induct students into a longstanding cultural practice of classic puzzles;

to challenge students to think more deeply than just at the level of arithmetical operations;

as recreation, like crossword puzzles or for sheer playfulness.

Story problems have played a significant role in the development of algebraic techniques. They have played, and could continue to play, a vital pedagogic role as students learn to use algebra to cope with 'as-yet-unknowns', and to express generality. By working on problems used in previous centuries, insight is gained into sociocultural contexts at different times in the past.

Many people have negative memories of story problems at school. This could be a combination of lack of success, use at the end of a topic and lack of appreciation by teachers of the huge potential for mathematical thinking afforded by story problems.

10.1 FROM ARITHMETIC TO ALGEBRA

Quickie 10.1

Write down two numbers.

Write down two numbers which total 36.

Write down two numbers with a difference of 8.

Write down two numbers with a total of 36 and a difference of 8.

Comment

Did you consider the freedom of choice available to you in the four sections, and how that freedom was more or less restricted? If you were unaware of the choices available for the second and third, you would be unlikely to have access to any possibilities for the fourth apart from guessing.

These tasks vary from great freedom of the first part, in which any numbers can be written, to the two constraints in the final part which mean that only one pair of numbers is possible. Faced with the sequence of tasks which use relatively simple numbers, it is likely that you simply tried out numbers or even already knew the answers. Presented with the last task on its own, it is possible that you might consider an algebraic solution. This section looks at problems which can be solved both arithmetically and algebraically and considers approaches that learners might take.

Task 10.1.1a Triangle Context

Consider the two triangle problems below. How do they differ? Which is harder? How might you go about solving the two problems? How do you think a 14-year-old student might solve them? How might an 11-year-old student solve them?

> Triangle problem A: the base of an isosceles triangle is 4 cm. The other two sides are each twice as long as the base. What is the perimeter of the triangle?

> Triangle problem B: in an isosceles triangle the two longer sides are each twice as long as the base. The perimeter of the triangle is 20 cm. How long is the base?

Comment

Did you draw a diagram, or imagine it and think about lengths? Did you find the two uses of 'two' confusing, even if only momentarily?

The first problem makes use of arithmetic in moving from something that is known, the length of the base, to something that is unknown, the perimeter. The second problem, which is essentially an undoing of the first problem, can be seen as much harder. In this case, there is a move from an unknown quantity, the length of the base, to using given information about the perimeter in order to work out the length.

This question was given to 11-year-old students on a written test. They did not make formal use of algebra as older children might do, but produced a range of solutions using arithmetic. Some of these solutions involved suggesting a length for the base and then calculating the perimeter to see if it was 20 centimetres. Other solutions involved dividing twenty by five.

Task 10.1.a Why Five?

Why might someone have divided by five?

What are some of the dimensions of possible variation and associated ranges of permissible change for triangle problem B?

Comment

To come up with five, it is likely that you 'see' the triangle as made up of $2 + 2 + 1$ copies of the base.

You could change the perimeter, and change the relation between the base and the equal sides. The base could also be smaller than the equal sides. You could also have a quadrilateral with one side twice, one side three times, and one side half (say) of the fourth side, and so on.

Types of strategies

Solutions which rely on suggesting a number and seeing whether it works are sometimes called 'trial and error' or 'trial and improvement'. In fact, answers which rely on picking a number and testing it can be classified in various ways. The issue here is whether and how you can identify someone else's strategies from looking only at their 'working'.

One thing to consider when looking at a solution is whether, when the first number guessed is incorrect, the choice of next number to be tried is informed by the checking of the first. When looking at written solutions, it is difficult to know whether a learner was being systematic in making subsequent guesses. It is also hard to know what the learner did in cases where the first number tried proves to be correct. It is possible that this was luck, or a sensible guess given the limited number of possible solutions. It may also be the case that the learner calculated the answer in a way that they did not record but instead recorded the checking procedure. Some possible ways of solving the problem above and similar problems are given in the list which follows.

Guess and test: a number is guessed and tested by doing some arithmetic. Then another number is guessed. There is no evidence of being systematic or learning from previous choices.

Try and improve: a number is tried and checked and there is some evidence that the next trial is in some way informed by the previous result (for example, in deciding whether to try a larger or a smaller number). Further trials are again informed by the results obtained so far.

Spot and check: a number is tried and checked and found to be correct. Despite absence of evidence of systematic trial, the chances of correctly guessing without mental work are assumed to be low.

Using structure: the numbers tried or the checking procedure gives some evidence for having made use of some structural aspect of the problem.

Denoting the as-yet-unknown: some expression is used involving one or more unknowns. The unknown may be manipulated (different occurrences combined, isolated from coefficients, …) or it may appear rather like a unit, unmodified and unmanipulated.

Task 10.1.2 Children's Solutions

Consider the solutions given in Figure 10.1 to triangle problem B: 'in an isosceles triangle the two longer sides are each twice as long as the base. The perimeter of the triangle is 20cm. How long is the base?'

These solutions were given by 11-year-old students in a written test. Use the classification of methods given above to classify each solution.

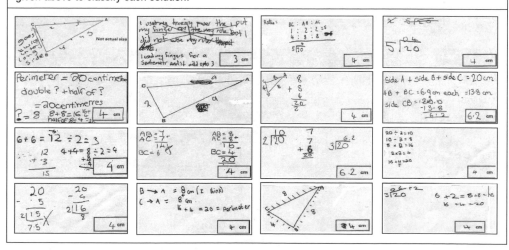

Comment

Just looking at what learners write down it is neither easy nor always even possible to decide between different approaches. Was it a lucky guess, or was it a response to structure? Most of the solutions given here fall in to the first three categories in that they represent some variation on trial and improvement (check results for numbers). Research based on a sample of 451 children answering this question found that over half giving the correct answer used the 'spot and check' method (Evens and Houssart, 2002). Examples in the last category were rare and none are shown here.

There are differing views about whether trial and improvement methods are helpful or unhelpful in developing pupils' algebraic thinking. Often trial and improvement is seen as an intermediate step from arithmetic to algebra, since the 'trying out' of various numbers could be seen as a step towards using variables in place of the trial value. On the other hand, there is resistance to trial and improvement from some, partly on the grounds that learners proficient with such methods are unlikely to want to learn algebraic methods. Such a view is put forward in a report by the Royal Society (1997) which suggested that trial and improvement may actually constitute an obstacle to the learning of algebraic methods because it involves working forwards from a known starting number to find the unknown, whereas algebraic methods involve working from an unknown number. There is a danger in *always* seeing trial and improvement as an inferior method to formal algebra. Such methods may be appropriate for particular problems. The algebraic approach is most useful when a method for solving a whole class of problems is needed.

Pause for Reflection

Task 10.1.R Reflection

What aspects of a task are likely to prompt 'trial and improvement'?

Comment

Looking for the solution to a single problem is more likely to prompt trial and improvement.

10.2 USING LETTERS

Quickie 10.2

Find two numbers with a total of 50 and a difference of 10.

Now find another way of solving the same problem … and another.

Does a model or diagram help?

Try the same problem with different numbers, such as a total of 47.358 and a difference of 3.57. Which method do you prefer now?

An important step in the move towards algebra is the confidence and stance to denote and operate with something that is as-yet-unknown. Frequent exposure to 'empty boxes', and being introduced to 'letters as numbers', leads to the use of a letter as a label rather than as an as-yet-unknown value; this often blocks learners' development of algebraic thinking. For example:

Two 10-year-old children were asking for help with a puzzle about cows and chickens in a farmyard, among which there were 30 heads and 68 feet. The children were happy to try specific numbers to see if they worked. They were happy to acknowledge that they did not know how many cows there were, and to suggest x for the number of cows (not c which might have been a more comprehensible shorthand but could be confused with 'chicken'). But they could not act as if x actually was the number of cows. They could not formulate arithmetic expressions using x, nor see what was meant when they were asked to state what they knew about the cows and the chickens using x.

The children described above took the first step in using letters but did not use the letters to form an expression. In the example shown here, an 11-year-old child, tackling the question about triangles introduced earlier, uses a question mark to denote the side of the triangle which is not yet known.

The example displays the important step of forming an expression using the unknown but does not go on to rearrange this expression to give an answer. This could be for several reasons, including the possibility that the answer was spotted at this point. However, this example does make the important point that being able to form expressions using unknowns is of limited use without the skills required to manipulate the expression which arises.

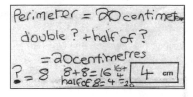

Discerning and labelling an unknown is not the same as recognising and expressing relationships involving that object. To move from arithmetic thinking in which the aim is to get answers to each particular problem, to algebraic thinking in which the aim is to find answers to classes of problems, there are three elements of importance:

- paying attention to *how* you do calculations (and sequences of calculations) in order to get a sense of how you 'do questions like this', for example, using Say What You See and Watch What You Do;

- using readily identifiable large or 'funny' numbers and *not doing* arithmetical calculations so you can see the structure (see tracking calculations in Chapter 3);

leading to

- using letters (or other symbols) to express relationships as calculations so that the arithmetic does not collapse and bury those numbers.

For example,

Solve the equations $3x - 4y = 11$ and $4x - 3y = 13$ can be seen as:

think of two numbers;

now find two numbers satisfying the first equation (and by implication, all such pairs);

now find two numbers satisfying both constraints.

Triangle problem B: in an isosceles triangle the two longer sides are each twice as long as the base. The perimeter of the triangle is 20 cm. How long is the base?

can be cast as, think of an isosceles triangle and imagine the base changing from very small to very large. Now suppose the two equal sides are each double the base. How can the triangle change under these constraints? Suppose now the perimeter is 20cm. What must the base be?

Contrast this with

Triangle problem A: the base of an isosceles triangle is 4 cm. The other two sides are each twice as long as the base. What is the perimeter of the triangle?

Here, as soon as you discern elements (base, sides) you are given calculations to do which are arithmetic, since they force you to find the new element in terms of previously specified ones.

Have you ever been engaged in a long and repetitive task and wondered how much longer it was going to take? Here is a version of this context:

Task 10.2.1 Half-life

On visiting the town where I was born, I realised that I had been away for one-third of my life. How long will it be before I will have been away for half my life?

Try to see the situation in terms of freedom and constraint, so that expressed generality turns into as-yet-unknown.

Comment

Since you do not know how old I am, you can treat it as a generality which may be constrained, and hence as an as-yet-unknown number. Call it A for age in years. Then I spent $A/3$ away and $2\,A/3$ growing up there. Now I might stay away, or I might be returning home to live.

Suppose I am away for a further Y years. Then I will have been away from home for $A/3 + Y$ and at home for $2\,A/3$, and these are to be equal, giving a relationship. From it, Y can be found in terms of A, and an answer given as 'as long as I have lived away so far'.

Suppose I am returning home and stay for Y years before leaving for Z more years, then $2\,A/3 + Y = A/3 + Z$ means that I must stay away as much as I have already plus as long as I stay in the future, to be away half my life.

Note that you could change the context by thinking in terms of a repetitive task such as marking homework books or doing a lot of exercises for homework, and ask yourself how much longer if, having done one-third of the tasks, how much longer it will be until you have done one-half. You could change the numbers by allowing the half and the third to be other fractions.

Once you are used to denoting the unknown by a letter, it seems entirely natural. But it is a sophisticated move which both troubled and excited mathematicians in the past, and which can trouble and excite young mathematicians of the present. It is only a major barrier where learners have not had previous exposure to, and developed confidence it, expressing their own mathematical generalities.

François Vièta (1540–1603) (also written Viète) claimed to be the first to discover the 'previously buried gold' of the ancient mathematicians, enabling him to solve not just 'this and that' problem singly, … but to solve any problem of this kind'.

Klein (1934, p. 165) also says that 'Viète arrived at the conception of a mode of calculation which is carried out entirely in terms of "species" of numbers called *logisticae speciosa* (in contrast to calculations with determinate numbers)' (Klein, p. 165). The notion of *species* is well caught by what has been called here 'expression of generality' or as Klein says, the 'provisionally indeterminate'. By contrast, Viète and others used the term *cosa* meaning 'thing', to denote an as-yet-unknown number.

Pause for Reflection

Task 10.2.R Reflection

What aspects of a task are likely to prompt 'trial and improvement', and what could be done to prompt learners to think more algebraically?

Comment

Looking for general methods rather than the solution to a single problem is more likely to prompt algebraic thinking. What matters is not the solution to the current problem, but whether learners feel they will be able to solve similar problems in the future. Familiarity with generalising is much more likely to support algebraic thinking than is a background of algebra as 'using letters'. Experiencing pleasure in using their power to generalise is more likely to attract learners to algebra than doing 'other people's algebra'.

10.3 STORY PROBLEMS

Quickie 10.3

A bottle and a cork cost 24*d*. The bottle cost 2*d* more than the cork. What was the price of the cork? (Ballard, 1928)

Comment

Although expressed as a story problem, structurally this is a variation on the previous quickies.

Approaching Story Problems

It has often been advocated that learners be trained to recognise cue words which tell them what operations to perform on the numbers in a problem. The effort is hampered by the fact that it is usually possible to rephrase a problem using words that indicate a different operation to the one learners need to perform.

Task 10.3.1a Rephrasing

Underline the words in the following problem which signal calculations, and overline words which signal relationships.

Jenny has five apples which is two more than John has. How many have John and Jenny together?

Which operations are most commonly associated with those words? Are they appropriate in this case?

Rephrase the following tasks so that words which cue specific operations are either absent, or misleading.

Jenny has 2 oranges, and Alan has one more orange than Jenny. How many oranges has Alan?

Alan has 3 oranges and Jenny has 2. How many more oranges has Alan than Jenny?

Comment

Although these hardly count as story problems, and certainly do not call upon algebraic thinking in any overt manner, the search for key or cue words highlights the weakness of this as a method.

One of the issues for younger learners about choosing an appropriate operation is that what one person sees as a subtraction problem, another may see as counting on, and hence as addition.

Task 10.3.1b Rephrasing

Construct some shopping contexts in which the words used signal inappropriate operations.

Comment

Here are some examples:

Haircuts which take off more than 4 inches have doubled in price to £24. What was the old price of such cuts?

A clothes shop has a whole box of spare hangers. An offer says 'take away any 5 for 50 pence'. How much would it cost to take away 10?

At a weight watchers' clinic, J has to pay £10 each week that she gains weight. One week her weight increases by 7 lb. How much does she need to pay?

Are you dubious that learners might misinterpret? Test out your conjecture. Try telling learners that 'some people thought this meant … ' and see what their reaction is. Do they appreciate the pitfalls?

People suffering from forms of dyslexia typically react to verbal cues from the starts of words before processing them fully, and so are particularly prone to being cued inappropriately if they read a problem to themselves.

One major purpose for using story problems is that learners meet unfamiliar problems which require some interpreting, some imagining of the situations in order to detect appropriate relationships and then find a way to solve the problems.

Sorting

One way to develop confidence with story problems is to sort a collection of them in different ways. Sorting offers the possibility of diverting attention away from 'doing' and onto 'how might this be done?', while at the same time providing a reason to engage in talking (even Say What You See) before rushing to record solutions.

Task 10.3.2 Same and Different

What is the same and what different about these story problems? Sort or classify them in some way which distinguishes between them according to mathematical rather than contextual structure.

What two numbers are those, whose difference is 14 and whose sum when added together, is 48? (Saunderson, 1740, Book ii, problem 76, p.107)

Two soldiers shot 100 bombs; the first shot 40 more than the other: How many did each one shoot? (Bézout, 1792, p. 38)

Two purses together contain 300 sovereigns. If we take 30 out of the first and put them in the second, then there is the same sum in each. How much does each contain? (Wright, 1825, p. 203)

A man rows down the stream at the rate of six miles an hour and against the stream at a rate of three miles an hour. What is the rate of the stream? (Ballard, 1928)

Comment

Most textbooks and problem sets aimed at the use of algebra include, as Saunderson does here, a sum-and-difference problem. The third recasts a 'difference of 60' by thinking in terms of adjustments to make them equal, and this will re-emerge shortly.

Strategies

In this subsection, three strategies are suggested which are quite different from the usual suggestion to train learners in recognising words which cue specific arithmetical operations. The strategies proposed here help the learner to probe the meaning and structure of problems.

Checking a Convenient Trial Value

One approach is to try some sample values as if they might be solutions. The purpose is not so much to hope that you get the right answer, but to use the numbers as confidence-inspiring objects with which you can express relationships hidden in the wording of the problem. Then you replace the guessed solution with letters, and end up with equations to solve.

For example, with Task 10.3.4d, try $A = 30$ and $B = 10$. Then $2 \times (30 - 7)$ is supposed to be the same as $3 \times (10 + 7)$. But interest does not lie in the arithmetic. Having discerned this as a relationship given in the problem, and recognised it as a relationship which must hold for the correct solution, the equation $2(A - 7) = 3(B + 7)$ can be written down with perhaps more confidence. Of course in this instance the previous work has already made use of these expressions, but where it seems difficult to locate relationships, the approach of using specific values can be of assistance. The aim is to be able to go straight to expressing the 'generality' using symbols for as-yet-unknown values.

Entering the Situation (Using Mental Imagery)

One of the strengths of mental imagery is that it enables people to enter into situations which are at least partly novel. It is also the means by which mathematics is used to model situations: you imagine the situation, pay attention to the features which seem significant, recognise relationships amongst quantities and then express those in symbols.

Task 10.3.3 Re-telling

Try telling your own version of the bottle and cork problem to someone, paying attention to how you prepare to do this, and what it is like when you do it.

If the person you tell it to balks at doing the problem, get them to tell it back to you and see if that makes any difference.

Comment

Did you think to change the context or the numbers? What about using simply the context of numbers? Would it make any difference?

Drawing a Diagram

You saw in Chapter 8 that diagrams can be very useful as a means of recording a sense-of relationships implicit in a problem. Drawing a diagram *can* sometimes support learners in thinking about relationships or constraints implicit in the problem.

In Singapore, for many years learners were taught to use bar diagrams to represent story problems as an aid to solving them. The basic idea is to represent known and unknown quantities as lengths of bars, here illustrated based on the quickie for this section.

Task 10.3.4a Corker

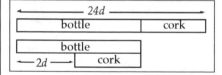

A bottle and a cork cost 24*d* [pennies]. The bottle cost 2*d* more than the cork. What was the price of the cork? (Ballard, 1928) Interpret the diagrams in relation to this problem, then use them to 'read off' the price of the cork and the bottle.

What do you need to do in order to move from a problem situation to a diagram?

Comment

Notice the difference between interpreting someone else's diagram and drawing your own. There is always an issue when using someone else's, even where it makes sense, as to how they knew what to draw and in what relationship.

Certainly you need to discern relevant details. That is what is required to decide what quantities to depict. You also need to recognise relationships between and among those details, which is what suggests the way you juxtapose the various bars.

For example, in the case of the bottle and the cork the data give the sum of the prices of the two objects, and the difference. By placing the two diagrams so that the bottles line up, it is evident that twice the price of the cork is 2*d* less than 24*d*, so the cork costs 11*d* and the bottle 13*d*.

As with any technique which is trained as behaviour without attention to the associated awareness, you need to avoid becoming dependent on diagrams.

Solving the particular is rarely of any abiding interest. What *is* of interest is the generality, which is what Diophantus initiated in his book of problems. Given the sum and the difference of two quantities, each can be found by using a similar method, which can be abstracted away from the diagram. To do this you need to discern what actions were used in the particular case, recognise relationships amongst quantities, and let go of the particulars (bottle, cork, 24d, 2d) in order to work with the general. For example, you can interpret the diagram as saying that 'you adjust half the sum by half the difference to get the two values'. This is a generality which has to be reconstructed by use of sense-making powers such as specialising and generalising, or relating to the diagram with specific numbers but seeing them as general or generic. What is of maximum value is becoming familiar and more confident with working with generality, that is learning to solve problems rather than memorising a method for solving each class of problems.

Task 10.3.4b More Corker

Interpret the diagram as a means to read off the price of the bottle.

Comment

The diagrammatic approach has enabled a solution to be read off without the use of any algebra at all.

Algebra only becomes useful if you are trying to express a general method, or if you consider a wider class of problems by exploiting one or more DofPV, or if the problem is too complicated to see immediately. But what you do with a diagram to solve a particular problem can also be expressed in symbols. For example, the following is a more complicated variant on the cork and bottle problem.

Task 10.3.4c Ages

Draw bar diagrams for the following two story problems.

Two persons, *A* and *B*, were talking of their ages: says *A* to *B*, seven years ago I was thrice as old as you at that time; and seven years hence I shall be just twice as old as you will be: I demand their present ages? (Mole, 1788, problem V, p. 129)

There are two types of canon ball: six of the stronger type, with ten of the second, makes 304 pounds; and ten of the first type with 15 of the second type makes 408 pounds. We ask what is the weight of each type of canon ball? (Bézout, 1792, p. 61)

Comment

Having discerned the fact of two ages, presented at two different times, a diagram such as the following might emerge. Note that it is not necessary to have copies of bars exactly the right length because no actual measurement is involved. What does matter is that the diagram indicates which ends are to be considered as aligned.

Task 10.3.4d Ages with Diagrams

Interpret the following diagrams as pertinent to the ages problem. What do *A* and *B* represent?

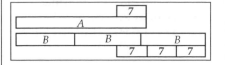

Comment

At first glance, *A* and *B* are labels for bars whose lengths depict (but do not measure) the present ages of two people. A quick glance at the diagrams reveals that A is both $3B - 2 \times 7$ and $2B + 7$ so *B* must be 21. Again it is not the immediate solution that matters but the articulation of the diagrammatic reading in symbols.

Starting from $A - 7 = 3(B - 7)$ and $A + 7 = 2(B + 7)$, *A* can be expressed both as $3B - 21 + 7$ and as $2B + 7$, so these must be equal, making $B = 21$. What really matters is discovering that, inspired by using replications of bars, you can add and subtract equations as objects, with a view to simplifying the coefficients and eliminating one variable. Then you set about solving that equation. Of course, there is some clerical work to follow, finding the value of the other variable and checking that the proposed values really do solve the original equations.

Which ways of 'seeing' structure in the cork and bottle problem, or the ages problem, is most helpful for generalising or extending to other similar problems? The issue here is not to find a 'best' form to be used in future, but rather to pay attention to the features which make extending and generalising more or less apparent. It is much more effective pedagogically if learners decide for themselves which forms of representation are of most assistance to them, rather than having a particular one imposed upon them.

Here is a different task on which to try the diagram technique.

Task 10.3.5 Meeting Point

Two men depart on one day and in one hour, that is to say, one leaves Paris to go to Lyon which is a hundred leagues by road, and the other man leaves Lyon to go to Paris and makes the journey in 7 days. And the one who is going from Paris to Lyon makes the journey in 9 days. To determine after how many days they will meet each other. (Chuquet, 1484, p. 204)

Comment

Chuquet gives an incorrect answer to his problem, but correctly answers another in which the trips take seven and eight days. Even textbook authors can make mistakes.

Pause for Reflection

The three strategies outlined are of course far from being exclusive. It is likely that when faced with a challenging problem, all three strategies might be used.

Task 10.3.R Reflection

Try using one of the approaches described here on a story problem which is not immediately easy for you, to try to discern the pros and cons of that approach. There are more story problems in the next section and in the challenges section at the end of the chapter.

Comment

Just trying one may not give much insight, but it is important to build up your own experience so that you can be sensitive to the needs of learners whom you may be supporting. Look for opportunities to try out and become more adept at using each of the three approaches.

10.4 EXPLOITING STORY PROBLEMS

Quickie 10.4

Given a triangle, is it possible to construct three circles, one centred at each of the triangle's vertices, so that each pair of the circles just touch each other?

Comment

Is this even a story problem? It is certainly stated in words, and needs interpreting. The context is geometry.

Here a rough diagram of a triangle and circles is helpful in order to see what the problem is about. Then it is necessary to discern what the task is asking for, and what elements of the triangle are involved. Denoting these by symbols makes it easier to express the relationships arising from the fact that the circles touch in pairs. The task then becomes algebraic, isolating the symbols for the quantities sought, in terms of quantities which, although not specified in particular, could be expressed with symbols. Did you need to use numbers for three sides of the triangle, or were you able to work with generalities?

Story problems can be exploited in several ways:

getting learners to make up their own by varying the language, trying to obscure or bury the operations required, including adding in extraneous data;

getting learners to make up their own variations by looking for dimensions of possible variation, including context, explicit numbers, and implicit structural numbers;

getting learners to alter the structure, for example changing what is to be found and what data is given.

When learners compose variations for themselves, they are more likely to recognise the structure of a task when they meet it in the future. When they appreciate how tasks are constructed, rather than being surprised by tasks, they can gauge the challenge and recognise that they could have posed a more challenging or more complicated one for themselves.

Looking for Structure

Task 10.4.1 Sums and Products

What is the same and what is different about the structure in the following story problems?

To divide a given number into two, having a given difference (Diophantus, c. 250 CE, 1964, p.130).

To divide a given number into two, having a given ratio (Diophantus, 1964, p. 130).

To find two numbers in a given ratio such that their difference is also given (Diophantus, c. 250 CE, 1964, p. 131).

Notice that the word 'divide' here means to split a number into the sum of two parts.

Comment

These are the first three problems in Diophantus' collection. They are very similar, but with 'difference' in the first replaced by 'ratio' in the second. The third combines the two. Notice that difference and ratio are the two ways of comparing quantities arithmetically.

The problems in Task 10.3.2 are also sum-and-difference problems. Looking for what is the same and what is different may begin with superficial features such as context or specific cue words, but the aim is to get learners to probe beneath the surface. The notion of dimensions of possible variation is intended to do just that.

Exploiting Story Problems Using Dimensions of Possible Variation

One way to stimulate learners to see beyond a single problem to a general class of problems is to use the notion of dimensions of possible variation. As with any task, there are explicit numbers which could be varied, although there may be implied constraints due to the structure of the situation in the story; there are implicit numbers which could be altered; and the context could be altered. More radical changes involve altering what is data and what is to be found.

Task 10.4.2 Using Dimensions of Possible Variation

What DofPV are suggested by these variants appearing in the same textbook?

Find the two numbers whose sum is 50, and whose difference is 16. (Thomson, 1874, problem 1, p. 206)

Six horses and five cows cost £205, and five horses and six cows cost £191. Find the cost of a horse and a cow respectively. (Thomson, 1874, problem 3, p. 207)

A man has two horses, and a saddle worth £7.10s. If he puts the saddle on the first horse, he is then worth double the other; and if he puts the saddle on the second horse, he is worth £15 less than the first. What is the value of each horse? (Thomson, 1874, problem 11, p. 207)

A crew can row $10\frac{1}{2}$ miles downstream in one hour and $5\frac{1}{2}$ miles upstream in the same time. What is the rate of the current in the river, and of the crew on still water? (Wells and Hart, 1923, p. 237)

Comment

The 'horses' problem following on from the first problem suggests different multiples in place of sum and difference. A narrower class of problems arises when there are three or more unknowns, and you are told, for example, the sums of each of the pairs formed by three numbers. Notice that this is the structure behind the quickie in this section.

Another version with three or more numbers is to be given, for each number, the amount by which it is less than the sum of all the other numbers.

Task 10.4.3 Dimensions of Possible Variation

What DofPV are suggested by the following variants of sum and difference problems?

A bookseller sold 10 books at a certain price and afterwards 15 more at the same rate. Now at the latter time he received 35 shillings more than at the former. What did he receive for each book? (Bland, 1832, p. 144)

A cask which held 146 gallons was filled with a mixture of brandy, wine and water. In it, there were fifteen gallons of wine more than there were of brandy and as much water as both wine and brandy. What quantity was there of each? (Bland, 1832, p. 144)

Two robbers, after plundering a house, found that they had 35 guineas between them and that if one of them had had 4 guineas more he should have had twice as many as the other? How many had each? (Bland, 1832, p. 149)

A mercer, having cut 19 yards from each of three equal pieces of silk and 17 from another of the same length, found that the remnants taken together were 142 yards. What was the length of each piece? (Bland, 1832, p. 149)

Comment

In each case there are two quantities, and two pieces of information about combinations of them. A similar situation could arise if someone knew what they paid at a café for, say two of one item and three of another on one occasion, and some other combination on another occasion.

The next task varies an implicit structural number, to generalise to a wide class of problems all of which can be solved by the same overall method.

Task 10.4.4a All Others Less One

Find a method for finding a set of numbers given the amounts by which each number is exceeded by the sums of all the others. Why do you need to have at least three numbers to do this? Can it always be done uniquely?

Suppose you are told for each number in a set, the sums of all the other numbers. Devise a method for finding all the numbers, when it is possible. Are there any constraints on the sums in order for there to be a solution?

Comment

You might have chosen to work with two numbers, then three, then four, being systematic and specialising in order to 'keep a grip'. You might be tempted to go directly to the general case and mentally extend your sense of structure and 'what to do' in general.

The idea from the case of sum and difference of two numbers, of adding both constraints together to give twice one of the numbers has an analogue in both of these tasks: adding up all the constraints gives some useful information which can be used to find the individual numbers. There are similarities with the problem of finding the middle number in a magic square given the row–column–diagonal sum.

Notice also the connection with characterising (section 6.1) and with freedom and constraint.

In the previous task, the aim was to find a method which works no matter how many numbers are in the set (more than two, finitely many). The next task involves cisterns, which, along with fountains and basins, provided a familiar context in medieval problem sets, perhaps because water distribution was frequently a concern.

Task 10.4.4b Taps

What DofPV are you aware of stimulated by the following classic tasks?

If one tap fills a basin in one hour, and if a second tap takes two hours, how long will it take both of them together to fill it?

If a child sets out from school walking at a pace which will take 20 minutes to get home, and an adult sets out from home at the same time, walking at a pace which will take 10 minutes to get to the school, how long will it be before they meet?

Comment

Freudenthal (1991, p. 37) reports a young girl reasoning as follows about the basin. The final basin will have some water from the first tap and some from the second. Since the first runs twice as fast, it will contribute 2/3 of the water in the full basin, so it will take 2/3 of an hour to provide its share. The second contributes 1/3 of the basin, but since it takes twice as long, it will take 2/3 of an hour to provide its share. Hence the basin will be filled in 2/3 of an hour.

Another approach is to let b be the volume of the basin, and to express the rate of filling as $b/1$ (basins-full per hour) and $b/2$ (basins-full per hour) respectively. So in time t, the two taps will have contributed $bt/1$ and $bt/2$ respectively. If the two taps fill the basin in time t, the sum of these two is the whole basin b. So $bt/1 + bt/2 = b$. This leaves $t = 1/(1/1 + 1/2) = 2/3$.

Another approach is to imagine running the two taps for a period of time, say 2 hours. Then the total amount of water would be 3 basins-full. So a single basin-full would be achieved in 2/3 of an hour.

One approach to the second task is to express the speed of the child as $d/20$ miles per minute, say, and the adult at a pace of $d/10$ miles per minute. In m minutes, they will have walked $md/20$ and $md/10$ respectively, which is a total of $md/10 + md/20 = d$. Thus $m = 1/(1/10 + 1/20) = 20/3$. Notice the similarity with the taps.

Think of the distance between school and home as the basin, being 'filled' by the distances the people walk. The problems become identical, apart from the actual numbers.

The pedagogic issue is to locate what it is about the two tasks which signal that they are really the same mathematically, but with different settings. Once you have worked on a number of apparently different tasks, you develop familiarity with structure.

Task 10.4.4c Generalising

Use each of the approaches described with the taps, to write down a method of dealing with n taps each filling the basin in a specified number of hours, different perhaps for each one. How long will it take if all the taps work together?

Comment

Further structural variations that can be found in later problem sets involve being told the times taken for various taps in combination, and being asked for either the overall time or the time for individual taps.

Task 10.4.4d Dimensions of Possible Variation in Varied Contexts

Explore different DofPV for tasks like the tap and the journeys. What other contexts can you come up with?

Comment

Here are some other variants which might suggest further DofPV:

A motorcyclist was sent by the post office to meet a plane at the airport. The plane landed ahead of schedule, and its mail was taken towards the post office by horse. After half an hour the horseman met the motorcyclist on the road and gave him the mail. The motorcyclist returned to the post office 20 minutes before he was expected. How many minutes early did the plane land? (Kordemsky, 1956, p. 116)

Three men are going to make a journey of 40 miles. The first can walk at the rate of 1 mile per hour, the second walks at the rate of 2 miles per hour, and the third goes in a buggy at the rate of 8 miles per hour. The third takes the first with him and carries him to such a point as will allow the third time to drive back to meet the second, and carry him the remaining part of the 40 miles, so as all may arrive at the same time. How long will it require to make the journey? (Jones, 1912, p. 26)

Another version of the same strategy of using DofPV explicitly is to offer learners several similar tasks and then to ask them what is the same and what different, as in Task 10.4.2.

But problems do not always have to be given in the particular. The next task offers an opportunity to think in general rather than in particular, and to see through the general to construct your own particular.

Task 10.4.5a Heaps

Solve the following problem, preferably without recourse to a particular case until after reasoning with generalities.

Person A having taken any number he pleases out of a heap of counters, another person, B, is told to take p times as many. The person who conducts the game specifies p but does not know how many counters A took. A is now told to hand to B a certain specified number, q, of the counters which he holds, and B is told to give in exchange to A p times as many counters as A has left. Show that B will have at the end $(p + 1)q$ counters. Give a numerical illustration. (Nunn, 1919, problem 3, p. 150)

Comment

Note that the result is independent of the number of counters in the original heap.

Does a picture of heaps and removals, or a bar diagram help? What if anything do diagrams offer as a staging point on the way to working solely with symbols?

You might like to make up your own variants, perhaps with three people rather than two, making sure that the result is independent of the number in the original heap.

Pause for Reflection

Task 10.4.R Reflection

What could be done to prompt learners to think more algebraically?

Comment

Looking for general methods rather than the solution to a single problem is more likely to prompt algebraic thinking. What matters is not the solution to the current problem, but whether learners feel they will be able to solve similar problems in the future. Familiarity with generalising is much more likely to support algebraic thinking than is a background of algebra as 'using letters'. Experiencing pleasure in using their power to generalise is more likely to attract learners to algebra than doing 'other people's algebra'.

10.5 PEDAGOGIC ISSUES

Pedagogic Strategies

The quickies in this chapter use the notion of *freedom and constraint*. Starting from a very free choice of objects and then adding extra constraints one by one is a style of task which affords learners access to potentially difficult problems (meeting all the constraints at once). It also demonstrates a useful strategy; if you can obtain a general solution to a less constrained problem, then you can impose the constraint and reach an algebraic condition that has to be satisfied, which might result in an equation you can solve.

When working on 'real-life' problems, learners have to decide what situational knowledge is relevant, and what not. From a mathematician's point of view, the aim is to locate the essential structural relationships, and to work with those. But learners may not be clear about what these structural relationships are.

Task 10.5.1 Really?

What responses do you think learners might give to the following tasks?

79 children are going on a school trip. If a coach holds 36 children, how many coaches will be needed?

There are 26 sheep and 10 goats on a ship. How old is the captain?

What differences might there be in response to the first if it were a real situation?

Comment

The expected answer to the school trip problem is 3 because 2 coaches will only hold 72 children, so an extra coach is required. In reality, many teachers faced with this situation would hire a minibus or use parents' cars rather than incur the expense of an extra coach for so few children. In reality you would not send 79 children on a trip without several adults, but this is not mentioned in the question.

Amazingly, many learners of all ages give the captain's age as 36. The same task, and many variants have been tried in several different countries with closely responding results[2]. Learners who have decided that mathematics is not supposed to make sense, but that an answer is always required, manage to produce an answer using the given numbers, but without 'entering' the situation of the problem.

Research suggests that children do better on problems such as these if they know the implicit rule that you do not take 'real life' too far. Children who tackle the problem for real are in danger of getting sidetracked by issues such as minibuses and extra adults, leading them either not to complete the problem at all or to give an answer that is considered to be 'wrong'.

Role of Context

One reason for putting problems in context is that it is sometimes felt that they make more sense to learners. Many people also expect children to find it easier to tackle a problem presented in words using a familiar context than one using formal algebraic notation.

Task 10.5.2 Mind Your Ps and Qs

Consider the two problems below which were both written for 11-year-old pupils. Both are variants of the quickie presented at the start of this chapter. Which of the two would you expect more children to answer correctly? What strategies and errors would you expect for each?

p and q each stand for whole numbers.
p + q = 1000
p is 150 greater than q.
Calculate the numbers p and q.

Two girls have 60 stickers altogether.
Jenny has 8 more stickers than Hilary.
How many stickers does Jenny have?

Comment

The p and q question appeared on a written test for 11-year-old pupils, which allowed children to use a calculator. Although it proved too difficult for many of them, research based on around 450 papers showed 23% of children answering correctly. Among those answering correctly, direct methods such as finding half of 1000 then adding and subtracting 75 were more common than answers using trial and improvement or spot and check methods.

The stickers question was written in an attempt to make the same idea accessible to more 11-year-old pupils. In fact this did not seem to work, since only some 15% of children answering correctly. A common incorrect answer was 38, and some children answered 68.

Researchers who have looked at the effects of using recognisable contexts in story problems on tests have found that learners who were supposed to be helped by having a mathematics problem set in a familiar context often made too much use of their knowledge of such situations (Cooper and Danne, 2000; Verschaffel, Greer and de Corte, 2000). They are more likely to go for pragmatic and practical approaches than to access the intended mathematical problem. But, then, the learners in the research did not have the benefit of a teacher apprised of the many strategies available to turn story problems from a fearsome burden into an opportunity to think algebraically and creatively.

Task 10.5.3 Difficulties with Context

The following incident is drawn from a lesson with a set of Year 5 children all considered to be low attainers in mathematics. Suggest reasons why the children were finding the problem so difficult. Formulate an alternative strategy to the one the teacher tried, or a way of adapting his strategy.

The children were given a worksheet containing story problems. The teacher went through the problems, helping with the reading and asking the children how they would go about solving the problems. The children gave answers such as 'add', 'take-away' or 'times', with answers often given quickly one after the other suggesting the children might be giving all the likely words until the teacher said yes. The teacher concentrated on one problem that involved 24 people going to a party in 8 cars, with the same number of people in each car. The children did not offer a strategy for solving this problem so the teacher drew 8 cars. He drew them all unusual shapes and said who they might belong to, using names of children in the class. Some of the children became quite excited at this point and seemed to be listening for their own names. The teacher completed the problem, but there was little evidence that the children were following his reasoning.

Comment

Involving children by using their particular names could serve to help them identify with the problem, but perhaps over identify so that they attend only to 'their' car and who else is in it, rather than attending to the intended structure. Further difficulties arise when learners try to make use of practical knowledge about a posed situation, such as knowing that people wouldn't necessarily put equal numbers in each car, or might stuff an extra person in one car to avoid taking another one.

Dimensions of Possible Variation

Dimensions of possible variation play a central role in the use of story problems to pedagogic advantage. Getting learners to discern features which could be changed is likely to awaken them to structural relationships and so assist them to express structural relationships, as well as to gain that sense of well being when you realise you can now solve a whole class of problems.

Solving not just one problem but a class of problems is a form of seeking what is invariant (the method) and what is permitted to change (the context, the overt numbers, implicit or structural numbers), and which of the quantities involved is given as data and which are to be found.

Same and Different

Same and different, and variations on this theme which involve sorting or classifying, are useful for getting learners to experience thinking about problems before diving in to do the first operation that comes to mind on whatever numbers are to hand. This applies particularly to story problems.

Developing flexibility between using diagrams, tracking trial solutions, and imagining themselves in the situation of a story problem so as to recognise structural relationships are steps along the way to gaining confidence in and familiarity with working with generalities and symbols.

Structure of Attention

The notion of structure of attention may lie behind the reluctance shown by some learners not just to using letters, but to treating letters as quantities rather than simply as labels. If their attention is on the whole of a problem (perhaps generated by dislike of long passages or uncertainty about how to proceed), if it is on entities but not relationships, then the learners are not likely to make sense of the structure implicit in a problem. If they are used to being clear from the start 'what they have to do', then they are ill-equipped to deal with novel situations.

ACKNOWLEDGEMENT

Children's responses to the triangle question and to P&Q and stickers are drawn from a research project carried out jointly between the Centre for Mathematics Education at the Open University and the Mathematics Test Development Team at the Qualifications and Curriculum Authority. The questions are reproduced with permission from the QCA.

NOTES

1 Cardano was the first to publish formulae for the solution of cubic equations, which he learned about from Nicolo Tartaglia (1499–1557) (having said he would never reveal the method, he went ahead and published) and the solutions of quartics which his son in law Lodovico Ferrari (1522–65) managed to discover using Tartaglia's ideas for the cubic. It was not until the nineteenth century that it was proved that there are no similar formulae for solving all equations of any degree than higher 4.
2 See for example Verschaffel, Greer and de Corte (2000) for an account of research on this and other problems, and the effects of alerting learners to the issue of reality *vs* problem-land, or Baruk (1985) or Freudenthal (1991, pp. 68–73).

11 Reasoning

Chapter 11 is about the power of algebraic thinking and manipulation to reason about numbers. Section 11.1 introduces the categories of 'always, sometimes, and never' true. Section 11.2 considers more advanced reasoning with generalities through looking at the structure of the 'number triangle' often associated with Pascal, but published centuries earlier in China. Section 11.3 uses diagrams as the source for reasoning about inequalities and number-lines. Section 11.4 provides further experience of reasoning with generalities by using the number triangle to construct formulae for sequences and extending the notion of number from positive counting numbers with zero to negative numbers and beyond. Section 11.5 considers the shift in thinking needed to move from being convinced by a few cases, to expressing that generic case in general, and proving.

The approach being taken in this book is that reasoning only becomes possible when learners have developed confidence in expressing generality.

11.1 REASONING ABOUT TYPES OF NUMBERS

Quickie 11.1

Is it true that between any two distinct rational numbers (numbers which can be expressed as fractions) there is another rational number?

Construct an argument using decimal notation.

Comment

One such argument is based on the notion of the mean of the two numbers.

Making deductions in particular and reasoning algebraically in general appear on the surface to be merely a matter of manipulating symbols. But those manipulations only make sense when you think in terms of 'all I know is … '. For example, to show that the sum of two odd numbers is always even but their product is always odd, you need to start with not just one expression for a general odd number, but two, capturing the properties of being odd within the way they are expressed. You could for example think diagrammatically or symbolically.

Diagrammatically

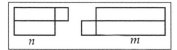

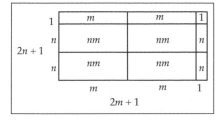

Note: symbols inside regions denote their area.

Symbolically

Let *n* and *m* be any integers.

Then $2n + 1$ and $2m + 1$ represent any two odd numbers.

Then $(2n + 1) + (2m + 1) = 2(n + m) + 2 = 2(n + m + 1)$ which is even, being of the form $2k$ for some integer *k*.

Furthermore, $(2n + 1)(2m + 1) = 4nm + 2n + 2m + 1 = 2(2mn + m + n) + 1$ which is odd, being of the form $2k + 1$ for some integer *k*.

Notice how generality is signalled by using unspecified lengths, and how the RofPCh of each letter needs to be specified (as well as what it is counting or measuring). The reader is free to see the lengths as particular but also as arbitrary. What matters is not the particular lengths but the relationships between copies of the same lengths. Notice, too, how the addition diagram is relatively self-explanatory, but the multiplication diagram benefits from being shown what the components are, and so identifying how the oddness of the two numbers is being represented.

Notice how both the diagrams and the symbols begin with expressing the oddness of the two given but general numbers, then working solely with that in order to express the sum and product, before finally interpreting the result as a property of the result, which is also general rather than particular. The tasks in this chapter provide opportunities to experience that shift from property to definition-axiom, in the sense of 'the property is all that is known about the object'.

Interpreting and Justifying Generalities

Each mathematical assertion, such as the statement of equality of two expressions, or the statement that one expression is greater than another, may be true always, no matter what values are taken by the variables, sometimes, for some values, or never, for any values. For example, the expression $x^2 = {}^-2$ is never true (within the real numbers), whereas the statement $x^2 > 4$ is true whenever *x* is itself greater than 2, or less than $^-2$.

Task 11.1.1 Sometimes–Always–Never

For each of the following, decide whether it is always, sometimes or never true. If it is sometimes true, decide for which numbers it is true.

For any number, there is a larger number.

There exists a number which is larger than every number.

For any two distinct numbers, there is a rational number between them (not the same as the quickie).

For any number, there is another number closer to zero.

For any two numbers, there is a multiple of the first which is larger than the second.

The product of two numbers is greater than either of them (multiplication makes bigger).

The difference of two numbers is less than either of them.

The quotient of two positive numbers is smaller than either of them (division makes smaller).

The quotient of two numbers is smaller than the first and larger than the second.

Comment

How do you set about testing such conjectures? Trying some particular cases helps of course, but it can also help to try extreme cases: something very large and positive, something very small and positive, and the same for negatives. It may help to place numbers mentally on a number line.

The question of whether some statement is always, sometimes or never true is a useful catchphrase to introduce to support the development of a conjecturing atmosphere (see Chapter 14), and also to engage learners in constructing objects for themselves rather than always dealing with mathematical objects created by someone else. Giving learners opportunities to make choices enables them to exercise creativity within the bounds of the imposed constraints.

Convincing yourself that something is always true calls upon algebraic thinking. You can work from particular cases and then express a generality, but such an expression remains a conjecture until you show that the assertion remains true no matter what numbers have been chosen within the constraints. Sometimes it is possible to use a picture which displays the essence of what is going on; often diagrams are either impossible, or too complicated.

Symbols are useful for demonstrating that some assertion is always true no matter what values are chosen for the variables.

The statement that 'One more than the sum of two consecutive numbers is even' can be looked at diagrammatically:

One more than the sum of two consecutive numbers can readily be rearranged to form an even number.

The 3-ness and 4-ness are merely place holders for longer shapes representing other pairs of consecutive numbers, just as the diagrams in the introduction use unspecified lengths to indicate generality.

A slightly more convincing picture might indicate the arbitrary nature of the pairs which could make the two consecutive numbers any size. Note that the diagram does not cope well with negatives.

An algebraic statement can be fashioned as follows:

Let n and $n + 1$ be any two consecutive numbers.

Then $1 + n + (n + 1) = 2n + 2 = 2(n + 1)$ which is an even number.

Starting off with 'let n and m be two consecutive numbers' would be possible, but then a relationship has to be built between n and m in order that the constraint that they be consecutive is expressed in symbols. It is no good trying to manipulate general numbers via symbols without expressing all the constraints of the situation.

Here is an opportunity to try some reasoning with symbols for yourself.

Task 11.1.2 Interpreting and Justifying

For each statement, decide whether it is (always) true, and if so, try to convince yourself, then convince a friend. If it is false, try to modify it so that it is (always) true. A variety is provided so that you have experience of the wide range of possibilities.

One more than the sum of four consecutive numbers is even.

From three consecutive numbers form the product of the first two and the last two. Their sum is twice a perfect square.

One more than four times the product of two consecutive numbers is a perfect square.

One more than the product of two numbers differing by two is a perfect square.

One more than the product of four consecutive numbers is the square of one less than the product of the two middle numbers.

The difference of two consecutive numbers is an odd number.

The sum of two consecutive triangular numbers is a square number.

The sum of three consecutive triangular numbers is one more than three times the middle triangular number.

The product of three consecutive numbers is the middle number less than a perfect cube.

The sum plus the product of three consecutive odd numbers is the middle number less than a perfect cube.

The sum of three consecutive numbers is divisible by 3; sum of five consecutive numbers is divisible by 5; . . . .

The sum of four consecutive numbers is divisible by 2; sum of six consecutive numbers is divisible by 3; . . . .

Product of two consecutive numbers is divisible by 2; product of three consecutive numbers is divisible by 6, ...

One more than eight times a triangular number is always a perfect square. And vice versa.

Comment

This task is intended to provide experience of denoting general numbers by letters, incorporating into that some structure such as being consecutive numbers, or being odd or even numbers.

Did you think about DofPV? For example, the second one can be extended to taking three consecutive numbers in arithmetic progression, and forming the products of the first and last of theme. Furthermore, given five consecutive numbers, the sum of the products of the first pair, second pair, and third pair, is three times the product of the second, third, and fifth.

The vice versa of the last assertion is not always true. Only odd squares can arise as one more than eight times a triangular number.

Notice the similarity between characterising (as discussed in Chapter 6) and the subtle move from perceiving a property to deducing from definitions.

Saying that 'every something has such and such a property' is perceiving a property (for example, every sum of two consecutive numbers is odd, is proposing a property of the numbers which result from adding two consecutive numbers).

Testing whether this property characterises all the things that have that property is shifting to the question of whether everything which has that property arises in that way (for example, is every odd number the sum of two consecutive numbers?).

You have to start with just the property, and try to deduce relevant things from it. For example, given the number $2n + 1$, can it be the sum of two consecutive numbers? All you have to go on is the $2n + 1$. It requires some insight, perhaps informed by experience of summing pairs of consecutive numbers, to see that $2n + 1 = n + (n + 1)$ and so it does indeed come from a sum of two consecutive numbers as conjectured.

Pause for Reflection

The shift from perceiving a property abstracted from some relationships themselves detected among some specific objects, to reasoning solely on the basis of those properties is one of the reasons why mathematical reasoning has proved difficult to teach effectively. Until learners are perceiving properties as attributes that objects may or may not have, they are not in a position to reason about objects which have those properties. The significant shift involves ignoring things you may know about particular objects, and concentrating solely on the announced properties. This idea is taken up further in subsequent sections.

11.1.R Task Reflection

What are the significant features of reasoning with generalities arising from this section?

Comment

Perhaps the most important feature is that when you want to have two general numbers, you need to use distinct letters. But the use of distinct letters does not force the numbers to be different! The distinct letters enable them to be different, but they may in particular circumstances turn out to be the same! It is also necessary to state the RofPCh of each letter (here it has usually been integers), and what that letter denotes ('let n be the number of … ').

11.2 REASONING ABOUT GENERALITIES

Quickie 11.2

Is it true that between any two distinct rational numbers there is an irrational[1] number?

Comment

Notice how, in this case, the decimal notation perspective is more helpful than the fraction notation for rational numbers.

This subsection considers some of the properties and uses of a triangle of numbers first written about in China probably by Jia Xian[2] in the eleventh century CE. In the Middle East, Omar Khayyam (c.1050–1123) described and used the triangle. In Europe it was explored by Blaise Pascal (1623–62) in the 1650s and published posthumously in 1665.

The Jia Xian Triangle

Task 11.2.1 The Jia Xian (Pascal's) Triangle

Look for and express some relationships which you detect between the entries in the following triangle (presented in three different ways), so that you could extend it as far as necessary.

```
1                              1          1 1 1 1 1 1 1 1
1 1                        1      1       1 2 3 4 5 6
1 2 1                   1    2    1        1 3 6 10 15
1 3 3 1               1   3    3   1        1 4 10 20
1 4 6 4 1           1   4   6   4   1        1 5 15
1 5 10 10 5 1     1   5   10   10  5   1     1 6
1 6 15 20 15 6 1  1  6   15   20   15  6   1  1
```

Comment

The second display is as displayed by Jia Xian, except that he used Chinese number notation.

The third is as displayed by Pascal.

Did you think to use Say What You See, or even Watch What You Do as you made a copy for yourself? Did you compare the three triangles before or after looking for details within one of them?

Looking at the last full line in the left hand display and trying to locate a source for the 15 and the 20 is likely to suggest the relationship that each number is the sum of the number above and the one to its left (in the left hand display), the sum of the two numbers above (in the middle display) or the sum of the numbers immediately above and immediately to the left in the right hand display. This is enough to generate succeeding lines, although it could be tedious if you wanted to generate the hundredth line.

Did you notice that the sum of the entries in a row is a power of two?

Having detected the counting numbers in the second column or in the diagonal in the right-hand display, you might be tempted to look at the third column or the next diagonal. You might recognise these as the triangular numbers. The next line of numbers represents the number of objects in a pyramidal array of objects such as oranges or cannonballs.

This triangle of numbers is important because it links together numbers arising from different contexts. For example, looking at the columns in the first display reveals familiar sequences (constant, triangular) and so serves to generalise those. They will be examined more closely in section 11.4 in the context of finding formulae for mystery sequences. Looking at the rows reveals the numbers which arise in binomial expansions, a topic studied by John Wallis and Isaac Newton, and which also arises in situations involving counting the number of choices when selecting from a range of objects.

Task 11.2.2 Binomial Expansion

Multiply out the brackets for as many of the following as you feel you need to, in order to see how to get the coefficients of one from the coefficients of the preceding one. Use the expansion obtained from one line to help work out the next.

$(a + b)^1 =$

$(a + b)^2 =$

$(a + b)^3 =$

$(a + b)^4 =$

$(a + b)^5 =$

$(a + b)^6 =$

Comment

It is worthwhile doing the multiplications enough times to become aware of how the coefficients for one row are obtained from the coefficients of the succeeding row. This should remind you of the patterns you found in the previous task.

Expanding powers of brackets can be thought of sequentially as in the previous task, but they can also be approached directly. Suppose you want to multiply out $(a + b)^5$:

$$(a + b)^5 = (a + b)\,(a + b)\,(a + b)\,(a + b)\,(a + b)$$

Each term in each bracket has to be multiplied by each term in every other bracket. So if you choose, for example, three *a*s and thus two *b*s, in how many different ways can you make this choice? Well, you have to choose three *a*s from five brackets, and then there is no further choice possible for the *b*s since they have to come from the remaining two brackets not yet selected. There are two common notations for such choices:

$$_nC_r \text{ and } \left(\begin{smallmatrix} n \\ r \end{smallmatrix} \right),$$

which both mean *the number of ways of choosing* r *things from* n.

For example, $\left(\begin{smallmatrix} 5 \\ 3 \end{smallmatrix} \right)$ means the number of ways of choosing 3 things from 5, which in the bracket expansion above means the number of times in the expansion that there will be an $a^3 b^2$ term contributed, that is, the coefficient of that term. So $\left(\begin{smallmatrix} 5 \\ 3 \end{smallmatrix} \right)$ is a notation for the coefficient of $a^3 b^2$ in that expansion. It is important to notice that having chosen three brackets to contribute an *a* from among five brackets, the other two brackets have to be *b*s. Put another way, choosing *r* things from *n* is the same as choosing $n - r$ things from *n*. So

$$\left(\begin{smallmatrix} n \\ r \end{smallmatrix} \right) = \left(\begin{smallmatrix} n \\ n - r \end{smallmatrix} \right)$$

It often happens in mathematics that notation is used to denote something which is known only by its property or properties, such as $\sqrt{2}$ (whose characterising property is that its square is 2), and $\left(\begin{smallmatrix} n \\ r \end{smallmatrix} \right)$ which is the answer to a counting problem. In fact, a great deal is known about combination numbers arising from their definition. The next task begins an exploration by providing some algebraic reasoning to read, follow and then reconstruct for yourself.

Task 11.2.3a Combination Properties

Suppose you want to calculate $\left(\begin{smallmatrix} n \\ r \end{smallmatrix} \right)$, that is, the number of ways of choosing *r* things from *n*. One thing you could do is pretend that you already know the number of ways of selecting from $n - 1$ things. Then if you want to choose *r* things from *n*, you put one thing aside from the *n*. Now you can choose *r* things from the remaining $n - 1$, or you can choose $r - 1$ things from the $n - 1$, together with the thing put aside. These are the only ways of selecting *r* things from *n*.

Pause, and think back over the reasoning, perhaps closing the book, or your eyes and reconstruct the reasoning for yourself. What did you have to do to make sense of the argument? What connections might there be with the patterns in Task 11.1.1?

Why would you expect $\binom{n}{r}$ to be equal to $\binom{n}{n-r}$?

Comment

Did you for example, resort to particular examples, in which case, did you do enough so as to experience the general structure and be able to express the generality for yourself? Did you follow the reasoning in general, perhaps by allowing the *n* and the *r* to express generality that you could sense?

   To choose *r* things from *n* involves choosing *not* to choose *n − r*, so the number of ways of choosing *r* from *n* is the same as the number of ways of choosing *n − r* from *n*.

   In how many ways can you select 0 objects from *n*? Although it seems a bit silly, it is the sort of question mathematicians ask themselves in order to extend notation, and it turns out to be very useful. One way to approach it is to observe that it should be the same as the number of ways of choosing *n* things from *n* (the things not chosen, as it were), which is 1. To a mathematician there is one way to choose no things from *n*, namely to choose none.

   The next task again involves following algebraic reasoning about generalities, then reconstructing it for yourself.

Task 11.2.3b Combination Calculations

Suppose you want to know $\binom{n}{r}$, that is, the number of ways of choosing *r* things from *n*. One thing you could do is reason as follows. There are *n* ways of choosing the first object, *n* − 1 ways of choosing the next, and so on until there are *n* − *r* + 1 ways of choosing the *r*th object. So there are *n*(*n* − 1)(*n* − 2) ... (*n* − *r* + 1) ways of choosing *r* objects from *n*.

However, this method of choosing distinguishes the order in which things are chosen. In the case of the brackets, it distinguishes choosing an *a* from the first bracket and a *b* from the second, from choosing a *b* from the first and an *a* from the second. So having chosen *r* things from the *n*, you have counted each choice many times, indeed, the number of times you can reorder *r* things. Once you have chosen *r* things, there are *r* ways of selecting the first one, (*r* − 1) ways of selecting the second, and so on down to 1 way for the *r*th. This makes *r*(*r* − 1)(*r* − 2) ... (1) ways of ordering the *r* things. This means that this is the number of times the same combination of *r* things from *n* has been counted in the count above. Putting it all together, The number of ways of choosing *r* things from *n* is $\frac{n(n-1)(n-2)\,\ldots\,(n-r+1)}{r(r-1)(r-2)\,\ldots\,1} = \binom{n}{r}$.

Close your eyes and reconstruct the argument for yourself. What did you have to do to make sense of the argument? Check this direct calculation gives the correct answers for the sixth row of the table, and for the seventh row which you will have filled in for yourself.

Comment

This 'formula' gives a direct method of calculation for $\binom{n}{r}$. You will have found that, for example,

$$\binom{7}{3} = \frac{7 \times 6 \times 5}{3 \times 2 \times 1} = 35$$

which is the sum of the 15 and the 20 in the row above in the Jia Xian triangle.

Since it is rather tedious to write all those products out when calculating with these numbers, mathematicians use the symbol ! (pronounced 'shriek' or 'pling' in computing contexts, but 'factorial' in mathematics, so 3! is 'three shriek' or '3 pling', or 'factorial 3'). The symbol denotes the product of all the numbers from 1 up to and including the number. Thus $3! = 1 \times 2 \times 3$ and $5! = 1 \times 2 \times 3 \times 4 \times 5$.

A more succinct way of writing $\binom{n}{r}$ is obtained by inserting $(n-r)!$ in both numerator and denominator, to yield

$$\binom{n}{r} = \frac{n!}{r!\,(n-r)!} \ .$$

What meaning could be ascribed to $0!$? Where is it needed? It is needed to make sense of $\binom{n}{0}$ which should be the same as $\binom{n}{n} = 1$. The factorial version says that $\binom{n}{n}$ $= \frac{n}{n!\,0!}$ and since this should be 1, it forces $0!$ to be 1. Another way to reason is that since $n! = n \times (n-1)!$, when $n = 1$, $1! = 1 \times 0!$ So $0!$ must be 1. This is another example of mathematicians extending meaning to make arithmetic consistent.

Task 11.2.4 Putting It All Together

Express a relationship between $\binom{n}{r}$, $\binom{n-1}{r}$ and $\binom{n-1}{r-1}$ which also expresses a pattern you discerned in the number triangle in Task 11.1.1 and in Task 11.1.2.

Using the direct means of calculating $\binom{n}{r}$, show that your expressed pattern is actually correct.

Comment

The first is the sum of the second and the third, expressing the basic method of extending the Jia Xian triangle line by line.

This is only the beginning of patterns and relationships to be discovered in the Jia Xian triangle. Other things you can do include:

replacing each entry with its remainder on dividing by some pre-chosen number, then looking for patterns and both predicting how they continue and proving that this is indeed the case;

finding formulae for sequences of numbers along other diagonals.

Leibniz's Triangle

The German mathematician Gottfried Leibniz who independently invented the calculus found a fraction triangle which is quite remarkable, and provides an opportunity to work on something possibly a little less familiar than the Jia Xian triangle.

Task 11.2.5 Leibniz's Triangle

Look for some relationships among entries in this triangular array of numbers. Find a link with the Jia Xian triangle as well.

$$\frac{1}{1}$$

$$\frac{1}{2} \qquad \frac{1}{2}$$

$$\frac{1}{3} \qquad \frac{1}{6} \qquad \frac{1}{3}$$

$$\frac{1}{4} \qquad \frac{1}{12} \qquad \frac{1}{12} \qquad \frac{1}{4}$$

$$\frac{1}{5} \qquad \frac{1}{20} \qquad \frac{1}{30} \qquad \frac{1}{20} \qquad \frac{1}{5}$$

$$\frac{1}{6} \qquad \frac{1}{30} \qquad \frac{1}{60} \qquad \frac{1}{60} \qquad \frac{1}{30} \qquad \frac{1}{6}$$

Comment

Did you think to use Say What You See or even Watch What You Do?

Were you content with one or two relationships? Did you find resonances with patterns and relationships in the Jia Xian or Pascal Triangle?

Pause for Reflection

11.2.R Task Reflection

Did you find your attention caught up in details about the number triangles rather than in the process of reasoning algebraically?

Comment

Learning to reason algebraically involves drawing upon confidence with symbols and with symbol manipulation. But spending learning time just working on manipulation is likely to obscure the interesting aspects of algebraic thinking (proving that something is true for an infinite number of possibilities such as for all numbers). Engaging in reasoning about infinite classes of numbers is one of several contexts in which learners can experience the use of symbol manipulation on the way to developing mastery.

11.3 REASONING WITH AND FROM DIAGRAMS

Quickie 11.3

Is it true that between any two distinct irrational numbers there is a rational number?

Think decimal notation; find a general argument.

Previous chapters have made extensive use of diagrams. Sometimes you have been asked to make algebraic sense of a diagram, and other times diagrams have been used to try to make sense of algebra. The two-way movement is vital if diagrams are to be of any use. Of course the most useful diagram is the one that the learner draws for themselves, for a diagram in a text is similar to text in that it has to be interpreted. You have to ask yourself what the important elements and aspects of the diagrams are (discerning details), what relationships are being expressed (what can change and still the relationships are preserved) and what properties the objects in the diagram are supposed to have. This section makes use of mental images of number lines and then returns to graphing of relationships. It includes some diagrams which come from Babylonian and Persian mathematicians and which justify the name 'completing the square' for the solution of quadratic equations.

Reasoning with Inequalities

Reasoning with inequalities is much like reasoning with equalities, as long as you watch out when performing operations on them. The first task uses graphs to support an image of what inequalities mean. Then rules for manipulating inequalities are developed by calling upon your experience and knowledge of the particular, and inviting you to generalise.

Task 11.3.1 Regional Order

From the graph of the three straight lines, determine for which values of x, L_1 lies both above L_2 and below L_3.

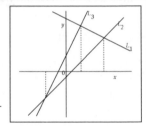

The dotted lines show how the x-axis is divided into intervals corresponding to the intersections of the lines. For each interval decide the 'order' of the lines, from lowest to highest. What happens to the order as you move from region to region along the x-axis?

Comment

As you move along the x-axis, the relationship between the lines stays the same over an interval, and then when you get to a crossing point determined by two lines, those two lines change their order. Note that there only four intervals, but there are six ways to arrange three things in order, so there are two 'orders' which are impossible: L2 > L1 > L3 and L2 > L3 > L1. In other words, if L2 is greater than either of L1 or L3, then it must be smaller than the other one. In general, with three linear expressions, at least two of the six arrangements will be impossible.

Inequalities are normally thought about on a number-line.

Task 11.3.2a Order on the Line

Imagine a number line. If two numbers n and m are announced, how will you decide whether n lies to the left or to the right of n?

Suppose now that m lies to the right of n. In what order will you find $n + 3$ and $m + 2$? $2n$ and $2m$? $n/2$ and $m/2$? $-2n$ and $-2m$? Generalise.

Comment

Did you think to try examples with n negative or with both n and m negative?

The next task invites a move away from images in order to develop rules for manipulation of inequalities.

Task 11.3.2b Rearranging Inequalities

Starting from the true statement that 2 < 3, perform operations on both sides of the inequality in order to show that the following are also true. Generalise each operation (but take care.)

$$2 \times 5 < 3 \times 5 \qquad\qquad ^-2 > ^-3 \qquad\qquad 2 + 4 < 3 + 4 \qquad\qquad 2 - 5 < 3 - 5$$

Now perform the same operations on the inequality $a < b$ to obtain rules for manipulating inequalities.

Comment

Did you think to imagine 2 and 3 on a number line, and to consider the effects of each operation on the pair of numbers $(2, 3)$, indeed on the interval between them?

Notice that this task suggests that when you are manipulating an inequality and you lose confidence in what happens when negative numbers are involved, you can try out a particular case for yourself as a check.

Task 11.3.2c General Inequalities

Someone knew $a < b$ and also that $c < d$. They concluded that $a - c < b - d$. Find counter-examples, and explain what they did incorrectly. What correct implications can you deduce?

Some one knew that $a < b$ and wanted to deduce that $1/b < 1/a$. Is this always valid?

Comment

From $c < d$, it follows that $^-c > ^-d$; adding two inequalities going in opposite directions just does not work ($2 < 3$ and $5 > 4$ but $2 + 5$ is neither < nor > $3 + 4$). Notice the difference between making sense of this counter-example provided, and constructing your own counter-example.

To go from a to $1/a$ requires a division: dividing both sides of the inequality by ab gives $1/b < 1/a$ BUT only as long as ab is positive, otherwise the inequality sign would reverse.

Reading inequalities from a diagram is one thing; manipulating them symbolically is another. The next task is a symbolic version of a particular case of the three lines in Task 11.3.1.

Task 11.3.3 Order! Order!

For what values of x is $3 - 4x \leq ^-5 \leq 4 - 3x$?

For what values of x is $^-5 \leq 3 - 4x \leq 4 - 3x$?

For which orders of the three expressions are there no possible values of x?

Comment

Did you try particular values for x? How can you move from successfully finding a few values to finding all possible values? Did you think of graphing?

Notice that a single inequality imposes a constraint on the freedom of x; a second inequality usually restricts that freedom further, to the extent that there may be no numbers satisfying all the constraints.

The previous tasks invited use of mental diagrams of number lines. Here is a different context in which inequalities arise:

Task 11.3.4 Reading Inequalities

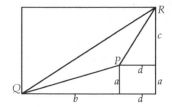

Express a relationship between the slopes of the three diagonal lines *PQ*, *PR* and *QR*. Then express those slopes as fractions using *a*, *b*, *c* and *d*.

What constraints are there on the position of the point *P* to preserve your inequality?

Comment

Notice connections with Task 9.2.1a, Thales, where the ratios were equal. What happens in the diagram when *a*/*d* and *c*/*d* are equal? Where is the point *P* then?

It is worthwhile gaining confidence with the inequality by trying it out in sufficiently many cases, chosen so as to illustrate the various possibilities concerning signs, and locating the corresponding position of *P*.

Completing the Square

Most algebra textbooks over the last 50 years or more have tackled quadratic equations by starting with factoring before moving on to the apparently more abstract general formula for quadratic equations. Leonard Euler (1707–83) took the opposite point of view in his landmark textbook, *Elements of Algebra* (1770) which was translated into English, from a French translation, in 1822. He followed the solution of linear equations with the solution of quadratics, in a development mirrored by the following tasks.

The programme is to solve equations of the form $ax^2 + bx + c = 0$.

Task 11.3.5a Very Simple Quadratics

What is the simplest quadratic equation?

Comment

Perhaps it is $x^2 = 0$, but a broader class of simple ones are quadratics of the form $x^2 = -c$, achieved by allowing *b* to be 0 and *a* to be 1. This is a good example of the use of specialising to a simpler case which is easier to solve. Of course, such an equation can be solved only if *c* is negative or zero, and there are two roots. It is convenient to say that there are two roots even when they are both the same.

Note that many learners thrown into symbols without plenty of experience in expressing generality, think that $-c$ means a negative number, when here, *c* has to be negative in order to make $-c$ positive.

Task 11.3.5b Simple Quadratics

Now construct a slightly more complicated class of quadratic equations which can be solved almost immediately.

Comment

The equation $ax^2 = -c$ can be solved by dividing through by a. Note that it is now possible to find solutions only when a and c have opposite signs. Clearly a cannot be zero.

Having moved from the very particular special case ($x^2 = 0$) to the much more general ($ax^2 = -c$), there remains the question of how to deal with the b.

Task 11.3.5c Quadratics

Starting with the large square as having side x, and the rectangle having side b, interpret the following diagram as a way to solve $x^2 + bx = c$.

Comment

The little square added on has side length $b/2$. The diagrams can be interpreted as showing that

If $x^2 + bx = c$, then $(x + b/2)^2 = c + b^2/4$, and vice versa.

If $(x + b/2)^2 = c + b^2/4$ then $x^2 + bx = c$.

The diagram has its roots in Babylonian tablets of 2000 BCE, and features in the algebra texts of Omar Khayyam and al-Khwarizmi.

Reasoning with Number lines

The next task invites reasoning about midpoints of segments on a number line. The idea is to move beyond the need for particular examples, but to be ready to use one when it becomes too hard to deal with the general by itself.

Task 11.3.6 Mid-points

Find the mid-point of the portion of the number line from 2 to 6.

Work out a method for finding the mid-point in general, given the end points.

Test your method on some intervals of your own choosing (including using negatives). Ask someone else to see if they can follow your instructions, and whether they agree that it does always give the mid-point.

The *mid-interval* of an interval is the middle interval formed by dividing an interval into three equal portions and choosing the middle one. How long are each of the mid-intervals of the two intervals left after removing the mid-interval of some interval?

> Is it true that the mid-point of the mid-interval of some interval is the same as the mid point of the interval formed by the mid-points of the two intervals left after removing the mid-interval of the original interval?

Comments

The intention of the last two parts is to experience working on making sense of someone else's generality. There is deliberately no diagram provided, in order to prompt you to draw your own. It is entirely natural to ask for, and then construct your own particular or special examples. The purpose of using particular examples which are more confidence inspiring than the vague verbal generalities, is to try to see for yourself what those generalities might be saying: in other words, to specialise in order to support your own re-expression of generality. Learners can create their own similar sorts of conjectures by compounding mid-point calculations.

Try making up a complicated compound mid-point calculation for yourself.

Note that one DofPV associated with this task is to change from mid-point to third-point, or some other fraction. You could even compound the operations using different fractions: for example, 'the one-third point of the interval between the two-thirds points of two intervals is the same as the ... '. By engaging in tasks like this, learners gain confidence and fluency in using a number line to support their thinking. One of the advantages of the empty number line is that it supports thinking in general as well as thinking using particular numbers.

Pause for Reflection

11.3.R Task Reflection

How if at all did using a number line help you to reason with inequalities?

Comment

Diagrams can sometimes provide a stimulus for reasoning by converting diagrammatic relationships into algebraic symbols. Conversely, a diagram can be used to illustrate algebraic calculations. Diagrams can assist learners to learn to reason with general rather than with particular numbers.

11.4 REASONING WITH GENERALITIES

Quickie 11.4

Is it true that between any two distinct irrational numbers there is an irrational number?

This section provides more opportunities to reason, in this case extending what is meant by *number*.

Extending Meaning

The mathematical theme of extending and contracting meaning plays itself out many times in the extending of the term 'number', as learners meet first counting numbers, then counting numbers with zero, then integers, then fractions (positive and negative) then decimals. Since the rules of arithmetic are an extension of the old rules to the new 'numbers', mathematicians want to be certain that such extensions do not introduce any contradictions. The way they do this is to 'construct' the extensions out of the old familiar numbers: they use the counting numbers to construct objects which act like the integers, they use the integers to construct objects that act like fractions, and so on. This section offers a little taste of these constructions, focusing on the construction of subtraction from the positive counting numbers with zero.

Task 11.4.3 Building Positive and Negative Integers from Scratch

Let N^+ denote the natural numbers together with 0. Let Z denote the set of pairs of natural numbers: $\{(a, b) : a$ and b in N^+. Addition is defined on the elements of Z as follows: $(a, b) + (c, d) = (a + c, b + d)$.

(a, b) and (c, d) are different names for the same thing if and only if $a + d = b + c$. Two such pairs are said to be *equivalent*.

List some specific pairs which are equivalent to (different names for) the pair $(2, 1)$.

Express the generality of all such pairs (be careful not to use the notions of negative or of subtraction).

Do the same for the pair $(1, 2)$.and for the pair $(0, 0)$.

Comment

The pairs $(3, 2)$, $(4, 3)$, and more generally of the form $(n + 1, n)$ are all equivalent to $(2, 1)$.

The pairs $(2, 3)$, $(3, 4)$ and more generally of the form $(n , n + 1)$ are all equivalent to $(1, 2)$.

Intuitively, equivalent pairs all have the 'same difference' except that the word 'difference' is not needed to describe them. The pairs equivalent to $(k, 0)$ all 'act like' the positive number k, while the pairs equivalent to $(0, k)$ all act like ^-k for any positive number k. Thus out of the positive numbers with zero emerge the positive and negative numbers, without any need to use the word 'negative'. Of course when doing arithmetic it is convenient to use such a shorthand.

The next task shows that you can add and multiply these pairs of numbers, and that it does not matter which representative you choose of all the equivalent ones, in order to do the arithmetic.

Addition: $(a, b) + (c, d) = (a + c, b + d)$

Multiplication: $(a, b) \times (c, d) = (ac + bd, ad + bc)$.

Task 11.4.3a Multiplication

Check out for yourself by trying some particular cases why the multiplication rule is as it is.

Comment

An alternative approach would have been to invite you to work out how to tell someone to multiply pairs, so that they got the answers expected for 'differences'. Did you think to relate this to the expansion of brackets $(a - b)(c - d) = (ac + bd) - (ad + bc)$?

The next task indicates the kind of work that is necessary in order to demonstrate that the operations proposed do actually mirror the operations intended, when each pair is identified with and interpreted as its corresponding integer.

Task 11.4.3b Arithmetic

The number pairs (2, 4) and (5, 7) are equivalent, as are (6, 5) and (9, 8). What happens when you add or multiply (2, 4) and (6, 5), and when you add or multiply (5, 7) and (9, 8). Are the two answers equivalent?

It is necessary to show that if you add or multiply two representative pairs, you get an answer equivalent to the answer you would get if you had chosen other pairs equivalent to your originals. Here is an argument. Your task is to try to say to yourself in words what is involved and how it works.

Suppose (a, b) and (A, B) are equivalent, and suppose (c, d) and (C, D) are equivalent. This means that $a + B = A + b$ and $c + D = C + d$. Adding the first of each type gives $(a, b) + (c, d) = (a + c, b + d)$; adding the second of each type gives $(A, B) + (C, D) = (A + C, B + D)$. Are these two answers equivalent?

It is necessary to show that $A + C + b + d = a + c + B + D$. But this follows by adding the two facts known about the original equivalent pairs: $(A + b) + (C + d) = (a + B) + (C + d)$ which says the same thing.

For multiplication a little more work needs to be done: $(a, b) \times (c, d) = (ac + bd, ad + bc)$ and $(A, B) \times (C, D) = (AC + BD, AD + BC)$. Are these answers always equivalent? This is needed so that multiplication makes sense.

To show these two pairs to be equivalent, it is necessary to show that $ac + bd + AD + BC = AC + BD + ad + bc$. All that is known is $a + B = A + b$ and $c + D = C + d$.

It takes some real insight to discover that by adding the same thing to both expressions, and using the facts that $a + B = A + b$ and $c + D = C + d$, the two expressions come to be the same, as expected and intended.

Left-hand side	Right-hand side
$= (ac + bd + AD + BC) + aD + bC + Ac + Bd$	$= (AC + BD + ad + bc) + aD + bC + Ac + Bd$
$= a(c + D) + b(d + C) + A(c + D) + B(C + d)$	$= D(B + a) + d(a + B) + c(b + A) + C(A + b)$
$= (a + B)(c + D) + (b + A)(d + C)$ (use what is known)	$= (D + c)(a + B) + (d + C)(A + b)$ (use what is known!)

The two expressions are the same (using what is known). All the calculations have been done with positive whole numbers, without invoking the 'as-yet-unknown' operation of subtraction. Thus it does not matter which representatives you use, which pair of positive numbers, multiplication will always give the same answer as for any other equivalent pair.

Comment

You may have found yourself tempted to skip over the symbols and just accept what is asserted. But this is what makes mathematics hard for learners, when they skip over details looking for 'what they have to do', and so miss out on using their own powers to make sense of something which can act as a model for their future behaviour.

Following complex reasoning is a good experience when trying to promote learners to reason, as it highlights the sorts of places where you need to pause and think, check on an example, or puzzle out why the next step was taken. By working on your own awareness of these features of complex reasoning, you can improve your own explanations and justifications, as well as prompting learners to fill in more detail in their attempts to justify statements.

As was indicated at the beginning, the intention here is not to have internalised the argument, but to experience the way in which mathematicians construct new objects from old so as to be certain that what they are doing remains consistent. A very similar line of reasoning shows how to construct rational numbers as pairs of integers, where (a, b) acts the way you want the fraction a/b to act. Similar constructions can be performed to mirror the arithmetic of numbers of the form $a + b\sqrt{5}$ and other similar sets of numbers obtained by changing 5 to another integer. For example, $(a, b) \times (c, d) = (ac + 5bd, ad + bc)$ mimics multiplication of $a + b\sqrt{5}$ and $c + d\sqrt{5}$. All you need to use about $\sqrt{5}$ is that it is a symbol denoting a number whose square is 5.

Pause for Reflection

The central idea and experience from this section is paying attention to what you have to do in order to follow someone else's reasoning, in order to be more sensitised to what learners need when you are justifying an assertion to them.

11.4.R Task Reflection

What did you do when you encountered a gap, a step that was not immediately clear? Were you able to resist the temptation to abandon ship and to use a particular example of your own devising, or to scan ahead to try to see where the reasoning was going?

Under what circumstances do you find yourself proceeding in 'inchworm' manner, or in 'grasshopper' style? What might you learn from this about supporting learners?

Comment

Great care must be taken with descriptions of behaviour. Once the person is labelled, it can be difficult to notice contrasting behaviour. Sometimes inchworm behaviour is highly appropriate; sometimes grasshopper behaviour is more appropriate. The sensitive teacher not only detects these behaviours, but prompts learners, even provokes learners, into adopting the other strategy when it seems appropriate.

11.5 PEDAGOGIC ISSUES

Quickie 11.5

Show that between a rational and an irrational there lies at least one rational and at least one irrational. You may need to consider what happens when the rational is the larger, and when it is the smaller of the two.

Comment

You should find that the reasoning you used in the previous quickies works here too: you look at the decimal names of the numbers. Since the numbers are distinct, there must be a position at which the digits first differ. That is where you can tinker a bit and introduce a terminating decimal (which is therefore rational) and a non-terminating non-repeating decimal (which is therefore irrational).

The odd thing is that in a very real sense, there are many more irrationals than rationals. The reason is that although it is possible to set up a one-to-one correspondence between the rationals and the counting numbers (so that the rationals are 'countable', even though infinite), it is impossible to set up a one-to-one correspondence with the irrationals. No matter how you try, there are always infinitely many left over.

Pedagogical Strategies

Instead of asking learners to do a lot of exercises, to 'do what they are told', it can change learners' attitudes considerably if they are invited to make choices for themselves. For example, doing only enough so that you can see something, or so that you can do another similar task in the future, puts the onus on the individual learner.

Mathematical Themes

Extending and contracting meaning is a very common phenomenon in mathematics. This is similar to what happens when first learning language. When you encounter a new word there is a tendency to use it in a broader sense than in common use, and then for the range of meaning to contract. You might like to look out for this phenomenon in people you work with: it is very difficult to notice in yourself except at the point where the meaning contracts and you realise you have been using the word a little too lavishly.

A related theme in mathematics is the use of symbols to store properties. For example, labels are given to fractions, which display their components (2/3 as an operation is to take two lots of one-third of); roots and indices similarly display their structure $\sqrt[5]{3} = 3(\frac{1}{5})$ and trigonometric functions simply provide a name, as in $\sin(x)$, $\tan(45°)$, $\cos(\pi/3)$. In each case the name is a convention and you have to be told what it means in order to use it. In this way, mathematicians extend their grasp over numbers, and in a similar manner, over more complex mathematical objects such as equations and functions.

Mathematical Powers

The power to specialise is immensely useful as a step to making sense and then re-generalising for yourself. It is not the only strategy however. The whole point of algebra is to get to the point where the symbols are doing the work for you; your job is to make sure that the calculations are done correctly!

Task Structures

In section 11.2, some of the tasks were deliberately structured to invite you to experience particular instances, and then to express more generally for yourself, 'rules' for manipulating inequalities. More generally, it is almost always possible to engage learners in particular cases which they can do for themselves by calling upon what they know, but in such a way as to be able to generalise for themselves. This makes it more likely that they will be able to reconstruct the technique for themselves when needed, especially if they engage in discussion about what is efficient, how the technique works, what wrinkles or obstacles might appear, and so on.

It is important however, not to fall into a trap in which tasks always or even almost always provide 'simple cases' from which learners are expected to generalise. Often simple cases can be done by other, specific methods and therefore do not give access to a generality,. For example, adding fractions like 1/2 and 1/4, or 1/3 and 1/6 do not immediately lead to a method for adding 1/2 and 1/3, though they may inform such a method. Getting learners to specialise a generality is just as important as getting them to generalise from particular cases.

In Task 11.3.6, Mid-points, the idea was to try to work with general intervals rather than with particulars. The task could be presented with just the last part, the very complex statement, as an opportunity for learners to battle their way to make sense of it, before making up their own even more complicated versions. It is the opportunity to be creative and to make choices which motivates learners, and, when they use their own powers to make sense of something, they actually get some pleasure from the experience.

NOTES

1 An irrational number is a number which when expressed in decimal form does not have an endlessly repeating 'tail'.
2 See Kangshen, Crossley and Lun (1999 p. 178).

12 Graphs and Diagrams

Much has been said in earlier chapters about graphs and how they provide a powerful pictorial representation of relationships. The defining characteristic of a graph is that it uses position (on the page) to convey information. Naturally, because a page is two-dimensional, each point on a graph will provide two pieces of information – usually (but not always) taken to be the horizontal and the vertical distance from a fixed point of reference (the origin). The axes are useful to help guide the eye to the exact location of the point in question and the scales on the axes help to quantify the two distances in units of measure that everyone can agree on.

For many learners there appears to be a rather uneasy relationship between graphs and their axes. The two opening sections of this chapter look at this from two complementary points of view. Section 12.1 considers situations where the graph stays fixed but the axes are allowed to move around in the form of a viewing window that can be used to focus on a particular segment of the graph. Too often, however, this can give a misleading impression by stressing just one (possibly unrepresentative) sector and ignoring the rest. Additionally, it is possible to stretch or squash the scales in one direction, which can alter one's perception of the story that the graph is telling.

Section 12.2 considers this the other way round; keep the axes fixed and consider what happens when you move a graph around. In particular, what effect does shifting and stretching a graph have on its equation and how can this idea help students to understand the notion of families of functions?

Section 12.3 explores some interesting iteration formulae, including the Greek mathematician Hero's method for calculating square roots. This is followed by section 12.4 in which you are asked to explore staircase diagrams for graphing iterations.

Finally, section 12.5 considers some of the pedagogic implications of graphing.

12.1 GRAPHICAL IMPRESSIONS

Quickie 12.1

What is the least amount of information needed to define the position of a point in one dimension, two dimensions, three dimensions, ... *n* dimensions?

As has been indicated in the introduction, it is *position* that is the key characteristic of how graphs convey information. The 'tools of the trade' for defining the meaning of a point on the graph are the *origin* (a fixed point of reference), the *axes* (two fixed lines of reference), the *labels* on the axes (identifying which variables are being depicted) and the *scales* on the axes (which fix the units of measure).

A pictorial representation may sometimes be worth a thousand words, but there are times when the story it tells is of corruption and fraud! This section provides some simple data sets for you to investigate and present graphically in different ways in order to investigate how graphs can mislead and confuse. If possible, try to use one or more of the following ICT tools:

computer graph plotting package,

computer spreadsheet, or

graphics calculator.

Task 12.1.1 That's a Bit Steep!

Between the years 2000 and 2004, the percentage of pupils from a particular school who gained five or more grade C passes or better at GCSE were as follows:

Year	2000	2001	2002	2003	2004
% of pupils	47	49	49	51	52

(a) Plot these results as a line graph.

(b) The school management wishes to create a favourable impression with parents. Now plot them in such a way as to exaggerate the improvement in the results. What is the mathematical basis of this 'trick'?

(c) Plot the data again but use a different 'trick' to exaggerate the improvement in the results.

Comment

Detailed comments on this task are set out below.

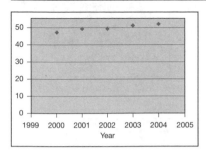

Scattergraph showing percentage of pupils achieving the target grades, over time

Using a spreadsheet:
(a) Enter the data as shown here.

Plot the data as a scattergraph using the 'XY(Scatter)' option (note that the points have not been joined up because the data are discrete – the examinations are taken only once per year so intermediate points have no sensible meaning).

(b) This is not a very impressive graph – the slope upwards is much too shallow to create the desired effect. If you aim is to give an impression of a more dramatic improvement, try chopping the vertical axis at, say, a value of 46. This will give a graph that looks like the one here. (Note that this version is actually the default scatter plot provided by Excel.)

The mathematical basis of providing a misleading visual comparison by chopping the vertical axis is that this alters the ratios of the heights of the points as measured from the

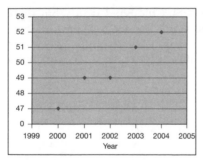

horizontal axis. For example, the relevant percentage figures for 2002 and 2004 are, respectively 49, and 51. Numerically, the 2004 figure is bigger that the 2002 figure by a factor of 51/49 or 1.04 (in other words, 51 is 4% more than 49). However, cutting the axis at 46 reduces these figures, visually, to 3 and 6 percentage points respectively and gives the visual impression that the 2004 figure is twice as great as the 2002 figure.

Another way of making a graph look steeper is to shorten the horizontal axis (or, if you prefer, lengthen the vertical axis. The final version has been created by stretching it vertically and squashing it horizontally.

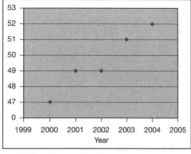

Original graph …

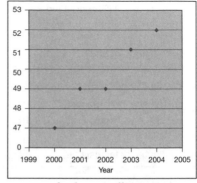

… stretched vertically …

A useful mental image for thinking about adjusting the starting position on the horizontal and vertical axes is the idea of a 'viewing window' that can blank out the entire graph apart from the area of interest inside. This window can be moved around the graphing area, focusing attention of particular sections at a time. Also, the viewing window can take on any rectangular shape. The diagram indicates a variety of positions and shapes that can be given to the viewing window.

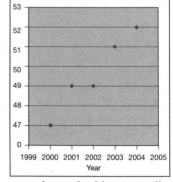

… and squashed horizontally

The viewing window

The graph

The next task will give you the opportunity to experiment with viewing windows in various positions on the graph and of differing size and shape in order to see some of the diverse stories that can be told by the same batch of data.

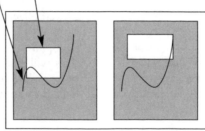

Task 12.1.2 The Viewing Window

A school head was concerned with behaviour problems in her school and decided to look at the records of exclusions since the school began in 1987. Between the years 1987 and 2005, the numbers of pupils excluded annually were as follows:

Year	1987	1988	1989	1990	1991	1992	1993	1994	1995	
Exclusions	7	11	14	16	23	28	27	26	25	

Year	1996	1997	1998	1999	2000	2001	2002	2003	2004	2005
Exclusions	24	26	32	37	38	39	40	41	42	44

(a) Plot these results as a line graph.

(b) Choose a suitable viewing window to show how the number exclusions in recent years have (i) fallen, (ii) risen slowly (iii) risen rapidly.

Comment

Detailed comments on this task are set out below.

(a) The graph as plotted on a spreadsheet will look something like this:

Using a graphics calculator, it will look like this:

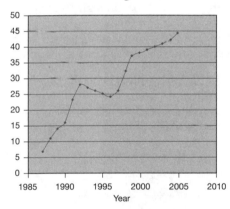
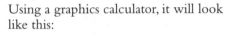

Finally, here it is on a graph-plotting package.

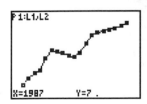

(b) (i) The term 'recent years' is ambiguous and open to multiple interpretations, so the time span can be selected to match the story you want to tell. The number of exclusions *fell* between 1992 (28 exclusions) and 1996 (24 exclusions), so this suggests these minimum and maximum settings for the viewing window:

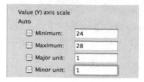

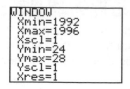

Window settings for the spreadsheet graph   Window settings on a graphics calculator

Using these settings, the graphs that follow show a pleasing decline on pupil exclusions in 'recent years'.

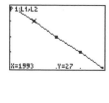

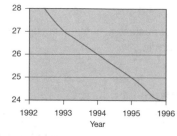

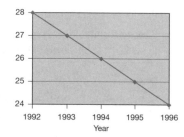

On the graphics
calculator   ... on the spreadsheet   ... on a graph plotter

(ii) The most rapid rise took place between 1996 and 1999, so positioning the viewing window here gives these graphs, which appear to show a very rapid rise in exclusions:

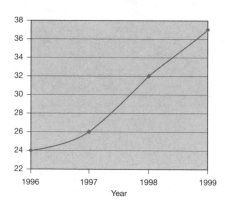

(iii) Finally, the gentle rise in the number of exclusions took place between 1999 and 2005, producing viewing windows that look like this:

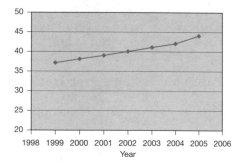

Note, however, that the scale on the vertical axis here needed to be manipulated in order to achieve this 'gentle' rise (the values chosen here run from 20 to 50 exclusions). As you saw earlier, depending on the range of values chosen, the graphs will look as steep as you want to make them. For example, adjusting the scale on the vertical axis to match the range 37–44 of exclusions will ensure that the graph runs from the bottom left corner to the top right corner, as follows:

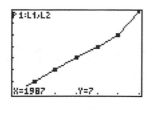
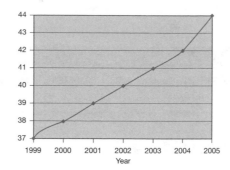

The issues of which viewing window to choose and what scales are chosen on the horizontal and vertical axes are thorny ones for all mathematical learners. The examples chosen in this section have been based on graphs drawn from data but the problem applies also to algebraic graphs. For example, the line $y = x$ is sometimes also referred to as the '45° line'. It may not be obvious to students that this line only makes an angle of 45° to the horizontal when the scales on the two axes are the same. This is often not the case, particularly when the representation is created on a non-square screen. For example, the so-called 'standard' window setting (Zstandard) of a graphics calculator runs from −10 to 10 on both axes. But, because of the oblong nature of the screen, this means that tick marks are unequally spaced and any displayed graphs and shapes are distorted. Here are the standard graphics calculator window settings and, alongside, you can see the resulting distortion on the slope of the line $y = x$ and on the shape of a circle:

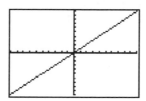
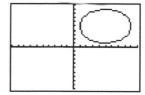

Standard window setting   The line $y = x$ looks too 'flat'.   A circle looks squashed

Now, 'square up' the axes (using the Zsquare command on the calculator) and this is the result.

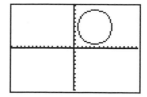

Square window setting   The slope of the line $y = x$ Now *that's* a circle
                                looks correct.

Pause for Reflection

Task 12.1.R Reflection

Can you recall seeing graphs in newspapers, magazines, or government reports that might benefit from careful analysis of the scales and axes?

12.2 SHIFTING AND STRETCHING GRAPHS

Quickie 12.2 Letters and Variables

In algebra, letters are used to represent variables, but some variables are subtly different in nature than others. Consider the equation $y = ax + b$. How would you characterise the distinction between the variables x and y and the other two letters, a and b?

Section 12.1 looked at the potentially distorting impression that can result from applying, to a graph, viewing windows of different size and shape and in different positions. To use the language of earlier chapters of this book, in each example you looked at the graph was *fixed* and the axes were *allowed to vary*.

In this section you are asked to consider the complementary relationship between a graph and its axes; here the axes will be fixed and you will consider what must be done to the equation of the graph to shift and stretch it. This will help to introduce a useful way of thinking about graphs and functions, namely to think of them as belonging to 'families', the members of which are connected in certain predictable ways. Once these principles have been learned for a particular family of lines or curves, they apply to *all* families of lines or curves.

An ideal medium for investigations of this sort is a graph–plotting package (for example, 'Autograph', 'TI Interactive!', and so on) and this is the medium used here. The early tasks will be spelt out in some detail but the later ones will require you take most of the initiative yourself.

Shifting Curves

The following task asks you to explore the notion of a 'family' of curves based around the simplest form of the sine curve, $y = \sin(x)$.

Task 12.2.1 Adding and Subtracting a Constant

The family of sine curves can take many different forms; for example:

$y = 3\sin(x) + 1$, $y = {}^-2\sin(x + 3) + 5$, $y = 2\sin(x - 4) - 1$, and so on.

The simplest form of all is $y = \sin(x)$, and this is the starting point of this investigation.

(a) Plot the graph of $y = \sin(x)$.

(b) Now plot the following graphs:

$y = \sin(x) + 1,$

$y = \sin(x) + 2,$

$y = \sin(x) -1.5,$

$y = \sin(x) -0.5,$

Look at the various graphs that you have drawn and answer the following question:

What is the effect of adding or subtracting a constant to the basic graph of $y = \sin(x)$?

Comment

Detailed comments on this task are set out below.

The basic graph of $y = \sin(x)$, plotted in a suitable viewing window, is shown in the first diagram. The other four graphs follow:

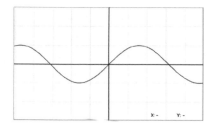

$y = \sin(x)$

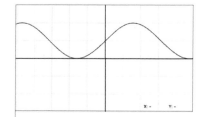

$y = \sin(x)+1$

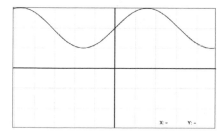

$y = \sin(x)+2$

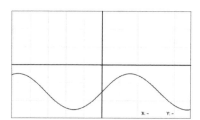

$y = \sin(x) - 1.5$

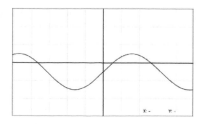

$y = \sin(x) - 0.5$

There seems to be a clear visual pattern here – the effect of adding or subtracting the constant term is to shift the curve vertically either up or down, depending on whether it is added or subtracted. But is this a general principle that can be applied to other families of curve? This question is the basis of the next task.

Task 12.2.2 Generalising

Articulate for yourself the effects on the graph of adding or subtracting a constant to an equation. Use graph-plotting software to check that your 'general principle' really does apply to all other functions.

(a) Plot the line $y = x$. Then explore what happens to the line when a constant is added or subtracted.

(b) Plot the line $y = x^2$. Then explore what happens to the curve when a constant is added or subtracted.

(c) When a constant is added to or subtracted from a function and the new graph is plotted, what stays the same and what changes?

(d) Consider some general function $y = f(x)$. How would you shift the graph of $y = f(x)$ to create the graph of a second function $y = (x) + c$, where c is a constant?

Comment

Detailed comments on this task are set out below.

(a) The basic graph of $y = x$ looks like this:

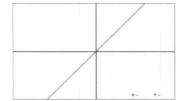

Here is the effect of adding and subtracting a constant:

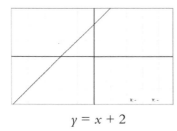 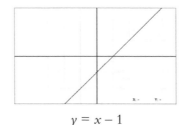

$y = x + 2$ $\qquad\qquad\qquad$ $y = x - 1$

It appears that these linear graphs have altered their position in the way that one might expect; adding 2 to the function shifts its graph up by 2 units and subtracting 1 unit shifts its graph down by 1 unit. However, one problem with linear graphs is that, to the eye, these shifts could equally well appear to be sideways. The reason for the uncertainty is that linear graphs are uniform so there is no distinctive portion of the graph to follow with the eye as it is transformed to a new position.

(b) The graph of $y = x^2$ looks like this:

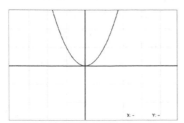

Here is the effect of adding and subtracting a constant:

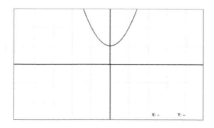
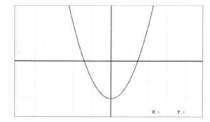

Adding 1: $y = x^2 + 1$ Subtracting 2: $y = x - 2$

As before, these graphs have altered their position in the way that one might expect; adding 1 to the function shifts its graph up by 1 unit and subtracting 2 units shifts its graph down by 2 units.

(c) When a constant is added to a function, the new graph shifts upwards by the amount of the constant. When a constant is subtracted from a function the new graph shifts downwards by the amount of the constant. In general, adding a constant to a function alters the *position* of a graph but not its *shape*.

(d) The answer to this question is to shift the graph *upwards* by an amount c. Note that when c takes a negative value (say, $^-4$) an upwards shift of $^-4$ units is equivalent to a downwards shift of 4 units.

Horizontal Shifting

You have seen that adding and subtracting a constant has the effect of shifting a graph up and down. But how can you shift it to left and right? Again, this is the sort of investigation that is much more rewarding when using graph-plotting software.

Task 12.2.3 Shifting Left and Right

(a) Using the basic functions $y = \sin(x)$, $y = x$ and $y = x^2$, investigate the effect of replacing the x with $(x + 1)$, $(x + 2)$ and $(x - 1)$.

(b) In general, how would you shift the graph of $y = f(x)$ to create the graph of a second function $y = f(x - b)$, where b is a constant?

Comment

(a) Here are a few illustrative examples:

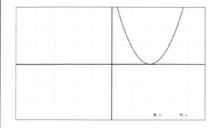
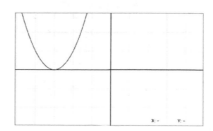

Replacing x with $x - 2$: $y = (x - 2)^2$ Replacing x with $x + 3$: $y = (x + 3)^2$

Task 12.2.3 Shifting Left and Right (continued)

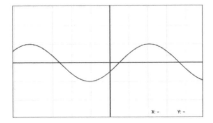 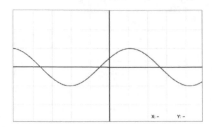

Replacing x with $x - 0.5$: $y = \sin(x - 0.5)$ Replacing x with $x + 0.5$: $y = \sin(x + 0.5)$

Replacing x with $x - 1$ shifts the curve to the right by 1 unit.
Replacing x with $x + 3$ shifts the curve to the left by 3 units.
Replacing x with $x - 0.5$ shifts the curve to the right by 0.5 unit.
Replacing x with $x + 0.5$ shifts the curve to the left by 0.5 units.

(b) The answer to this question is to shift the graph to the right by an amount b. Note that for a function such as $(x + 3)^2$, b takes a negative value $^-3$. A rightward shift of $^-3$ units is equivalent to a leftward shift of 3 units.

Stretching

So far you have investigated shifts in two directions (vertically and horizontally) Algebraically, these shifts are equivalent to changing to function $y = f(x)$ to the form $y = f(x - b) + c$, where b represents the horizontal shift and the c represents the vertical shift. These two transformations amount to altering the position of the graph but leaving its shape unaltered. However, the third major transformation is to *stretch* the curve by inserting a multiplicative factor, usually denoted by the letter a. The complete generalised curve is therefore normally written as:

$$y = af(x - b) + c$$

This general function can be built up from the basic form $y = f(x)$ by the following three transformations.

$y = f(x) + c$ First, shift the curve upwards c units …
$y = f(x - b) + c$ … then shift the curve right b units …
$y = af(x - b) + c$ … and finally stretch the curve by a factor a.

Task 12.2.4 Stretching

(a) Use the graph-plotting software to confirm that the effect of inserting the factor a in a general function $y = f(x)$ will have the effect of stretching the curve. Investigate the transformation starting with simple functions and then using various values of a, such as 2, 3, 0.5, 0.2, $^-1$, $^-3$, etc.

(b) What general principles can you discover about the effect on the graph of the scale factor, a?

Comment

(a) Here are a few illustrative examples.

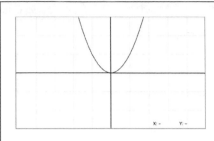

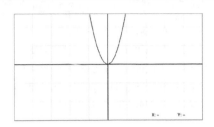

The original curve: $y = x^2$

Setting the scale factor, a, to 3: $y = 3x^2$

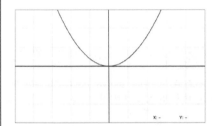

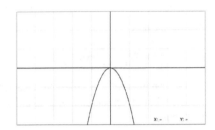

Setting the scale factor, a, to 0.4: $y = 0.4x^2$ Setting the scale factor, a, to ⁻2: $y = -2x^2$

(b) In general:

values of $a > 1$ have the effect of making the function appear tall and narrow,

values of $0 < a < 1$ have the effect of making the function appear short and wide,

values of ⁻1 $< a < 0$ have the effect of turning the curve upside down and making it appear short and wide,

values of $a <$ ⁻1 have the effect of turning the curve upside down and making it appear tall and narrow.

The Same but Different

To end this section, you are asked to consider a more philosophical question about families of functions, namely, are all linear, quadratic and sine functions basically the same? To set the scene for this question, consider these two congruent triangles.

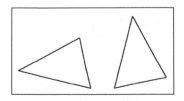

They are identical in shape and size, but have a different position and orientation. Note that the triangles are still congruent to each other regardless of position and orientation.

Now consider any two straight lines (say, $y = 3x$ ⁻2 and $y =$ ⁻2$x + 5$). All that distinguishes these lines is their position and orientation. Thinking about 'congruence', these two lines are therefore identical, since two simple transformations, a translation and a rotation are all that are required for one to become identical to the other. The next task asks you to apply this thinking to two different families of function.

Task 12.2.5   Quadratics and Sine Functions

Now apply the same sort of thinking to answer the following two questions:

(a) Are all quadratic curves essentially the same?

(b) Are all sine function curves essentially the same?

Note that there is an additional complication with quadratic and sine functions, namely that their shape is affected by the introduction of a scale factor.

Comment

Learners often meet quadratic functions before sine functions. It is worth nothing that changes in sine functions are more easily interpreted than changes in quadratic functions.

Pause for Reflection

12.2.R   Task Reflection

What is the difference between the variations considered in section 12.1 and the variations considered in this section: what is the same and what is different; what is invariant in each case, and what is permitted to change?

12.3   STEP BY STEP

Quickie 12.3

Take a simple number, say 4 and apply the sequence 'divide by 2 and add 3'. Keep applying the sequence to each new answer until it appears to settle down.

Now take a different starting number and repeat the process. What do you notice?

This section looks at iterative or recursive formulae. Such formulae have two key characteristics:

As the names suggest, these involve repeating a procedure over and over.

The formulae apply term-to-term (rather than position-to-term: see Chapter 4 on the use of this terminology).

Most people are rather surprised with the result of the quickie investigation that you have just carried out. It may be surprising enough that the sequence seems to settle down to a stable value (a limit) but it is even more counterintuitive that the value of this limit is independent of the starting number.

These sorts of investigations are much easier and more engaging when supported by ICT, allowing you to generate them quickly and easily, so enabling attention to be directed to the patterns and a search for an explanation of what lies behind it.

Iterating with a Graphics Calculator

Task 12.3.1 Exploring Sequences with a Graphics Calculator

Using the home screen of a graphics calculator, explore the sequence 'divide by 2 and add 3'.

Comment
Comments are given below.

Here is a possible 'What if … ' approach based on using a graphics calculator.

Step 1 Try a couple of simple examples — only a few iteration steps are shown.

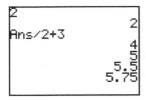 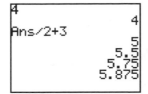

Step 2 What if I tried starting numbers bigger than 6?

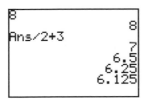 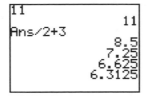

Step 3 What if I tried negative starting numbers?

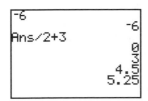 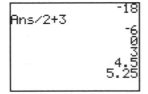

Step 4 What If I tried non-integer starting numbers?

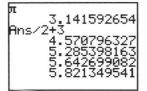

Letting these iterations run for a few hundred steps suggests that the endpoint really is 6, regardless of the starting point.

Using a Spreadsheet

One key feature of using a spreadsheet is that, once the underlying formula is in place in a particular cell, it can quickly be 'filled down' for 10, 30, or 100+ terms. Also, once the numbers are in place, they can easily be plotted graphically.

Task 12.3.2 Iterating with a Spreadsheet

Using a spreadsheet, explore the sequence 'divide by 2 and add 3'. When you have generated some data, try graphing them so as to represent the 'settling down' pattern visually.

Comments

Comments are given below.

The spreadsheet will look something like the one on the left.

	A	B	C
1	Step	Sequence	
2	1	4	START
3	2	5	
4	3	5.5	
5	4	5.75	
6	5	5.875	
7	6	5.9375	
8	7	5.96875	
9	8	5.984375	
10	9	5.9921875	
11	10	5.99609375	
12	11	5.998046875	
13	12	5.999023438	
14	13	5.999511719	
15	14	5.999755859	
16	15	5.99987793	
17	16	5.999938965	

	A	B	C
1	Step	Sequence	
2	1	41	START
3	2	23.5	
4	3	14.75	
5	4	10.375	
6	5	8.1875	
7	6	7.09375	
8	7	6.546875	
9	8	6.2734375	
10	9	6.13671875	
11	10	6.068359375	
12	11	6.034179688	
13	12	6.017089844	
14	13	6.008544922	
15	14	6.004272461	
16	15	6.00213623	
17	16	6.001068115	

	A	B	
1	Step	Sequence	
2	1	-248	START
3	2	-121	
4	3	-57.5	
5	4	-25.75	
6	5	-9.875	
7	6	-1.9375	
8	7	2.03125	
9	8	4.015625	
10	9	5.0078125	
11	10	5.50390625	
12	11	5.751953125	
13	12	5.875976563	
14	13	5.937988281	
15	14	5.968994141	
16	15	5.98449707	
17	16	5.992248535	

Note that the starting number, 4, is entered into cell B2. The 'divide by 2 and add 3' formula is entered into cell B3 and filled down column B. Once the spreadsheet has been created, it is simply a matter of entering some other starting value into cell B2 to see, directly, a new set of values. Whatever number is entered into this cell, the result is always the same – the sequence tends towards a limit of 6. Two more examples are shown above on starting values of 41 and ⁻238:

The benefit of including the step values in column A of the spreadsheet is that the results can now be plotted as a scatterplot. Note that these sequences are based on a series of discrete steps, so line graphs would not be appropriate. The scatter plot for the first ten terms of the first of the spreadsheets above will look like the following:

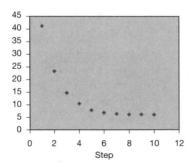

Task 12.3.3a More Sequences with a Spreadsheet

(a) Using a spreadsheet, explore some more sequences like the sequence you have just investigated – 'divide by 2 and add 3', by altering some dimensions of possible variation.

(b) Try to create a sequence that settles down to the number 10.

(c) Using an algebraic method or a logical argument, try to find a convincing explanation connecting the sequence rule to the final number that each sequence settles down to.

Comment

Comments are given below.

(a) The spreadsheet based on the sequence 'divide by 5 and add 2' settles down to a limiting value of 2.5.

(b) There are many possible ways of setting up a sequence so that it settles down to a particular value. Here are three different sequences that all settle down to the same value, 10. They are, 'divide by 2 and add 5', 'divide by 5 and add 8' and 'divide by 4 and add 7.5'. They are displayed in columns B, C and D respectively of this spreadsheet.

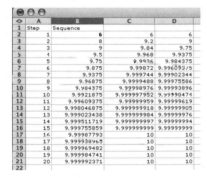

(c) An argument or proof showing how the sequence links to the final number needs to be based on an important fact about such sequences, namely that, when it gets close to a stable value, it looks as though it is actually at that stable value. A stable value is unchanged by applying the iteration process. To take the first sequence (divide by 2 and add 3) as an example, you can let both the final number and its preceding value equal N. So, the following formula connects these two values:

$$N = N/2 + 3$$

solving for N gives the answer 6, confirming the result from Task 12.3.2. This method can be used to demonstrate that the other sequences proposed all have a stable value of 10.

Task 12.3.3b Pythagorean Iteration

Use the method for finding stable values to find the stable values for the Pythagorean iteration in Task 9.2.4, namely $\sqrt{2}, \sqrt{1+\sqrt{2}}, \sqrt{1+\sqrt{1+\sqrt{2}}}, \ldots$. Graph the equations $y = x$ and $y = \sqrt{1 + x}$ and use the staircase construction to see the iteration process converging to one of the stable values.

Comment

It may be worth contemplating the dimensions of possible variation in this iteration sequence. Sometimes they will settle down at a stable value, but sometimes they get larger and larger, or oscillate between two values.

Hero's Square Roots

Hero was a celebrated mathematician and engineer who lived in Alexandria in the first century BCE. Amongst several inventions, he discovered the principle of feedback control devices. His self-filling wine bowl, for example, had a hidden float valve that automatically sensed the level of wine in a bowl. When guests ladled out wine, the bowl mysteriously refilled itself.

Hero's method for estimating square roots was also based on the principle of a feedback loop. Suppose Hero wanted to find the square root of 10. His approach was to guess an answer (say, 3) and then apply the following sequence several times: Divide 10 by the guess, add the guess, then divide the answer by 2. This gave a sequence of ever-improving guesses.

Task 12.3.4 Be a Hero!

(a) Using a calculator, run Hero's sequence four or five times and then compare your result with the calculator answer for the square root of 10.

(b) Set up a graphics calculator or spreadsheet to run Hero's method for finding square roots, based on roughly 10 iterations.

(c) Using an algebraic method or a logical argument, try to find a convincing explanation for Hero's method.

Comment

Comments are given below.

(a) On a graphics calculator, the initial value, 3, is entered. Then, repeatedly apply the formula: $(10/\text{Ans} + \text{Ans})/2$. Note that for each iteration the value of Ans is the most recent estimate.

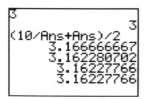 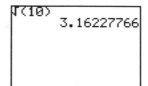

As you can see from the screenshots, Hero's square root algorithm settles down very quickly indeed – usually only three or four iterations are needed to produce an estimate of a square root to ten figure accuracy.

(b) A six-line graphics calculator such as the following could be used to provide ten iterations of Hero's method. The number whose square root you want to find is labelled N and the initial estimate of the square root is S. An explanation for each command is given here.

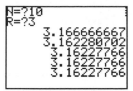

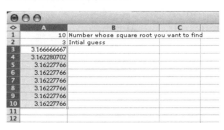

Enter values for the number N and your initial estimate S.
Set up a loop with ten iterations.
Apply Hero's formula.
Display the value of R, the current estimate of the square root.
Pause.
End the loop.

Execute the program. Each time the latest value of R is displayed, the program pauses. Press <ENTER> to move it on to the next iteration.

In the spreadsheet set-up, notice that the value whose square root you wish to find is entered into cell A1. The first guess is entered into A2 and the initial formula is entered into cell A3; this is: =(A$1/A2+A2)/2. This is then filled down. Note the use of the dollar sign in the formula to refer to the value in cell A1 – this ensures that the cell reference to A1 does not alter as the formula is filled down.

To find the square root of a different number, simply enter it into cell A1.

(c) An explanation for the solution is based on the same principle mentioned in the comments to Task 12.3.3 part (c), namely that, when settling down has taken place, the final estimate is very nearly equal to the value preceding it, and at the stable value, the iteration makes no change. Let this estimate for the square root be labelled S. Then the formula for estimating the value of the square root of 10 can be written as:

$$S = (10/S + S)/2$$

Multiplying out the brackets and rearranging, gives:

$$S^2 = 10, \text{ and therefore}$$
$$S = \sqrt{(10)}.$$

Replacing the particular value 10 with N provides the following general iterative formula for finding the square root, S, of any positive number, N:

$$S_{new} = (N/S_{old} + S_{old})/2$$

Hero's method, although over 2000 years old, is extremely efficient and is essentially the same algorithm that is built into modern calculators to calculate square roots.

Pause for Reflection

Task 12.3.R Reflection

Rehearse in your mind the technique for locating stable values of an iteration.

Can you construct an iteration which does not settle down, even though there is a stable value?

Comment

Just because you have a stable value for an iteration process, there is no guarantee that it will settle down at all, or it may only settle down for certain starting values. Deeper study of this topic belongs in an introduction to the calculus. New=Old^2 has 1 as a stable value but no static value settles down to 1.

12.4 GRAPHING ITERATIONS

Quickie 12.4

Iterative methods are designed to generate a sequence of numerical values that may or may not settle down to a particular value. Why might there be advantage in graphing the results of iteration? How might you get a picture of an iteration process?

In this section you are asked to explore ways of representing iterations graphically. In the comments to Task 12.3.2 you saw a graphical representation of the results of the iterative procedure 'divide by 2 and add 3'. Here the values were plotted on the vertical scale and the step number on the horizontal. Now, in Task 12.4.1 you are asked to take a different approach. The aim here is to lead gradually to the notions of staircase diagrams for plotting iterations.

One-dimensional Plot

Before developing alternative ways of graphing iterative values, it would be helpful to clarify the notation that will be used.

Each term value will be labelled T_0, T_1, T_2, etc., where T_0 is the initial starting value (in this case, 2).

The 'divide by 2 and add 3' function will be labelled F. Writing, say, $F(4)$ means the value of the 'divide by 2 and add 3' with 4 as the input value.

Using this notation, the first five iterations of this procedure can be written as follows:

$T_0 = 2$
$T_1 = F(2) = 2/2 + 3 = 4$
$T_3 = F(4) = 4/2 + 3 = 5$
$T_4 = F(5) = 5/2 + 3 = 5.5$
$T_5 = F(5.5) = 5.5/2 + 3 = 5.75$

Task 12.4.1 A One-dimensional Plot

(a) Plot these values on a one-dimensional horizontal line.

(b) What is stressed and what is ignored in this representation?

Comment

(a) The one-dimensional representation should look something like this:

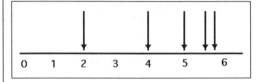

(b) This representation stresses the particular values that are generated by the iteration formula but ignores the term values. In other words, the one-dimensional graph gives no clue as to the sequence of the values being depicted. It fails to signal an important feature of the iteration process, namely that the output value for one iteration becomes the input value for the next, and it fails to make use of the second dimension.

Staircase Diagrams

The staircase diagram is an attempt to solve the problem mentioned in the comments to the previous activity, in that it provides a clear and powerful pictorial image of how each new output value becomes the input value for the next iteration. To achieve this, you must return to a two-dimensional representation but this time with different variables depicted on the axes. But most students find staircase diagrams rather daunting when they first come across them. For this reason, they are presented here in two stages in Tasks 12.4.2 and 12.4.3. The first of these tasks sets out a simple principle of what is involved in plotting iterative values graphically and the second task looks at how this might be done more elegantly.

But first, here is the rudimentary staircase diagram.

Task 12.4.2 A Rudimentary Staircase

The graph shows input value on the horizontal scale and output value on the vertical scale. Try to follow the first few stages through now step by step. The straight line graph represents the 'divide by 2 and add 3' rule that you have been using. So, it takes the form of $y = x/2+3$.

Step 1: (a) Input the starting value, 2. This can be represented as a vertical line from an input value 2 to the function line. (b) Read off the corresponding output value, 4. This can be represented as a horizontal line from the function line to the vertical axis.

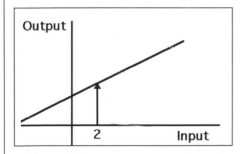 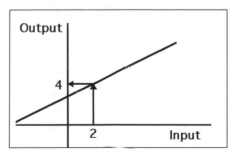

Step 2: The output value 4 now becomes the input value for the next iteration. (a) Input this value as a vertical line from 4 to the function line. (b) Read off the corresponding output value, 5. This can be represented as a horizontal line from the function line to the vertical axis.

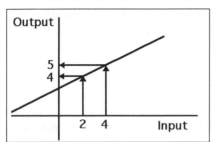

Continue subsequent steps in this manner until it settles down.

(a) What are the coordinates of the point where the sequence settles down? What is the significance of this point?

(b) Can you think of a more efficient way of creating this sequence graph?

Comment

(a) The graph settles down at the point (6,6). There are two features worth noting about the point where $x = 6$, $y = 6$:

(i)   This point lies on the line (check this by substituting the values $x = 6$, $y = 6$ into the equation $y = x/2+3$.

(ii) The x and y values are equal; in other words, this is the only point on the line where the input value is equal to the output value (which is the condition of settling down).

(b) Each new step begins by taking the output value from the previous step and making it the new input value. As carried out here, this is a rather cumbersome process as it involves taking particular values from the y-axis and measuring them out on the horizontal axis. It might be considerably speeded up if the line $y = x$ were included on the graph. You will be asked to explore this simplification in the next task.

Task 12.4.3 A Fancy Staircase

(a) Repeat the iterative graph that you have just drawn in Task 12.4.1 but this time include the line $y = x$. Try to use this line to speed up your drawing.

(b) Compare this version of the drawing with the one that you created in the previous task. What are the gains and the losses in including the $y = x$ line?

Comment

(a) As before, the first iteration starts at the value 2 on the Input axis and a vertical line is drawn to the line $y = x/2+3$. But now, instead of moving horizontally to the *left* to read off the corresponding output value, the movement is to the *right*, to meet the line $y = x$, ready for the next iteration. This effectively collapses the following two steps into one:

Read the output value off the vertical axis.

Turn this value into an input value by marking off the same interval on the horizontal axis.

It is this stage that most students find difficult to grasp, for good reason, in that the thinking is fairly dense.

Another version is to start on the x-axis at some point; go up to the graph, across to the line $y = x$, then up (or down as need be) to the graph again, then across to $y = x$, then up or down again, continuing in this fashion. The effect of going across to the line $y = x$ is to transfer the current height into a distance along the x-axis.

Continuing in this manner produces a series of steps that eventually end up at the point (6,6). It is not difficult to see from the final picture why this is often referred to as a 'staircase diagram'.

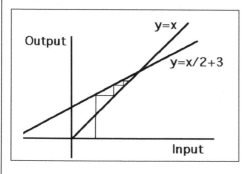

(b) The inclusion of the $y = x$. line has certainly streamlined the process and probably speeded up your drawing of the iterations, but there is certainly a cost in terms of clarity about what is going on. How comfortably might you have understood this more sophisticated procedure had you not already gone through the underlying thinking in Task 12.4.2? This points to a wider in mathematical learning, namely that there is often a trade-off between algorithmic efficiency and transparency of method. It might be argued that, since machines are increasingly carrying out algorithms very quickly indeed (even for inefficient methods), inefficiency of method may be a price worth paying so that students can gain a clearer understanding of the big underlying ideas.

Pause for Reflection

The simple process of tracking the coordinates of each of the points on the staircase is a useful exercise in learning to interpret the graphs of equations: they are not simply end products, rather, they are intended to be informative, and so it is valuable to learn how to interpret them.

12.4.R Task Reflection

What has using graphs to think about iterations highlighted for you about reading and interpreting graphs?

12.5 PEDAGOGIC ISSUES

Algebraic versus Statistical Graphs

Most teachers would probably agree that students find algebraic graphs difficult yet they seem to have a good intuitive understanding of statistical graphs based on everyday data. This finding was recorded by Daphne Kerslake in her chapter entitled 'Graphs' in Hart et al., 1981. The research was carried out on roughly 1800 pupils aged 13–15. They found that: '(V)ery little difficulty was experienced by the pupils with elementary items on block graphs, and the use of rectangular coordinates to plot points, when the numbers involved were integers. About 90 per cent of the pupils were successful at such items.'

However, the movement from everyday to algebraic graphs, combined with the transition from discrete to continuous variables caused major problems. In one of the tasks set, the pupils were asked to plot the points (2,5), (3,7) and (5,11) and join them with a straight line. They were then further interrogated about what they had drawn: 'many pupils found difficulty with the idea that there are any more points on the line than those they had plotted. Several said that there were no points between (2,5) and (3,7), while others thought there was just one (presumably the mid-point)'.

The pupils were also provided with paired data (height and waist measurements of five pupils) and asked to plot them as a scatter plot. They were then asked, 'Should we join up the points on the diagram?' The commonest answers to this were based not on the nature of the data or the meaning of any lines used to join up the points but on the *appearance* of the graph. This was true both for many of pupils who thought the points should be joined up as well as for some of those who did not.

'Yes, I think this because it would be more accurate and look neater.' (Philip aged 14 years)
'Yes, because it would look tidier.' (Jane aged 13 years)
'No, because the points would be all in a mess.' (Simon aged 13 years)

Perhaps unsurprisingly, pupils also found it difficult to identify graphs from their visual appearance. They were given the graphs $y = 2x$, $y = 2$, $x = 2$ and $x + y = 2$, then asked to indicate which of the four was $y = 2x$, and then to give the equation of the other three.

Their success levels, in percentages, are summarised in the table.

	13 years	14 years	15 years
$y = 2x$	18.8	18.2	26.9
$y = 2$	16.7	10.3	14.3
$x = 2$	15.2	9.8	14.0
$x + y = 2$	5.9	3.9	5.1

Task 12.5.1 How Good Are Children at Identifying Graphs?

How do you respond to these figures? What explanations, if any can you offer for them? What are their implications for the level and pacing of graph teaching at school?

Comment

It may not be surprising that the pupils performed best with the first function, $y = 2x$. This may be due, partly, to the fact that this was the only one for which the equation was provided. But another possible explanation is that the bulk of children's experience with linear functions is when they are presented in the standard form of $y =$ some expression in x. The so-called simple cases of $y = 2$ and $x = 2$ do not fall into this category and so are seen as difficult by many children. The same argument applies to the implicit equation, $x + y = 2$, for which the standard rules for identifying the gradient and y-intercept are hard to apply without first rearranging the equation − a step too far for those many students whose algebraic manipulation skills are shaky.

A surprising result is the apparent drop in performance levels in pupils between the ages of 13 and 14. A general failure to improve during this year was noted in a number of the other mathematical test items carried out by CSMS, but no clear explanation was offered. It may be that at this time of great physical and emotional change, many adolescents feel that the challenge of linking algebraic graphs and their algebraic functions does not merit their full attention!

Levels of generality

In section 12.2 you were offered the following quickie task: 'In algebra, letters are used to represent variables, but some variables are subtly different in nature than others. Consider the equation $y = ax + b$. How would you characterise the distinction between the variables x and y and the other two letters, a and b?'

In truth, this is of course no quickie! On the contrary, this question touches on a major source of confusion for students about the nature of algebraic variables. For example, at one level, the equation $y = 2x + 3$ is a *particular* (linear) relationship between two variables, x and y. However, because x and y are able to vary, this equation is *general* in that it represents an infinite number of ordered pairs that satisfy this relationship. How, then can a linear relationship achieve generality? This can be done by considering the broader class of all linear relationships – what was referred to earlier as the 'linear family'. This movement from particular to general is achieved by generalising the two defining characteristics of linear equations – the gradient and intercept – and indicating their variable nature by allocating them letters rather than numbers. Thus, the equation $y = ax + b$ not only represents an infinite set of points on the plane but also an infinite set of equations. Note that, whereas the particular equation $y = 2x + 3$ represents an infinite number of points on a particular curve on the plane, the generalised linear equation $y = ax + b$ covers *all* possible points on the plane.

It seems that there are two distinct types of variable here. The values taken by the x and y variables represent the input and output values but the values given to a and b are what particularise the general family of linear equations. Variables that do this are usually referred to as *parameters*.

Task 12.5.2 Parameters

(a) Can you think of examples in school algebra and beyond where the notion of a parameter is important?

(b) How do the notions of a 'parameter' and 'families of graphs' link to the mathematical themes of this book (these are summarised in section 15.2 of Chapter 15)?

(c) Section 15.5 of Chapter 15 lists a number of pedagogic strategies that you might use with pupils to help them gain a clearer understanding of algebraic ideas. Choose one of these strategies and use it to explore how you might help pupils gain an insight into some of the big ideas underlying the graphing of algebraic relationships.

Comment

(a) The general quadratic equation $y = ax^2 + bx + c$ has three parameters, a, b and c. The notion of parameter crops up in many areas of mathematics. For example, the 'normal distribution' in statistics refers to the common bell-shaped curve that is a useful model for the distributional pattern of many natural phenomena (birth weight, leaf size, gestation period, and so on). The two parameters that define the normal distribution are the mean and the standard deviation – the mean determines where the distribution is located and the standard deviation how widely it is spread.

(b) The ideas of 'freedom and constraint' are relevant to the notion of a family of graphs and to the importance of parameters in defining that family. For example, pupils can be provided with a particular equation such as $y = 2x - 5$ and asked to find an example of another line parallel to it ... and another, and another. Now can they find another line that cuts through the y-axis in the same point ... and another, and another? This topic could also be addressed through considering the notion of 'invariance and change'. For example, if a sequence of linear graphs all slope from bottom left to top right, what is the same about them? In other words, what is allowed to change and what must stay the same? An equivalent question can be applied to quadratic curves – for the curves to be 'smiley faces', what is allowed to change and what must stay the same?

(c) The pedagogic strategy of 'turning a doing into an undoing' can be usefully applied to the teaching of families of curves. For example, pupils may start with the standard linear graph $y = x$, asked to make it steeper by doubling the gradient (giving $y = 2x$) and finally shifting it upwards by 5 units (giving $y = 2x + 5$). Now, what steps are required to return the new graph to its original state? Does the order matter (on this occasion the answer is 'no')? Another strategy, 'same and different' will be useful here also. Pupils could be given a variety of different linear or quadratic curves, asked to look at them two at a time and say what is the same and what is different about them. This exercise should help direct their attention to the underlying generality of linear families and help them gain insight into the meaning of the parameters a and b in the equation $y = ax + b$.

Introduction to Block 4

This final block serves as summary, review, and reflection on the previous three blocks, with attention particularly on pedagogic implications. Here the mathematical powers, mathematical themes, pedagogic constructs and pedagogic strategies which have been used throughout the book are reviewed and summarised in one place.

Chapter 13 begins with some important themes which pervade mathematics and which serve to link and unify topics that otherwise might seem rather disparate. Even within algebra, the topics presented to learners often seem disconnected, largely because the encounter is based on mastering techniques without drawing on these themes or upon learners' powers. The remainder of the chapter considers the structure of mathematical topics, culminating in a framework which can be used to inform preparation for teaching any mathematical topic.

Chapter 14 begins with a description of some of the natural powers which all learners possess and which are vital for mathematical thinking generally, and particularly for algebraic thinking. These are the powers which need to be activated and developed through work on specific topics, and you will have experienced them when working on tasks throughout the book. It goes on to elaborate on the various pedagogic constructs and strategies made use of in and by tasks throughout the book.

Chapter 15 starts with the importance of opportunity and encouragement for learners to generalise. The subsequent sections exploit the notion of dimensions of possible variation in augmenting and using tasks to make them pedagogically effective. The chapter ends with a brief summary of the roots of algebra, by which it is possible to chart a route to algebra for learners, and some of the directions in which algebra blossoms as learners move into sixth form and beyond.

13 Themes and Structure

Section 13.1 recapitulates some of the underlying mathematical themes which pervade and serve to unify mathematical topics. The next three sections each focus attention on an aspect of the human psyche: awareness, emotion and behaviour as they impact upon learners' encounters with a mathematical topic. Examples are drawn from factoring quadratics, solving simultaneous equations, and graphing equations. Section 13.2 draws attention to the sorts of things one would like to have come to learners' minds in the context of a topic. This is how learners educate their awareness. Section 13.3 considers motivational aspects of problem situations and applications associated with a topic which support learners in harnessing their emotions. Section 13.4 considers aspects of training behaviour in the context of a topic: gaining competence in procedures and methods. Section 13.5 then integrates these three aspects in a single framework which has proved useful for analysing and preparing to teach any mathematical topic.

13.1 MATHEMATICAL THEMES

There are certain themes which pervade mathematical topics, serving to reveal connections and links which might otherwise go unnoticed. The themes summarised here all have important manifestation in algebra, as will have emerged throughout the book.

Freedom and Constraint

Most mathematical problems can be seen as starting from a very general, relatively free situation (consider one, or two, or three, or more numbers; consider a shape in the plane or in three dimensions, ...), and then imposing constraints upon that freedom, upon those possibilities. The problem is usually to construct one or more objects which satisfy all those constraints, though sometimes it is necessary to demonstrate that the constraints are too demanding and that nothing can satisfy them all. A useful way to get learners to become more aware of the choices and freedom available to them is to use the pedagogic strategy of *another and another*.

Looking for freedom and constraint can be helpful in several ways. Stimulating learners to become aware of choices that they can make, and prompting learners to make choices, contributes to a sense of involvement and participation which is the principal source of motivation. Seeing mathematics as a constructive and often creative activity makes a change from the more usual view of mathematics as a collection of techniques for solving predetermined problems. More psychologically, the mathematical notion of a *variable* captures and encodes a sense of freedom which is going to be constrained, and the expression of a generality describes freedom within constraint. Learner difficulties are sometimes associated with imposing extra implicit constraints which aren't actually either necessary or desirable. For example, learners might implicitly assume that an answer has to be a whole number, or positive. Furthermore, difficult or unfamiliar problems can often be tackled by removing some of the constraints and expressing the general class of solutions to the new problem, before then going on to impose the extra constraints.

Task 13.1.1 Saying it Differently

Express in symbols (write an expression for) all numbers which are one third more than a whole number multiple of 1/2. By rearranging your expression and then translating into words, find at least two different ways to express the same numbers verbally.

Comment

Using n as a variable for all possible whole numbers, the numbers sought are of the form $1/3 + n/2$. This can be written as $(3n + 2)/6$ and also as, for example, $(n + 1)/2 - 1/6$. Expressed verbally these come out as 'one sixth of a number of the form two more than a multiple of 3', and as 'one sixth less than a multiple of one half'.

You might have found yourself puzzling over these for a moment, perhaps specialising to try particular cases.

Here is a sophisticated version of tasks appearing in earlier chapters, such as Task 0.2 and Quickie 1.2.

Task 13.1.2 Three-Sum

Find three expressions that sum to $5x + 7y + 4$.

Find another three expressions.

And another three.

Now do the same again but this time, arrange that all of the coefficients are positive.

Comment

Had you thought of allowing negative coefficients, or was it the last prompt that released this possibility? Was your final set of three more ambitious (perhaps using fractions)? Had you thought of allowing fractions, numbers like $\sqrt{3}$ or π? Had you thought of including other variables which cancelled out?

At each stage of constructing expressions, it is possible to catch a sense of 'how much freedom is there left?' When the coefficients all have to be non-negative, there are some choices which cannot be extended to a full solution. How many triples are there then which work? That leads to an opportunity to generalise: treat the 4, 5 and 7 as DofPV which could be changed.

Any question involving equations and inequalities can be seen as a sequence of constraints imposed on some set of numbers. Each additional constraint may cut down the choices. Sometimes it is even useful to think in terms of the constraints being imposed sequentially rather than all at once, thus easing an otherwise difficult looking task.

Doing and Undoing

Whenever someone finds a way of 'doing' a calculation or of solving a problem, there is available the 'undoing' or reverse problem: if this is the answer, what other questions or situations like this would give the same answer. For example:

> Given a fraction, find the decimal (perhaps ending with a repeating pattern) equivalent; given a decimal ending with a repeating part, find a fraction which is equivalent to it.
>
> Given a pair of numbers calculate the difference; given the difference, find pairs of numbers that have that difference.
>
> Given two whole numbers you can multiply them together; given a number, find pairs of numbers that could be multiplied together to give it (factoring). The same idea applies to algebraic expressions: the undoing of expanding or multiplying out of brackets is factoring.
>
> Given a pair of numbers, you can calculate their least common multiple; given a number, what pairs of numbers have that number as their least common multiple?
>
> Given values for x and y, construct statements which are true using x and y (setting up equations for others to solve); given information (facts, true statements) about x and y, find their values (solving equations).

Notice that while a 'doing' usually gives a single answer, the corresponding 'undoing' often gives rise to a whole class of answers. It often requires considerable creativity as well as ingenuity to solve 'undoing' problems. Trying particular cases (specialising) in order to detect some underlying common structure (generalising) is often a good way to proceed.

There is a close connection between 'undoing' and characterising. 'Undoing' a calculation or the use of a technique is essentially interchanging the givens (the data) and what is sought. Characterising is used when the question arises as to the class of all possible inputs (data, givens) which give rise to the same answer or all possible answers arising from the use of a given technique. For example, when thinking about greatest common divisors of two numbers, you can ask how, given a number, to find pairs of numbers which have that number as their greatest common divisor (undoing). You can ask for a characterisation of all such pairs. You can also ask what numbers can arise as the greatest common divisor of two numbers.

Task 13.1.3 Recognising

If you double any whole number and add 1 you get a new number. What numbers can arise in this way?

If a service costs £12 for the first hour and £7 for each succeeding hour, what prices can arise?

If you add some consecutive odd numbers you get a number. Which numbers arise in this way?

Comment

The first is straightforward because it is familiar: an odd number. The second is familiar from the quickies in Chapter 1: numbers of the form 12 more than a multiple of 7, but it is set in a work context. The third has layers of complexity and is much more obscure. One response might be that the result is always a difference of two squares. An undoing applied to the third asks whether any difference of two squares is the sum of some consecutive odd numbers.

Extending and Restricting

Arithmetic and then algebra can be seen as repeated use of extending the meaning of 'number'. Starting with whole or counting numbers, these are extended to include zero, which is then referred to as a 'number'. Adding numbers together is a generalisation of the operation of 'adding one' to a number. When negatives are introduced, the whole collection is also referred to as 'numbers', though sometimes they are called *integers* (positive, negative and zero) to identify them specifically. When *fractions* are introduced as operations, they are quickly identified with their effects on the unit, 1. So 'taking one-third' slips into 'one-third' as an object, and then referred to as 'a number'. Fraction (operations) which give the same result (such as 4/6 of and 6/9 of) as positions on the number line, are referred to as 'the same number'. Fractions become 'numbers', with the integers as members. The notion of 'number' has extended considerably.

Combining fractions with negatives produces the positive and negative fractions, also known as *rational numbers*, and again referred to as 'numbers', sometimes as 'rationals'. The rationals include the whole numbers and the integers as special cases, as rationals with a denominator of 1. Note that 2/3 and 3/2 are both fractions, but can be thought of as standing for all of the fractions equivalent to them respectively and, so, as rational numbers. The process of extending continues, to include irrational numbers, decimal or real numbers, complex numbers and beyond.

As well as meaning being extended, it is also often fruitful to restrict attention. For example, in order to appreciate the fact that whole numbers can be uniquely factored into products of primes, it is useful to discover that there are 'sets of numbers' which do not factorise uniquely into 'primes'. The next task illustrates this.

Task 13.1.4 New Primes

Verify that the product of two numbers, both one more than a multiple of 3, is itself one more than a multiple of three.

Find the first three numbers of the form $3n + 1$, where n is a positive whole number, which factorise into the product of two numbers which are themselves of the form $3n + 1$. (These are called 'composite' numbers within this restricted domain; those that do not factorise in this way are 'prime' in this restricted domain.)

Factorise 100 as the product of two numbers of the form $3n + 1$, in as many ways as possible. What is the significance of what you found?

Comment

Did you find yourself having to remember that you are restricting your attention to numbers of the form $3n + 1$? In the context of these numbers, which are closed under multiplication, the notion of primes makes sense (numbers which cannot be factored into products of numbers of the same form other than themselves and one) but 100 can be factored in two different ways: there is no unique factorisation into primes in this restricted set of numbers. This task illustrates that restricting attention to a subclass of objects can produce unexpected results or properties which are not the same as the properties of the whole class. Thus numbers of the form $3n + 1$ form a restricted system of numbers closed under multiplication but which do not have the property of unique prime factoring.

Did you think to generalise by considering DofPV?

Extending meaning is closely related to considering the range of permissible change (RofPCh) of a parameter or feature of a concept, task, expression, etc. For example, learners often, as in Task 13.1.2, Three-Sum, implicitly assume a narrow range of permissible change of parameters. By inviting them to consider explicitly what the RofPCh might be their appreciation of the scope and range of a technique or concept can be broadened considerably. Conversely, if learners have a narrow sense of the RofPCh in a situation, they may not appreciate what the 'fuss' is about.

Invariance and Change

Mathematics is rarely concerned with very specific facts, such as that $3 + 4 = 7$. Rather, it is concerned with generalities, and these can often be approached by thinking about what is allowed to change, and what remains invariant in the midst of that change. For example, in $x + y = 10$, the presence of the letters x and y suggest that their values can change, but that the 10 is taken to be invariant.

Task 13.1.5 Invariance

What is changing and what is the same about the three following expressions as a whole?

$3 + 5 = 2 \times 4, \qquad 5 + 7 = 2 \times 6, \qquad 3 + 7 = 2 \times 5?$

Comment

Invariants include the number of numbers appearing (two each side of the equals sign), the signs $+$, $=$ and x which are common to all, and the multiplier 2. What is changing are the numbers on the left which are all odd (an invariance), and the last number is half way between the numbers on the left.

Human senses (seeing, hearing, touching, smelling, tasting, and perhaps a less choate 'sense of structure') all work by detecting change. But change only makes sense if there is something that is not changing (or not changing so much) as a background against which to detect the change. It is often useful to switch from stressing what is changing, to stressing what is staying the same and back again in order to appreciate the significance of a collection of objects or 'examples'.

In several tasks you have been asked to consider what was the same and what different about two or more 'objects'. The idea is to make use of learners' power to select attributes and to detect pattern or similarity. This leads to seeing particular objects such as numbers, shapes, pictures, relationships such as $3 < 4$, and so on, as particular cases of a general class of such objects. Once the objects are seen as representative of a whole class of 'similar' objects, a phenomenon has been identified, based around that sameness. This is the essence of generalisation, seeing the general through the particular.

To appreciate sameness-and-difference requires that you discriminate features, some of which are shared by all objects being considered but which might not be shared by all possible objects (sameness), and some which can be used to distinguish between the objects (difference). For example, recall the issue of counting 2p coins in Task 1.5.1: they all look the same; what is being counted is their materiality while their 'value' is ignored. In trying to transform a task they have been set into a task they can do, learners often stress features that are not what the teacher is stressing. The result is that they may find generalities being asserted by the teacher rather opaque!

When you stress certain features apparently shared by all the objects, and ignore differences, you are engaged in abstraction or generalisation. You are classifying according to those selected features, opening up the possibility of considering other objects with those same features, but perhaps differing in some other respects which are currently being ignored. As Caleb Gattegno[1] (1987) said, stressing and ignoring is the basis for generalisation, for classification. For example, in order to appreciate that 1/2, 2/4, 3/6, 4/8, etc. all represent the same rational number and that they are deemed to be 'equivalent fractions', it is necessary to discern not only the fact that there are two numbers separated by a slash, but also that in each case the second or 'bottom' number is double the top. But this relationship is merely an artefact unless there is an associated awareness of / as a division sign, and a sense that each of the divisions, as operators, gives the same result as taking one-half or dividing by 2. This is unchanging, invariant, amidst the change of fraction name or form. Only then does it make sense to treat the relationship as a property of fractions, and to think about 'equivalent fractions'. More generally, amongst all objects 'you can imagine' which share the features you are stressing, those features remain the same, remain invariant, while other features are permitted to change. So understanding a concept involves appreciating what aspect or feature is to be stressed and so considered to be invariant (in the case of equivalent fractions, the effect of operating the fraction on a unit, or the 'value' of the fraction) and what can change (in the case of equivalent fractions, the form or presentation of the fraction).

Multiple Interpretations

Although mathematics is considered to be precise and rigorous, it achieves its power and use through ambiguity, or put more positively, through permitting multiple readings or interpretations of symbols. For example:

⁻3 can be seen as an integer (negative three) or as the result of an operation on whole numbers $(0 - 3)$.

2/3 can be seen as an instruction to divide two units into three equal parts, or what is very similar as an operator (take two-thirds of something); it can also be seen as the answer to that division; as a fraction; as the value of a fraction (a rational number); and as the value of a ratio, not to say a position on the number line or the name of a number.

$3x + 1$ can be seen as a calculation instruction to be applied to an as-yet-unknown number x; as the result of that calculation; as an expression of generality where x represents the number of some objects or attributes; as the specification of a function; as part of the description of a graph $(y = 3x + 1)$.

24 and $2^3 \times 3$ are different ways of presenting or naming the same number, as are $23 + 1$, $48/2$, $4^2 + 2 \times 4$ and so on.

$(x - 2)(x + 3)$ and $x^2 + x - 6$ and $(x + 1)x - 6$ are different ways of presenting or naming the same expression or function, among others.

In each case, it is vital to be able to move flexibly and instantly between different representations and interpretations in order to function efficiently and effectively with numbers and expressions.

Learning From and Through Experience

Five mathematical themes have been put forward: freedom and constraint, doing and undoing, extending and restricting, invariance and change, and multiple interpretations. The claim is that these not only pervade mathematics, but often serve as links and connections between otherwise apparently disparate topics. Put another way, learning mathematics can be perceived as exploring the variety of ways in which these themes are developed and instantiated or exemplified in different mathematical concepts and topics. By being aware of these as themes you can draw upon them when structuring tasks, so that learners encounter the themes, and you can use the themes explicitly with learners as prompts to get them to make choices and to develop and extend their appreciation of concepts. For example, when stuck on a problem, learners can be invited to ask themselves what freedoms and constraints they are assuming; when they think they have finished a task they can be invited to ask themselves whether a 'doing' could be converted into an 'undoing'; when learners are being introduced to an extended meaning of a term with which they thought they were familiar, you can be sensitive to their surprise and confusion at finding old ideas being extended or varied; when symbols are introduced you can draw attention to the multiple ways of interpreting those symbols, because that is once of the sources of power and effectiveness of mathematical symbols.

13.2 AWARENESSES AND ABSENCES

Mathematical concepts and topics are not simply 'ideas', nor are they simply 'definitions' or formulae. Rather, they are a complex tapestry of interwoven thoughts and images, connections and links, behavioural practices and habits, emotions and excitements. When something becomes a topic to be taught in school, it is because someone recognised that a class of problems could be solved by using a technique, which depends on being aware of certain concepts, which are themselves ways of perceiving, ways of stressing some features and ignoring others. This and the next two sections introduce the notions of awareness, emotions and behaviour as components to the structure of a topic, which is then summarised in section 13.5.

Awareness

Task 13.2.1 Coming to Mind

What comes to mind when you encounter the terms *factoring*, *simultaneous equations* or *graphing equations*?

Comment

You are likely to think of multiplying and expanding brackets (which is the undoing of factoring), ways of thinking about factoring numbers and quadratic expressions, perhaps even the quadratic formula. You are likely to have images of straight lines meeting on a graph, and both straight lines and parabolae. Terms such as *x*-intercept and *slope* are also likely to be lurking somewhere.

The totality of thoughts, images, ideas, associations, related topics and concepts which come to mind constitute your awareness in the moment. As thoughts come, other awarenesses may also come to mind. These are the awarenesses which are dominant for you in association with the term or topic. The important question is which of these you want to come to learners' minds as a result of work on the topic. Similarly, you can ask of any set of exercises what awarenesses are or could be coming to learners' minds as a result of working on the tasks. Thinking in this way orientates you towards choosing how to introduce, develop and complete work on each and every mathematical topic.

A powerful way to think of awarenesses is tied up with dimensions of possible variation and ranges of permissible change: what are the dimensions of possible variation of which you are immediately aware, and which come to mind upon further thought? Do learners appreciate the range of permissible change that you are aware of in each dimension? If not, how might you stimulate them to extend those ranges, to appreciate the full generality necessary to appreciate the concept or topic?

Absence

Learners for whom some aspects of a concept or topic do not come to mind may be disempowered. Furthermore, some ideas that do come to mind are not always appropriate or even correctly formulated, so associated with *awarenesses* are *absences*: things that learners often forget about, misconceptions and misconstruals that you notice learners having to work their way through at various times, and classic errors which learners seem prone to making.

Researchers have collected the wide range of errors and slips made by learners over the years. Some of them have persisted for hundreds of years.[2]

$1/a + 1/b$ is added to get $1/(a + b)$ or $2/(a + b)$. This was commented on in the nineteenth century as an example of something learners do even though they would not do the same thing with numerical fractions.

$(a + b)^2$ is expanded as $a^2 + b^2$; $(a + b)^3$ as $a^3 + b^3$; etc.

$3x + 4$ is contracted or compacted to 7 or $7x$, ignoring the letter completely; $2a + 3b$ becomes $5ab$ or $6ab$.

$2a + 3b$ is treated as 2 apples + 3 bananas making, perhaps, 5 fruit. Known as fruit salad algebra, this error shows up when single letters are treated as short forms for objects starting with that letter, so in $3y$ the y is seen as standing for yachts, yams, or yogurts but not for a number.

Confusing $2cm$ or $2m$ and $2 \times m$ where m is a number not a unit of measurement.

Treating a as 1, b as 2, and so on, rather than as standing for *any* number whatsoever.

Treating letters as always having a single value rather than as standing for any or all numbers.

Thinking that x and y, being different letters, must stand for different numbers.

Thinking that two occurrences of the same letter can stand for different numbers, such as, 'let $2n$ be any even number; then $2n + 2n$ represents the sum of any two even numbers'.

Thinking letters stand only for whole numbers, and not for fractions or decimals.

Confusion between $a \times b$ and $a + b$ written as ab; not seeing 2 3/4 as 2 + 3/4 but confusing it with juxtaposition in algebra as $2 \times 3/4$. Using ab instead of $10a + b$ to represent a two digit number.

When x is 3, interpreting $4x$ as 43.

Applying operations in order from left to right (so $2 + 3 \times 4$ is 20) rather than using the convention that multiplication and division bind more strongly that addition and subtraction. Calculators and computer software are contexts in which these errors crop up particularly.

Using idiosyncratic notation such as $x + 2 \times 3$ to mean the area of a rectangle with sides $x + 2$ by 3, instead of using brackets; not realising that $1 + (2 \times 3)$ and $(1 + 2) \times 3$ give different values, especially when larger numbers are involved.

Confusing $12 \div 4$ and $4 \div 12$ (reading one as '4 guzinto 12' and the other as '12 divided by 4').

Not accepting or recognising $2l + 2b$ as an answer to the perimeter of a rectangle which is l by b, either because they expect a single symbol or even a number as an answer.

One of the issues is whether these sorts of 'mistakes' are slips because attention is fully involved in some other aspect, or whether they represent incomplete or flawed sense making. Which they are will make a difference in how they are dealt with. In section 13.4, ways of exploiting classic learner errors are proposed.

It can be very helpful, especially when preparing to teach a topic or when refreshing your sense of a topic before teaching it again subsequently, to have kept a record of awarenesses (images, ways of thinking, links, sense of 'essence' of a topic etc.) that you notice at different times, and pages devoted to errors, absences, and confusions which you detect learners experiencing. The next two sections will suggest further pages for such a notebook, so that in total you might want to have either a separate notebook for each topic, or at least three pairs of facing pages devoted to each topic.

13.3 HARNESSING EMOTION

Every mathematical topic arises because someone works out how to solve a class of problems. The solution may involve new concepts, a new technique, or a new way of thinking. A curriculum designer then decides that the concept and the technique are important and also within the reach of learners, and so the topic is introduced. Unfortunately what often happens is that the concept and the technique are all that remain when the topic is described in the curriculum. Access to the original situation which puzzled someone and led to the solution may be missing, yet this is where the potential motivation lies. The didactic transposition comes into force.

Encountering Surprise

Being surprised by something ignites interest. If that interest can be sustained so that it turns into a flame, then learners 'have been motivated'. Every mathematical topic has an element of surprise in it, otherwise it would not be a topic! For example, the fact that some quadratics factorise but others do not can be experienced as a (mild) surprise, leading to wanting to sort out how to identify the ones that do factorise.

Discovering that most 'curves' drawn on a coordinate grid do not have 'nice equations' can be a surprise, but it is possible to characterise all the graphs which are associated with specific kinds of expressions (linear, quadratic, exponential, trigonometric, …). Solving a pair of simultaneous linear equations may not be much of a thrill, but discovering that all possible pairs of equations which have that same solution can be thought of geometrically as pairs of lines which pass through the corresponding point, could be surprising, if encountered by the learner rather than simply through being told by a teacher.

The Role of Contexts

The emotions are the source of energy. Emotions need to be harnessed, that is, directed into focusing attention rather than dissipating attention, and the best way to do this is to invoke surprise, and to expect learners to exercise their powers. It can help learners if they appreciate the sorts of problems that people encountered which are resolved by the topic, and contexts in which that topic and its techniques are likely to arise. This is no mere window-dressing, with a few applications stuck on at the end which only the quick working learners ever get to. It means assisting learners to relate the contexts in which typical problems arise to their own experience. It does not mean basing everything only on authentic problems which people outside of school encounter. It means making contexts realistic (capable of being realised and appreciated) by learners. This may take the form of imagining some situation, making use of some authentic problematic situation, drawing on historical information and putting learners in some mathematical context in which a problem arises. For example, take factoring quadratics, which occupies so much curriculum time.

Task 13.3.1 Contextualising Factoring
What problem does factoring resolve? In what sort of contexts might it appear and be useful?

Comment

One response might be that to factorise a quadratic is to reveal its roots (indeed this is true of any polynomial); the reason for this is that the product of some expressions being equal to zero forces one or more of those factors to be zero. It all comes down to a property of zero. But factoring might be a topic because it is seen as something that can be both learned and assessed. If you want to solve a quadratic equation it is most efficient to use a formula achieved by completing the square. Factoring is more useful when doing theoretical work with quadratics. For equations of higher degree beyond four, there are no such formulae to use.

Where might factoring be useful? Whenever you have a situation which cannot immediately be resolved by doing arithmetic, you set up as-yet-unknowns, express the constraints symbolically, and end up with equations, or sometimes with inequalities. To solve equations (and inequalities, for that matter) it is most convenient if the equation factors; otherwise you have to use approximate methods.

The same questions can be applied to simultaneous equations, indeed to any topic. For example, seeing expressions as related to equations and drawing their graph is a relatively new idea (sixteenth or seventeenth century) and resolves a problem of how to get a kinaesthetic sense of relationships expressed in symbols. Prior to the widespread use of symbols, mathematics was perceived geometrically, so the move to symbols was a response to the need to be able to calculate answers to problems.

Some people like to have an overview before committing themselves to specific tasks; others are happy to engage immediately. Mathematics is well known for the use of 'motivating examples', but often these involve contexts which are anything but familiar to learners. At the other extreme, such examples can be drawn as often as possible from everyday situations which learners recognise they are likely to meet. As long as the work on the topic is not confined to such contexts, it can help learners see why they are being asked to engage with the topic. Some teachers find that a strong motivating force is a sense of meeting and overcoming a challenge, through the use of learners' own powers.

Using Powers

Human beings get pleasure from using their powers. They often become frustrated when other people do things for them which they are on the edge of being able to do for themselves, to the extent that learners sometimes decide that those powers are not wanted in the mathematics classroom, and so they stop using them even where there is an opportunity.

Developing algebraic thinking both exercises and develops those powers in everyone, particularly the pleasure of encompassing a wide range (even better an infinity) of possibilities under one expression of generality. That is why so much emphasis has been put on expressing generality in this book. Using their own powers in a supportive atmosphere also reveals to the individual the fact of those powers, something learners may not even be aware of until it is drawn to their attention. There is nothing so strongly motivating as realising you can do something that is valued and valuable. The exercise of your own powers, independently, is a major source of pleasure for human beings, whereas dependency on others breeds discontent.

Making Choices

Everyone makes choices. Sometimes choices can be hard to make, and advice is sought. But sometimes there is no choice at all. If mathematics lessons continue to restrict the possibility of making sensible and informed choices, then some learners are likely to make the only choice they can: not to participate, and to make things difficult for others.

An alternative is to invite learners to make choices wherever possible. They can make up their own examples on which to test conjectures, and make up their own exercises to challenge or demonstrate their appreciation of a technique or method. Instead of setting them a series of exercises for homework or for a lesson, you can suggest that they 'do enough of the exercises' so that they can describe to someone how to 'do a task of this type'. Already their attention is directed out of the particular and towards the general: what does 'of this type' mean? This is where the notion of DofPV is really useful, and with it, the associated RofPCh. What can you change in the exercises and still you can use the same technique? (Notice the simultaneous use of invariance and change.) As learners develop confidence and experience of expressing generality, they can try to express a general (or sometimes several different generalisations) exercise 'type', and then show how to 'do it'. Of course, this will produce a general formula. The quadratic formula is a case in point: it expresses how to re-express any quadratic in a form which displays the roots, and it even copes with quadratics which have no real roots. Similarly, techniques for solving pairs of simultaneous (linear) equations apply to more equations in more unknowns.

Learners need to recognise the 'type' of a question so as to know what technique(s) to use; the best way to do this is to get them to (re)generalise for themselves, to become aware of the variety of choices possible (DofPV and associated RofPCh) which constitute the space of possibilities. But making choices also exercises personal involvement and hence enhances motivation.

Learner Constructions

A rich domain for making choices is to get learners to construct mathematical objects for themselves. Examples of this style of task appeared in Tasks 3.1.2, 3.2.2 and 3.4.1.
    For example:

Task 13.3.2 Construction

Construct a number which leaves a remainder of 3 on dividing by 7. And another; and another. As discussed in Section 3.5, this task structure is likely to lead learners to getting a sense of a whole class of such objects.

Now construct a number which as well as leaving a remainder of 3 on dividing by 7, also leaves a remainder of 2 on dividing by 5.

Comment

Of course, you can start from scratch for the second part, but you can also systematically consider particular examples from the results of the first part, and then detect or expose some structure which enables you to write down all such numbers, as a generality.

Other examples are easy to come by:

> Construct a quadratic which has two roots with the same numerical value but opposite in sign; and another; and another; … generalise

> Construct a pair of simultaneous equations for which the solutions (roots) are 2 for x and 3 for y. How simple can you make your equations? How complicated can you make them so that the solutions are not obvious (but stick to linear equations)? What are some easier intermediate forms? What are all the equations whose graphs go through the point (2, 3) and what do they look like?

> Construct three straight lines not passing through a common point, and write down the inequalities whose solution set is the points within the bounded triangular region formed by those lines.

Any problem which asks for a solution to some constraints can be seen as a construction task, where you start from no constraints and then gradually add the constraints on one at a time. In each case, you express the most general objects possible which satisfy the current constraints.

Making Sense Mathematically

The world of the twenty-first century is full of situations which require some form of mathematical thinking in order to make sense of them. Sections 1.2, 5.2 and 9.2 offered some examples of these involving possible algebraic thinking, especially where a situation is likely to arise repeatedly so that a policy (formula) is required. Situations do not have to be based in activity outside of the classroom, since mathematics itself presents many such situations. The sequence idea in Task 7.3.3 presents such a situation, as does Task 5.2.4b, Perforations, and many if not most of the other tasks in this book.

13.4 PRACTICE MAKES ... ?

Every topic involves technical terms and phrases or sentences which express relationships and properties. Becoming familiar with those technical terms means not only having a sense of what they mean, but actually making use of them in order to express your own thinking. Associated with every topic are collections of words, phrases and sentences which it is worth recording in a notebook as a reminder for the next time the topic is to be taught. Sometimes learners come up with humorous or interesting variations, which are also worth recording so that they can be used, or circumvented, in the future, as seems relevant. Often things that learners say are based on things they think they have heard the teacher say, so by reminding yourself before starting a new topic of some of the things that might derail or confuse learners, you can avoid some of the mistakes that arose in the past.

Every technique or method has more than a sequence of actions to be performed. It has 'inner incantations' or 'things that you say to yourself' as you carry out the procedures, and it involves choices as to what to do next which may depend on the situation. In order that learners can 'get through an examination' in time, but, more usefully, in order that learners can focus their attention on the main problem they are trying to solve rather than on the details of a specific technique, and in order that they can also be watching out for slips in the use of the technique, they need to free up some attention.

What is being practised when learners are set collections of exercises to complete? Are they actually developing facility in the use of particular concepts and techniques (that is, are they learning the ins and outs of particular concepts and the use of particular techniques)? Are they developing fluency by integrating the use of those concepts as technical terms to express their thinking, and by automating or habituating the techniques so that they do not need to devote full attention to the mechanics? Encouraging learners to try to articulate how you do 'one like these' and to describe what makes something 'like these' contributes to their awareness of the topic rather than just working at training their use of techniques.

Each topic also involves one or more methods, and ways of thinking which in some sense define or delineate that topic. This is what learners will need to automate.

Facility and Fluency

The issue then is how best to promote learners in developing both facility and fluency. Asking learners to engage in a set of tasks which essentially repeat the same technique over and over can be effective in developing fluency if it is a race against time, so that attention is directed to trying to be as quick as possible. However, there are other ways of encouraging learners to practice a technique. The most effective is to engage them in a task in which they find themselves constructing their own examples on which to use the technique because their attention is directed towards some other more general goal, naming locating, checking and justifying some general conjecture. For example, suppose you want to prompt learners to set up and solve pairs of simultaneous equations. Setting them a task such as the following might have the desired effect:

Task 13.4.1 Fluency with Equations

Write down the equations of a pair of straight lines which intersect at a known point. Can you find a point somewhere in the plane for which adding 2 to the first coordinate and 1 to the second puts it on your first line, but subtracting 2 from the first and subtracting 1 from the second puts it on your second line?

Comment

There are several ways of tackling this task. Learners who really know what they are doing can use their geometrical awareness to inform their choices, but most learners will find themselves constructing examples and solving them, thereby not only giving them practice, but attracting at least some of their attention to the overall goal, and so reducing the attention they devote to the exercise of the technique. Since an expert uses a minimum of attention while a novice tends to use a great deal, such tasks help novices become more expert. Another example is given in section 14.3.

Learner facility and fluency can be tested by giving them sample tasks to do in a limited time. Learner awareness is best revealed by asking them to construct relevant objects meeting suitable constraints, and inviting them to push the boundaries of the dimensions of possible variation and associated ranges of permissible change of which they are aware.

Using Classic Errors

A useful source of explorations involves classic errors that learners have made in the past. By collecting these for each topic as suggested in section 13.2, you equip yourself to confront similar errors in the future. For example,

Some learners conjectured that the equation of the line through the point $(0, 1)$ with slope 3 is $y = 3x + 1$ because you start at $(0, 1)$ and you go 1 unit to the right, and 3 up.[3]

This could be a classic case of learners attending to features inappropriately, having formed the conjecture that the slope is the coefficient of x divided by the constant term. What might be an appropriate response?

Offering a counter-example may convince learners, but it may only be seen as a passing incident which does not actually challenge their conjecture, which itself may not actually be explicitly formulated. Getting the learners to articulate the conjecture and then to test it for themselves turns the initiative over to them, and reinforces the notion that in mathematics the authority lies within mathematics, not with individual people. One way to locate the specific error or inappropriate conjecture being used by the learners is to ask them to use the same approach with other lines, say with the same slope but through other points, or with fractional slopes and passing through other points. Sketching these on a graph, or using a graphics calculator is likely to throw up some counter-examples. But what matters with counter-examples is not learning that a conjecture was wrong but, rather, becoming imbued with the sense that mathematics consists of conjectures and justifications, as well as, in this case, learning to focus attention appropriately when looking for slope and y–intercept.

13.5 STRUCTURE OF A TOPIC

Every mathematical topic consists of three strands, corresponding to the previous three sections, because these reflect the structure of the human psyche: awareness, emotion and behaviour or, more currently, cognitive, affective and enactive aspects of human psychology and sociology. When preparing to teach a topic, whether for the first time or when refreshing before teaching 'yet again', it can help to review the three strands.

The awareness strand encompasses the ideas and thoughts that you find come to mind as you think about the topic, and hence that you would like to come to learners' minds as well. This includes mathematical themes, images, diagrams and the like. This strand also includes 'absences': the classic errors that learners make, whether as slips when not paying sufficient attention, or more deeply based misconstruals of what they have encountered. These are worth collecting over the lifetime of your teaching as they indicate ways in which learners attend to what they are presented which may not be what was intended, and so indicate places where further care might be valuable when teaching the topic next time.

The emotional or affective strand includes both the problematic situations which originally gave rise to the topic, together with other situations which learners might be able to appreciate, and also the range of other situations in which the topic or some aspect of it is likely to arise. This goes beyond 'applications', to include situations in which the ways of thinking have proved relevant.

The most familiar aspect of a mathematical topic is the techniques or methods which learners are expected to master in order to solve test questions. But there is more to behaviour than methods. For example, every topic involves the use of special terms, phrases and sentences which both orientate and demonstrate the relevant ways of thinking. Every technique or method is accompanied by 'things you say to yourself as you are doing them', perhaps reminding yourself about choices, or about tricky bits that you sometimes get wrong. These 'inner incantations' are just as much part of the behaviour associated with a topic. Section 6.3 used this structure to consider overtly the topic of area and perimeter.

Of course the three strands, awareness, emotion and behaviour are tightly interwoven. Language patterns that learners do not quite get correct can lead to classic errors and misconstruals of the types illustrated in section 13.2 as well as in Chapter 10. Awarenesses which are incomplete can block access to the use of an appropriate concept or technique, and so on. The three strands provide a structure which can serve, not as a mechanical 'form-filling' exercise, but as a reminder of aspects to think about when preparing to teach any topic. Hence the value in keeping notes for each topic which can be augmented when learners display new and interesting behaviours, emotions and awarenesses, and which serve as a quick reminder of the complexity of a topic when it is time to teach it again.

The most powerful way to engage learners' full attention and involvement is to activate all three strands of their psyche, and the best way to do this is to involve learners in making choices and in using their own mathematical powers, which are discussed in the next chapter.

NOTES
1 See also the ATM Gattegno reader (ATM (1989) *A Gattegno Anthology*, ATM, Derby.)
2 Based on Leslie Booth in *Routes to Roots of Algebra*, itself based on research at Chelsea College (CSMS and SESM) led by Kath Hart. See Hart Mason, J, Graham, A., Pimm, D. and Gowar, N. Milton Keynes, The Open University.
3 Example is due to Dave Hewitt.

14 Powers, Constructs and Strategies

Chapter 14 summarises the core components of the approach to teaching and learning algebra presented in the book.

Section 14.1 begins with a summary of some of the basic and natural powers which all learners possess, and which can be exploited in mathematics lessons so that learners feel that their powers are being used, rather than being suppressed or ignored. Section 14.2 summarises the pedagogical constructs which have been used explicitly and implicitly throughout the book. Section 14.3 summarises the principal pedagogic strategies used throughout the book.

14.1 MATHEMATICAL POWERS

> Walking home from school, Olivia (7) was asked by her brother 'what is 8 times 45?' She worked it out by repeated doubling of 45, then said 'Hey, every number is a half of another number' … pause … 'every number and every number-and-a-half is half of another number'.

Olivia demonstrated natural powers of locating relationships, proposing properties, and making and testing conjectures which generalise particular cases.

Human beings naturally try to make sense of their experience. Sense (in the sense of understanding) requires interpreting current experience in terms of past experience. Sense is made by using natural powers to collect, classify, assimilate, accommodate and reject sensations whether physical or imagined, remembered or constructed, literal or metaphoric.

Working on the tasks in previous chapters will, it is to be hoped, have reminded you of fundamental powers which you, and your learners, all possess. This section summarises and highlights these mathematical powers, drawing attention particularly to four pairs of powers which learners bring to lessons.

Imagining and Expressing

Every child can imagine, whether they use mental pictures, words, kinaesthetic responses, have a vague sort of 'sense-of', or some combination of these. It is by means of imagination that people are able to contemplate what is not actually present, whether it is a pattern continuing into the future or an experience from our past. Imagine standing at the entrance to your kitchen; which way would you turn to get a fork? These sorts of questions can be answered because it is possible to 'be', mentally, at the entrance of your kitchen. Sometimes your body knows the answer, so you imagine yourself moving and then watch which way you moved in order to find out.

What can be expressed, whether in pictures, movement, words or symbols, is only a small part of that rich world called experience. Learning to write stories exercises connections between speech and imagery; learning to write algebraic symbols exercises connections between awareness of patterns and generality, and symbols. The advantage of algebraic symbols over words and pictures is that the symbols are more easily manipulable, once they have become familiar and confidence-inspiring.

Through mental imagery you have access to very large, very small, or very negative numbers or indeed to the infinite, as in imagining a decimal name for the square root of two. (In a sense, root two 'knows' *all* its decimal digits, but human beings can only ever find out a finite number of them.) It is through the power to imagine that you access generality, for it is a sense of potential, of encompassing all possibilities, of denoting the as–yet–unknown that is captured in an expression involving words, pictures, numbers and symbols.

The next task links imagery, particularly visceral or kinaesthetic imagery, with generality.

Task 14.1.1 Shady Circles

In the first block of circles below, quickly shade in every third dot starting from the second, counting from left to right and running on from row to row.

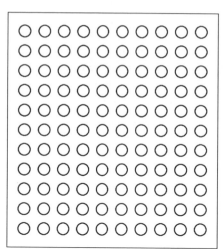

Pay attention to *how* you do it.

In the second block, shade in every seventh starting from the third.

Comments

Many people find that at some point they switch almost unconsciously from counting circles to following a pattern. At first they may not be confident of the pattern, and so keep counting as well, but then the pattern takes over. If you did not notice this, try another version for yourself.

Try counting from left to right in one row, then right to left in the next, alternating the direction with each succeeding row, to see how long it is before your body takes over and expresses the emerging pattern. Try changing things like the number of circles in a row, the count and the starting value. Try using a calendar arrangement of numbers in place of the dots, or some other tabular array of numbers, to see what effect having the numbers present makes.

The switch from cognitive counting to bodily or visceral pattern response is a moment of transition which is highly significant and very useful (and has been called Watch What You Do in this book). It is an example of spontaneous expression of generality. By catching this moment, the kinaesthetic can be verbalised as a pattern, turning from an action into a description of a relationship.

The power to imagine is usefully called upon explicitly and can be developed with practice. If imagination is not called upon in mathematics, then a powerful link to the emotions is neglected, and motivation-interest may suffer. If expression in multiple forms is not encouraged, then learners may form the mistaken impression that mathematics does not offer opportunities for creativity. If learners encounter a very limited range of images, and a very limited range of expressions, they are likely to form the erroneous impression that mathematics is a very limited domain of human experience.

Experiencing and expressing generality is entirely natural for learners. The issue is whether that power is being called upon and developed in mathematics lessons, or whether it is being left to one side where it is likely to atrophy, at least in the mathematics context, through non-use.

Specialising and Generalising

Very young children display the power to generalise as well as specialise: in order to talk, young children need to generalise, for words such as *dog* are by their very nature general, and they need to specialise when identifying a specific object described in words. Freudenthal (1979, p. 235) illustrates this beautifully in describing an incident with his grandson: Bastiaan starts to ask about two women, one in a wheelchair: 'What did the lady say to the lady [hesitation] that pushed the wheelchair?' He recognises in the moment the ambiguity and acts to correct this. Such 'shifts' are an integral part of learning to use language. If every experience was individual and unique, our brains would soon reach memory overload. It is precisely because people can generalise that they can categorise and so make sense of experience through stressing (and consequently ignoring).

The whole point of arithmetic is not to learn number facts, but to learn general methods. No one would imagine asking learners to memorise all possible two-digit additions. Rather, learners are expected to discern and integrate into their functioning, methods for doing such operations. Any method of doing an action in different situations or with different data is a generality. It involves the learner constructing if not expressing awareness of a generalisation. Indeed, even number names are generalisations, nouns abstracted from multiple contexts, so that 1, 2, 3 become as concrete and specific as one ball, two balloons, three bicycles are for younger children.

Mathematicians see generalising as lying at the very heart of mathematics. For example, Charles Saunders Peirce was a famous American mathematician and philosopher who thought deeply about the nature of mathematics: 'Another characteristic of mathematical thought is that it can have no success where it cannot generalize' (Peirce, 1902, p. 1778). Every technique learners meet is an expression of generality. Every time a choice is possible, a generality is lurking. Expressing generality is the lifeblood of mathematical thinking and of algebra in particular. It is the source both of 'algebraic expressions' and of the rules for manipulating those expressions.

Generalising happens spontaneously when someone imagines a process continuing. It might be something simple like adding one, over and over, leading to the generality that there can be no largest integer because 'you can always add one more'. It might be something more complicated like imagining doubling and subtracting 1 over and over again, or thinking of a graph as extending on and on for ever in both directions, not just confined to what can be seen on a screen (mental or material). It might be something quite subtle such as that no matter what two numbers you add (or multiply) the answer is independent of the order, or that you can factorise any whole number uniquely into a product of prime numbers. Sometimes generalising is so quick that you do not realise there may be other ways of perceiving and hence generalising.

When you see the sequence 1, 2, 3, 4, 5 it is natural to assume the continuation 6, 7, 8, … . However, depending upon the context, the sequence may continue in a different way. It might be part of a bus list, in which the next term is 35. This is why it is vital, whenever a pattern is detected, whenever relationships are surmised, to base all conjectures on some agreed source which generates the sequence or pattern.

Hand in hand with *generalising* goes its reverse process, particularising, or as the famous Polish–American mathematician and mathematics teacher George Polya referred to it, *specialising*. Both processes are important, as Polya pointed out: 'we need to adopt the inductive attitude [which] requires a ready ascent from observations to generalizations, and a ready descent from the highest generalizations to the most concrete observations' (Polya, 1957, p. 7, 1962).

The reason for trying a particular case of something more general is to try to see what is going on through the example, through watching *how* you do the example. The purpose of the specialising is to make sense, to enable a reconstruction of the general, expressed in a more familiar language and a more manipulable symbolism. For example, when faced with a conjecture such as 'the sum of an even number of consecutive odd numbers is divisible by double the number of numbers', trying some cases gives a sense of what the conjecture is about.

Conjecturing and Convincing

Conjecturing is a way of working, an ethos, in which ideas are developed through learners thinking out loud or explicitly in some other way. *Everything* that is said is thought about and tested by those who are listening. People speak because they are uncertain and hope to get some help from others in how to articulate what they think they are 'seeing' or thinking. It is a way of working in which everyone takes responsibility for making sense of what is said, and anybody can be asked to explain their thinking, that is, to try to convince others. One of the most important things that a school can contribute in the way of developing learners' powers is to engender a conjecturing atmosphere.

In a conjecturing atmosphere, when someone says something that is not quite understood by another, someone might ask for or offer an example, or might focus on a detail and ask pointedly for elaboration. In a conjecturing atmosphere, people do *not* say 'That's wrong', they say 'I invite you to modify your conjecture', or they say 'What about … ' and offer a possible counter-example.

Mathematical thinking really only gets going when there are competing conjectures or when there is something to justify. If learners feel that answers are always either right or wrong, they may become reticent about offering their ideas. If conjecturing is valued, and especially if modifying conjectures is valued and praised, then mathematical thinking is more likely to flourish.

Conjecturing is about being aware of the status of some assertion: is it reasonable? Is it always true? Is it sometimes true? Is it never true? How do I know? If I cannot justify it by convincing someone else, then it remains a conjecture, something which I think may be true, and for which I have some possible evidence.

Trying to justify why you think something is the case by trying to convince someone else is most helpful in sorting out what you think, for as you start to explain it, things either tend to fall into place or fall apart. The person being explained to can learn from the experience by learning to ask probing questions ('give me an example', 'what if … was different?', 'how do you know?', 'why must …?' and so on), which in turn develops expertise in convincing others. Thus learning to be sceptical when listening to others trying to convince is an important part of learning to convince people yourself, for you learn to internalise the sorts of objections that others are likely to make.

When ideas are coming thick and fast it is sometimes hard to hold on to what you think is actually the case. Consequently one of the features of a conjecturing atmosphere is making a record of current conjectures. Like all mathematicians, learners sometimes run out of time when exploring some idea. A sensible place to leave off work is to make a record of current conjectures, and a summary of available evidence. Developing this practice provides a satisfactory way of leaving a topic or a project and going on to something else.

Organising and Classifying

Human beings make sense by organising and classifying experience. Putting dishes and laundry away are forms of imposing order on the material world, and act as useful metaphors for working in the mental, symbolic worlds, and social worlds.

One of the reasons for organising is that it reduces confusion. It simplifies the multitude of experiences and forces acting upon you. The desire to impose order is manifested very early. Every experience is classified (unconsciously) in order to assimilate it into current schema and so 'make sense of it'. If it resists classification, then it is either rejected out of hand or schemas are altered in order to accommodate it (Piaget, 1971). Having acknowledged the desire and value of organising, it is useful to probe just how it is that organising comes about.

Each act of sorting involves stressing some (relevant) features and ignoring others, which in turn requires being able to discriminate those features. Sorting tasks are really excellent for getting groups of learners to express their thinking to each other and to negotiate different ways of seeing. Some learners will learn from others ways of discerning that had not previously come to mind. Others will find their way of perceiving supported or confirmed.

Task 14.1.2 Sorting Expressions

Sort the following expressions in some way that seems sensible perhaps by using different labels to distinguish the different groups.

$x^2 + 2x + 1$	$2x + 1$	$x^2 + 4x + 3$	$3x + 2$	$3x - 1$	$x^2 + 2x + 3$
$4x + 3$	$x^2 + 4x + 6$	$x^2 + 2x + 2$	$2x - 1$	$x^2 + 4x + 4$	$4x - 1$

Now think of a different context in which a different organisation might be sensible.

Comment

Sorting is usually for a purpose; different purposes will produce different sorting, through different ways of seeing. For example, distinguishing between quadratic and linear might be useful when thinking about graphs; distinguishing the quadratics which factorise from those that do not, or even those that are perfect squares, those that factorise but are not squares, and those that do not factorise might be useful in the context of finding roots. The linear expressions could be distinguished on the basis of whether there is a plus or a minus sign, or whether they give the same remainder when divided by the coefficient of the x, or whether when set equal to zero would produce a positive or negative answer for the unknown value of x.

The act of sorting serves to reveal the qualities which are being used to sort, which are by necessity, generalities, properties. Qualities or features seen as similar, relate objects in the group together, and these arise by stressing some aspects and consequently ignoring others. But there is a subtle shift from seeing similarity to seeing things classified according to some property. To identify a property, and then to see if objects possess that property is quite different from being aware of relationships which, in fact, do constitute 'having that property'. Learners may be aware of the presence of x and numbers in expressions such as $2x + 3$, but not be aware of the property of being linear, that is of having the form $mx + b$, even though they recognise $2x + 3$ and $4x - 5$ as being similar.

Symbols both express and help to crystallise the notion of form, of property. Mathematicians make a further move by trying to find out all they can about objects sharing a specified property or properties by deducing what must follow as a consequence. This is the process of characterising which was developed in Chapter 6 and featured in Chapters 9 and 11.

Summary

Four mathematical powers have been presented as pairs:

> Imagining and expressing;
> Specialising and generalising;
> Conjecturing and convincing;
> Organising and classifying.

These are powers often called upon when learners are trying to make sense of mathematics. The conjecture underlying this book is that it is by prompting learners to use, and hence develop those powers, that algebraic thinking is best promoted.

14.2 PEDAGOGIC CONSTRUCTS

Pedagogical constructs are distinctions which have proved to be useful for thinking about teaching mathematics. They have been found useful:

> when planning a lesson or a sequence of lessons;
> in the midst of teaching, when they come to mind in the form of possible actions;
> for retrospective analysis and in preparing to learn from recent experience.

Dimensions of Possible Variation (DofPV)

A task that cannot be extended and generalised is unlikely to be pedagogically effective. Talking about *dimensions of possible variation* is a reminder to look for all the different features that are needed for the concept and also the features of particular examples which are not actually needed. There are close similarities to the productive questions promoted by Brown and Walter (1983): 'what if … were changed?' and 'what if not … ?'. Different people are aware of different dimensions of possible variation at different times, so that getting learners to reveal what they are aware of as variable can inform teaching. Furthermore, each dimension of possible variation has an associated, sometime implicit, *range of permissible change*. Asked to complete $7 = ? + ?$, some learners will confine themselves to positive whole numbers, others will use negatives, others fractions, and others decimals. In each case, what a learner reveals is part of their sense of freedom and constraint.

Often the *dimensions of possible variation* that learners perceive and the corresponding *range of permissible change* to which they constrain their answers are not the same as those imagined by the teacher. If the teacher is talking from one view, what is said may make little sense to a learner with a different view. By being aware of this, a teacher can take action to attract learner attention appropriately .

The notion of *dimensions of possible variation* applies to tasks as well as to concepts, and indeed to the different ways in which tasks can be presented. With any task it is possible, and usually fruitful, to ask what can be changed and still the same method applies. Often there are specific numbers to change, but there are other changes to be made as well. If a teacher develops and even uses explicitly the notion of *dimensions of possible variation* with respect to tasks, then learners can be encouraged to seek not just the solution to a single task, but try to characterise the general class of tasks which succumb to the same technique. They can be prompted and stimulated to generalise for themselves. Learners who are aware of classes of tasks are much more likely to do well than those for whom each task is new and different.

With and Across the Grain

Following a pattern, sometimes by watching what your body does almost automatically, can be thought of as 'going with the grain' (Watson, 2000). For example, the generalising in Task 14.1.2 showed how your body can take over and manifest a pattern. As you become aware of the flow and the underlying pattern, you are in a position to express a generality. Going with the grain and detecting relationships is important, but it is not, in itself, learning. In order to round it off and actually learn something from the process, it is important to pause and to 'go across the grain'. This means stopping and making sense of the generality expressing the pattern, trying to see what it might be telling you.

In Task 14.1.1 (Shady Circles), this means seeing why the pattern goes the way it does, in diagonal lines. Following the pattern leads to an expression of generality, but what is valuable is the insight achieved in 'going across the grain' and interpreting each equation or each expression as an instance of a general statement of equality that always holds. Following patterns in tables of numbers (as in section 5.4) uses powers of pattern detecting and following, but the purpose of such pattern following is to experience the generality, and then to interpret that generality as a statement about arithmetic. For example, tracking the pattern flow backwards into the negative numbers reinforces the rules of arithmetic for calculating with negatives.

Manipulating–Getting-a-Sense-of–Articulating (MGA)

As long ago as 400 BCE, Plato praised Egyptian teachers who invited learners to work with physical objects when learning arithmetic. But apparatus is only useful if it can eventually be dispensed with, otherwise learners become dependent on that particular apparatus. The point of using apparatus is to 'get a sense of' some pattern or relationship, some property or structure, and then to begin to articulate the 'sense' to yourself until it becomes fluent. The apparatus can be returned to if a situation becomes too complicated, but the apparatus is intended to provide experience and images (visual and kinaesthetic) which are internalised and integrated into learners' functioning.

Manipulating–Getting-a-sense-of–Articulating (MGA) can be seen as a spiral of ongoing development, in which objects which are familiar and confidence-inspiring are manipulated in some setting in order to get a sense of some structure, enabling articulation (in diagrams, pictures, words and symbols) which becomes more and more succinct and more and more 'articulate'. These articulations (usually in symbols but also in diagrams) themselves become the components for further manipulations.

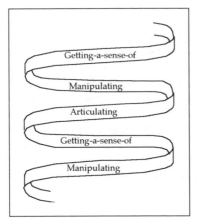

Whenever you encounter a statement that is not very clear, perhaps because it is very general or because it uses technical terms, it can help to turn to some example which is confidently manipulable. This may take the form of something physical, or it may consist of symbols, as long as you are *confident in using those symbols*. Comments and suggestions on some of the tasks have tried to encourage you to do this, but also to be aware of just how powerful and effective it can be as a strategy.

Do–Talk–Record (DTR)

Manipulating is not learning, merely opportunity to learn and preparation for learning. Doing tasks is not learning, only an opportunity for learning. Getting learners to talk about what they are doing, trying to articulate to others the sense they are making, contributes to the possibility of making some sort of record of what they are doing. That record may use diagrams, pictures, words and symbols. Trying to record can inform your talk; talking can inform what and how you 'do'. What is important, and what is signalled by the DTR framework is the importance of paying attention to how you do something, not just to getting it done.

Discussion between learners can be highly effective, as long as it is mathematical in nature, that is, supported by a conjecturing atmosphere in which everyone listens, constructs examples and possible counter examples, and tries to articulate for themselves. Only when it becomes convenient to use labels to refer to objects, whether present or only imagined, known or unknown is it necessary and appropriate to move to formal labels (symbols).

The triple construct Doing–Talking–Recording can act as a reminder that the point of doing is to get better at articulating something, that recording emerges out of articulation as well as feeding ever improved articulation, and that articulation emerges out of paying to attention to how you are doing something, as well as improving that doing through articulating.

Enactive–Iconic–Symbolic and Different Worlds

Jerome Bruner's terms *enactive, iconic* and *symbolic* were introduced in Chapter 2 and developed in Chapter 8. A fourth world, which Bruner drew attention to later in his career, is the world of social practices and interpersonal relations. People operate within this fourth world through representations drawn from the other three. Thus people demonstrate with objects, describe and draw images, and use formal symbols. The social is where people encounter and become enculturated into the use of objects, diagrams and descriptions, and formal symbols.

Rather than preferring one world over others, or letting one world dominate others, what is most valuable is achieving a balance among all four. Practices are picked up through being in the presence of other people using them. For example, in classrooms in which 'same and different' are used frequently and effectively, learners pick them up; in classes where conjecturing is the norm, learners pick up the associated practices; in classes where individual methods are valued but also challenged and stretched in order to be more efficient, learners actually become more mathematically sophisticated and mature.

See–Experience–Master (SEM)

When a new idea is encountered, it is not always taken in immediately. For example, when you encounter a new word, you may use it in too broad and general a meaning, before it contracts back into common usage. So too, meeting new ideas is sometimes like experiencing a train rush through a station: lots of excitement and noise, but not a lot of detail grasped. With continued exposure over time, experience becomes richer and more detailed. After a while, that experience includes increasing competence and fluency, leading to 'mastery' of the techniques and familiarity with the ideas. 'Doing things', manipulating familiar and confidence-inspiring objects, getting a sense of structural patterns, relationships and properties, and articulating these with increasing succinctness and fluency is how substantial learning comes about.

By giving each of the first three blocks of this book a parallel structure, often returning to the same theme but at a more sophisticated level, you were offered opportunity to see ideas go by, but to re-encounter them several if not many times in different ways. This mirrors how people learn naturally in situations outside school.

Theorem in Action

Learners often make use of properties or facts without really being aware of them. Gerard Vergnaud (1981) called these 'theorems-in-action'. For example, young children act as if addition is commutative without being aware that is what they are doing; learners write the next term in a sequence of expressions without being aware of how they are doing it. Theorems in action are not always correct: some learners write down $a^2 + b^2$ as the expansion of $(a + b)^2$, others cancel terms in the top and bottom of fractions almost indiscriminately.

At some point it is worth drawing learners' attention to things that they are assuming without questioning, in order that these can be questioned and checked. Sensible discussion can only take place if there are agreed foundations from which to build, and learners have experience of conjecturing and reasoning. For example, it is no use inviting learners to guess what $(^-1) \times (^-1)$ should be, unless they are used to using patterns in arithmetic to justify their actions.

Structure of Attention

When confronted with something unfamiliar, attention is either on the whole, or on some part of that whole. After what may be a moment or a long time, details start to emerge: some aspects or parts are distinguished or discerned from amongst the rest. Put another way, at first, there are details which are either not seen at all, or ignored, as when learners are invited to read an expression such as $3x + 2$ out loud and omit the x.

For example, have a go at the next task and do not be put off by what you see. Rather, try to notice what you do to get beyond your first reaction!

Task 14.2.1 Attention!

Say (to yourself, to a friend, to a goldfish!) what you see below. Start simply!

$$Y = \frac{(x - b)(x - c)}{(a - b)(a - c)} A + \frac{(x - a)(x - c)}{(b - a)(b - c)} B + \frac{(x - a)(x - b)}{(c - a)(c - b)} C$$

What do you notice about how your attention moves, about what you attend to?

Comment

On first seeing a complicated algebraic expression like this you might find yourself over-whelmed by all the letters and complexity. You might then become aware of the horizontal bars, the plus signs, and the capital letters. This gives access to the fractions each of which is a product involving x in two factors in the numerator and some lower case letters in the denominator. Notice that your attention shifts from term to term, sometimes on the whole term, sometimes checking for detailed similarities to another term. Using the power to focus selectively, you might be drawn to say the first fraction, and observe things that are the same about numerator and denominator, and how they differ. This could lead to noticing that inserting a for x makes the first fraction have a value of 1, while inserting b or c for x makes it zero.

This equation is an example of what is called *Lagrange interpolation polynomials*, which seem to have been first published by Edward Waring in 1779, rediscovered by Leonard Euler in 1783, and published by Joseph-Louis Lagrange in 1795 (Jeffreys and Jeffreys, 1988).

Until you discern details, which involves focusing attention, you cannot do any-thing but be aware of the whole. As you focus on a detail, discerning it from what is around it (stressing and consequently ignoring) you become aware of relationships. Here, there are relationships within a part such as within one of the fractions, and also between the parts (each has a capital letter, …).

Having analysed each of the terms (fraction, with capital) and located some simi-larities between them, it is possible to change the way you are thinking and to ask, for example, whether all the possibilities are present. This is a step towards property-making or 'proposing properties': isolating a relationship or a similarity and then looking to see if other objects have that same relationship.

The upshot of this example is that it illustrates how human attention shifts rapidly between different ways of attending and different foci of attention. Sometimes there are several of these going on either simultaneously, or in swift succession. In summary, there can be:

awareness of or focus on wholeness: the identification of an object (which may be a part of some other object);

a shift to awareness of or focus on discerned details comprising that object (creating sub-objects);

a shift to awareness of relationships or similarities between features comprising sub-objects at any level of detail;

a shift to awareness of or focus on properties that (sub-)objects might satisfy;

a shift to awareness of or focus on properties as definitions or as axioms on the sole basis of which, deductions can be made.[1]

The suggestion is that these shifts in the structure of attention are going on all the time, and not necessarily in any specific sequence. Attention is too will-o'-the-wisp to be subject to predetermined sequences.

What Makes an Example Exemplary?

In Chapter 2, mention was made of a learning paradox: in order to appreciate a concept it is useful if not necessary to have an example; to see what an object exemplifies requires that you already appreciate the general of which it is a particular case. To see this more sharply, consider the following two types of task.

Task 14.2.2 Exemplary

Compare the two tasks:

Construct a fraction which illustrates the fact that not all fractions lie between 0 and 1.

What features of fractions does 6/4 illustrate?

Comment

The second seems much harder than the first. You have to see through the particulars of one object and try to see what could be changed, and yet some relationship or property remain valid. For example, it illustrates the fact that not all fractions lie between 0 and 1 (the previous part probably signalled that to you). It also illustrates that some fractions can be simplified or reduced by removing common factors between the numerator and the denominator. The fraction 6/4 also illustrates a fraction which is harder to display diagrammatically than fractions between 0 and 1; furthermore, it is an example of a fraction with a terminating decimal. It is, however, not an example of a fraction that is negative.

When presenting an example to learners, whether illustrating a concept or property, or showing how to use a technique in a particular case, it is worthwhile paying attention to which features are generic and to be treated as a DofPV, which aspects of the RofPCh are indicated, and which features are extraneous and irrelevant. Emphasis can then be placed on the important ones through the use of colour and voice tones. Offering several examples can be more helpful, but only if learners appreciate what is the same as well as what is different about the various examples. In other words, are the various DofPV being highlighted by not varying too many features at once, and are the RofPCh sufficiently clearly exposed?

With worked examples, the sequence of calculations is usually easy enough to carry through, but what learners often get stuck not knowing what calculation to do next: where do numbers and properties used in the technique come from? When a learner asks about a worked example, 'where did you get that three', it is tempting to repeat the calculations around that point, but the learner may be asking how you knew to do those calculations and in that order.

14.3 PEDAGOGICAL STRATEGIES

This section reiterates some of the pedagogical strategies suggested by the constructs in the previous section, and used or suggested throughout the book.

Say What You See; Watch What You Do

Presenting learners with a picture, a symbolic expression, a set of exercises, or a worked example, and asking them simply to 'Say What You See' can be very instructive. It helps learners to take in the whole, to discern details and to learn from details others have discerned. Where someone describes something that others are unclear about, there is opportunity to reinforce a conjecturing atmosphere and to get learners to work on asking specific and pointed questions, instead of 'say that again'. Asking each person to say just one thing each, in turn, enables many or most to contribute something. Doing all this without physically pointing can strengthen learners' control over both their mental imagery and their verbal descriptions of what is present in their attention. Over time, Say What You See can become something that individuals do for and with themselves as they tackle the unfamiliar and the complex.
Dave Hewitt writes about Watching What you Do:

> There is a difference between counting and watching yourself counting. It is observing how you count, rather than just counting, which leads to statements about counting [and so to a general formula] ... A certain awareness is required to be able to count ... but a second level of awareness is needed to observe and articulate how that counting is being carried out ... . (Hewitt, 1998, p. 20)

The same applies to any other context. The MGA, DTR and SEM constructs can act as reminders to prompt learners to pay attention to how they are doing something rather than simply 'getting it done', using some version of Say What You See or Watch What You Do.

When trying to detect underlying structure or pattern it often helps to try some particular cases for yourself. This is an example of specialising, and just as with any specialising, what matters is not the answers you get, but attending to what you actually do (Watch What You Do). This means monitoring your actions, especially the ones that spring from nowhere, as it were. It does not mean slowing down and being careful, but rather maintaining speed while being awake to what you are doing. Thus an instruction to 'copy and complete' a table is most likely to turn into a clerical exercise in which learners pay little or no attention to what is going on. Doing one or two special cases with full attention to the 'how', perhaps even tracking the arithmetic rather than doing it all (see, for example, Task 3.4.3a) is often much more informative than a page full of calculations all done mechanically.

Same and Different

A useful question to initiate mathematical thinking is to ask learners what they see as the same, and what different about, two or more objects. These objects could be numbers, problems, diagrams, physical objects, sequences of numbers or objects, and so on. The aim of the question is to draw attention to aspects that are different, that can change, and at the same time, to aspects which are invariant and so do not change. This supports awareness and articulation of generality.

Presenting learners with two or more objects and asking them to look for what is the same and what is different has many virtues. First, it passes initiative to learners; secondly, it exercises their attention and their control of that attention, including the power of mental imagery; thirdly it provides the basis for the exercise of powers of specialising and generalising; fourthly, it reinforces the mathematical theme of invariance in the midst of change.

Looking for what is the same and what is different is closely related to 'going with and across the grain' (see below).

Brown and Coles (2000) demonstrated that when used frequently, looking for similarities and differences ('same 'n' different') can be internalised and used spontaneously by learners.

Easy–Hard–Peculiar–General

Asking learners to make up their own task similar to ones in a set of exercises can be very revealing of the DofPV and associated RofPCh of which they are aware. Asking explicitly for DofPV and associated RofPCh draws attention away from the mere doing of tasks and onto awareness of types of tasks.

Asking for an easy example enables everyone to make a start; asking for a difficult example (and what makes it difficult) sometimes shows learners that in fact there are not any difficult ones; at other times it shows up lack of confidence with decimals or large numbers. Asking for one which will challenge others in the class, or learners in another class, or even one or more teachers, introduces an element of competition and challenge. Variants include a task which shows that you know how to do tasks of this type. Learners can also be asked to describe how to recognise a task of a given type.

Another and Another

A good way to encourage creativity and playfulness is to ask learners to construct an object meeting certain constraints, then another, then another. When they hear other people's ideas some will resolve to be more adventurous next time. Some will be carefully conservative in case they are then asked to do something tricky with their example, but after a while they will see that this is not to be the case. Asking for objects which meet increasingly restrictive constraints enables learners to appreciate the impact on freedom of choice that additional constraints are likely to have, thereby supporting their sense of what a variable is.

Turn a Doing into an Undoing

Most tasks, no matter how routine, can be transformed into challenging tasks requiring insight and creativity simply by converting a 'doing' into an 'undoing'. Asking learners to characterise all the problems of a given type which will give a specified answer, and asking for a description of all the numbers which can be answers to a problem of that type enriches their awareness of generality, their experience of characterising objects mathematically, and stimulates a shift from individual problem to type of problem.

An example of doing and undoing of particular pertinence to algebra is *building and stripping*: start with some known facts about some numbers, say $x = 1$ and $y = 2$. Then build up more and more complicated expressions of facts about x and y, discovering how to make more complicated ones from simpler ones. Then take some of the deduced facts and use them as starting points. By undoing, complex expressions can be reduced to simpler ones. By learning how to make things more complicated, learners discover how to do the reverse and make them simpler. This is the origin of techniques for solving problems. More generally, if learners are engaged in constructing tasks they are more likely to recognise appropriate techniques when they meet questions on examinations.

Scaffolding and Fading

Jerome Bruner and colleagues drew attention to the fact that learners' attention is often fully taken up with details of a computation or a problem, and that the role of the teacher is to be 'consciousness for two' (Bruner 1986, pp. 75–6), holding onto awareness of the larger goal and not getting lost in the details. So arose the notion of *scaffolding* to refer to the support provided by the teacher. For example, if a teacher asks the same question repeatedly over several weeks, such as 'what is the same and what different?', 'what is changing and what is staying the same?' or, when learners are stuck, 'have you tried a simpler example?' or, when learners are uncertain what to do next, 'what did you do last week in this situation?', learners may find themselves prompted to make progress.

However, learners may easily become dependent on teacher prompts, and may not even be aware of the form or nature of those prompts. It is necessary therefore to make the prompts gradually less and less direct. For example, shifting from 'can you give me an example' or 'what might be a particular case', to, 'what did I suggest last time?', 'what question do you think I am going to ask you?', or 'what did we do last time this happened?' prompts the learner to become aware of the teacher's scaffolding, and thus to internalise it for their own use. At first such 'meta-prompts' may result in learners being somewhat taken aback and bemused, but they soon work out what is being asked of them. Eventually the prompts become so indirect and so infrequent that learners find themselves using them spontaneously for themselves. Many authors (Floyd et al., 1981; Seeley Brown, Collins and Duguid, 1989; Love and Mason, 1992) independently pointed out that what is important about scaffolding as prompts to support learners is the fading of the prompts, so that learners use them spontaneously for themselves (Brown and Coles, 2000).

Learner Constructed Examples[1]

Whenever someone in a class says something that is not clear to others, someone can either propose or ask for an example. If someone thinks the statement is false, then they can try to produce a counter example. Example construction is quite difficult at first, but where it becomes a regular part of the way of working, learners benefit from using their own powers to make sense of what others say and do, rather than accepting without questioning.

Learners can be given opportunities to express their creativity and to make choices for themselves by asking them to construct objects meeting certain constraints (as in tasks). In the process, learners display some of the DofPV and associated RofPCh of which they are aware. Asking them to construct another and another (see above) may prompt them to explore the boundaries of their confidence and so extend the range of examples of which they are aware and with which they are confident.

Where learners can be invited to explore a conjecture which involves them in constructing examples to test out, which in turn call upon the use of some technique that they need to practise, learner attention is drawn out of the practice and onto the conjecture being tested. The result is that they become more expert, for experts require little attention to carry out a technique whereas novices usually require nearly full attention. Moving from novice to expert means integrating the technique so that it requires less and less attention to perform, so that attention can be directed towards larger goals.

When learners move from being satisfied to complete an assignment, to being confident they could solve a similar problem in the future, they are beginning to educate their awareness concerning the topic as a whole, and not just the mechanics of techniques. When learners are invited to construct sample tasks for themselves which illustrate their prowess in solving a class of problems, they are making global sense rather than simply getting through the work. When learners can describe or even express a general class of problems which they can solve with a given technique, and when learners can set challenging questions of a similar nature, they are enabling themselves to reconstruct the technique at a future occasion. They are more likely to perform well on tests and exams, even when they meet unfamiliar problems.

Diverting Attention in Order to Automate

An expert is someone who does not need to place their full attention in the carrying out of that expertise. Caleb Gattegno (1987) argued that in order to develop competence and fluency it is necessary to divert your conscious attention away from what you are doing, rather than into it. Dave Hewitt (1996) developed this idea, suggesting that by setting learners tasks which involve them in specialising by constructing their own examples which require the use of a technique to be automated, learner attention can be drawn away from the doing in order to keep track of what the results of the doing say about the task in hand. Thus, to get learners to practise factorizing quadratics, it makes sense to set them a task which involves them in needing to construct and factorise several or many quadratics for themselves, as part of their investigation. The same applies to any technique. The next task provides two examples.

Task 14.3.1 Fractions and Factors

Notice that:

$$\frac{1}{2} - \frac{1}{3} = \frac{1}{6}; \quad \frac{1}{3} - \frac{1}{4} = \frac{1}{12} = \frac{1}{6} - \frac{1}{12} = \frac{1}{11} - \frac{1}{132} = \ldots; \quad \frac{1}{4} - \frac{1}{5} = \frac{1}{20} = \frac{1}{10} - \frac{1}{20} = \frac{1}{19} - \frac{1}{380} = \ldots$$

Describe a method for finding all such re-presentations of the difference of two fractions like these.

The quadratics $x^2 + 5x + 6$ and $x^2 - 5x + 6$ both factorise. What other pairs of quadratics which differ only in the sign of the linear term, both factorise?

Comment

In both cases, learners do a lot of examples in pursuit of a greater goal, thus not only practising the associated skill, but in a context in which it is to their advantage to become adept at the calculations.

This book does not offer practice exercises; instead you are invited to engage in ever more sophisticated tasks and challenges, with a view to competence and fluency developing through use while meeting further challenges, rather than in repetition of tasks of the type already encountered. It has been assumed that where you have felt the need for more routine practice, you can construct it for yourself, but that competence and fluency develop through meaningful use in context not from mindless rehearsal.

Teaching Techniques

It is very tempting to isolate a technique which will serve learners well on examinations, and then teach them the technique through worked examples and plenty of practice. But on an examination it is necessary for learners first to recognise each question as belonging to a type, and to have the appropriate technique come to mind. If learners are led, through suitably constructed tasks, to construct viable and efficient methods for themselves (usually through discussion and reflection) then they are more likely to remember the technique or to be able to reconstruct it when needed, and more likely to recognise its relevance. They are also more likely to be able to adapt a technique to a novel situation than if they have been trained in the specifics of a technique.

NOTE

1 Based on Watson A. and Mason, J. (2002), Student-Generated Examples in the Learning of Mathematics, *Canadian Journal of Science, Mathematics and Technology Education*, 2 (2) pp. 237–49, which was expanded into Watson, A. and Mason, J. (2005) *Mathematics as a Constructive Activity: the role of learner-generated examples*, Mahwah, NJ, Erlbaum.

15 Final Reflections

Chapter 15 pulls the ideas in the book together.

Section 15.1 starts with the notion that every mathematics lesson involves generalisation and hence specialisation, and the use of other powers as well. Section 15.2 considers ways of augmenting and exploiting tasks so that they do make use of children's natural powers. Section 15.3 suggests that any single task is most usefully thought of as a representative of a whole class or domain of related tasks, and that it is through awareness of those possibilities that choices are informed both when preparing a lesson or group of lessons and in the moment as learners work on a task.

Section 15.4 summarises the philosophy and approach promoted in this book, including the roots of algebra. There is also a brief historical overview of how these developed historically, ending with an indication of how algebra develops beyond school mathematics.

15.1 GENERALITY IN EVERY LESSON

The fundamental thesis being put forward in this book is that expressing generality lies at the heart of (school) mathematics. Without confidence and familiarity with expressing generality, the rest of algebraic thinking makes little or no sense at all. Put another way which will by now be familiar, *a lesson without the opportunity for learners to express a generality is not in fact a mathematics lesson.* Every teaching page of a textbook, every work-card must have some implicit or explicit generality, otherwise it is at best a clerical exercise and at worst a waste of learners' time and energy.

If there is a statement of a general method or technique, then the generality is explicit, although often this is ignored by learners who go straight to the worked examples and then the exercises. If they are able to find relationships between worked examples and exercises, then there is an opportunity to become aware of a generality; if there is some structure to the exercises which means that there is something the same about them, something invariant, while the different exercises illustrate different dimensions of possible variation, then there is an implicit generality; if a new idea or concept is being introduced, or a technical term, then deciding what makes something an example, and what makes something not an example involves implicit generalisation, for the concept consists of the dimensions of possible variation and the associated ranges of permissible change which maintain something being an example.

Thus: *Every teaching page of every mathematics textbook not only includes opportunities, but signals a need to generalise, in order to appreciate what the page is about.*

Consider the exercise taken from Wentworth (1890), p. 80 after a page encouraging learners to multiply out in their heads.

Find the product of

1. $3x - y$ and $2x + y$.	6. $10x - 3y$ and $10x - 7y$.
2. $4x - 3y$ and $3x - 2y$.	7. $3a^2 - b^2$ and $2a^2 + 3b^2$.
3. $5x - 4y$ and $3x - 4y$.	8. $a^2 + b^2$ and $(a - b)$.
4. $x - 7y$ and $2x - 5y$.	9. $3a^2 - 2b^2$ and $2a + 3b$.
5. $11x - 2y$ and $7x + y$.	10. $a^2 - b^2$ and $a + b$.

What generalities might Wentworth be intending learners to experience and even to express as a result of this short exercise?

A plausible but unfortunate conjecture might be that mostly you use x and y except when there are squares, and then you use a and b. Presumably the intention is to work at dealing with negative signs. Learners might also be expected to appreciate, if not express, the product of $ax + by$ and $cx + dy$ when a, b, c, d are integers (but notice how the role of the negative sign disappears in the generality).

Task 15.1.R Locating Generalities

Take any teaching page from a textbook and find as many implicit generalities as you can.

What support or prompts might be needed in order to engage learners' powers to generalise in order that they make contact with those opportunities?

Comment

Look for dimensions of possible variation in each task, and consider for which dimensions there is sufficient variation present for learners to become aware of it as a dimension of possible variation.

Learners can be invited to construct other examples 'like those presented' in a dimension which you specify. Learners can also be invited to locate dimensions of possible variation for themselves. Within each dimension there is also the question of the range of permissible change, which may lead to considerable discussion and debate.

15.2 AUGMENTING AND EXPLOITING TASKS

Tasks as presented in textbooks and in other curricular schemes are not necessarily as richly relevant to your particular learners as they might be. On the basis of an analysis of the structure of a topic, as outlined in Chapter 13, and in light of the mathematical powers which your learners might need to work on specifically, it is useful to augment and modify textbook tasks in order to maximise their pedagogical effectiveness. This section makes use of the notion of dimensions of possible variation and the related notion of range of permissible change as a device for alerting yourself to possible developments of tasks.

Dimensions of Possible Variation

Brown and Walter (1983) recommended making a list of all the features of a task, and then asking 'what-if' one or more of these features changed. Following Marton and Booth (1997) it is useful to think of these dimensions of possible variation. Marton's view is that awareness of dimensions-of-possible-variation is what is meant by understanding. Understanding grows when learners become aware of further dimensions that can be varied, or when they become aware that the range-of-permissible-change is greater than previously thought.

Thus in order to appreciate the three-times table, you need to be aware that the multiples can change (one lot of, two lots of, three lots of …) and that the 'unit' remains the same: 3. To get other tables, you change the 3. In order to understand arithmetic progressions you need to be aware that they are constructed by adding a fixed constant to multiples of a fixed number, and that this is the same thing as adding the same number repeatedly to get more and more members of the sequence.

One application of dimensions of possible variation is to task modification: each task or problem has a number of associated features, any of which could be varied. For example, it is well known that many learners, while confident and comfortable with number naming, reading, and writing, make slips when it comes to transitions around powers of ten, giving rise to the following task:

Task 15.2.1 Task Features

What are the principal features of the following task?

Say out loud the whole number which comes after 29, after 49, after 99, after 3 999, after 379 999.

Comment

There are some small numbers, some middle-sized numbers and some big numbers; they all end with one or more 9s; you are asked for the next number. The challenge is to make sure when naming the number that you change the correct place value!

Any or all of these features could be altered: perhaps the small numbers are not needed, or perhaps the large numbers are a bit too large; you could be asked for the number before rather than after, or even two before or two after; the numbers might then be more effective if they did not end in 9.

A further feature is that you are asked to do something to a number provided. You could also be asked to make up a number which might be tricky for some people to name the next number (or the number before it); in this way you could find out whether learners were aware of the potential complexity of 9s in naming numbers.

Note that this task has some generic features (some dimensions of possible variation): you take a feature which sometimes gives learners difficulty, or something to which you want to draw their attention. You then construct a task which involves them 'tripping over' the difficulty or the awareness, preferably by asking learners to construct objects, and to engage in some sort of same and different or invariance in change activity. Being aware of DofPV enables you to decide what features to alter.

In order to become aware of a dimensions-of-possible-variation, learners need to be exposed to two or more examples which vary in that dimension (while other dimensions are held fixed), and to experience them in quick succession. If learners do not experience variation in a dimension, they are unlikely to become aware of it *as* a dimension in which something can be changed. If too many things are varied at once, learners have no background against which to be aware of change and hence of a dimension of possible variation. So if you want learners to generalise, say, then at least at first you will expect them to generalise along dimensions in which you display some variation. To express a generality is to be aware of a particular dimension of possible variation, and to indicate this dimension by means of an expressed generality (using words or symbols).

> ## Task 15.2.2 Seeking DofPV
>
> For each of the following, what dimensions of possible variation are in the task itself?
>
> What is the same, and what different about the left and right hand sides of these two equations?
>
> $86 + 43 = 83 + 46$; $92 + 57 = 97 + 52$;
>
> Find a quadratic expression which not only factorises, but also has the property that if you change the sign of any or all of the coefficients the new expressions also factorise.
>
> When graphing a quadratic, what is the difference between the form $y = ax^2 + bx + c$ and the form $y = a(x + b/2a)^2 + c - b^2/4a$?

Comment

For the first, there is an implied dimension of variation in the changing of individual digits, but changing the number of digits is much less obvious as a dimension of possible variation, as is adding three numbers rather than two. By contrast, changing addition to subtraction would require more subtlety in the 'exchanging of digits' between numbers, and changing to multiplication leads to characterising situations in which the answers are the same. Telling learners the numbers can have any number of digits takes away the frisson of pleasure in realising that it probably works for any sized numbers.

For the second, learners have to start by simplifying or specialising, and this may reveal implicit dimensions of possible variation. For example, most will probably consider only expressions with leading coefficient of 1, at least to begin with. They would be helped considerably by being given two or three examples, such as $x^2 + 5x + 6$ and $x^2 + 13x + 30$. The main feature is that in trying to find expressions which factorise, they will end up constructing a lot of their own, and trying to factorise them, thereby gaining practice in factoring.

When graphing, the second form reveals the coordinates of the extreme value (maximum or minimum) and the roots.[1]

The point about appreciating dimensions of variation is not to 'learn' them, but to learn to recognise them yourself, because this is what lies behind 'learning a method or technique'. Learners can be encultured into seeking dimensions of possible variation for themselves as a way of extending and enriching their appreciation of both concepts and classes of tasks to which a particular technique is applicable.

Range of Permissible Change

Any feature which can be changed, that is, any DofPV, can only be changed to a certain extent. Often some property or relationship is presented with whole numbers but actually works for any numbers at all, but other times the numbers involved have to be integers or fractions, or special kinds of numbers. For example, the fact that the sum of three numbers, whose remainders when dividing by three are all two, is always divisible by three, has several DofPV: the divisor, the remainder, the number of numbers being added. If the remainders all stay the same, then the number of numbers has to be the same as the divisor for the property to work, so there is a constraint on the freedom of the RofPCh of those parameters. Varying the remainder might lead to the fact that if you have one number with each possible remainder on dividing by three, their sum will also be divisible by three. However, here the RofPCh for the divisor three is odd numbers only.

Each DofPV has an associated RofPCh, and it is often the case that learners' sense of the RofPCh is much more restricted that the teacher's. Consequently it is something worth being aware of, and bringing to attention every so often when generalities are being uttered.

Dimensions of Possible Variation in Task Presentation

There are many different ways to introduce tasks. Falling into a habit of using only one method may give learners the impression that that is the only way. It may also make them dependent so that when something different happens, they are unable to cope. At the other extreme, using a different method every time may give the impression that there is no rhyme or reason to how tasks arise, and may actually put learners off. Learners like consistency, but also challenge. Getting the balance right is a constant process of adaptation and experiment.

Doing Calculations

Almost any task can be presented as a sequence of calculations to be performed, just as a collection at the end of a chapter might list a number of exercises to be done, or a worksheet display a number of examples to work on. To be pedagogically effective, there has to be something which arises from doing the tasks, such as a surprise (perhaps all the answers are the same, such as 42, or just 2, or perhaps they are all related in some evident way) and or exposing some invariant relationship despite the changes from task to task. Note that it is vital that learners do more than simply tackle each task in turn: they need to be alert to potential relationships amongst answers (go across the grain).

Distributed Work and Pooling resources

Different groups of learners can work on different versions of a task, in order to accumulate large numbers of examples. Perhaps a number of particular examples are required in order to seek an invariant relationship, so each member embarks on their own example. Perhaps each group has a different looking task, yet all the answers turn out to be the same, or each group starts from the same starting point, but makes it more complex in some manner of their own (start with a solution and generate a question to which it is the solution, within some specified topic or use of specified technique).

Groups can decide for themselves to split the work and pool their resources, or work can be allocated by the teacher.

When a situation develops in which it seems desirable to have a number of different examples to look at in order to try to see what is going on, the learners can divide up the work amongst themselves and then pool their results.

After a period of working on a problem, learners can offer their ideas for making progress in a plenary discussion so that others can pick up on fruitful ideas.

After a period of learners formulating their own questions concerning some situation, they can pool their ideas and decide which questions look tractable and interesting to pursue.[2]

Start Simple or Start Complex?

If learners are always given 'simple' or simplified tasks to begin with, their power to simplify for themselves in order to appreciate what is going on may atrophy. Yet this is what is needed when tackling complex or unfamiliar problems both within school and outside it.

When starting with a complicated or general problem, the implicit invitation is for learners to make up their own simpler versions first. In this way the learner participates more fully, being more interested in working on subtasks constructed by themselves than on a teacher's worksheet.

Start with the General or Start with the Particular

The teacher poses a general problem and invites learners to try their own special cases in order to work out how to do the general.

The teacher can pose a few specific problems and invite the learners to do these and to make up their own like it, leading to trying to describe how to 'do this kind of question' in general.

What is the Same and What is Different … ?

Two or three 'examples' are presented, and learners are invited to decide what they think is the same and what different about the objects presented. Then they are invited to construct their own which is the same as a specified one, and one or more that are different in some way.

By varying some feature, attention is drawn to that as a dimension of possible variation. Within that dimension, what is the possible range of change?

Start with Learner-Generated Examples

Begin by asking learners to construct an example of an object with which they are likely to be familiar. Perhaps then, impose a constraint and ask for an example meeting that constraint; then add an additional constraint. The example and constraint could be relevant to the next topic or aspect of the topic to be developed. Asking learners to construct objects both calls upon them to exercise choice and creativity, as well as revealing something of the dimensions of possible variation and the corresponding ranges of permissible change of which they are aware (and willing to invoke). Using this strategy over a period of time is likely to encourage learners to become more confident, more creative, and more adventurous when they see that what is valued is variety and risk taking. Within a conjecturing atmosphere it is useful when some examples offered do not meet the constraints, so that properties and definitions can be clarified collectively. For example:

> To develop work on solving quadratics, learners could be asked to construct a quadratic equation with roots of ±3, say.

> To develop work on graphing straight lines learners could be asked to write down the equation of a line parallel to the x-axis; and another; and another.

Starting in Silence

The teacher writes on a board, or displays their writing with an overhead projector or interactive white-board. The writing is done *in silence*, pausing in slightly exaggerated form after each calculation or transformation to show that learners should be doing the calculation themselves. This continues for at least two or three exemplary calculations. Learners can then be invited to come up and offer similar examples. The only comment made by the teacher, if any is needed, is to draw a happy or sad face beside them depending on whether they fit or do not fit what the teacher has in mind. Alternatively, learners can all write down the next two or three examples, discuss with each other, offer to the whole group etc. Once someone thinks they know what is going on, they are expected to offer examples which will reveal this to others, without actually stating it in words.

Starting in silence helps focus attention and concentrate thinking. Most learners enjoy trying to puzzle out some relationship or property. Variants include individual learners or a small group of learners taking the teacher's role of presenting the starting example and deciding which ones fit and which do not. Objects on which to work could be any mathematical objects, such as a triple of numbers satisfying some property, an equation of a particular form, a graph with a particular property, input and output values of a function.[3]

Collective Multiplicity

The teacher asks each child to choose an object (a number, a shape, a graph, a calculation, a technique, as appropriate) and to write it down, select it from cards etc. Then a sequence of actions is described to be performed on the object. At the end of several calculations there must be some invariance, something that is the same about all the 'answers'. Either they are all the same, or they all bear an obvious relationship with the starting object.

The fact that so many starting points all produce the same relationship is intended to raise the question of whether it always works, to experience the generality of a technique or procedure applied to many different examples. For example:

> Take a pair of numbers which differ by 3. Add 4 to the larger and 7 to the smaller. What do you notice about your answers? This can be made much more complex of course.

> Draw a square on squared paper. Draw a rectangle with sides respectively one more and one less that the sides of your square. Which is bigger in area, and by how much? Which is bigger in perimeter and by how much? Of course they will all differ in area by 1, with the square being bigger, but have the same perimeter.

Undoing a Doing

The teacher performs a calculation or action upon an object and gets an answer. Then the teacher offers a potential answer and asks what object could have been used to start with. It may not be necessary actually to do the calculation, just to indicate the underlying calculation.

Using Mental Imagery

Instead of using a worksheet, try presenting a task orally. Learners may wish to close their eyes in order to cut out other distractions. To be effective, it helps to change the language of the task slightly so that you are giving instructions in the imperative, and to ask that learners not draw anything. Ask them to imagine a situation or object which you describe, and perhaps to do some calculations with it, or some transformations on it. Over a period of time, learners will be able to do quite a lot in their minds before needing to resort to paper. For example:

> Imagine the graph of a straight line. Translate (slide) it until it goes through the origin. Now rotate it about the origin until it has a slope of 3/2. Now imagine a

copy on top of it, which you then slide sideways (parallel to the x-axis) until it goes through $(1, 0)$. Where does it cross the y-axis? Etc.

Think of a number; add two; multiply by the number you first thought of; add one; take the square root; subtract one. You should have your starting number. (Or subtract the number you first started with … you should all have one as the answer.)

Lists such as these are only of value if they prompt some particular action such as reminding you of a possibility. Then you imagine yourself in a situation using the idea, and preferably, go and do the preparation immediately that will be needed to make use of that idea. For example, varying the format for introducing tasks gets learners away from falling into a routine habit. Variation prompts being on your toes and having to think freshly.

The notion of DofPV and associated RofPCh are powerful ideas which can be used to improve the effectiveness of tasks, and of learners' experience of working on pre-prepared tasks. Learners can also use them to improve their studying, by seeking the dimensions of possible variation in example, or of a set of exercises. There are of course close links between DofPV, the strategy of asking what is the same and what different, and the mathematical theme of invariance in change.

15.3 TASK DOMAINS

It is of little lasting value to a learner to 'get the answers' to a task unless they are better placed to get answers to similar tasks in the future. It is vital therefore for learners to be engaged not simply in 'doing tasks' but in becoming aware of the class of tasks of which these are representative. By learning to look for themselves for dimensions of possible variation in tasks, and by explicitly asking themselves what the range of permissible change might be in each of those dimensions, learners are being called upon to use their power to generalise, and to discern different features which could change in other manifestations. Thus by extending tasks themselves, and by trying to 'do' not just individual tasks but classes of tasks, they are in a better position to re-construct a method they need when they meet something not too familiar in the future.

The tasks used in this book, in common with all mathematical tasks, are merely representatives from a variety of related tasks which can be accessed using the notion of dimensions of possible variation. Thus each task comes from and is illustrative of what is usefully referred to as a *task domain*, from the French word *demesne*, and often used in the context of animals roaming their domain. The idea is that as a teacher it is important to be aware of a larger domain, and that it is possible to develop in learners the habit of exploring that domain for themselves. Learners who are quicker at resolving set tasks can be encouraged to extend and vary tasks for themselves.

Task Domain One: Historical Roots

Although algebra as the use of letters of the alphabet to stand for numbers emerged in Medieval times (notably François Viète and René Descartes) with roots extending back to Diophantus, the use of 'things' to stand for an as-yet-unknown seems to go back into the earliest recorded mathematics. Indeed, the original Medieval term for unknown was *thing*, based on translations of Arabic texts in which much of the mathematics of earlier times were preserved and developed. Euclid (around 300 BCE) is famous for his organisation of mathematical thought, and describes a study of number through geometry (as distinct from use of arithmetic in the marketplace for buying and selling): numbers were conceived of as lengths, and were for them distinguished from numbers denoting areas. There is some evidence (Eves, 1993) that Babylonian scribes were less concerned to distinguish between number as length and number as area, and were not averse to adding the two together, something which Euclid and contemporaries would have avoided at all costs and by means of different subterfuges. Algebra as developed by Arabic scholars during the so called 'dark ages' (500 to 1000 CE) began as the expression of geometrical relationships and propositions, and only gradually shed the diagrams and the reliance on geometry, a Euclidean legacy.

This domain offers some examples of geometrical propositions taken from a translation of Euclid, with a view to converting into diagrams, and then from the diagrams into symbols used in algebra in order to reveal algebraic relationships which are thought of as rules for manipulating symbols. The purpose of this and the next domain is to illustrate how tasks can be seen as representative of a wider domain of exploration.

Task 15.3.1a Diagramming Text and Texting Diagrams

For the two propositions shown, use the diagram to help make sense of the text. Then use symbols to denote lengths to obtain symbolic statements of Euclid's geometrical theorems. Pay attention to what you do with your images in order to see the diagram as speaking the generality implied by the text rather than as a statement about particular lengths shown.

Euclid Book II Prop 4

If a straight line is divided into any two parts, the square on the whole line is equal to the sum of the squares on the two parts together with twice the rectangle contained by the two parts.

Euclid Book II Prop 5

If a straight line is divided equally and also unequally, the rectangle contained by the unequal parts, together with the square on the line between the points of section, is equal to the square on half the line.

Task 15.3.1b Diagramming Text and Texting Diagrams

For the two diagrams, produce a text which 'speaks the area diagram' *before* converting to symbols.

Euclid Book II Prop 6

If a straight line is bisected and produced to any point, the rectangle contained by the whole line thus produced, together with the square on half the line bisected, is equal to the square on the straight line made up of the half and the part produced.

Task 15.3.1c Diagramming Text and Texting Diagrams

What happens to the diagrams if 'lengths' turn out to be negative? Do the propositions remain true?

Comment

Various approaches can be developed for dealing with negatives, such as using directed segments (arrows) to indicate positive and negative directions, but this requires the development of 'rules' for manipulating such diagrams.

The domain associated with these tasks has many different aspects. For example, different geometrical-algebraic results can be depicted, as appeared in sections 1.2, 5.2 and 9.2. Familiarity with starting with an algebraic statement and seeking an appropriate diagram, and with starting with a diagram and expressing it in symbols develops flexibility rather than addiction to one or other direction as preferred.

Task Domain Two: Simultaneous Equations

The covert aim is to get learners to practice solving simultaneous equations. The approach taken is to engage learners in exploring a phenomenon which involves the creation and solution of many sets of simultaneous equations. Note the use of the heading *suggestions* because words like *hint* imply that there is a correct answer hidden behind a veil which you are to discover, whereas suggestions may be found to be helpful, or may not, depending on the direction of your own thinking. What is important is for learners to exercise and develop their mathematical powers and to make further contact with important mathematical themes, while at the same time practising techniques.

Task 15.3.2a The Phenomenon

Solve the pair of equations $2x + 3y = 5$ and $7x + 5y = 12$

Solve the pair of equations $2x + 4y = 6$ and $8x + 5y = 13$

Solve the pair of equations $2x + 5y = 7$ and $9x + 5y = 14$

What do you notice about the solutions? What is it about the equations which might account for this? How might this show up on a graph?

Suggestions

The questions seem innocuous at first. Solutions could be found by guess and test, by graphic calculator, by graphing, or by algebraic manipulation. The fact that they all have the same answer may not be noticed by learners so eager to finish the tasks that they do not think about the answers, but the subsidiary questions draw attention to something common to them all. In a class, learners at different tables could be given different problems, yet all would find the same answer, perhaps generating surprise and the question of what it is about the coefficients which makes this happen.

Some learners may be able to guess the solution, or even to come to it by noticing a connection between coefficients and the common solution to all the pairs. Learners could then be challenged to write down other pairs of equations which would have the same solution.

The next task illustrates the use of dimensions of possible variation as a prompt to expressing a phenomenon which connects not only the individual cases in the previous task, but extends and generalises it.

Task 15.3.2b What is the Phenomenon?

What dimensions of possible variation are there in the phenomenon presented in the previous task?

Suggestions

There are relations between the first of each pair; there are also relations between the coefficients of each equation. The solutions are all the same because of a property possessed by the coefficients of the equations in each pair.

You could vary the coefficients, preserving only the property that the sum of the coefficients of x and y is the constant term.

You could vary this relationship too: suppose the constant is always twice the x coefficient minus three times the y coefficient, for example.

The next task could have been used as an entry task for learners with more confidence in solving simultaneous equations.

Task 15.3.2c The Phenomenon II

Solve the pair of equations $4x + 5y = 6$ and $7x + 8y = 9$;

Solve the pair of equations $3x + 5y = 7$ and $9x + 11y = 13$;

Solve the pair of equations $17x + 14y = 11$ and $8x + 5y = 2$.

What do you notice about the solutions? What is it about the sets of equations which might account for this? Generalise!

> *Suggestions*
>
> Try reading the equations in each pair out loud, to reveal a relationship amongst the coefficients.
>   As in the previous task, different tables could be given different pairs of equations.
>   What is the class of all such properties between coefficients which lead to the same solution? For example, could the constant term be the sum of the squares of the coefficients of x and y?

   The core of these tasks was to attract learner attention to looking for relationships and formulating properties which link pairs of equations with the same solution. In the process the learners are likely to find themselves setting up and solving other equations for themselves, thus rehearsing the solution of equations while their attention is focused on seeking those relationships. Learners who work out that they can substitute values in for x and y to test conjectures are developing a richly interconnected sense of simultaneous equations rather than seeing them as based on an isolated technique on which they might be tested.
   The next task develops the exploration implied in the previous task, and is only included here to indicate a direction of development which could be prompted arising from work done on the previous task.

Task 15.3.3 Imposed Relations

The coefficients of the equation $ax + (a + d)y = 4 + 2d$ are arbitrary numbers (a ≠ 0), belonging in sequence to an arithmetic progression. Interpret the rewriting of this equation as $a(x + 1) + (y - 2)(a + d) = 0$ in terms of one point on the line. What does this say about any pair of equations whose coefficients belong to an arithmetic progression? Must the coefficients come from the same arithmetic progression? Must the coefficient of y be the arithmetic mean of the coefficients of x and the constant? Does it matter if the coefficients of x and of y are interchanged in one or both equations?

Show that all equations of the form $ax + (a + c)y/t = c$ pass through the point $(^-1, t)$.

Suggestions

Notice the use of t as a parameter: fixed for a time, but able to vary to create a class of generalisations. Notice the prompt to check that the generalisation using t actually encompasses previous known examples.

Task 15.3.4a An Inverse Phenomenon

Construct all the linear equations which go through the point $(^-2, 1)$. Express a relationship between the coefficients, and use this to generate particular pairs of equations in which the coefficient relationship might be exposed so that learners could recognise it and generalise for themselves.

Suggestions

Choosing examples requires care with the numbers so that, for example, none is repeated (otherwise it is hard to trace the effects of each instance of the same number), and any necessary relationships are reasonably evident (they don't require arithmetic calculation, perhaps).

. This task has some dimensions of possible variation, including changing the point that all equations are to pass through.

Task 15.3.4b An Inverse Phenomenon

Select a point and characterise all pairs of equations that pass through that point. Generalise.

Comment

There is no intention that learners should or even could learn to recognise from the coefficients what the solution is. That is the role of the technique of solving equations. The purpose of this and related tasks is to engage learners in both the 'doing' and the 'undoing', as well as engaging them in seeking relationships and appreciating that a solution represents a point common to the two lines. Furthermore, by working on these tasks they are experiencing invariance (of a relationship amongst coefficients) in the midst of the coefficients themselves changing.

Summary

The point about these task domains is the variety of ways in which tasks can be presented and developed by varying different dimensions of possible variation. Coefficients can be fractions, or decimals, or even complex numbers as long as they satisfy other constraints. Constraints can be seen not just as singular and particular but as representative of a class of possibilities (that is, they too possess dimensions of possible variation). Approaching constraints this way makes it easier to see how, when the situation seems too complex, you might simplify a complicated one (that is, to specialise) in order to see what is going on before then re-complexifying.

15.4 ROOTS AND BLOSSOMS OF ALGEBRA

This section briefly indicates how algebra emerges from the use of learners' natural powers to make sense mathematically. Although it is commonly thought that algebra is an extension of, or development from arithmetic, arithmetic actually calls upon algebraic thinking, because of the implicit generalities which learners are expected to internalise. As Dave Hewitt put it: 'Arithmetic is impossible without algebra' (Hewitt, 1998, p. 20).

> It is awareness of awareness which is involved in working algebraically. Arithmetic is concerned with the result … Algebra is concerned with organising the counting, finding a structured way to get the result. To be able to count requires a way of counting, a way of structuring and organising counting. To be able to count requires you to work algebraically. (Hewitt, 1998, p. 20)

The term *generalised arithmetic* is often used to describe or define algebra, but there are even two interpretations of this: algebra as 'doing arithmetic with letters', and algebra as the expression of the rules of arithmetic (associativity, commutativity, distributivity) and the extension of those rules to the symbols in which those rules have been expressed. Merely doing arithmetic with letters has proved fruitless for countless generations of learners.

Algebraic thinking is rooted in and emerges from learners' natural powers to make sense mathematically. At the very heart of algebra is the expression of generality. Exploiting algebraic thinking within arithmetic, through explicit expression of generality and through 'tracking arithmetic' (section 3.4) makes use of learners' powers to develop their algebraic thinking and hence to appreciate arithmetic more thoroughly. Algebraic symbols are a language for expressing generalities. As fluency and facility with expressions of generality develops, the expressions become more succinct, and hence manipulable.

The force and desire to manipulate comes from several sources. One is from recognising that different looking expressions sometimes purport to express the same thing. For example, if $1 + 3s$ and $4 + 3(s - 1)$ arise as two different ways of seeing how to count the number of 'sticks' in a single row of unit squares or the number of segments for a pine tree diagram.

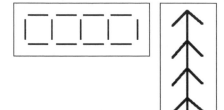

Then since both expressions express the same thing, there must be a way to demonstrate this simply by rearranging the expressions, without recourse to the original diagram. Another source for desire to manipulate algebraic expressions is from recognising properties of numbers in arithmetic and generalising these (hence generalised arithmetic). Another source for purposeful algebraic manipulation is from wanting to develop calculation techniques to manifest graphical properties. For example, when two graphs intersect, how can you find the coordinates of the intersection from the equations of the graphs? A further source comes from everyday applications such as pricing policies (see Chapter 8).

In parallel with expressing generality is the use of symbols to denote as-yet-unknown numbers so that relationships can be expressed (a form of expressing generality). Facility in manipulating symbols will develop while exploring and expressing. Routine practice on exercises is only of value if attention is attracted away from the technical aspects of manipulation, and used to direct progress towards some other goal, perhaps a conjecture being explored.

As manipulative facility develops, attention will turn to the solution of equations and inequalities which arise during explorations and from expressing relationships described in words within problems and problematic situations. This parallels the development of algebraic techniques historically. Moving to the expansion of brackets, simplification of strings of symbols, and the solution of one or more equations without plenty of previous experience of expressing their own generalities often leaves learners mystified as to what they are supposed to be doing and why.

The claim has been made that a lesson without an opportunity for learners to generalise cannot be considered to be a mathematics lesson. In other words, in every topic, in every exercise, in every task, there are opportunities for generalisation. Generalising is not just something that is done in mathematics, but rather is the essence of any learning. At the most practical level, being aware of a class of problems (a problem type) which can be solved by use of a particular technique is much better preparation for a test or examination than is pedestrian solving of individual problems without any form of reflection or sense-making. At the emotional–motivational level, learners are much more likely to enjoy lessons in which they get to use their own powers, such as 'seeing the general through the particular' and 'seeing the particular in the general'. Furthermore, generalising, encompassing a range of apparently disparate particulars in a single generality releases energy and stimulates learners. Inviting learners to be explicit about the dimensions of possible variation and the associated ranges of permissible change of which they are aware associated with a concept or a technique lets them take the initiative, to construct pertinent examples, and to reinforce their understanding.

Finally, when the rules of arithmetic (commutativity of addition and multiplication, associativity, distributivity, the roles of zero and one, and both additive and multiplicative inverses) are expressed in general, they comprise the rules for manipulating algebraic symbols, precisely because algebra is a generalisation of arithmetic. School algebra is generalised arithmetic not because letters are used in place of numbers, but because the language of algebra expresses general properties of numbers and of arithmetic calculations.

In summary, the roots of algebra are found in

> *expressing generality*: encountering the use of words and symbols for expressing unspecified, arbitrary numbers and other objects with particular attention to the use of diagrams and to number tracking as contexts for fostering awareness of generality;
>
> *multiple expressions*: encountering multiple expressions for the same generality and thus being led to the possibility of rules for manipulating expressions independently of their source;
>
> *freedom and constraint*: encountering the use of symbols to stand for the as–yet–unknown or the as-yet-unspecified and translating constraints into equations and inequalities, leading to the need for techniques for solving equations etc.;
>
> *experiencing structure*, leading to *generalised arithmetic*: expressing in general the rules of arithmetic, ending up with the rules for manipulating algebraic expressions as well.

These four strands provide a structure to inform every mathematics lesson. When combined with exposure to mathematical themes (section 13.1) and with encouragement for learners to use their own mathematical powers (section 14.1), all within a conjecturing atmosphere, algebraic thinking develops.

Significant Moments in the History of the Development of Algebra

Algebra did not spring spontaneously into being. It took many centuries to be developed. The psychological and pedagogic roots and the struggles of some learners are mirrored in the historical record. Here are some of the highlights.

	Dates	Modern country	Objects/people	Contribution
		China	Chinese manuscripts (lost)	Reasoning about general methods
	2000–1000	Egypt	Rhind papyrus	Reasoning about general methods
BCE		Iraq	Cuneiform tablets	Quadratic equations, systems of equations, Pythagoras' theorem
	1000–500	India		Square root
	500–300	Greece	Plato (427–347 BCE)	
		Egypt	Euclid (c.325–265 BCE)	Axiomatic presentation of mathematics geometrically

	Dates	Modern country	Objects/people	Contribution
CE	0–200	Jordan	Nichomachus (c.50–c.150)	Figurate numbers
	200–300	Egypt	Diophantus (c.200–c.284)	Collection of problems purely about numbers
	500–600	Italy	Boethius (c.480–c.525)	Elementary word problems collected
	800–1000	Iraq	Mohammed ibn-Musa al-Kwarizmi	First algebra text. His name gives us the word 'algorithm'; the title of his book gives us the word 'algebra' derived from al-jabr meaning 'completion' or 'adding the same to both sides'.
	1000–2000	China	Jia Xian Triangle	Used to solve equations
		Iran	Omar Khayyam	Geometric solution of quadratic and cubic equations
	1200–1300	Italy	Leonardo of Pisa (Fibonacci) (c.1180–1240)	Book of the Abacus for use by merchants
	1500–1600	Italy	Girolamo Cardano (1501–1563)	Solution of general cubic equation; tentative use of complex numbers
		Italy	Raphael Bombelli (c.1526–1573)	Use of negatives following rules of signs for their arithmetic
		France	François Viète (1540–1603)	Use of letters and how to manipulate them. Solution of equations and general problem solving methods using algebra
	1600–1700	France	René Descartes (1596–1650)	Use of Thales' theorem for arithmetic of segments; converting geometry into algebra
		England	Isaac Newton (1642–1727)	Shift from solving word problems to solving equations as the subject of algebra; use of complex numbers
	1746	France	D'Alembert (1717–1783)	Proof of fundamental theorem of algebra: every polynomial of odd degree n with integer coefficients has a real root; every polynomial with integer coefficients can be factored as a product of quadratics and linear expressions with integer coefficients

Source: based on Bashmakova and Smirnova (2000).

Whence Algebra?

Having worked on some of the ideas in this book, you may have begun to appreciate that algebra is much more than the use of letters in place of numbers, much more than the solution of simultaneous linear equations, much more than the factoring of quadratic expressions. School algebra is about expressing generality and about developing confidence in manipulating those generalities.

If children in primary school are encountering the roots of algebra and of algebraic thinking as they deal with arithmetic, if adolescents in the middle years are called upon to develop algebra into a manipulable symbol system which can be used to express a wide range of generalisations about number and relationships, as well as to resolve a wide class of problems, and if sixth-formers use algebraic thinking to master new techniques and new ideas associated with a wider class of problems, where does algebra go next? How does it develop?

The answer is that algebra continues to be a manipulable language in which to express generalities concerning relationships, but whereas in school algebra those generalities are concerned with number (and only a restricted class of numbers, the reals), 'higher algebra' goes beyond by making a shift. The language of algebra is used to capture and to express the idea of structure itself.

Whenever you express a generality about numbers you are describing or capturing some structure. It may be the structure of odd numbers (all of which are of the form $2n + 1$ for n an integer), or the structure of numbers which can be expressed as the sum of two square integers (all numbers for which prime divisors that are 1 less than a multiple of 4 appear to an even power). But just as mathematicians around the time of Newton were turning from using algebra to express problems in symbolic terms, to seeking methods for solving the resulting equations, so mathematicians turn their attention to the structure of sets of numbers as a whole. Furthermore, they use not just familiar numbers, but number-like objects. In every case, those objects, which share all or most of the properties of the rationals or the reals, are studied because they assist in the solution of more complex problems, just as the complex numbers are needed in order to solve all quadratics. So attention turns to properties which characterise numbers, such as associativity, commutativity, distributivity, the properties of 0 and 1, and the presence or absence of additive and multiplicative inverses.

Algebraic thinking goes even further. Whereas the roots of algebraic language to express generality can be found in the desire to count objects making up some structured array or diagram (counting matchsticks, counting the number of ways of choosing things from a bigger set, etc.), 'higher algebra' uses the structures which are revealed by generalising numbers, as the replacement for numbers themselves. A 'structure' involves both objects and operations on those objects, just as arithmetic comprises numbers, and operations on those numbers (addition, subtraction, multiplication, division).

For example, instead of merely counting the number of faces on a die sitting in a tight fitting box, mathematicians ask themselves 'what is the structure of the operations you can perform on the die as you put it back in its case?' The objects are the ways of reorientating the die before it goes back in the box; the operation is composing two of these transformations, that is, performing one and then another. This goes beyond simply counting the number of ways of putting it in its box. The answer turns out to have some similarities with the structure of numbers.

As another example, suppose you are standing in a garden which has a pole, bird-bath, sculpture, or some other obstruction at the centre. You fasten a hosepipe to a tap on the boundary, then walk around the garden watering, ending up back at the tap. Then you start tugging on the hosepipe trying to pull it in. But of course it may be wound around the obstruction. Instead of asking 'in how many different ways can the hosepipe be wound around the obstruction?', mathematicians ask 'what is the structure of all the different ways?' The objects are the ways the hose can be wound around, and the operation is joining the nozzle end of the first hose to the tap end of a second hose to make a longer hose. It turns out to be a useful way for characterising surfaces which arise in a wide variety of contexts, and (of course) it generalises vastly.

One of the significant developments in mathematics which took place around the beginning of the twentieth century was to turn attention to transformations, including functions, as the objects amongst which relationships are sought, and of which properties are formulated. So starting from numbers used to count, expressions of generality about numbers are seen as particular cases of functions; transformations of sets of functions are then studied; then transformations of these transformations, and on and on.

The important thing to appreciate about school algebra is that it is an important step in a long line of exciting developments which enable mathematicians to recognise, reason about, and characterise, a succession of more and more sophisticated mathematical structures, which in turn enable them to solve more and more complex problems. A good deal of modern mathematics can be seen as developing a language in which to express and manipulate increasingly complicated and sophisticated relationships and properties.

NOTES

1 Rina Zazkis and Karen Gadowsky (2001) describe notations as being transparent with respect to certain features, so the second form is transparent (once you know how to read it) for the roots, just $777 + 1$ is transparently one more than a multiple of 7 whereas 120 is not.
2 This strategy was developed and exploited particularly by Afzal Ahmed.
3 'Starting in Silence' was developed initially in the context of the 'funtion game' in which input and output values are offered and either accepted or declined, developed particularly by Laurinda Brown.

Epilogue

You have been invited throughout the book to integrate encounters with some of the important aspects of algebra and ways of thinking about, and interacting with learners. The overall design has been to engage you in tasks in order to accumulate experience which can then be used to make sense of pedagogic remarks. Only after thoughtful reflection does it make sense to think about implications for teaching. Through engaging in algebraic thinking, with frequent invitations to pause and reflect, you have been prompted to reconsider and reconstruct what has been experienced. This approach to professional development is summarised by the triple Adult–Process–Classroom (APC for short), and is recommended as a structure for working with colleagues, as well as when working with learners in classrooms. Start from recent experience; use that experience to make sense of past experience by reflecting on processes, re-entering significant and salient moments, recalling details, and most especially, imagining yourself in a typical classroom situation making use of a task type or strategy. Working in this way, striving to be more disciplined in noting actions to take and things to look out for in classrooms, and in planning for the future by imagining yourself acting the way you would like to, is the beginning of a science of education. Caleb Gattegno (1970) and Hans Freudenthal (1983) both strove to outline such a science, but their writings can at best be inspiration. The real science is what you choose to do, yourself, in your situation.

I cannot change others;

I can however work at changing myself (Mason, 2002).

It is amazing what an influence this can have on others.

References

Ahmed, A. (1987) *Better Mathematics: A Curriculum Development Study Based on the Low Attainers in Mathematics Project (LAMP)*. London: HMSO.

Association of Teachers of Mathematics (ATM) (1989) *A Gattegno Anthology*. Derby: ATM.

Ballard, P. (1928) *Teaching the Essentials of Arithmetic*. London: University of London Press.

Baruk, S. (1985) *L'âge du capitaine: de l'erreur en mathématiques*. Paris: Éditions du Seuil.

Bashmakova, I. and Smirnova, G. (2000) *The Beginnings and Evolution of Algebra*. Dolciani Mathematical Expositions 23. Washington, DC: Mathematical Association of America.

Battista, M., Clements, D., Arnoff, J., Battista, K. and Borrow, C. (1988) 'Students' spatial structuring and enumeration of 2d arrays of squares', *Journal for Research in Mathematics Education*, 29 (5): 503–32.

Bednarz, N. and Janvier B. (1996) 'Emergence and development of algebra as a problem solving tool: continuities and discontinuities with arithmetics', in N. Berdnarz, C. Kieran and L. Lee (eds), *Approaches to Algebra: Perspectives for Research and Teaching*. Dordrecht: Kluwer Academic. pp. 115–36.

Bell, A. (1996) 'Algebraic thought and the role of a manipulable symbolic language', in N. Berdnarz, C. Kieran and L. Lee (eds), *Approaches to Algebra: Perspectives for Research and Teaching*. Dordrecht: Kluwer Academic. pp. 151–4.

Bell, A., Rooke, D. and Wigley, A. (1978) *Journey Into Maths*. Nottingham: Shell Centre.

Bézout, E. (1792) *Cours de Mathematiques, à l'usage du corps de l'artillerie*. Paris: Musier.

Bills, C., Bills, E., Mason, J. and Watson, A. (2004) *Thinkers*. Derby: Association of Teachers of Mathematics.

Bills, J. (1996) 'Shifting sands: students' understanding of the roles of variables in "A" level mathematics'. Unpublished PhD thesis, Open University, Milton Keynes.

Bishop, A. (1988) *Mathematics Education and Culture*. Dordrecht: Kluwer.

Bland, M. (1832) *Algebraical Problems: Producing Simple and Quadratic Equations with their Solutions*. Cambridge: J. Smith.

Brissenden, T. (1980) *Mathematics Teaching: Theory and Practice*. London: Harper and Row.

Brousseau, G. (1997) *Theory of Didactical Situations in Mathematics: Didactiques des Mathématiques, 1970–1990*, in N. Balacheff, M. Cooper, R. Sutherland and V. Warfield, (trans). Dordrecht: Kluwer.

Brown, A. (2002) 'Patterns of thought and prime factorisation', in S. Campbell and R. Zazkis (eds), *Learning and Teaching Number Theory: Research in Cognition and Instruction*. Journal of Mathematical Behaviour monograph. Westport, CT: Ablex. pp. 131–7.

Brown, L. and Coles, A. (2000) 'Same/different: a "natural" way of learning mathematics', in T. Nakahara and M. Koyama (eds), *Proceedings of the 24th Conference of the International Group for the Psychology of Mathematics Education*, Hiroshima: Nishiki Print Co. Vol. l2, pp. 153–60.

Brown, S. and Walter, M. (1983) *The Art of Problem Posing*. Philadelphia, PA: Franklin Press.

Bruner, J. (1966) *Toward a Theory of Instruction*. Cambridge, MA: Harvard University Press.

Bruner, J. (1986) *Actual Minds, Possible Worlds*. Cambridge, MA: Harvard University Press.

Butler, W. (1838) *Arithmetical Questions on a New Plan: Intended to Answer the Double Purpose of Arithmetical Instruction and Miscellaneous Information Designed for the Use of Young Ladies*. 12th edn. London: Harvey and Darton.

Campbell, S. and Zazkis, R. (eds.) (2002)' Learning and teaching number theory: research in cognition and instruction', in C. Maher and R. Speiser (series eds), *Mathematics, Learning and Cognition: Monograph Series of the Journal of Mathematical Behavior (vol. 2)*. Westport, CT: Ablex Publishing.

Chevallard, Y. (1985) *La Transposition Didactique*, Grenoble: La Pensée Sauvage.

Chuquet, N. (1484) *La Géométrie*. Paris: J.Vrin.

Cooper, B. and Dunne, M. (2000) *Assessing Children's Mathematical Knowledge: Social Class, Sex and Problem-Solving*, Buckingham: Open University Press.

Courant, R. (1981) 'Reminiscences from Hilbert's Gottingen', *Math Intelligencer*, 4 (3): 154–64.

Day, J. and Kalman, D. (2001) 'Teaching linear algebra: issues and resources', *College Mathematics Journal*, 32 (3): 162–8.

De Morgan, A. (1865) 'A speech of Professor De Morgan, President, at the first meeting of the London Mathematical Society', *Proceedings of the London Mathematical Society*, 1 (1866): 1–9.

De Morgan, A. (1943), *On the Study and Difficulties of Mathematics*. 4th edn. Chicago, IL: Open Court.

Dewey, J. (1902) *The Child and the Curriculum*. Chicago, IL: University of Chicago Press.

Dewey, J. (website) *My Pedagogic Creed*, available at www.rjgeib.com/biography/credo/dewey.html.

Diophantos (trans. Heath) (1964) *Diophantus of Alexandria: A Study in the History of Greek Algebra*. New York: Dover.

Dweck, C. (1999) *Self-Theories: Their Role in Motivation, Personality and Development*. Philadelphia, PA: Psychology Press.

Elgin, D. (2004) 'Do it wrong, get it right', *Mathematics in School*, 33 (1): 14–15.

Eliot, G. (1855) 'Thomas Carlyle', in *G. Eliot, Selected Essays, Poems and Other Writings*. (Reprinted 1990.) Harmondsworth: Penguin. pp. 343–8.

Evens, H. and Houssart, J. (2002) 'Sum and difference problems at KS2', *Proceedings of BSRLM*, Leeds, July, 24 (2): 21–6.

Eves, H. (1993). *Lectures in the History of Mathematics*. History of Mathematics vol. 7. Providence, RI: American Mathematical Society and London Mathematical Society.

Festinger, L. (1957) *A Theory of Cognitive Dissonance*. Stanford, CA: Stanford University Press.

Floyd, A., Burton, L., James, N. and Mason, J. (1981) EM235: *Developing Mathematical Thinking*. Open University course. Milton Keynes: Open University Press.

Freudenthal, H. (1978) *Weeding and Sowing: Preface to a Science of Mathematics Education*. Dordrecht: Reidel.

Freudenthal, H. (1983) *Didactical Phenomenology of Mathematical Structures*. Dordrecht: Reidel.

Freudenthal, H. (1991) *Revisiting Mathematics Education: China Lectures*. Dordrecht: Kluwer.

Gattegno, C. (1970) *What We Owe Children: The Subordination of Teaching to Learning*. London: Routledge and Kegan Paul.

Gattegno, C. (1987) *The Science of Education Part I: Theoretical Considerations*. New York: Educational Solutions.

Gerofsky, S. (1996) 'A linguistic and narrative view of word problems in mathematics education', *For the Learning of Mathematics*, 16 (2): 36–45.

Gibson, J. (1977) 'The theory of affordances', in R.E. Shaw and J. Bransford (eds), *Perceiving, Acting, and Knowing*. Hillsdale, NJ: Lawrence Erlbaum Associates.

Gillings, R. (1982) *Mathematics in the Time of the Pharoahs*. New York: Dover.

Gray, E. and Tall, D. (1994) 'Duality, ambiguity, and flexibility: a proceptual view of simple arithmetic', *Journal of Research in Mathematics Education*, 25 (2): 116–40.

Greeno, J., Smith, D. and Moore, J. (1993) 'Transfer of situated learning', in D. Detterman and R. Sternberg (eds), *Transfer on Trial: Intelligence, Cognition, and Instruction*, Norwood, NJ: Ablex. pp. 99–167.

Halmos, P. (1980) 'The heart of mathematics', *American Mathematical Monthly*, 87 (7): 519–24.

Halmos, P. (1985) *I Want to be a Mathematician*. Washington, DC: MAA Spectrum.

Halmos, P. (1994) 'What is teaching?', *American Mathematical Monthly*, 101 (9): 848–54.

Hart, K., Kerslake, D., Brown, M., Ruddock, G., Küchemann, D. and McCartney, M. (eds) (1981) *Children's Understanding of Mathematics 11–16*. London: John Murray.

Hewitt, D. (1992) 'Train spotters' paradise', *Mathematics Teaching*, 140: 6–8.

Hewitt, D. (1996) 'Mathematical fluency: the nature of practice and the role of subordination', *For the Learning of Mathematics*, 16 (2): 28–35.

Hewitt, D. (1998) 'Approaching arithmetic algebraically', *Mathematics Teaching*, 163: 19–29.

Jeffreys, H. and Jeffreys, B. (1988) 'Lagrange's interpolation formula', in H. Jeffreys and B. Jeffreys (eds), *Methods of Mathematical Physics*. 3rd edn. Cambridge: Cambridge University Press. Sect. 9.011.

Jones, S. (1912) *Mathematical Wrinkles: A Handbook for Teachers and Private Learners*. Nashville, TN: Jones.

Kangshen, S., Crossley, J. and Lun, A. (1999) *The Nine Chapters on the Mathematical Art: Companion and Commentary*. Oxford: Oxford University Press.

Karpinski L.C. (1965) *The History of Arithmetic*. First published 1925, Chicago, IL: Rand McNally. Reprinted 1965, New York: Russell and Russell.

Klein, J. (1992) *Greek Mathematical Thought and the Origin of Algebra*. E. Brann (trans.). New York: Dover. (First published in 1934.)

Kordemsky, (1975) *Moscow Puzzles: 359 Mathematical Recreations*. A. Parry (trans.), M. Gardner (ed.), Harmondsworth: Penguin. (First printed in 1956.)

Love, E. and Mason, J. (1992) *Teaching Mathematics: Action and Awareness*. Milton Keynes: Open University Press.

MacGregor, M. and Stacey, K. (1993) 'Cognitive models underlying students' formulation of simple linear equations', *Journal for Research in Mathematics Education*, 24 (3): 217–32

Marton, F. and Booth, S. (1997) *Learning and Awareness*. Mahwah, NJ: Lawrence Erlbaum Associates.

Mason, J. (1988) *Expressing Generality, Project Update*. Milton Keynes: Open University Press.

Mason, J. (2002) *Researching Your Own Practice: The Discipline of Noticing*. London: RoutledgeFalmer.

Mason, J. and Johnston-Wilder, S. (2004a) *Fundamental Constructs in Mathematics Education*. London: RoutledgeFalmer.

Mason, J. and Johnston-Wilder, S. (2004b) *Designing and Using Mathematical Tasks*. Milton Keynes: Open University Press.

Mason, J., Graham, A., Pimm, D. and Gowar, N. (1985) *Routes To Roots Of Algebra*. Milton Keynes: Open University Press.

Mole, J. (1788) *Elements of Algebra; to which is prefixed, a choice collection of arithmetical questions, with their solutions, including some new improvements worthy the attention of arithmeticians*. London: G.G.J. and J. Robinson.

Moshovits-Hadar, N. (1988) 'Surprise', *For the Learning of Mathematics*, 8 (3): 34–40.

Nemet-Nejat, K. (1993) *Cuneiform Mathematical Texts as a Reflection of Everyday Life in Mesopotamia*, American Oriental Series, vol. 75. New Haven, CT: American Oriental Society.

Nunn, T.P. (1919) *Exercises in Algebra [Including Trigonometry], Part I*. London: Longmans, Green and Co.

Olney, E. (1870) *The Complete Algebra; embracing simple and quadratic equations, proportion and the progressions, with an elementary and practical view of logarithms; a brief treatment of numerical higher equations and a chapter on the business rules of arithmetic treated algebraically*. New York: Sheldon and Co.

Peirce, C.S. (1902) *The Essence of Mathematics*, (reprinted 1956) in J.R. Newman (ed.), *The World of Mathematics*. New York: Simon and Schuster. p. 1779.

Piaget, J. (1971) *Biology and Knowledge*, Chicago, IL: University of Chicago Press.

Plato, *Plato: Five Dialogues*. G.M.A Grube (trans.), revised by J.M. Cooper. Indianapolis, IN: Hackett.

Polya, G. (1957) *How to Solve It*. New York: Anchor.

Prestage, S. and Perks, P. (2001) *Adapting and Extending Secondary Mathematics Activities: New Tasks for Old*. London: Fulton.

Robson, E. (2000) 'Mesopotamian mathematics: some historical background', in V. Katz (ed.), *Using History to Teach Mathematics: An International Perspective*. Washington, DC: Mathematical Association of America. pp. 149–58.

Royal Society, Joint Mathematical Council of the United Kingdom (1997) *Teaching and Learning Algebra Pre-19, Report of the Royal Society/JMC Working Group*. London: Royal Society.

Sanford, V. (1975) *The History and Significance of Standard Problems in Algebra*. New York: American Mathematical Society Press.

Saunderson, N. (1740) *The Elements of Algebra in Ten Books*. London.

Seeley Brown, J., Collins A. and Duguid, P. (1989) 'Situated cognition and the culture of learning', *Educational Researcher*, 18 (1): 32–42.

Stacey, K. and MacGregor, M. (2000) 'Learning the algebraic method of solving problems', *Journal of Mathematical Behaviour*, 18 (2): 149–67.

Stigler, J. and Hiebert, J. (1999) *The Teaching Gap: Best Ideas from the World's Teachers for Improving Education in the Classroom*. New York: Free Press.

Tahta, D. (1980) 'About geometry', *For the Learning of Mathematics*, 1: 2–9 .

Tahta, D. (1981) 'Some thoughts arising from the new Nicolet films', *Mathematics Teaching*, 94: 25–9.

Thomson, J. (1874) *New Practical Arithmetic for Grammar Departments*. 15th edn. New York: Clark and Maynard.

Van Hiele, P. (1986). *Structure and Insight: A Theory of Mathematics Education*. Developmental Psychology Series. London: Academic Press.

Vergnaud, G. (1981) 'Quelques Orientations Théoriques et Méthodologiques des Recherches Françaises en Didactique des Mathématiques', *Actes du Vième Colloque de PME*. Grenoble: Edition IMAG. Vol. 2, pp. 7–17.

Verschaffel, L., Greer, B. and de Corte, E. (2000) *Making Sense of Word Problems*. Lisse: Swets and Zeitlinger.

Viète, F. (1983) *The Analytic Art: Nine Studies in Algebra, Geometry and Trigonometry from the Opus Restitutae Mathematicae Analyseos seu Algebra Nova*. T. Witmer (trans.). Kent, OH: Kent State University Press. (First published 1591.)

Watson, A. (2000) 'Going across the grain: mathematical generalisation in a group of low attainers', *Nordisk Matematikk Didaktikk (Nordic Studies in Mathematics Education)*, 8 (1): 7–22.

Watson, A. and Mason, J. (1998) *Questions and Prompts for Mathematical Thinking*. Derby: Association of Teachers of Mathematics.

Watson, A. and Mason, J. (2002) 'Student-generated examples in the learning of mathematics', *Canadian Journal of Science, Mathematics and Technology Education*, 2 (2): 237–49.

Watson, A. and Mason, J. (2004) *Mathematics as a Constructive Activity: The Role of Learner-Generated Examples*. Mahwah, NJ: Lawrence Erlbaum Associates.

Wells, W. and Hart, W. (1923) *First Year Algebra*. Boston, MA: Heath.

Wentworth, G. (1890) *A School Algebra*. Boston, MA: Ginn and Co.

Wheeler, D. (1996) 'Backwards and forwards: reflections on different approaches to algebra', in N. Bednarz, C. Kieran and L. Lee (eds), *Approaches to Algebra, Perspectives for Research and Teaching*. Dordrecht: Kluwer Academic. pp. 317–25.

Whitehead, A. (1948) *Essays in Science and Philosophy*. London: Rider.

Whiteside, D. (ed.) (1972) *The Mathematical Papers of Isaac Newton, Vol. V 1683–1684*. Cambridge: Cambridge University Press.

Witmer, T. (trans.) (1968), *Ars Magna or The Rules of Algebra, Girolamo Cardano*. New York: Dover.

Wright, J. (1825) *Self Examinations in Algebra*. London: Black, Young and Young.

Zazkis, R. (2001) 'From arithmetic to algebra via big numbers', in H. Chick, K. Stacey, J. Vincent and J. Vincent (eds), *Proceedings of the 12th ICMI Study Conference: The Future of the Teaching and Learning of Algebra*. Melbourne: Department of Science and Mathematics Education, University of Melbourne. pp. 676–81.

Zazkis, R. and Gadowsky, K. (2001) 'Attending to transparent features of opaque representations of natural numbers', in A. Cuoco (ed.), *The Roles of Representation in School Mathematics*. Reston, VA: NCTM. pp. 146–65.

Index